CW01433429

28

XV or MOUNT EVEREST 29002

III or Pawhunri 23186

I or Chumalari 23944

XIII 27799

XVI 22215   XIV 24020   826

XII

IX or Kanchinjinga 28156

25304 Junnu   XI   VIII

V or Black Rock

X or Kabru 24015

VII or Pandim 22017

IV or Chumunko

VI or Narsing 19146

Kanglanamo 13000 ?

Tista R.

Arun R.

II or Gipmochi

Tumbok P.

Singelelah

Tambur R.

Tonglo

DARJILING

27

Senchal

Dumdangi 219

Khanchabari 338

Thakurgay 273

Ania   Baisi 242

s

Harpur 226

Ramgang 262

Nirpur 240

Lachmipur 237

Banderjula 251

Newani 274

Menai 237

Kamaldaha 230

Dipnagur

u   e

Sonakhoda

Dewangunj 221

Ghiba 218   a   l

Banghora 205

S   e   r   244

Kharkhari

Bharati 205

Chuni 208

Manikpur 216

Musaldanga 203   200

Tagria

Chotaki 255

Kesurbari

Latona 209

Ramnagur 195

Manulla 197

Lohagara

Garipur

26

Mohania

Dighi

Purneah

87   88   89

Edwd. Weller. Lithogr. Duke Strt. Bloomsbury.

Gaurisánkar, or Mount Everest, in the Himálaya of Nepál.

Lat North 27 59 07"   Long East of Green 86 54 40"   Height 29000 Engl feet

Original Aquarell by Hermann de Schlantweit June 1855

LEIPZIG F.A. Brockhaus.   LONDON Trübner & Co.   The Copyright is reserved.   Printed in Oil-colours by Storch & Kramer, Berlin

EVEREST

A THOUSAND YEARS OF EXPLORATION

Frontispiece
Gaurisánkar, or Mount Everest, in the Himálaya of Nepál
Original aquarell by Hermann de Schlagintweit, June 1855
Lat. North 27" 59' 17" Long. East of Green 86" 54' 40" Height: 29,000 Engl. feet

The original caption continues:
This is the highest mountain of our globe as yet measured. The drawing is taken from a mountain south east of Falut, at a height of 11,035 Engl. feet. As a mighty massif, it forms the prominent group of this view, though surrounded by many peaks of a height exceeding 20,000 Engl. feet. From its proximity to the tropics it stands out, as represented here, at midday in summer a most conspicuous object in the full rays of a nearly vertical sun, herein exhibiting a highly characteristic feature and presenting at the same time a most marked difference from the appearance of the Alpine peaks in higher latitudes. A very extensive glacier, of which the upper cirque de névé is seen on the left, descends to the south west. The name given to Gaurisánkar by the Tibetans, and by which it is generally known, to the natives of the nothernmost parts of Nepal, is Chingopamarí.

Note: This drawing caused considerable confusion in the identification of Mount Everest. In 1855 Hermann Schlagintweit suggested the name Gaurisankar for Everest but the true Gaurisankar was Peak XX, 23,440ft, which had already been identified by the Great Trigonometrical Survey and was about 36 miles west of Everest. Schlagintweit's drawing in fact shows Makalu, Peak XIII.

Endpapers
Front: Map to illustrate Col A S Waugh's paper on 'On Mounts Everest and Deodanga', 1858.

Back: 'The immediate region around Mt Everest' from the eight-page map drawn by Ted Hatch to accompany this monograph. (*See pages 320-327*)

EVEREST

A THOUSAND YEARS OF EXPLORATION

A Record of Mountaineering, Geographical Exploration,
Medical Research and Mapping

Michael P Ward

The Ernest Press

EVEREST. A THOUSAND YEARS OF EXPLORATION
A Record of Mountaineering, Geographical Exploration,
Medical Research and Mapping

First published in 2003
by The Ernest Press
17 Carleton Drive, Glasgow G46 6AQ

Designed and typeset by Johanna Merz
14 Whitefield Close, London, SW15 3SS.

Printed in China through Colorcraft Ltd., Hong Kong

ISBN 0 948153 71 7

Acknowledgements

So many people over so many years have contributed directly or indirectly to this monograph that it would be impossible to name them all. However, I would like to thank Dr David Somervell and James Somervell, FRCS, for permission to reproduce the striking painting by their father, T Howard Somervell, FRCS, which graces the dust jacket of this book.

I am grateful to the Alpine Club and the Royal Geographical Society for the help of their archivists and for permission to reproduce photographs, maps and other documents in their possession. I also thank Peter Clark, Keeper of Maps at the Royal Geographical Society; Dennis Davis for a photo from his collection; Denise Evans for permission to reproduce the drawing of her husband, Sir Charles Evans, FRCS; Hodder & Stoughton for the photograph of Norman Hardie; C S Houston for the drawing of Florin Perier which appeared in his book *Going Higher* (Little, Brown 1987); Brian Mullan for the portrait of Griffith Pugh; Mrs Anne Russell for the photograph of her father, George Ingle Finch, FRS; and Ken Wilson for permission to quote from W H Murray's autobiography *The Evidence of Things Not Seen* (Bâton Wicks, 2002).

Johanna Merz, Editor of the Alpine Journal from 1992 to 1999, has edited, typeset and helped in many other ways with the production of this work. Ted Hatch, of the Royal Geographical Society, has drawn many of the the maps, which accurately and artistically illustrate so much of the text. I thank them both.

Michael P Ward
September 2002

Contents

Author's Note

Because of their multi-cultural origins – including Tibetan, Chinese, Nepali, Indian, Mongolian and English – there are no approved spellings of Central Asian place names. These vary from text to text and from map to map. I have tried to be as consistent as possible between maps and text, but this has not always been possible, particularly in respect of the older maps. Similarly, the heights I have given vary between metric and imperial. On the older maps imperial heights were used, while most of the maps appearing in later chapters show heights in metric measurements. But since some place names appear on both the earlier and the later maps, consistency in the text has not been possible.

List of Plates

Frontispiece

'Gaurisánkar, or Mount Everest, in the Himálaya of Nepál'
Original aquarell by Hermann de Schlagintweit, June 1855
Lat. North 27" 59' 17" Long. East of Green 86" 54' 40" Height: 29,000 Engl. feet
(*Royal Geographical Society Collection*)

(Note: This drawing caused considerable confusion in the identification of Mount Everest. In 1855 Hermann Schlagintweit suggested the name Gaurisankar for Everest but the true Gaurisankar was Peak XX, 23,440ft, about 36 miles west of Everest. Schlagintweit's drawing in fact shows Makalu.)

Appearing between pages 232 and 233

1. Telephoto of the Everest Range taken by Dr A M Kellas from the south at Sandakphu. It shows Lhotse, Everest (South Col, South Ridge and NE Ridge) and Makalu. This was one of the earliest photographs of Everest ever taken, probably in 1920 or 1921. (*Alpine Club Collection*)
2. The fort at Kampa Dzong in Tibet. It was near here that Kellas died, possibly from high-altitude pulmonary oedema, during the approach march in 1921. The photograph dates from 1938. (*C B M Warren*)
3. The headstone for Kellas's grave on a hillside south of Kampa Dzong. (*Royal Geographical Society Collection*)
4. Gaurisankar (*left*) and Menlungtse, from the Chyubas range in Nepal. At one time Everest was called 'Gaurisankar', a name never accepted by the Survey of India, who had identified both peaks from a distance. (*M P Ward*)
5. Tinki Dzong, visited by the 1921 expedition on their way to Everest. In the background is the north side of the main Himalayan Range. (*Royal Geographical Society Collection*)
6. Members of the 1921 Everest reconnaissance expedition. (*From L*) *Standing*: Wollaston, Howard-Bury, Heron, Raeburn. *Sitting*: Mallory, Wheeler, Bullock, Morshead. Note Norfolk jackets, nailed boots, puttees, sweaters and plus fours. No windproof clothing or down jackets were worn or available, and frostbite was common. Down jackets were used routinely on Everest only from 1951 onwards. (*Royal Geographical Society Collection*)
7. George Ingle Finch on the 1922 expedition. Many years ahead of his time, Finch designed and wore a windproof down jacket. Unlike his contemporaries, he reached 27,000ft without suffering from frostbite or other ill effects of the intense cold at altitude. (*The Finch Collection, by kind permission of Mrs Anne Russell*)
8. Everest 1921. The North Col (east side) from the Lhakpa La. (*Royal Geographical Society Collection*)
9. Everest 1921. The Kangshung Face, South Col and Lhotse. (*Royal Geographical Society Collection*)
10. The famous picture of E F Norton climbing alone at 27,000ft on the north side of Everest. The photo was taken by Howard Somervell in 1924. (*T H Somervell. Royal Geographical Society Collection*)
11. The north, Tibetan side of Everest, with North Peak in the foreground, photographed in 1936. (*Royal Geographical Society Collection*)

viii

12. The 1951 Reconnaissance team: *clockwise from left* E Shipton, W H Murray, T D Bourdillon, H E Riddiford, E P Hillary, M P Ward. (*Eric Shipton*)

13. The Nuptse-Lhotse Ridge with Everest, midway, peeping over the ridge. Photo taken from Thyangboche in 1951 – the first view of Everest on this approach. (*Eric Shipton*)

14. W H Murray (*right*) and the author at Namche Bazar in 1951. (*Eric Shipton*)

15. Taken from Pumori in 1951, this was the first photo to show the full complexity of the south side of Everest. Unlike an aerial photo taken a few years previously which exaggerated the steepness of the Lhotse Face leading to the South Col, the photo taken from Pumori shows that the angle of the Face is actually relatively mild. Although the Khumbu Icefall looks formidable, avoiding it looks even more dangerous than to go straight through it – an unusual concept in 1951. E P Hillary can be seen in the right-hand bottom corner. (*Eric Shipton*)

16. The Khumbu Icefall, North Face of Lhotse and South Col seen during the 1951 Reconnaissance Expedition. (*W H Murray*)

17. 1951. The Upper Bhote Kosi valley, leading to the Nangpa La. T D Bourdillon in the foreground. The pundit Hari Ram crossed the Nangpa La in 1885. (*W H Murray*)

18. 1951. The Upper Hongu valley, with many glaciers. Ama Dablam in the background. This area was mapped by Norman Hardie in 1954-1955. (*Eric Shipton*)

19. Menlungtse and the Menlung Basin where in 1951 Eric Shipton and Michael Ward saw what they were told by Sherpas were tracks of the elusive yeti. The first 'on the ground' identification and naming of Menlungtse was made by Shipton and Ward in 1951. Its height and that of Gaurisankar had been known to the Survey of India for many years. (*M P Ward*)

20. Kantega and Tamserku, peaks of c. 21,000ft, seen from the Sherpa village of Khumjung. Note the contrast between the wooded valleys on the south, Nepalese side of Everest with the bare Tibetan plains on the North side as seen from Tinki Dzong in Plate 5. (*A E Gregory, Royal Geographical Society Collection*)

21. The Everest team a few days after the first ascent on 29 May 1953:
    From left C W F Noyce, A E Gregory, L G C E Pugh, G C Band, T D Bourdillon, M P Ward, W G Lowe,Tenzing Norgay, H J C Hunt, E P Hillary, C G Wylie, R C Evans, Dawa Tenzing, T D Stobart, and many Sherpas.
    (*Royal Geographical Society Collection*)

22. Everest seen from the air in 1953. The photo shows both the Tibetan and the Nepalese sides of the range and includes the North Ridge, the North Col (west side), the North Face, the Summit, the South Col, Lhotse, the Western Cwm and the Khumbu Icefall.

23. Dr L G C E Pugh (1909-1994) who was the physiologist on the 1952 Cho Oyu and 1953 Everest expeditions. His studies laid the foundation for the first successful ascent of Everest. (*By courtesy of Brian Mullan*)

24. Dennis Davis, surveyor to the 1955 Merseyside Himalayan Expedition, W of Everest. With Tashi Sherpa, he made the first ascent of Nuptse in 1961. (*Dennis Davis Collection*)

25. Norman Hardie, surveyor on the New Zealand Alpine Club Himalayan Expedition 1954, and on the 1955 Mount Chamlang Survey Expedition, S and E of Everest. In 1955, with three others, he made the first ascent of Kangchenjunga.
    (*Reproduced from* Kangchenjunga. The Untrodden Peak *by Charles Evans, Hodder & Stoughton, 1956.*)

Maps, Diagrams & Drawings

Preface

The last of the earth's three great geographical problems was solved when Hillary and Tenzing made the first ascent of Mount Everest on 29 May 1953. The North Pole had been reached on foot by Robert E Peary's party on 6 April 1909, and the South Pole by Roald Amundsen and his group on 14 December 1911. The technical mountaineering difficulties involved in climbing Everest are similar to those to be found on Mont Blanc (15,800ft), the highest point in Europe, first climbed in 1786. If these technical difficulties had been the only problems to be overcome, Everest would almost certainly have been climbed in the early 1920s when the first attempts were made from Tibet. The reasons for the delay until after the Second World War were not only the politico-geographical uncertainties which existed in the Everest region at that time, but also the major altitude problems, unique to Everest, posed by the last thousand feet (ie between 28,000 and 29,000 feet) and by the extreme cold to be found at that altitude. I have written this monograph on the mountaineering, mapping and medical aspects of the exploration and ascent of Everest because no contemporary publication gives a comprehensive account of these three interwoven strands. A study of all three is essential to a full understanding of the complicated factors involved.

The thousand-year exploration of the Everest region falls naturally into four parts. During the first phase, between AD 800 and 1921, the emphasis was on identification, and following a survey by Chinese lamas, the first European map of southern Tibet was published in France in 1733. Later, in the middle of the 19th century, the position and height of the mountain were determined from the Indian plains by the Survey of India. Although the Pundits, secret native explorers employed by the Survey, failed to find Everest's exact position during their route surveys in Nepal and Tibet, the peak was finally identified on the ground from Nepal in 1903 and from Tibet in 1904.

During the second phase, from 1921 to the outbreak of the Second World War, the Tibetan side of the Everest region was mapped, as was part of the unknown Nepalese side. During this period, too, mountaineers made ascents on the Tibetan side to 28,000 feet on several occasions, some using supplementary oxygen and others relying on acclimatisation alone. However, the last thousand feet defeated them all.

In the third and critical phase, from 1947 to 1953, Tibet closed her frontiers but, fortuitously, for the first time in history, Nepal opened hers in 1949. In early 1951 a new route up the Nepalese side of Everest was discovered by myself from photographs in the archives of the Royal Geographical Society in London, and from a hitherto disregarded map based on data provided by a 1933 aerial survey of the south side of Everest. At the same time, the Medical Research Council started working towards the elusive medical solution of the problem of 'the last thousand feet'. In the autumn of 1951, during a reconnaissance expedition to Nepal, the new route was confirmed as feasible, and in the spring of 1952, following extensive work by the Medical Research Council, the medical solution was verified at altitude on an expedition to Cho Oyu in the Everest region.

After two unsuccessful attempts on Everest by the Swiss in 1952, which reached no higher than 28,200ft, the first ascent was made in 1953, using for the first time adequate amounts of supplementary oxygen and other medical measures recommended by the Medical Research Council to counter severe altitude deterioration and disease.

The fourth and last phase covered the years following the first ascent, when the exploration and survey of the Nepalese side of Everest resulted in the publication of the first accurate and comprehensive map of both the Tibetan and Nepalese sides of Everest by the Royal Geographical Society in 1961.

During these years, too, growing interest in the medical aspects of cold and high altitude led to a pioneering scientific expedition to the Everest region in 1960-61, and another in 1981 when, for the first time, measurements were made on the summit of Everest. In addition, a number of long-term decompression chamber experiments were completed. These resulted in the emergence of a thriving medical sub-speciality – high-altitude medicine and physiology – which has helped in understanding the problems not only of the 100 million or so people who live at high altitude, and the millions who each year travel to altitude to climb, trek and ski, but also of those with chronic lung and heart disease who, though residing at sea level, may suffer interference in their oxygen transport system. Recently, too, genetic factors have been shown to be of importance in altitude adaptation.

In 1978 the last barrier was broken and Everest was climbed without the help of supplementary oxygen. In the year 2000, Everest was skied from summit to base camp in less than five hours. Although Everest may seem to be in danger of being down-graded like many of its 19th century Alpine counterparts, its ascent is still a formidable undertaking with an appreciable mortality.

At the start of the 21st century, with the ascent of all its major ridges and faces successfully accomplished, the mysteries of Everest, whether involving mountain exploration, medicine or mapping, are well on their way to solution.

Michael P Ward
July 2002

Chronology of Everest: AD 800 – Present

800	The Tibetan name 'Chomolungma' was given to Everest by inhabitants of the Rongbuk valley, southern Tibet.
1661	Fathers Grüber and d'Orville, Jesuit missionaries, traversed the Nyalam valley on their way from Lhasa to Kathmandu after a journey from Beijing to Lhasa.
1711-18	A survey was made by Curquin Zangbu and Lanben Zhainba, Tibetan lamas, trained by Beijing Jesuits. On their map, the name 'Jumu Langma Alin' appears in the position of Everest.
1712-27	Father Desideri, a Jesuit missionary, traversed the Nyalam valley on his way from Lhasa to Kathmandu, after working as a missionary in Lhasa.
1733	On J B B d'Anville's map, published in Paris, the name 'Tchoumour Lancma' appears in the position of Everest.
1847	'Peak b' was discovered during a routine survey from the Plains of India by J W Armstrong of the Survey of India. The name was changed to 'Peak h'.
1849-50	'Peak h', renamed 'Peak XV', was observed from six stations in India by J O Nicholson of the Survey of India.
1856	'Peak XV' was named 'Everest' by Andrew Waugh of the Survey of India in a letter to the President of the Royal Geographical Society in London. Its height was estimated at 29,002ft.
1857	The Alpine Club was formed in London. The altitude problems of Everest were discussed in the *Alpine Journal* and in the *Geographical Journal*.
1855-86	Everest was named 'Gaurisankar' (Peak 20) by the explorer H Schlagintweit but was wrongly placed in the position of Makalu (Peak 13). Neither the position nor the name was accepted by the Survey of India.

1868   The Pundit M.H., No 9 (Hari Ram) and Pundit G.S.S. (S D Singh) explored the Everest region from Tibet and Nepal for the Survey of India, but they failed to identify Peak XV (Everest).

1903-4   The first correct ground identification was made by H Wood of the Survey of India from 100 miles away in Nepal (1903) and Tibet (1904).

1904-13   J B L Noel and A M Kellas (at different times) attempted to explore the approaches to Everest. The nearest point, within 50 miles, was reached by Noel from the east in 1913.

1918-20   Overtures with regard to a possible expedition to Everest were made to the Tibetan Government by the Government of India, the Alpine Club and the Royal Geographical Society (RGS).

1920   Oxygen equipment was tested on Mt Kamet (Garhwal) by A M Kellas and H T Morshead.

1921   Decompression chamber experiments were conducted by Professor G Dryer of Oxford University, G I Finch and others.

The first British expedition to Everest – a survey, mapping and reconnaissance expedition – took place from Tibet. It was led by C K Howard-Bury. The East Rongbuk glacier route to Everest was discovered by E O Wheeler. The highest point reached, by G H L Mallory and G H Bullock, was the North Col at 23,000ft. No supplementary oxygen was used.

The first modern map of the north side of Everest was published by the Survey of India. It showed many names of peaks, passes and glaciers given by expedition members. The map was approved by the Tibetan Government and the RGS.

1922   Further experiments in a decompression chamber were carried out at Oxford by Professor Dryer, T H Somervell and others.

The second British expedition to Everest, led by C G Bruce, made an attempt from Tibet. G I Finch and J G Bruce reached a height of 27,400ft, using supplementary oxygen at 2 litres/minute in open-circuit sets. E F Norton, T H Somervell and G H L Mallory reached a height of 27,000ft without the use of supplementary oxygen. During a further attempt a fatal avalanche intervened, killing seven porters.

1922
(contd)

A survey of the Kharta and Arun valleys, east of Everest, was carried out by the Survey of India.

A meeting was held at the Royal Society of Medicine in London to discuss high-altitude medicine.

1924

The third British expedition, led by C G Bruce, made an attempt on Everest from Tibet. The highest point reached was by E F Norton to 28,000ft (using no supplementary oxygen) with T H Somervell in support. A second attempt was made by G H L Mallory and A D Irvine, using supplementary oxygen at 2 litres/minute and open-circuit sets. They failed to return and the highest point they reached is unknown.

Mapping of the West Rongbuk glacier and the Rongshar valley, west of Everest, was carried out by the Survey of India.

1923-35

Altitude research was carried out in Tenerife and South America by J B S Haldane, J Barcroft, B Mathews and others from the Universities of Harvard, Oxford and Cambridge. Some data from their research was applied to subsequent Everest expeditions.

1924-27

General mapping of Nepal was carried out, omitting glacial regions. Only native surveyors of the Nepal detachment of the Survey of India were used or permitted. No photographs were allowed.

1924-1932

Further British expeditions to Everest were refused by the Tibetan Government during this period.

1933

The fourth British expedition to Everest, led by H Ruttledge, attempted the summit from Tibet. The highest point reached was 28,000ft by P Wyn Harris, L Wager, and by F S Smythe climbing alone. Supplementary oxygen was taken on the expedition but not used.

Houston-Westland organised the first flight over Everest (from Nepal). Its purpose was to map the Nepalese side of Everest and to test engines at altitude. Entering Tibetan air space was prohibited.

1934

A solo attempt on Everest was made from Tibet by Maurice Wilson. His body was found the following year at 21,000ft.

1935

A request by the Alpine Club and RGS for permission to attempt Everest from Nepal was refused by the King of Nepal.

1935   **The fifth British expedition to Everest** was a reconnaissance and
            mapping expedition from the Tibetan side, led by E E Shipton. The
            highest point reached was only 24,000ft, but more peaks over 20,000ft
            were climbed than had been ascended worldwide before this date.
            As a result, the Everest map was re-drawn by the RGS.

1936   **The sixth British expedition to Everes**t, led by H Ruttledge from
            the Tibetan side, was ruined by adverse weather conditions. The highest
            point reached was the North Col at 23,000ft.

1938   **The seventh British expedition to Everest** from Tibet was led by
            H W Tilman. On the first attempt on the summit, by F S Smythe and
            E E Shipton, 27,400ft was reached without supplementary oxygen.
            A second attempt was made by H W Tilman and P Lloyd. They both
            reached 27,400ft. Lloyd, using supplementary oxygen at 2 litres/
            minute, moved faster and with significantly less overall fatigue than
            Tilman who used no supplementary oxygen. This was the first
            undisputed evidence that the use of supplementary oxygen increases
            climbing rate at high altitude.

1939-45   The Second World War intervened but some of the techniques of
            mountain warfare, developed during the war, were subsequently
            applied to the successful assault on Everest in 1953. Investigations
            included those at the Mountain Warfare Centre in the Lebanon,
            directed by W J Riddell and L G C E Pugh.

1945   A secret flight over Everest from India and Nepal was made by 684
            Squadron, RAF. Photographs taken on the flight were sent, poorly
            labelled, to the RGS and stored in their archives.

            The first map of both the Nepalese and the Tibetan sides of Everest
            was made at the RGS by M F Milne and A R Hinks. They made use of
            work done during the 1935 reconnaissance expedition and combined
            this with information gained from photographs taken on the 1933
            Houston-Westland 'Flight over Everest'.

            A proposal by Eric Shipton for an Everest expedition from Tibet in 1947
            was considered by the Alpine Club, but a letter from the Viceroy of
            India made it clear that there was no possibility of sending an expedition
            to Tibet for the foreseeable future. The project was abandoned.

1946   C S Houston and R L Riley organised an experiment called 'Operation Everest' at Pensacola Naval Air Base, Florida, USA. They succeeded in replicating, in a decompression chamber, conditions at the summit of Everest. The experiment showed that it was theoretically possible to survive at this height without supplementary oxygen.

1947   A secret flight over Everest was made by K D Neame of the RAF, from India and Nepal. Photographs, poorly labelled, were sent to the archives of the RGS.

        E Denman, supported by Tenzing Norgay, made an unsuccessful secret expedition to the Tibetan side of Everest.

1949   Nepal opened its frontiers to foreigners for the first time, but the Nepal Government refused H W Tilman permission to go to Everest.

1950   Tibet closed its frontiers to foreigners.

        The first party of Westerners to visit the Nepalese side of Everest was an Anglo-American trekking group which included H W Tilman and C S Houston. While ascending Kala Pattar to 18,000ft, Tilman took the first photograph of the south side of Everest but failed to go high enough to identify a route to the summit.

1951   **Early spring**
        M P Ward examined maps and two or three thousand photographs in the archives of the RGS. From these he found cartographic and photographic evidence of a possible route to the summit of Everest from Nepal. However, the newly-formed Himalayan Committee of the RGS and the Alpine Club initially showed little interest in this evidence and failed to back a reconnaissance from the south.

        Early spring and summer
        At the Medical Research Council Laboratories in London, L G C E Pugh and M P Ward identified the solution to the main problem of the last thousand feet of Everest. They were able to show that, while only 2 litres/minute had been used on pre-war expeditions, the use of 4 litres/minute, in open-circuit sets, would significantly increase climbing rate at great altitude.

1951   R B Larsen made secret visits to both sides of Everest via the
(contd.) Nangpa La.

Autumn
A reconnaissance expedition, led by E E Shipton, explored the southern
approach to Everest. A feasible route to the summit was confirmed and
extensive exploration was carried out both east and west of Everest.

The Swiss having obtained permission for an attempt on Everest in
1952, the Himalayan Committee applied for permission for a British
attempt on Cho Oyu in the spring of 1952 and on Everest in the spring
of 1953.

1952   **Spring**
An attempt on Everest was made by the Swiss from Nepal. The highest
point reached was 28,220ft. Supplementary oxygen was used only
intermittently owing to design faults in the oxygen sets.

A British expedition, led by E E Shipton, went to Cho Oyu, west of
Everest. An attempt on the mountain was abandoned, since the only
feasible route lay in Tibet which was still forbidden. Exploration was
carried out on the Nepal-Tibet border north of the Tesi Lapcha pass,
and also on the Barun glacier, east of Everest.

During the same expedition, the solutions to the problems of the last
thousand feet of Everest, previously reached theoretically at the MRC
Laboratory in 1951, were tested and confirmed in the field by physiological research carried out by L G C E Pugh on the Menlung La
at 20,000ft.

Autumn
A second attempt on Everest was made by the Swiss from Nepal.
The highest point reached was just above 26,600ft. Supplementary
oxygen was used, but the sets were again ineffective. Extreme cold
and oxygen lack ended the attempt.

27,000ft was reached by Russians from Tibet.

On 28 July Eric Shipton was appointed leader of the 1953 expedition
but, after much controversy, he resigned on 11 September and was
replaced by John Hunt.

1953   **Spring**
A British expedition went to Everest from Nepal, led by John Hunt.
Other members of the party were: G C Band, T D Bourdillon,
R C Evans, A E Gregory, E P Hillary, W G Lowe, Tenzing Norgay,
C W F Noyce, L G C E Pugh, T Stobart (photographer),
M H Westmacott, M P Ward, C G Wylie.

The first ascent of the South Summit (28,720ft) was made by
T D Bourdillon and R C Evans on 26 May using closed-circuit oxygen
sets. These sets proved unreliable and dangerous and their failure
prevented the pair from reaching the summit.

The first ascent of the Main Summit (29,002ft) was made on 29 May by
E P Hillary and Tenzing Norgay using open-circuit oxygen sets at a
flow rate of 4 litres/minute.

On this expedition L G C E Pugh and M P Ward (Medical Officer) carried
out extensive medical research into the problems of climbing at high
altitude.

Autumn
Peaks south of Namche Bazar were explored by R C Evans.
J O M Roberts explored the Inukhu Khola, east of Everest.

1954   The height of Everest was fixed at 8,848m (29,028ft) by B L Gulatee
of the Survey of India. The new height was accepted by Chinese
cartographers from Tibet.

A meeting was held at the Royal Society, London, under the
chairmanship of Sir Bryan Mathews (who had been in overall charge of
scientific preparations for Everest) to discuss the problems of high
altitude.

1954-55   Exploration and mapping were carried out by N Hardie south and
east of Everest and Makalu. He explored the Barun glacier, the Iswa
Khola and other valleys.

1955   Exploration and mapping were carried out by A E Gregory and D Davis
west and south of Everest, including the Tolam Bau glacier and the Tesi
Lapcha region.

1960   A Chinese expedition made the first ascent of Everest from the north,
            Tibetan side. Wang Fu-chou, Chu Yin-hua and a Tibetan, Konbu,
            reached the summit.

1961   The first comprehensive map of the Everest region, drawn by
            G S Holland, was published by the RGS in London.

1960-61   The Silver Hut Medical Physiology expedition visited the Everest
            region (Nepal). This was the first expedition to winter in the Himalaya
            (at 19,000ft) using Polar techniques.

1978   On 8 May 1978 Peter Habeler and Reinhold Messner reached the summit
            of Everest without using supplementary oxygen.

1999   George Mallory's body was found by an American expedition at about
            27,000ft on the North-East Ridge of Everest.

2002   A comprehensive map of the Everest region was produced by E J Hatch
            and M P Ward, using recent Nepalese, Chinese, Russian and American
            sources.

1953-2002   During this period, all the major ridges and faces of Everest were climbed
            by mountaineers of many nationalities. Over one hundred ascents were
            made without using supplementary oxygen. Also, a thriving new sub-
            speciality emerged: high-altitude medicine and physiology.

Chapter 1

THE ABODE OF SNOW

Introduction

Everest straddles the frontier of Tibet and Nepal just south of the Tropic of Cancer, and clustered around it are some of the world's highest peaks in a tangled and spectacularly beautiful mass of passes, gorges, peaks and glaciers. Whilst Everest can be clearly seen from the plains of Tibet to the north, from the south, in Nepal, it is hidden until one gets close, when its height overwhelms all other mountains. Its position between two of the world's least politically accessible countries has meant that, unlike many other high yet easily visible peaks, like Kangchenjunga close to Darjeeling, it remained unknown to the Western world until the middle of the 19th century, and the first comprehensive map of the Everest region was not available until 1961.

Everest's other unique feature is that because it is a thousand feet higher than any other mountain, its ascent has always been primarily a medical rather than a mountaineering problem; for its position near the Tropic of Cancer at 28°N means that because the barometric pressure, and therefore the oxygen pressure, is higher, for a given altitude, in the tropics than in the polar regions, it is possible, but only just, to climb it without the help of supplementary oxygen. In doing so, however, the mountaineer is on a knife-edge between success on the one hand, and failure and possible death on the other. It is these twin factors of medical challenge and geographical inaccessibility that have given this peak an almost mystical status.

Everest is a sacred peak but it is not the most holy peak in Tibet, which is Mt Kailas (Kangrinboche), over 250 miles to the west. That mountain rises above the twin sacred lakes of Rakas Tal and Manasarowar. Tibetans have a special affinity with the mountains of their land, as they are believed to be a ladder or cord down which their ancestors descended to earth. Certain peaks, too, represent warrior gods, and many are sacred, being regarded as pillars or supports of the sky, or pegs that fasten the sky to the earth.

800-1804 Surveyors, Tibetan and Chinese. Jesuit missionaries. The Lama Map. J B B d'Anville's Map. Crawford's Nepal Map.

Since about AD 750, the Rongbuk monastery in southern Tibet, its valley and the surrounding region have been considered sacred by Tibetans because they are within sight of an immensely high peak, Chomolungma. This can only be Everest, for it dominates the whole region, though a similar name, Chomo Kankar, is mentioned in a Tibetan geographical text, with Chomo Uri as another name. There is no doubt, however, that the local Tibetan name for Everest is 'Chomolungma', for on the passport given in 1921 by the Prime Minister of Tibet to the first British reconnaissance expedition to Everest from the north, it states that 'a party of Sahibs is coming to see Chha–mo–lung–ma mountain'.

The word Chomolungma is usually considered to mean 'Goddess Mother of the World' or 'Goddess Mother of the Wind'. However, according to Tenzing Norgay, who with Edmund Hillary made the first ascent of Everest in 1953, Sherpa mothers used to tell their children that it meant 'The mountain so high that no bird can fly over it'.

The first time that the world's highest peak was found on a map followed the mapping of Tibet by the Chinese Emperor Kangshi. In 1708, following his conquest of China, the Emperor decided to have a map drawn of all his dominions, a task he gave to the Jesuit missionaries in Beijing. They started around the Great Wall and in each province found earlier Chinese maps. But none was available for Tibet, which initially was not included in the survey. As a result, a special embassy was sent to Tibet which stayed for two years, producing a map which in 1711 was sent to Father Régis in Beijing for reproduction. He declined to use it, however, as there were no fixed points, and distances had not been measured but were simply based on information derived from local hearsay.

Because of Tibet's obvious strategic and geographical importance and its possible wealth, the Emperor decided that an accurate map must be drawn. To this end he ordered two Lamas, Curquin Zangbu and Lanben Zhainba, who had learned geometry and arithmetic in a Chinese mathematical academy, to make a map of Tibet from Xining to Lhasa and as far west as the sources of the Ganges (and Tsangpo), near Mt Kailas. This work was completed by 1718 and was far superior to the 1711 map. By checking all reliable information, particularly about journeys between China and Tibet, the map had 'the exactitude which was worthy of the attention of the public'.

The Jesuit fathers' map was added to the great map of the whole of China, and was printed in the Man language in copperplate in 1719, and in the Han language in woodcut in 1721. A copy was sent to Louis XV, where it was kept in his private library in Versailles. The Jesuit Father du Halde had a copy made and sent it to the renowned French map-maker J B B d'Anville, asking him to reduce it and prepare it for publication. This map 'Carte Generale du Tibet ou Boutan ... Avril 1733' is to be found in du Halde's 'Description ... de la Chine' published in 1735. On this map the name 'Tchoumour Lancma' appears in the position of Everest, whilst a recent translation of the original Chinese ideogram by the Permanent Committee on Geographical Name gives 'Jumu Langma Alin'.

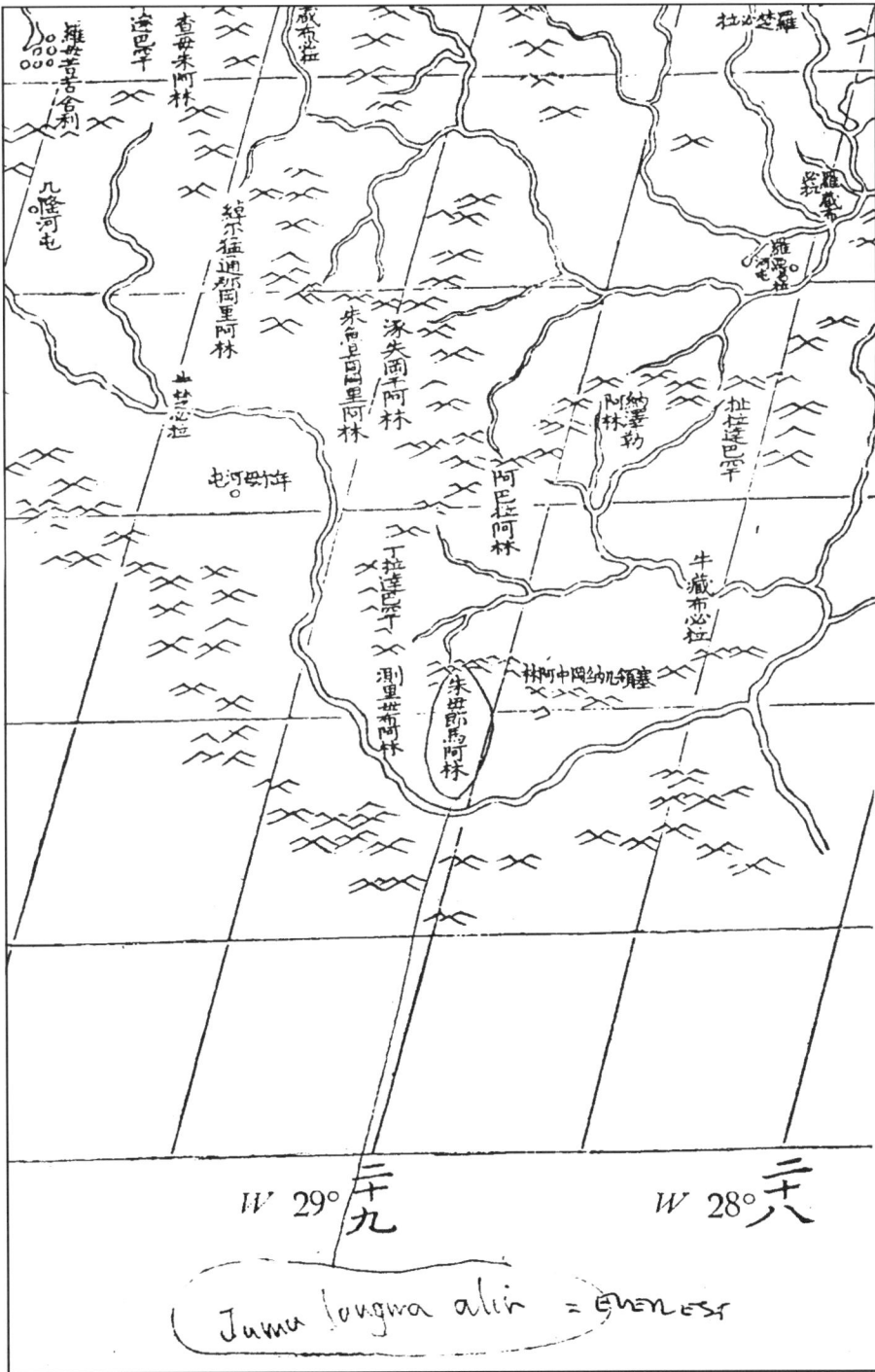

Detail from a map drawn by Jesuit fathers in Beijing from a survey
of the Everest region made by the Chinese between 1708 and 1718.

Fac simile of the part containing Thibet of "Carte generale du Thibet ou Bout-
...et des pays de Kashgar et Hami. Dressée sur les cartes et memoires des R.R.PP.
...uites de la Chine et accordée avec la situation constante de quelques Pays voisins.
...Le S.ʳ D'Anville, Geographe Ord.ʳᵉ du Roi. Avril 1733."

Part of d'Anville's map of Tibet, published in 1733, showing Tchoumour Lancma M. [Everest], Pari-dsong, Nialma (Nyalam), Tsanpou ou le Fleuve [Tsangpo River], Poutala [Potala] and Oujouk-linke [Signet Ring Lake or Yamdrok Tso]. Pays de Pouronké is Bhutan.

4

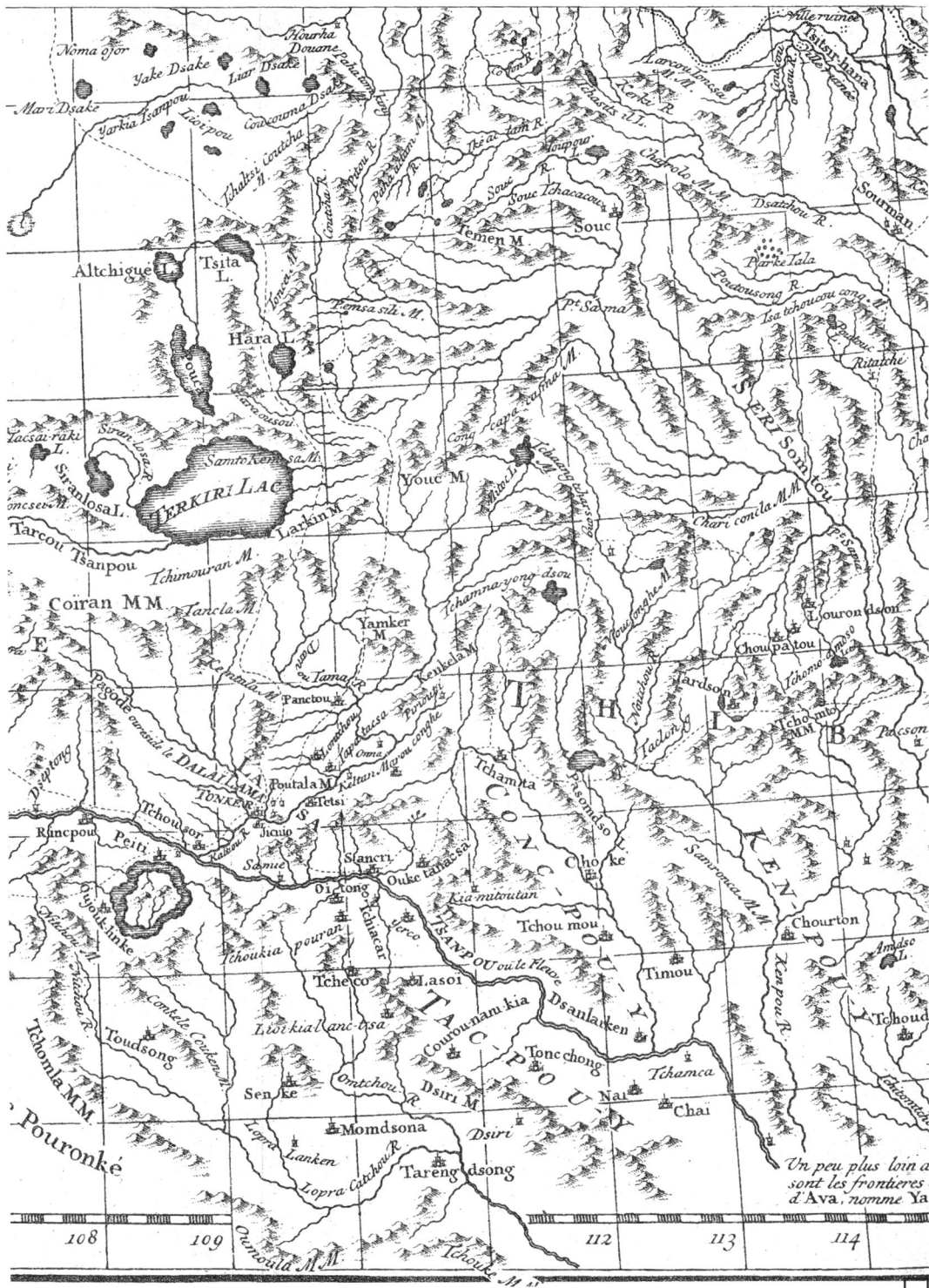

Noma ojor

Hourha Douane

Yake Dsake Liar Dsake

Mari Dsake

Yarkia Tsanpou Liorpou Coucouna Dsake Tchalis Tontcha Peka Kitan M

Tsakan M Iss at tam R

Toupou R

Souc R Souc Tchacacou

Larcou la ros. Senki R

Tatsin hana

Chigkolo M.M

Sourman

Dsatchou R

Temen M Souc Pu ke Tala

Poutousong R

Isa tchoucou cong

Altchigue L. Tsita L.

Hara L.

Temsa sili M.

Pt. Samal

Ritatche

SERI Som tou

Tacsai-raki L. Siran losa L.

Samto Kem sa M.

Conf capa cama M.

Youc M. Mari L.

Huang tchasseng

Noutouoghe M.

Chari conla M.M

Pe Sepac

Cha

Toncseu M. Siranlosa L. UERKIRI LAC Larkin M. Tarcou Tsanpou

Tchimouran M. Tancla M.

Coiran MM

Yamker M.

Tchamna yong dsou

Choupatou

Lourondson

Tchomo Amdso

Pagode ou reside le DALAI LAMA

Diuptong Kopulal M Panctou Tamar Keukela M

Tontchou Plottacsa Perugi Sit Omna Maron conghe

Poutala M. Tetsi

CO

Manchou

Yardson

Taclou M

Tchomta

COZ

Tcho mto Tchamti MM

Pacson

KEN

B

Rincpou Peiti Tchousor Rattou M

Jiulip Same

Stancri Oukc tähat sa Kia mitoutan

Pasomdso M.

Cho ke

Samvonca M.M

Chourton

Amdso L.

Oujok linke

Oi tong Tchiacar Jerco

Tchou mou

Timou

Kenpou R.

Tchoud

Tchoukia pouran

Tche co Lasoi

Tchomla M.M Toudsong

Sen ke

Liot kia lanc tsa

Omtchou Dsiri M.

Couounan kia Dsanlarken

TSANPOU ou le Fleuve

Tonc chong Nai

Tchamca

Chai

Pouronké

Lopra Lanken Lopra Catchou R.

Momdsona

Tareng dsong

Dsiri

Un peu plus loin a
sont les frontieres
d'Ava, nomme Ya

108 109 Oumould M.M Tchouke M.M 112 113 114

In the 17th century Jesuit missionaries visited Tibet in search of Nestorian Christian colonies, but none saw Everest as they were too far west, being based on Tsaparang. In 1661 Johann Grüber, an Austrian, and Albert d'Orville, a Belgian, who worked at the imperial observatory in Beijing, were the first Europeans to visit Lhasa. Unable to return to Europe by sea because of war with Holland, they travelled overland. Leaving Beijing on 13 April 1661, they passed through Xining, and gained the north-eastern edge of the Tibetan plateau by crossing the Kun Lun Shan (Burhan Buddha range), continuing south on a route closely followed by the present Golmud to Lhasa road. They crossed the central meridian range of Tibet, the Tanggula Shan, by a pass of 17,000ft, reaching Lhasa on 8 October. Here Grüber made the first sketch of the Potala, which appeared, together with a map of their route, in Kircher's *China Illustrata*, published in 1667.

Going west from Lhasa they followed the trade route along the Tsangpo river passing through Kampa Dzong and reaching Tingri. Walking south along the Nyalam gorge through the main Himalayan range they reached Kathmandu, the capital of Nepal, in January 1662. Everest is clearly visible from Tingri, but neither of these travellers left a record of seeing any particularly high peak, and neither did Father Desideri who reached Lhasa from India and western Tibet in 1716. Five years later he returned from Lhasa to Kathmandu via Tingri and the Nyalam gorge.

In 1793 a Nepalese embassy visited Beijing following the Sino-Nepal war, traversing the Himalaya by the Nyalam gorge and going along the Tsangpo valley to Lhasa. They too made no comment on any particularly high peaks. In Nepal, the first European to make a formal survey was Charles Crawford, a member of the mission staff in Kathmandu between 1801 and 1804. He calculated the latitude and longitude of Kathmandu and produced a large-scale map showing the heights of peaks around the capital. He also completed a map of the rest of the country, but again there is no mention of a particularly high peak. In 1804 the British Resident, Captain William Knox, and his staff including Crawford, were forced to leave Nepal, and Anglo-Nepalese relations deteriorated.

Although some years later a British Resident with a small staff returned to Kathmandu, no European visitors were allowed to visit Nepal nor even leave the confines of the Kathmandu valley except in exceptional circumstances. Nepal remained, for Europeans, a 'closed country' until 1949.

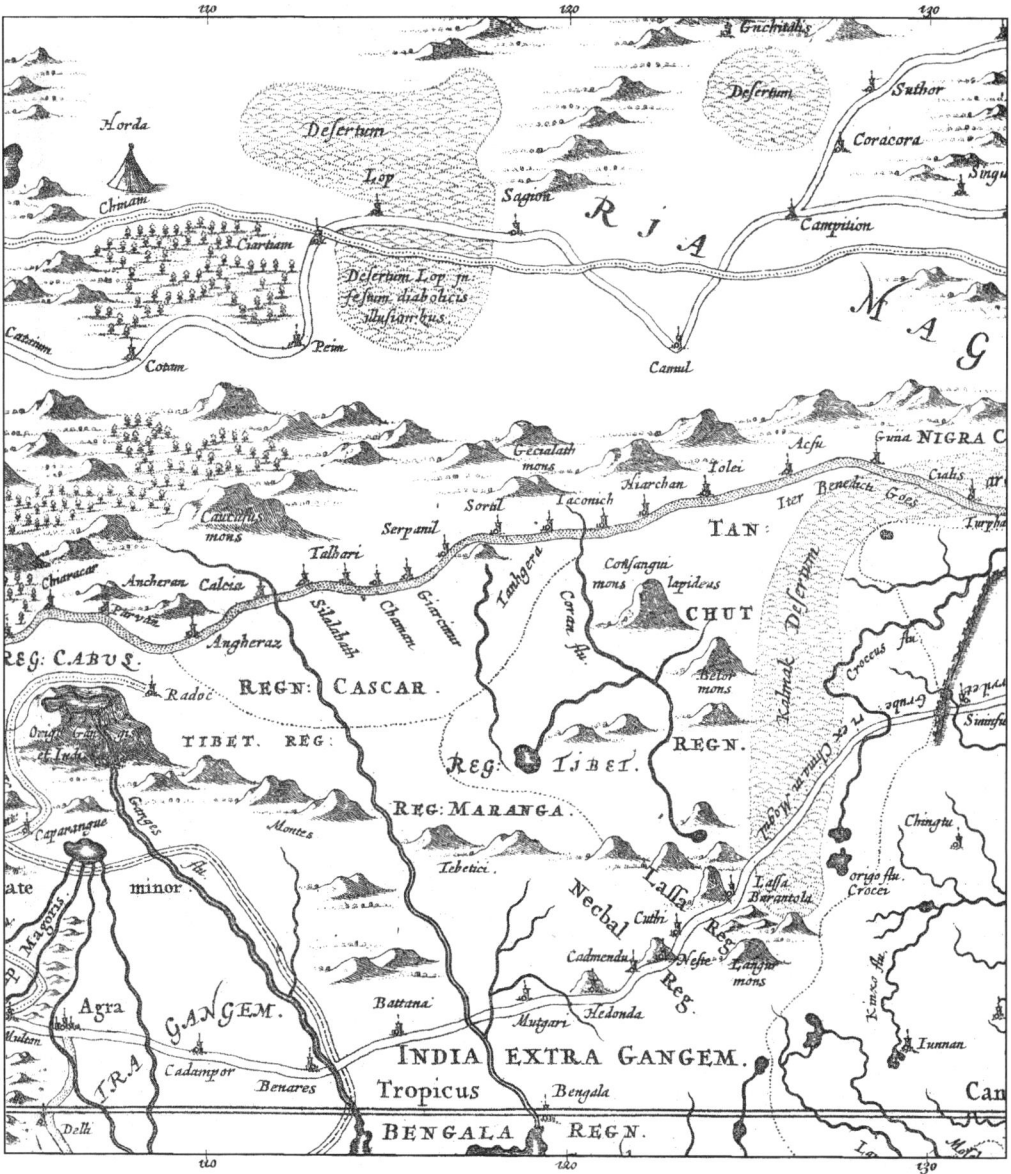

Part of the Map of Asia in Kircher's 'China Illustrata', Amsterdam 1667,
showing the route of Grüber and d'Orville from Xining to Kathmandu.
Note: Cadmendu, Cuthi, Lassa and Langur mountains.
There is no reference to Chomolungma.

Identification of Everest by the Survey of India (1846-1850). 'The Highest Peak in the World' and its different names.

Since the formation of the Survey of India in the early part of the 19th century, its officers had been mapping this vast and then little-known country. George Everest went out to India as an artillery cadet in 1806 and in 1818 became chief assistant to William Lambton, the founder of the Great Trigonometrical Survey. On Lambton's death, Everest succeeded him and from 1830 until his retirement in 1843 he held the combined posts of Surveyor-General and Superintendent of the Great Trigonometrical Survey. During this period he conceived and put into effect the gridiron system of triangulation which formed a rigid framework within which a detailed survey of the whole of India could be carried out.

Eventually this framework reached the foothills of the Himalaya, but was prevented from going further north to the peaks themselves owing to powerful local rulers, particularly in the independent kingdoms of Nepal, Bhutan and Sikkim.

However, starting around 1845, it was possible to measure the more prominent of the Himalayan peaks from the Indian plains, up to 150 miles away. First Dhaulagiri (Peak 42) in central Nepal, then Kangchenjunga (Peak 8) on the borders of Sikkim and Nepal, were considered to be world's highest peaks. As routine measurements continued, it gradually became apparent that in eastern Nepal, about 70 miles west of Kangchenjunga, there was an extremely high peak. First observed by a party led by J W Armstrong in 1846-47 as 'Peak b', it seemed to be one of a number of minor summits, many of which were nearly invisible. Then, between November 1849 and January 1850, the same peak, now designated 'Peak h', and then 'Peak XV', was observed by J O Nicholson from six stations, between 108 and 118 miles to the south, using a 24-inch theodolite.*

Andrew Waugh, the Superintendent of the Great Trigonometrical Survey, who had taken over from George Everest in 1843, asked his Chief Computer, Radhanath Sikhdar, to calculate and check the results. In 1852 a mean height of 29,002ft was obtained from individual readings from the six stations: 28,990ft, 28,992ft, 28,999ft, 29,002ft, 29,005ft, 29,025ft. Peak XV was clearly higher than any other peak by a margin of nearly 1,000 feet.

Because of atmospheric refraction, however, it was not until 1865 that the determination of the height of Everest was considered accurate and scientifically reliable enough to be regarded as fact. Because of this uncertainty, Everest was not marked on a map published in 1854 in Hooker's *Himalayan Journals*, nor on Hodgson's map of 1857 published in Trelawney Saunders' paper 'The Himalayan Mountain System' in *The Geographical Magazine* of 1877. It was, however, depicted with a height of 29,002ft in *The Geographical Journal* of 1858, and in the *Journal of the Asiatic Society of Bengal* of the same year, seemingly for the first time.

---

* See diagram on page 10.

In a letter to Sir Roderic Murchison, dated Dehra, March 1st 1856, Waugh wrote:

The revision has proceeded to some extent, and I am now in possession of the final values for the peak designated XV in the list in the Office of the Surveyor-General of India. We have for some years known that this mountain is higher than any other hitherto measured in India, and most probably it is the highest in the whole world.

I was taught by my respected chief and predecessor, Colonel Geo. Everest, to assign to every geographical object its true local or native appellation. I have always scrupulously adhered to this rule, as I have in fact to all other principles laid down by that eminent graduist.

But here is a mountain, most probably the highest in the world, without any local name that we can discover, or whose native appellation, if it have any, will not very likely be ascertained before we are allowed to penetrate into Nepal and to approach close to this stupendous snowy mass.

In the mean time the privilege, as well as the duty, devolves on me to assign to this lofty pinnacle of our globe, a name whereby it may be known among geographers and become a household word among civilized nations.

In virtue of this privilege, in testimony of my affectionate respect for a revered chief, in conformity with what I believe to be the wish of all the Members of the scientific department, over which I have the honour to preside, and to perpetuate the memory of that illustrious master of accurate geographical research, I have determined to name this noble peak of the Himalayas 'Mont Everest.'

The final values of the coordinates of geographical position for this are as follows, viz.:-

Mont Everest, or Himalaya Peak XV.

Latitude N.	Longitude E. of Greenwich	Height above Sea-level
27° 59' 16.7"	86° 58' 5.9"	29,002 Feet.

The above letter, from Andrew Waugh to Sir Roderic Murchison, President of the Royal Geographical Society (RGS), mentions the peak's coordinates and its average height of 29,002ft (8840m). The accepted height today is 29,028ft (8848m) (or 29,035ft/8853m in 1999) but this was not fixed until 1952–4 when a party of Indian surveyors under B L Gulatee measured the mountain from 50 miles to the south, in Nepal. Waugh suggests that the name 'Everest' be given to the peak not only to commemorate his outstanding predecessor but also because he believed that there existed neither local name nor 'native appellation'. In this he was wrong because the Tibetans had already given this peak the name Chomolungma, but they did not know that it was the world's highest mountain any more than the Survey knew its Tibetan name.

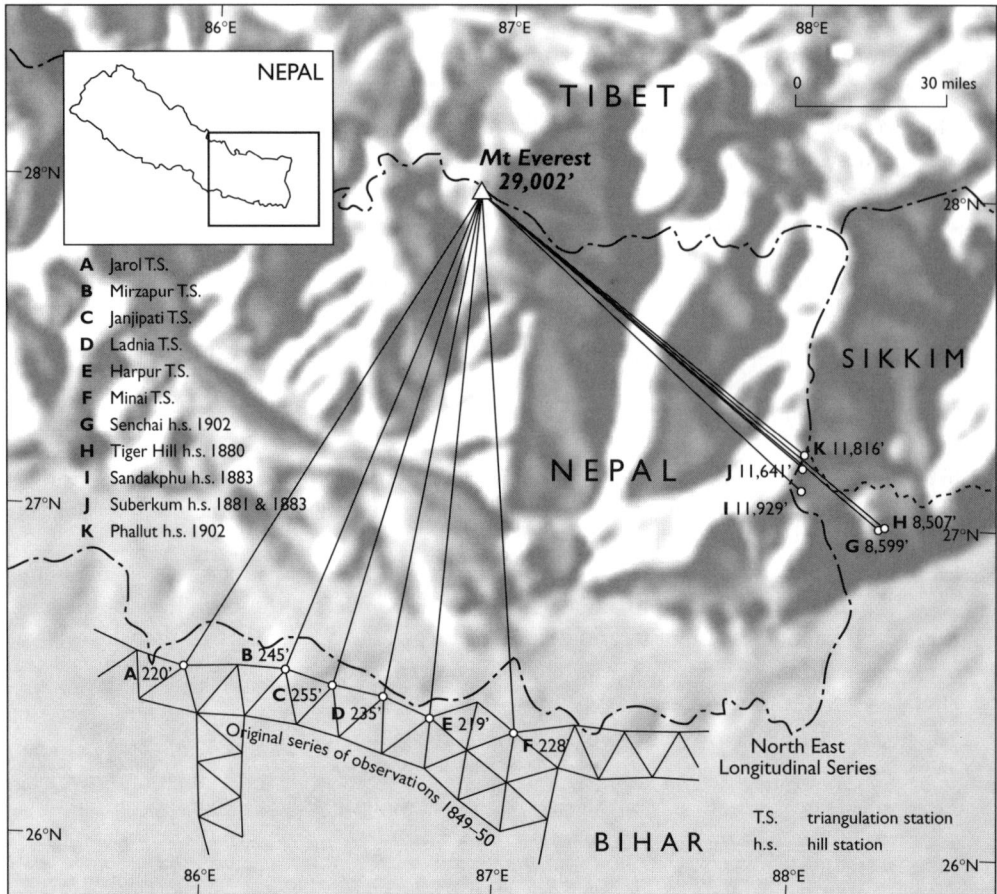

Observations to Mount Everest at the time it was first coordinated
and its height calculated, together with observations of 1880-1902.

Immediate controversy over the name began and another letter appeared in the
Journal of the RGS, from Brian Hodgson, British Resident in Kathmandu, who
considered that the Nepalese already had a name, 'Devadhunga' (Divine Rock).
This claim was later investigated and found to be incorrect. Born in 1800, Brian
Hodgson was Assistant Resident and then Resident in Nepal from 1825–43 and from
1845–58. He lived in Darjeeling before returning to England where he died in 1894.
As an acknowledged authority on Nepal and the Himalaya, he received from the
Maharajah of Nepal official summaries of routes through the Himalaya taken by
the embassies to Beijing. In those summaries, the word 'langur', as in 'Mahalangur',
was probably used to indicate the Himalaya though, as Hodgson wrote, the word
was used nonspecifically for a pass, a mountain, a mountain range or even a village.

In a report on the first survey of Nepal, undertaken by the Nepal detachment of
the Survey of India between 1924 and 1927, Sir Edward Tandy maintained that

there was little likelihood of there being a Nepalese name for Everest, as from Nepal it did not look an outstanding mountain.

Sir Charles Bell, Political Officer of Sikkim who looked after Tibet, made the point, in a letter to *The Times* on 8 August 1935, that the word 'Chamo-lung' means 'bird country' in which the Tibetan side of Everest lies, and 'Chomo-lungma' is spuriously applied to Everest. He concluded that the correct Tibetan name should be 'Kang Chamolung' as 'Kang' means 'snow'; the meaning then being 'The Snow of Bird Land'. The word 'Sagarmatha' was adopted by the Nepalese as their national name for Everest during discussions with the Chinese in the 1960s over their common border and about who 'owned' Everest. An early appearance of this word can be found in the Nepali literary journal *Sharda* in 1938. An article by the noted Nepalese historian Baburam Acharya interprets 'sagar' as 'sky' and 'matha' as 'forehead'. He implies that the name was a local one and unknown in Kathmandu until 1961. The present alternative names are Chomolungma (Tibetan), Qomo-lungma Feng (Chinese) and Sagarmatha (Nepalese).

J D Hooker in the Sikkim Himalaya (1848-1850)

Between 1848 and 1850 the botanist Joseph Hooker, a friend of Charles Darwin and later President of the Royal Society and Director of the Royal Botanic Gardens at Kew, explored the Sikkim Himalaya, at that time virtually unknown both botanically and geographically. The Survey of India needed information about the Tibetan borderlands adjacent to the dominant peak Chomolhari (Peak 1) on the Bhutan-Tibet border. The peak lies just east of the main route to Lhasa from Darjeeling, which crosses the Jelep La, descends into the Chumbi valley and passes through Phari. Such was the ignorance of the geography of the whole area that Hooker comments in his Himalayan journals: 'It was not then known that Kangchenjunga [Peak 8 and the world's third highest peak], the loftiest mountain on the globe, was situated on my route and formed a principal feature of the geography of Sikkim.' Whilst in Sikkim, Hooker stayed with Brian Hodgson, the former Resident in Kathmandu, and during his botanical explorations visited Tongloo to the south and west of Darjeeling on 8 November 1848. From here he had good views of Kangchenjunga and also of Chomolhari, but commented that to the west and north there was a 'white mountain mass of stupendous elevation called by the Nepalese, Tsungau. From the bearings I took of it from several positions it is in about latitude 27° 49' and longitude 86° 24' and is probably on the west flank of the Arun river.' Later he wrote: 'It is the only mountain of the first class in magnitude between Gosainthan (north-east of Katmandoo) and Kinchinjunga [sic].' Could this have been Everest?

The Schlagintweit brothers (1855-8) and Captain H Wood, Survey of India, in Nepal (1903) and Tibet (1904)

Among the first Europeans to attempt to identify Everest were the Schlagintweit brothers who made a number of exploratory journeys in the Himalaya and Central Asia on behalf of the East India Company. Hermann Schlagintweit painted a water colour of a mountain that he thought was Everest from the south at Phalut, near Sandakphu on the Singalila Ridge which runs south from Kangchenjunga. However, from both Phalut and Sandakphu, the most dominant peak is Makalu (Peak 13), Everest being an almost invisible summit to the west. To confuse matters further the title of this painting is 'Gaurisankar or Mt Everest'.

The name 'Gaurisankar' related to a visit that Hermann Schlagintweit made in 1857 to Kathmandu. Whilst there, he climbed a small hill, Kaulia, outside the town and saw a peak that had previously been named 'Devadhunga' and called it 'Gaurisankar', which is a corruption of the word 'Gauri-Pavarti' used by local shamans. As a result, for several years Everest was called 'Gaurisankar' by geographers and mountaineers. The Survey of India, however, accepted neither the name 'Gaurisankar' nor its coordinates, but Andrew Waugh was unsuccessful in getting surveyors into Nepal to resolve the problem.

The correct identification of Everest from Nepal had to wait until 1903, when Henry Wood of the Survey of India visited the hill, Kaulia, at the instigation of the Viceroy of India, Lord Curzon. Wood's survey clearly showed that Gaurisankar (Peak 20), well known to the Survey, was 36 miles west of Everest and it was later discovered that there are two separate peaks in the Gaurisankar group. They were identified on the ground for the first time from Nepal by Eric Shipton and myself during the 1951 Everest reconnaissance expedition. The two peaks are Gaurisankar (Tibetan name: Jobo Tseringma, Peak 20, 23,440ft) which was first seen from Tibet during the 1921 Everest reconnaissance expedition, and a *higher* peak, Menlungtse (Tibetan name Jobo Garu, Peak 19, 23,560ft) which, in 1951, Shipton and I named from the river at its foot which divides it from Gaurisankar.

In the late 19th century it was much more difficult for Europeans to travel in Nepal, outside the confines of the Kathmandu valley, than it was to travel in Tibet. In the 1870s a member of the British mission in Kathmandu wrote 'the country, except for 20 miles around the capital, is as unknown to Europeans as it was 50 years ago', and it was to remain so until 1949. Wright, for 10 years the residency surgeon, described Nepal as a country 'where every enquiry made by a European is viewed with the most tedious suspicion, where the collection of statistics is looked on as their folly and where above all Baron Munchausen himself would have been considered a marvel of accuracy and truthfulness'.

Everest was later identified from Tibet in 1904 by Captain H Wood during the Younghusband expedition to Lhasa. Thus the same surveyor, Henry Wood, was the first to identify Everest from the ground in both Tibet and Nepal in succeeding years, though from a distance of 100 miles.

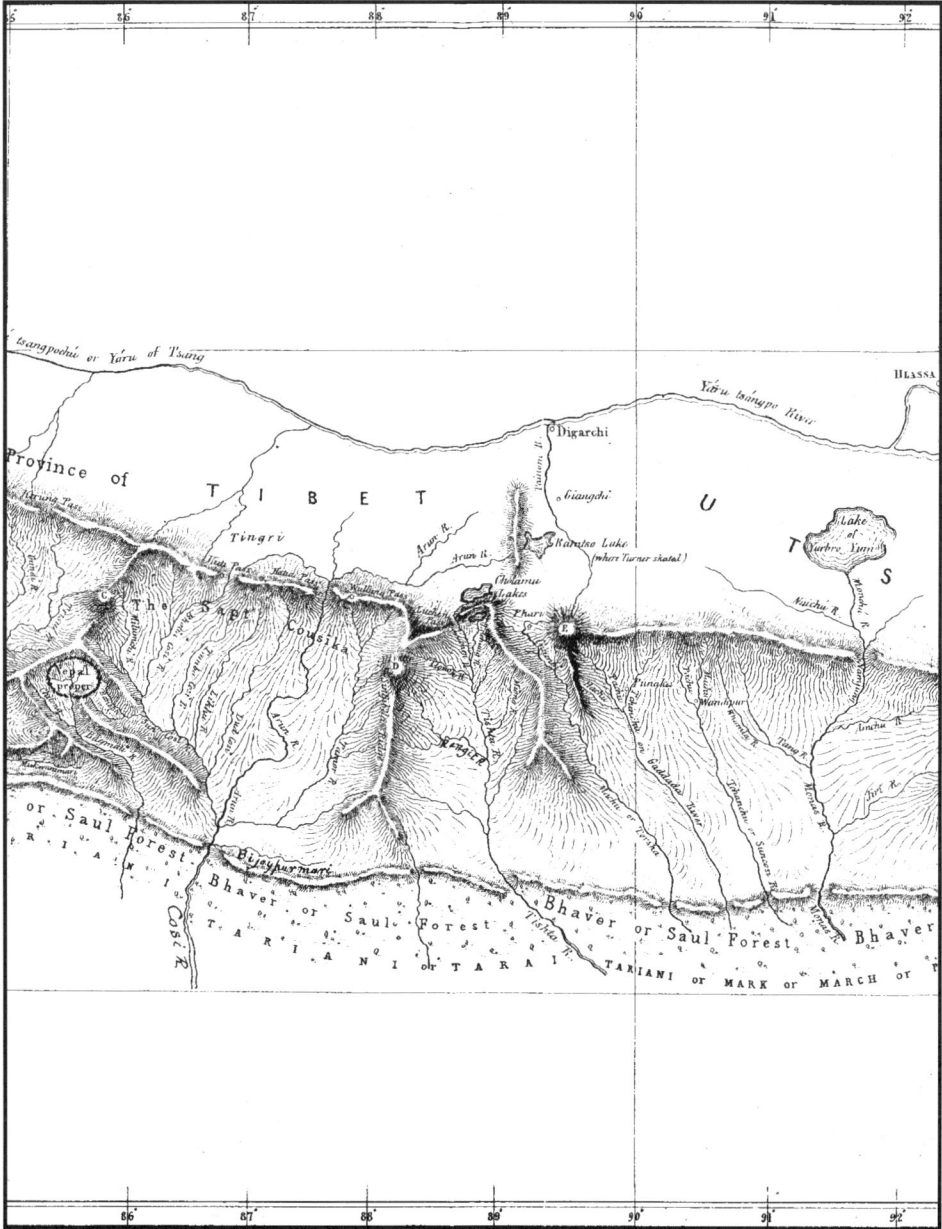

Hodgson's map of the Himalaya 1857
'Nepal proper' = Kathmandu, E = Chomolhari, D = Kangchenjunga,
C = Gosainthan.   Everest is not shown.

DIFFERENT NAMES FOR MOUNT EVEREST

Date	Name	Source
Unknown	Mi-ti Gu-ti Cha-pu Long-Nga	Tibet
	('You cannot see the summit from near it, but you can see the summit from nine directions, and a bird which flies as high as the summit goes blind.')	
c 800	Jo-mo Glung Ma	Tibetan
c 800	Jo-mo Glang Ma	Tibetan
c 800	Jo-mo Glan Ma	Abbot of Rongbuk
c 800	Jo-mo-Glan-Mahi Gangri	Abbot of Rongbuk
c 800	Gans-Ri Glan-Ma	Abbot of Rongbuk
1733	Tchoumour Lancma	d'Anville
1733	Jumu Langma Alin	Lama map
1856 (March)	Everest	Waugh
1856 (October)	Devadhunga	Hodgson
1857	Bhairavlangur	Hodgson
1857	Gnalthamthangla	Hodgson
1862	Gaurisankar	Schlagintweit
1885	Jomokangkar	Chandra Das
1899	Jomokankar (Chomokankar)	Waddell
1904	Chomo Kankar	Waddell and Chandra Das
1907	Chho Lungbhu	Natha Singh
1909	Chomo Lungmo	Bruce
1921	Chomo Uri	Howard-Bury
1921	Chomo Lungma	Howard-Bury (Tibetan)
1921	Chha-Mo-Lung Ma	Howard-Bury (Tibetan)
1952	Chumulongma	Chinese
1975	Qomolangma Feng	Chinese
1990	Sagarmatha	Nepali

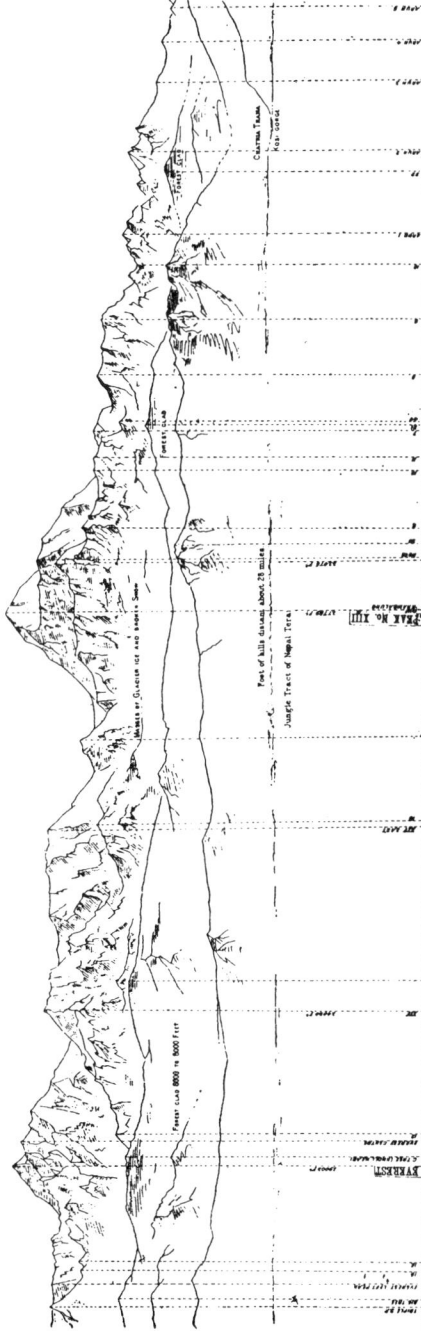

EVEREST AND "PEAK NO. XIII" from nearly due SOUTH, ON KOSI RIVER.

Lat. 26° 20' : long. 87° 5' (approx.).

(Distance of Everest about 114 miles, and "Peak XIII" about 117 miles.)

'Peak No. XIII' is Makalu

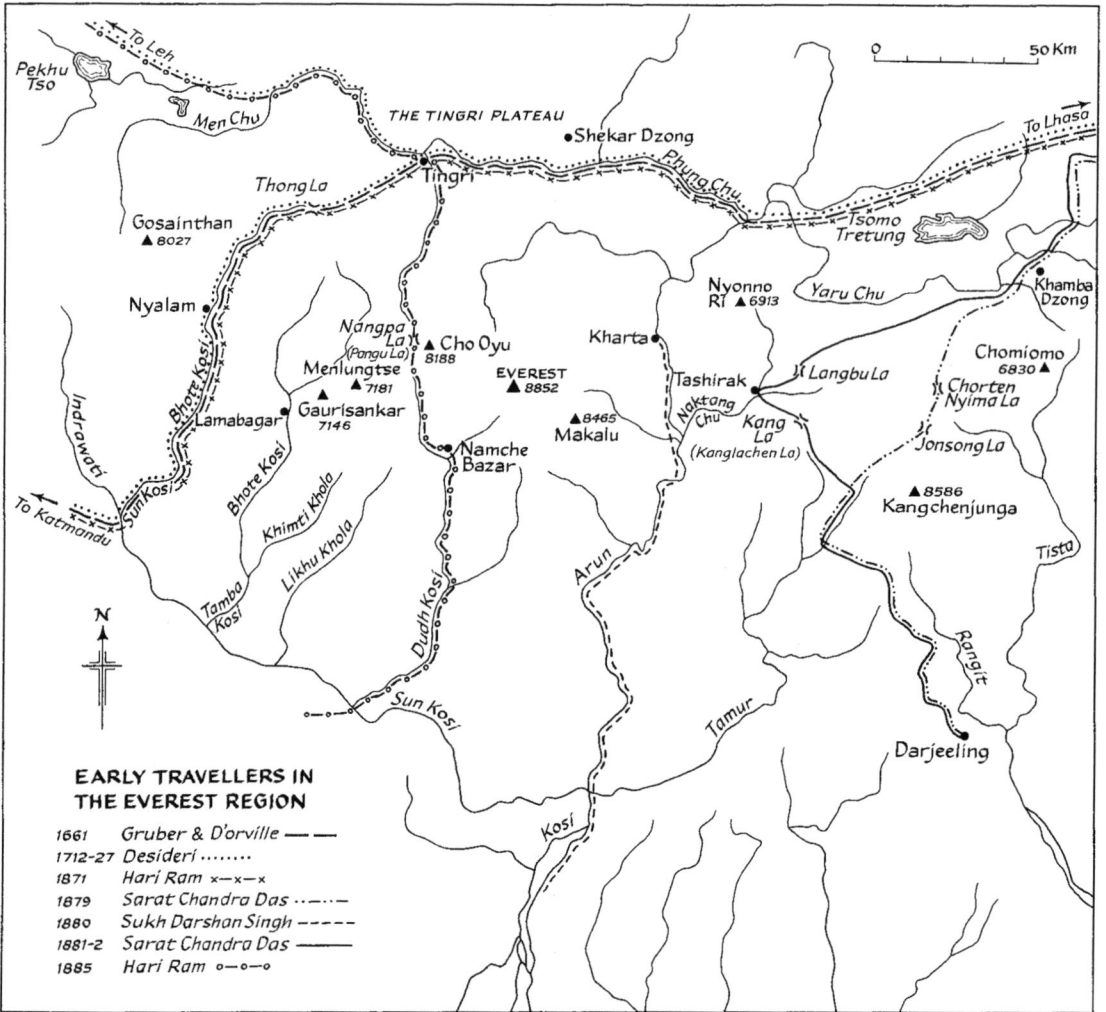

EARLY TRAVELLERS IN
THE EVEREST REGION

1661	Gruber & D'orville — —
1712-27	Desideri ....
1871	Hari Ram x—x—x
1879	Sarat Chandra Das ··—·—
1880	Sukh Darshan Singh − − − −
1881-2	Sarat Chandra Das ——
1885	Hari Ram o—o—o

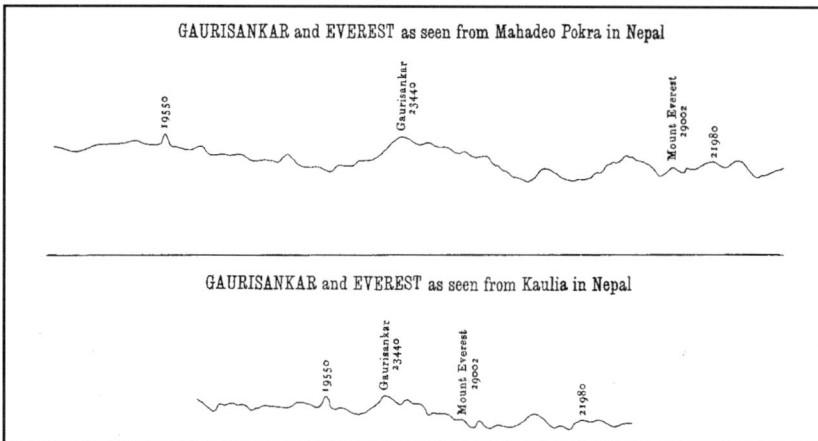

GAURISANKAR and EVEREST as seen from Mahadeo Pokra in Nepal

GAURISANKAR and EVEREST as seen from Kaulia in Nepal

PEAKS OF THE HIMALAYA IN 1858

Name	Height in ft.	Survey of India No.	Position
Chomolhari	23,944	I	Bhutan-Tibet
Gipmochi	?	II	? Sikkim
Pauhunri	23,186	III	Sikkim-Tibet
Chumonko	?	IV	? Sikkim
Black Rock	?	V	? Sikkim
Narsing	19,146	VI	Sikkim
Pandim	22,017	VII	Sikkim
? Kangchenjunga	?	VIII	Sikkim
Kangchenjunga	28,156	IX	Sikkim
Kabru	24,015	X	Sikkim
Jannu	25,304	XI	–
?	–	XII	Nepal
Makalu	27,779	XIII	Nepal-Tibet
? Chamlang	24,020	XIV	Nepal
Everest	29,002	XV	Nepal-Tibet
?	22,215	XVI	Nepal
?	22,826	XVII	Nepal
?	21,987	XVIII	Nepal
Menlungtse	23,570	XIX	Tibet
Gaurisankar	23,447	XX	Nepal-Tibet
?	19,540	XXI	? Nepal
Jibjibia East	21,853	XXII	Tibet
Gosainthan	26,305	XXIII	Tibet
Jibjibia West	22,891	XXIV	Tibet
Daya Bong	23,762	XXV	Tibet
?	24,313	XXVI	Tibet
?	23,313	XXVII	Tibet
Dhaulagiri	26,504	XXXXII	Nepal

BIBLIOGRAPHY

P V Angus-Leppan, 'The Height of Mount Everest' in *Survey Review 26*, 367-395, 1982.

Anon, 'The name of Mount Everest' in *Nature 127*, 686, 1931.

T S Blakeney, 'A Tibetan name for Everest' in *Alpine Journal 70*, 304-310, 1968.

C G Bruce, *Himalayan Wanderer*. Maclehose, 1934.

S G Burrard, 'The Everest controversy' in *Nature*, 42-46, 10 November 1904.

S G Burrard and H H Hayden, *A sketch of the geography and geology of the Himalaya mountains and Tibet*. Superintendent of Government Printing, Calcutta, India, 1907-1908.

S G Burrard, 'Mount Everest and its Tibetan names'. *Professional Paper No 26*. Geodotic Branch Office, Survey of India, Dehra Dun. 1931.

P Caraman, *Tibet. The Jesuit Century*. Halsgrove, Devon, UK, 1998.

J N Collie, 'The ranges North of Mount Everest as seen from near the Kang La' in *Alpine Journal 33*, 303-305, 1921.

J N Collie, 'A short summary of mountaineering in the Himalaya with a note on the approaches to Everest' in *Alpine Journal 33*, 295-303, 1921.

Ed. W A B Coolidge, 'Gaurisankar or Devadhunga' in Alpine Notes, *Alpine Journal 12*, 521-522, 1886.

D W Freshfield, 'Further notes on Mont Everest' in *Proceedings of the Royal Geographical Society 8*, 176-188, 1886.

Ed. D W Freshfield, 'Everest or Jomokangkar?', a note in *Alpine Journal 21*, 33-35, 1903.

D W Freshfield, 'The highest mountain in the world' in *Alpine Journal 21*, 317-320, 1903.

D W Freshfield, 'Mount Everest v. Chomolungma' in *Alpine Journal 34*, 300-303, 1922.

W R Fuchs, *Der Jesuiten Atlas der Kanshi Zeit. Monumenta Serica*. Monograph Series IV. Fujen University, Beijing 1943.

J De Graaf-Hunter, 'The Height of Mount Everest' in *Geographical Journal 121*, 21-27, 1955.

B L Gulatee, 'Mount Everest – its height and name' in *Himalayan Journal 17*, 131-142, 1952.

B L Gulatee, 'The Height of Mount Everest. A new determination (1952-54)'. *Survey of India Technical Paper No 8*, 1954.

J B du Halde, *Déscription Géographique Historique ... de l'Empire de la Chine et de la Tartarie Chinoise, Vol 4*. Le Mercier (Paris), 1735.

B H Hodgson, 'The native name of Mount Everest'. Letter in *Journal of the Asiatic Society of Bengal 25*, 467-470, 1856.

B H Hodgson, 'Route of two Nepalese embassies to Peking with remarks on the watershed and plateau of Tibet' in *Journal of the Asiatic Society of Bengal 25*, 473-497, 1856.

B H Hodgson, 'On the Physical Geography of the Himalaya' in *Journal of the Asiatic Society No 32, August*. Printed by J Thomas at the Baptist Mission Press, Calcutta, 1857.

J D Hooker, *Himalayan Journals* (2 vols.). Murray 1854.

C K Howard-Bury, *Mount Everest. The Reconnaissance*. Arnold 1922.

John Keay, *The Great Arc: the dramatic tale of how India was mapped and Everest was named*. Harper Collins, 2000.

E G H Kempson, 'The local name of Mount Everest' in H. Ruttledge, *Everest the Unfinished Adventure*. Hodder & Stoughton, 1937.

Kenneth Mason, *Abode of Snow*. Hart-Davis, 1955. Diadem/Mountaineers, 1987.

N E Odell, 'The Tibetan name of Mountain Everest' in *Alpine Journal 37*, 196, 1925.

N E Odell, 'The supposed Tibetan or Nepalese name of Mt Everest' in *Alpine Journal 47*, 127-129, 1935.

Ed. Edward Pyatt, 'The native name of Mount Everest: Sagarmatha?' in Editor's Notes, *Alpine Journal 82*, 258, 1977.

Trelawnay Saunders, 'The Himalaya Mountain System' in *Geographical Magazine*, July 1877.

Hermann von Schlagintweit, *Reisen in Indien Und Hochasien*. 4 Vols. Jena: Costenoble, 1869-80.

H A, and R Schlagintweit, *Results of a scientific mission to India and High Asia undertaken between the years 1854 and 1858, by order of the Directors of the Honourable East India Company*. 4 Vols. Brockhaus, London. Trubner, Berlin, 1861-66.

J R Smith, *Everest.The Man and the Mountain*. Whittles Publishing, 1999.

J R Ullman, *Man of Everest: the autobiography of Tenzing told to J R Ullman*. Harrap, 1955.

L A Waddell, 'The environs and native names of Everest' in *Geographical Journal 12*, 564-569, 1898.

L A Waddell, *Among the Himalayas*. Constable, 1899.

J T Walker, 'Notes on Mont Everest' in *Proceedings of the Royal Geographical Society 8*, 88-94, 1886.

J T Walker, 'A last note on Mont Everest' in *Proceedings of the Royal Geographical Society 8*, 257-263, 1886.

M P Ward, 'The Height of Mount Everest' in *Alpine Journal 100*, 30-33, 1995.

M P Ward, 'The Name of the World's Highest Peak' in *Himalayan Journal 53*, 27-35, 1997.

A S Waugh, Letter in *Proceedings of the Royal Geographical Society 1*, 345, 1855-57.

A S Waugh, Papers relating to the Himalaya and Mount Everest in *Proceedings of the Royal Geographical Society of London, No IX*, 345-6, 1857.

A S Waugh, 'On Mounts Everest and Deodanga' in *Proceedings of the Royal Geographical Society 2*, 102-115, 1858.

C Wessels, *Early Jesuit Travellers in Central Asia 1603-1721*. Martinus Nijhoff, The Hague, 1924.

H Wood, *Report on the identification and nomenclature of the Himalayan peaks as seen from Katmandu, Nepal*. Office of the Superintendent of Government Printing, Calcutta, India, 1904.

Turrell V Wylie, *The Geography of Tibet according to the Dzam-Gling-Rgyas-Bshad*. Text and English translation, Roma. Instituto Italiano per il medio estremo oriente, 1962.

Wang Yuxin, 'Qomolangma in Myths and Maps' in *High Mountain Peaks in China*. The People's Sports Publishing House of China. The Tokyo Shimbum Publishing Bureau of Japan, 1981.

COLONEL GEORGE EVEREST, FRS, 1843

Chapter 2

A SACRED AND SECRET SUMMIT

Formation of the Alpine Club in 1857

On 23 December 1857 the Alpine Club, the world's first mountaineering club, was formed in London. At its first summer dinner, on 18 June 1858, Hermann and Robert Schlagintweit were guests; so the possibility of climbing Everest is likely to have been in the minds of members of the club from the beginning. Its journal, first published in 1859 and called initially *Peaks, Passes and Glaciers*, became the *Alpine Journal* in 1863 and included in its early numbers articles concerned with extreme altitude. Mountain travel was still in its infancy, though Mont Blanc, Europe's highest peak, had been climbed on 22 August 1786 by Dr Michel-Gabriel Paccard, a medical general practitioner from Chamonix, and Jacques Balmat, a porter. The exploration of the Alps followed, hastened by the formation of both the Alpine Club and the Swiss Alpine Club.

The Matterhorn had its first ascent, from Switzerland, in 1865 by Edward Whymper in a party of seven – three of his companions and a guide falling to their deaths during the descent. The mountain's second ascent, from Italy, came a few days later. The exploration of the world's other great ranges followed and continues; many mountains, glaciers and valleys in the Himalaya and Central Asia remain unclimbed and unvisited to this day.

The Pundits, Hari Ram ('M.H.' or 'No 9'), S D Singh ('G.S.S.') and the first exploration of the Everest region, 1868-1886. L A Waddell's Tibetan Picture Map, 1898.

In the latter part of the 19th century, owing to political difficulties, the only way to learn about the topography of the Himalayan Kingdoms and Central Asia was secretly. Pundits – native explorers – were used by the Survey of India to make route maps and gather intelligence about these little-known lands. There was an urgent need for these maps because of the potentially destabilising effect of Russian expansion southwards into Tibet, which was even threatening the borders of India. British parties had not been very successful in their attempts to explore Tibet; some were murdered, others were imprisoned.

The use of trained native surveyors, or Pundits, was mainly the idea of Colonel T G Montgomerie who had been responsible for the survey of Kashmir and the Karakoram. As British military parties gradually penetrated Kashmir, the Pundits'

Nepal peaks from Sandakphu, showing Everest (29,002ft) and Makalu (27,799ft).
This contemporary drawing, dated 1886, was one of the first depictions of Mt Everest.

main efforts were concentrated in Tibet and its border lands. For the exploration of southern Tibet and eastern Nepal, Montgomerie chose Hari Ram, who came from the village of Milam in the province of Kumaon. The Milam people traded extensively with Tibet, spoke Tibetan, and were well known to the border guards; thus they were able to travel freely. Surprisingly, Hari Ram never identified Everest on his various journeys, though he circumnavigated the Everest region.

Joining the Survey in 1868 he took part in an expedition, probably as a training exercise, to the north and west of Everest, an area that had already been visited. During this journey he managed to clarify details of the Himalayan watershed that lay out of sight beyond those ranges visible from India. In fact, the minor range that separates the source of the Tsangpo, the largest river in southern Tibet, from the source of the Ganges is located north of the Himalaya and just south of the Tsangpo. Unfortunately, before he had completed his assignment, Hari Ram was apprehended by a Tibetan official and forced to leave the area.

Undaunted, he tried again in 1871, but was detained east of Everest on the Sikkim-Tibet border. Luckily he was able to ingratiate himself with a Sikkimese official whose wife was ill. Montgomerie always supplied his agents with a variety of medicines and Hari Ram also had with him the translation of a medical textbook. He matched up the lady's symptoms with those described in the book and gave her the appropriate drugs, awaiting the result with some trepidation. To his amazement the woman made a rapid recovery and the official, most impressed, provided the Pundit with a companion to vouch for him whilst in Tibet. They reached Xigatse on

17 September, and continued west to Tingri where, fearful of winter snows, Hari Ram crossed the Thong La (Kuti Pass) and descended the Nyalam valley, reaching Kathmandu in January 1872.

In 1885, after a visit to the Mustang salient – a peninsula of central Nepal that intrudes like a finger into southern Tibet – Hari Ram was again instructed to enter eastern Nepal. His mission was to follow the Dudh Kosi river to the Solu Khumbu region of NE Nepal, in which Everest lies, cross the Himalaya to Tingri, and return. Arriving at the residence of the Governor of Khumbu in mid-August, initially he was not allowed to cross to Tingri by the Nangpa La (Pangu Pass) because it had never before been crossed by a 'Hindustani or Gurkha'. Again his medical skills helped him and he was able to cure the Governor's daughter-in-law of goitre. Her husband was so indebted to him that he allowed him to cross the Nangpa La, the height of which he assessed at 20,000ft. He visited Tingri and from there turned west to the Palgu Tso Lake before returning to Kirong in Nepal.

The Nangpa La, 15 miles west of Everest, is an important glacier pass, open all year except for the three winter months. It is freely used even by families with small children, enabling Tibetans to breed yaks in the softer climate of Khumbu in Nepal. The pass is approached on the Tibetan side by a gradual ascent along the Kyetrak glacier and was visited by members of the 1921 Everest reconnaissance expedition. The steeper and narrower Nepalese approach was visited by W H Murray and T D Bourdillon during the 1951 Everest reconnaissance.

During his stay in Khumbu in 1885 Hari Ram would not have been able to see Everest from the route that he took. However, Everest is visible from Tingri and from much of his 1871 route in southern Tibet. From here it rears up as a dominant obelisk, dwarfing its mountain neighbours, but he made no mention in his report of seeing such a peak.

In 1880 another Pundit, the Hindu Sukh Darshan Singh (G.S.S.), was asked by the Survey to travel to Tingri by the Tambar valley in Central Nepal. This valley does not traverse the Himalaya and so he ascended a parallel valley further east which contains the Arun river. This rises in Tibet, where it is called the Phung Chu, and cuts through the Himalaya by a stupendous gorge, east of Everest. The Pundit G.S.S. continued up this valley to the Tibetan border at the Popti La, and crossed to the Kharta valley in Tibet but was not allowed to go any further north. The Tibetan side of this area, east of Everest, was first explored by the 1921 Everest reconnaissance party, whilst the Nepalese side was first visited by the 1951 Everest reconnaissance and again during the Cho Oyu expedition.

Thus, by the end of the 19th century, Everest remained a mystery mountain with its form not clear and its lower slopes unvisited.

Further indirect evidence about Everest came in 1898 from Dr L A Waddell, later medical officer on Francis Younghusband's mission to Lhasa in 1903-4. During a visit to the Yalung valley in eastern Nepal he gathered some notes on the topography and local names of Everest and was also given a Tibetan picture map of the region south of Tingri. This map shows a path running south from Tingri that appears to cross the main Himalayan chain by a pass, Chi'tsi. This could be either the Nangpa La (Pangu La) or a less obvious pass, the Phuse La, further west, which ends in the Rongshar valley. The mountains shown on this map are to the west of this pass and probably represent the Gaurisankar–Menlungtse group already mentioned, and not Everest, which is further east.

1892-1903 C G Bruce, F E Younghusband, Lord Curzon

Despite the failure to get near to Everest, the exploration of the Himalaya, and in particular the Karakoram, proceeded rapidly as access became politically easier.

One of the most important expeditions of this period was that led by W M Conway (later Lord Conway of Allington) to the Karakoram in 1892. This combined exploration with high-altitude medical science and made important contributions to both. It provided a link with the early Everest expeditions, since Charles Bruce, then a Lieutenant in the 5th Gurkhas and later leader of the 1922 and 1924 Everest expeditions, was a member of the party. In 1893 Bruce met Younghusband, then Political Officer in Chitral and well known for his formidable journey from Beijing to Kashmir. He suggested to Bruce that Everest might be explored from Tibet. Younghusband had already approached the Resident in Kashgar informally, suggesting that it might be possible to march via Yarkand through Tibet to Lhasa and explore the north side of the mountain, returning by Darjeeling to Bengal. This idea had the approval of Mortimer Durand, then Foreign Secretary of the Indian Government, but for political reasons it was never followed up.

The appointment in 1898 of Lord Curzon as Viceroy of India gave an added impetus to the Everest story. A brilliant politician and traveller, though not a mountaineer, Curzon had explored the source of the Oxus river in the Pamir. He had met Younghusband and also knew Douglas Freshfield, an important figure in both the Alpine Club and the Royal Geographical Society, to whom he wrote in 1898 saying that on a visit to Nepal he would seek permission to attempt Everest. But nothing came of that approach either.

At the start of the 20th century events in Central Asia brought Tibet into the political limelight, providing the impetus for exploring the approach to Everest from the north, Tibetan, side.

TIBETAN PICTURE-MAP OF MOUNT EVEREST RANGE
L A WADDELL, 1898

Part of the Pundit Map of the Mount Everest Region, 1875

The first approach to Everest from Tibet (1903-1904)

In 1902 the Viceroy, Lord Curzon, was alarmed at the increase in Russian influence in Tibet. Letters sent to Lhasa were returned unopened, and there were rumours that Russia and China had reached a secret agreement. Later that year, after much persuasion, the British Government approved a mission to Tibet, with military escort, to discuss frontier problems and commercial disputes. In the meantime J Claude White, Political Officer in Sikkim, visited the Sikkim-Tibet border to demarcate the boundary. From the northern slopes of a border peak, Chomiomo, he had a good view of Everest.

In July 1903 a mission led by Younghusband crossed the Sikkim-Tibet border bound for Gyantse in southern Tibet. This is a key village where the southern route from Tibet to India joins the east-west route from Lhasa to Leh along the Tsangpo valley. At Guru the Tibetans tried to check the British party and firing broke out. Following this incident the attitude of both the Tibetans and the British hardened, and negotiations broke down. Younghusband marched on Lhasa, the Dalai Lama fled and, in his absence, a treaty was signed by his officials which was later repudiated by the British Government.

This whole episode was considered to be the requiem for 'The Great Game' played by Curzon, Younghusband and others, but it placed Tibet squarely on the political agenda in Asia and had an important effect on future expeditions to Everest. This was because the countryside was not ravaged, there were no atrocities, and relations between Tibet and Great Britain remained remarkably good. As a result, the Tibetan authorities looked favourably on the British and accorded them special privileges, including visits to Mount Everest.

Another result of the 1903-4 mission was that it had provided a golden opportunity to survey southern Tibet and identify Everest. This task was given to C H D Ryder, C G Rawling, F M Bailey and H Wood and they followed the main east-west route along the south bank of the Tsangpo valley to the important trading post of Gartok. Henry Wood who, the year before, had identified Everest from the hill, Kaulia, in Nepal, was now able to identify the peak again from Kampa Dzong in Tibet; he confirmed that there were no higher peaks in the vicinity. A photo taken by J Claude White from Kampa Dzong in 1903 showed both Everest and Makalu.

The next year, 1904, H H Hayden, a geologist with the mission, took a further series of photos which extended over 50 miles of the Himalaya from Kangchenjunga to Everest, and these were lodged with the Royal Geographical Society.

Finally, Everest was clearly seen from a pass, the Kara La, 50 miles to the north. This was the first clear view a European had had of the peak, and it was the nearest anyone had approached to the mountain. Nearly twenty years were to elapse before its lower slopes were seen by Europeans.

C G Rawling described his view of Everest from the Kara La (17,900ft):

No sooner was the summit reached than we realised that, if a conical hill close by was climbed, we were certain to obtain a fine view of Mount Everest, and from a direction never before seen by Europeans.

The morning was cold, crisp and clear, so ... we climbed steadily until the crest of our observatory hill was reached; and well did it repay us, for to the south, and distant about fifty miles, though to all appearance much nearer on account of the rarefied atmosphere, lay the wildest part of the Himalayas fully exposed to view.

Towering up thousands of feet, a glittering pinnacle of snow, rose Everest, a giant among pigmies, and remarkable not only on account of its height, but for its perfect form. No other peaks lie near or threaten its supremacy. ... To the east and west, but nowhere in its immediate vicinity, rise other great mountains of rock and snow, each beautiful in itself, but in no other way comparing with the famous peak in solemn grandeur. It is difficult to give an idea of its stupendous height, its dazzling whiteness and overpowering size, for there is nothing in the world to compare it with. Its northern face had the appearance of a sheer precipice, but the distance was too great to decide upon this with certainty.

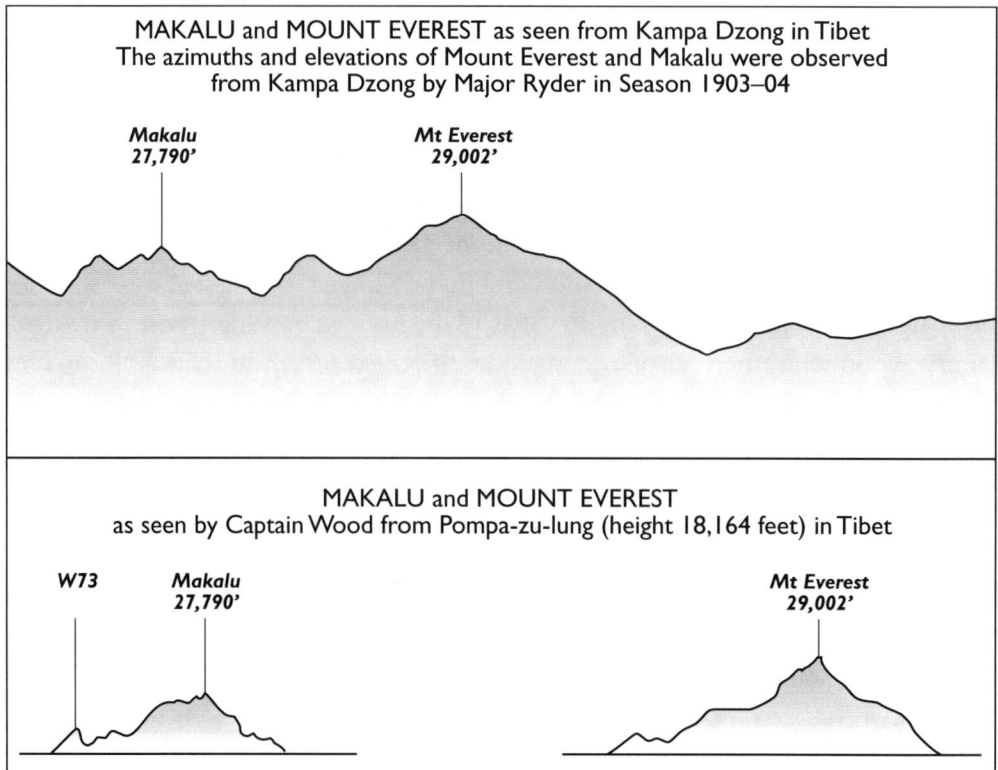

MAKALU and MOUNT EVEREST as seen from Kampa Dzong in Tibet
The azimuths and elevations of Mount Everest and Makalu were observed from Kampa Dzong by Major Ryder in Season 1903–04

Makalu 27,790'
Mt Everest 29,002'

MAKALU and MOUNT EVEREST
as seen by Captain Wood from Pompa-zu-lung (height 18,164 feet) in Tibet

W73   Makalu 27,790'
Mt Everest 29,002'

Attempts at exploration from Nepal (1905-1909) and from Tibet (1913) by Captain J B L Noel

Curzon remained keen to see Everest climbed but not from Tibet, as he thought that the effects of the Younghusband mission should be allowed to die down. In 1905, therefore, he wrote to Douglas Freshfield at the Royal Geographical Society (RGS) proposing an approach from Nepal, and an attempt on Kangchenjunga was also mentioned.

In 1907, as part of the 50th anniversary celebrations of the Alpine Club, C G Bruce, A L Mumm and T G Longstaff approached the RGS with the proposal that an expedition should enter Tibet, go to Kampa Dzong and continue to Tingri. An attempt on Everest would be made from the north, and the country to the east and west explored. In fact this was exactly the plan followed later by the first reconnaissance party in 1921. But this 1907 party was vetoed by the new Viceroy, Lord Morley, who thoroughly disapproved of Curzon's 'Forward' policy. Instead, this group visited the Garhwal where Longstaff, with the two Swiss Brocherel brothers as guides and a Gurkha soldier, Karbir, climbed Trisul (23,360ft). Their ascent and descent of 6,000 feet in one day was the forerunner of the small climbing parties which later in the 1930s carried out a great deal of Himalayan exploration.

Longstaff was a member of the 1922 Everest party and in 1906 had written one of the first medical treatises on mountain sickness. He also discovered the Siachen glacier in the Karakoram – one of the largest glaciers in the world outside the polar regions.

In the same year, 1907, as a result of pressure by Bruce and Longstaff, an Indian surveyor, Natha Singh, from the Survey of India but unaccompanied by a European, was allowed by the Nepal Government to make a hurried visit to Solu Khumbu, and here he heard Everest called 'Chho Lungbhu'. He was only able to draw the lower end of the Khumbu glacier because he had no plane table, and photography was not allowed.

In 1908 the Prime Minister of Nepal and the British Resident in Kathmandu, Major J Manners-Smith VC, discussed a joint Anglo-Nepalese expedition to Everest, and in 1909 the Nepal Durbar (Government) was prepared to permit this. But at the last moment the plan was cancelled by the British Government. While obtaining information about the mountain, C G Bruce heard it called 'Chomo Lungmo' by Sherpas from Solu Khumbu.

The next attempt to get to Everest was in 1913, from the east, by Captain J B L Noel. Born in 1890 and educated in Switzerland and the Royal Military College, Sandhurst, Noel was commissioned in the East Yorkshire Regiment and posted to India where he took local leave. His planned route to Everest, based on the 1881 account by the Pundit Sarat Chandra Das of his travels in the area, involved descending an eastern tributary of the Arun river to Tashirak (which had been ascended by Das on his way to Kampa Dzong from a little-used pass west of Kangchenjunga) and then crossing the main Arun river. With three Tibetans and himself in disguise, Noel followed the Teesta valley in Sikkim northwards towards the Himalaya. At the village of Thango he turned west following a tributary of the river until he was able to cross the mountain range of the Sikkim-Tibet border by a little-known pass, the Chorten Nyima La. Descending to the village of Mugk on the plains of southern Tibet he turned west, and crossed the Langbo pass (17,500ft). From here he could see Everest 40 miles away but there was at least one mountain range, the Nyonno Ri, in between. At the village of Tashirak, which had been visited by the Pundit Sarat Chandra Das on his way to Lhasa in 1893, Noel turned south until he was stopped by Tibetan soldiers. He managed to get to Quodo on the Nepal-Tibet border before returning to Sikkim and Darjeeling. After serving in the First World War, he joined the 1922 and 1924 Everest expeditions as a photographer. He died in 1989.

One other well-known traveller in Tibet, C G Rawling, who was a member of the 1903-4 Younghusband mission to Lhasa, planned a reconnaissance of Everest from the north in 1915, to be followed by an attempt on the summit, but the war intervened. The possibility of an aerial photographic reconnaissance of Everest was also considered at this time but the idea was not pursued.

A M Kellas (1868-1921), pioneer explorer and high-altitude physiologist

The person who knew more than anyone about the approaches to Everest and its physiological problems was A M Kellas, a lecturer in chemistry at the Middlesex Hospital Medical College in London. He had made his first Himalayan expedition in 1907 to the Pir Panjal range in Kashmir, and later to the Zemu glacier and Simvu in the Sikkim Himal. Between 1909 and 1920 he made further expeditions to Sikkim, Kashmir and Garhwal and his ascents included Langpo (22,800ft), Pauhunri (23,387ft), Chomiomo (22,430ft) and Kanchenjau (22,603ft), all peaks on the Sikkim-Tibet border. During this period he had reached 20,000ft and above on more occasions than any of his contemporaries and was one of the first to appreciate the value of using Sherpas as porters. He became increasingly interested in the physiological problems of high altitude and in 1917 proposed that an expedition should be mounted using a hut as a laboratory at 20,000ft near the summit of Kanchenjau in Sikkim. This was the forerunner of the Silver Hut physiological party that spent the winter of 1960-61 at 19,000ft in the Everest region.

Kellas's most remarkable contribution was in an unpublished manuscript, written in 1920, entitled 'A consideration of the possibility of climbing Mt Everest' and in

EASTERN APPROACHES TO EVEREST 1913

0   20   40 Km

Route of J.B.L.Noel ....

this he made many correct predictions, the most important of which was that the oxygen uptake near the summit of Everest was just under one litre (1000mls) per minute. The modern accepted value is just over this figure. He also calculated the maximum climbing rate near the summit (not using supplementary oxygen) as being 300-350ft per hour, which closely approximates to Reinhold Messner's progress of 350ft/hour in 1978 on the first ascent of Everest without supplementary oxygen.

Another point was that the 'limit of permanent acclimatisation to high altitudes', based on his own experience, was 20,000ft. The present caretaker at the Auconquilcha mine in Chile lives permanently at an altitude of 19,500ft. However, these individuals are born and bred at high altitudes; sea-level dwellers deteriorate if they spend long periods at this level, as was clearly shown on the Silver Hut expedition.

Finally, Kellas concluded that Everest could be ascended without the help of supplementary oxygen, which was finally proved to be the case in 1978.

Kellas's extraordinary prescience was ignored by Everest expeditions of the 1920s and 1930s. With J B L Noel, he was fascinated by the idea of exploring Everest and they often met at the Middlesex Hospital in London. Kellas had taught one of his native porters to use a camera and had sent him to Kharta and the Arun gorge to find a route to the east side of Everest. As a result, he knew of a hide-rope bridge across the Arun river which could be reached from Tashirak in southern Tibet. Once across the Arun, he would cross the Langma La, a pass used by shepherds to reach Kharta from the south. Into the west end of the Kharta valley a glacier flowed from a high but easy pass – the Lhakpa La – which led to the East Rongbuk glacier and Everest. Food depots would be left by Sherpas out of sight of Tibetan guards. Kellas asked Noel to join him in this daring piece of exploration but sadly the First World War intervened.

Longstaff summed up the feelings of climbers: 'People may realise the hopeless frustration of battering against political difficulties of access, (for) it was only such difficulties which for so long debarred us from exploring and attempting to climb Everest.'

Early photographs of Everest

Possibly the earliest photograph of Mount Everest was taken by Kurt Boeck in 1893. This shows the peak partially obscured by Makalu (Peak XIII). Other early photos are by Vittorio Sella taken from Chunjerma during his circumnavigation of Kangchenjunga in 1899 with D W Freshfield, and one by Bourne and Sheppard before 1903. The Kellas photograph reproduced in this monograph [*Plate 1*] was probably taken in 1920 or 1921. All these photographs are from the south and east of Everest. Photographs of the northern aspect were not taken until the Younghusband mission of 1903-1904 and on the 1921 Everest reconnaissance.

BIBLIOGRAPHY

Ed. John Ball, *Peaks, Passes and Glaciers*. Longman, Brown, Green, Longmans & Roberts, 1859.

K Boeck, *Himalaya Album. Twenty Photographs of the Indian Alps taken by K. Boeck*. Baden Baden, 1893. [See review in *Alpine Journal 17*, 374, 1893.]

W M Conway, *Climbing and Exploration in the Karakoram Himalayas*. T Fisher Unwin, 1894. With Appendix on 'Mountain Sickness' by C S Roy.

G N Curzon, *The Pamirs and the Source of the Oxus*. The Royal Geographical Society / Edward Stanford, 1896.

P Fleming, *Bayonets to Lhasa*. R Hart-Davis, 1961.

D W Freshfield, 'The highest mountain in the world' in *Alpine Journal 21*, 317-320, 1903.

H H Hayden and C Cosson, *Sport and Travel in the Highlands of Tibet*. R Cobden-Sanderson, 1927.

R L G Irving , *A History of British Mountaineering*.Batsford, 1955.

A M Kellas, 'A consideration of the possibility of ascending the loftier Himalaya' in *Geographical Journal 49*, 26-47, 1917.

A M Kellas, 'The possibility of aerial reconnaissance in the Himalaya' in *Geographical Journal 51*, 374-389, 1918.

A M Kellas, 'Sur la possibilité de faire l'ascension du Mont Everest' in *Congrès de l'Alpinisme*, Monaco, 1920.

A M Kellas, 'A consideration of the possibility of ascending Mount Everest' in *High Altitude Medicine and Biology, Vol. 2, Number 3*, 427-461, 2001.

T G Longstaff, *Mountain Sickness and its Probable Causes*. Spottiswode, 1906.

T G Longstaff, 'A Mountaineering expedition to the Himalaya of Garhwal' in *Geographical Journal 31*, 1908.

T G Longstaff, 'Glacier exploration in the Eastern Karakoram' in *Geographical Journal 35*, 622-658, 1910.

T G Longstaff, *This My Voyage*. Murray, 1950.

A L Mumm, *Five Months in the Himalaya*. Arnold 1909.

J B L Noel, *Through Tibet to Everest*. Arnold, 1927.

J B L Noel, 'A Journey to Tashirak in southern Tibet and the eastern approaches to Mount Everest' in *Geographical Journal 53*, 289-308, 1919.

I S Rawat, *Indian Explorers of the 19th Century*. Ministry of Information and Broadcasting. Government of India, 1973.

C G Rawling, *The Great Plateau*. Arnold 1905.

C G Rawling, *Military Report on Western Tibet including Changtang and Rudok*. Intelligence Branch of the Quarter Master General's Department. Simla, India, 1905.

Ed. W W Rockhill, *Sarat Chandra Das, Journey to Lhasa and Central Tibet*. Murray, 1902.

C H D Ryder, 'Exploration and survey with the Tibet Frontier Commission, and from Gyangtse to Simla via Gartok' in *Geographical Journal 26*, 369-395, 1905.

Unattributed note, 'Work of the Native Explorer M.H. in Tibet and Nepal in 1885-86' in *Proceedings of the Royal Geographical Society (New Series) 10*, 89-91, 1888.

L A Waddell , 'The environs and native names of Everest' in *Geographical Journal 12*, 564-569, 1898.

D Waller, *The Pundits: British Exploration of Tibet and Central Asia*. The University of Kentucky Press, 1990.

J B West, 'Highest inhabitants in the world' in *Nature 324*, 517, 1986.

J B West, 'Alexander M Kellas and the physiological challenge of Mount Everest' in *Journal of Applied Physiology 63*, 3-11, 1987.

J B West, 'A M Kellas. Pioneer Himalayan physiologist and mountaineer' in *Alpine Journal 94*, 207-213, 1989/90.

J B West, 'Introduction to a previously unpublished paper by A M Kellas' in *High Altitude Medicine and Biology, Vol. 2, Number 3*, pp 427-461, 2001.

J Claude White, *Sikkim and Bhutan*. Arnold, 1909.

Ed. George Yeld, 'Notes on Himalayan Exploration' in *Alpine Journal 23*, 50-51, 466-468, 1907.

Chapter 3

'THINNESSE OF THE AIRE'

Introduction

Because Everest is over 29,000ft high and a thousand feet higher than any other peak in the world, it is the only mountain where the medical problems involved in climbing it are even more challenging than the mountaineering problems. It was this fact that frustrated success for over thirty years and, at the same time, brought mountaineers into contact with medical scientists.

In the 19th century the only people who had been to a comparable altitude were balloonists, some of whom had died suddenly from oxygen lack. Mountaineers were now about to enter a region of the natural world where the dangers posed by high altitude could only be countered by the use of supplementary oxygen or long-term acclimatisation to oxygen lack.

Barometric pressure: Torricelli (1644) and Pascal (1648)

The idea that air, about a fifth of which consists of oxygen (the rest being nitrogen), had weight and exerted pressure on the earth's surface had to wait for the Renaissance before it was fully appreciated. Evangelista Torricelli, a pupil of Galileo, realised that the force of a vacuum was caused by the weight or pressure of the atmosphere. He also wondered if this pressure would be less on the tops of mountains than at sea level, and he made the first mercury barometer, probably in 1644, to measure this 'weight' of the atmosphere.

In 1648 the French mathematician and philosopher Blaise Pascal suggested that his brother-in-law, F. Perier, should take a barometer to the top of the Puy du Dôme (4,800ft) in Central France to see whether, as he believed, the barometric pressure was lower on the summit than at the base of the peak. He was right, and it fell by three inches during an ascent of '500 fathoms'. This proved that the pressure or 'weight' of air, and of the oxygen in the air, was less at altitude. It followed that less oxygen was driven through the walls of the lungs into the blood. This oxygen lack is the primary problem faced by man at high altitude and is the cause of mountain sickness and its complications.

In the early part of the 20th century another important observation was made by a German physiologist, Nathan Zunz, namely that barometric pressure varies with temperature. Later it was also found that, for a given altitude, it is higher in equatorial regions (such as Everest at 28°N) than in polar latitudes. For instance, the barometric pressure on the top of Everest on 21 October 1981, when it was measured for the first time, was 253 mmHg (against 760 mmHg at sea level), whereas if Everest had been in the position of Mt McKinley at 63°N, the pressure at its summit would have been 223 mmHg, which is much too low to be reached without the use of supplementary oxygen. Thus it is only Everest's geographical position in the equatorial region that allows it to be climbed without supplementary oxygen – a feat carried out for the first time by Reinhold Messner and Peter Habeler, Austrian mountaineers, in 1978.

PERIER PREPARES TO CLIMB THE PUY DU DÔME

Florin Perier measured the barometric pressure at the bottom and on the summit of the Puy du Dôme in 1648, and showed that it decreased as altitude increased.

Balloonists, Italian and English (1862-75). Paul Bert, the founder of high-altitude medicine (1878). Angelo Mosso (1898) and the first high-altitude laboratory.

The effect of sudden, acute oxygen lack is coma followed by death. The first individuals to be exposed to this hazard were balloonists who ascended rapidly to great altitudes in the 18th and 19th centuries. Though mountaineers are exposed to oxygen depletion more gradually, and can acclimatise as a result, the experiences of balloonists had a profound effect on Everest mountaineers. In particular, in 1875, two out of three Italian balloonists died after ascending rapidly to 27,000ft. The surviving third man, Tissandier, was about to become comatose when he was able to vent hydrogen,which enabled the balloon *Zenith* to descend.

This tragedy ensured that all Everest expeditions expecting to go higher than 27,000ft took with them supplementary oxygen. It also led to a profound misunderstanding between the effects of *acute* oxygen lack, as in balloon ascents, and *chronic* oxygen lack, as in ascents to altitude on foot (and in chronic lung disease).

Paul Bert, whom the Italian balloonists consulted before their ascent in *Zenith*, was Professor of Physiology in Paris. He is now considered to have been the 'father' of high-altitude medical studies, and wrote a classic work *La Pression Barometrique* in 1878. Bert considered that the symptoms of mountain sickness were caused by oxygen lack; but his work did not go unchallenged, particularly by Angelo Mosso, Professor of Physiology in Turin, who built a laboratory on Punta Gnifetti, a summit of Monte Rosa in the European Alps. Mosso thought that mountain sickness was caused by excessive carbon dioxide in the blood, produced by working muscles. This controversy was later settled in favour of oxygen lack as being the main cause of mountain sickness.

From the point of view of mountaineers, an important series of balloon ascents was made by the British meteorologists Coxwell and Glaisher in 1862. They both noted that on successive ascents to 27,000ft and above, without supplementary oxygen, a tolerance (or acclimatisation) to oxygen lack occurred. However, Glaisher, who lived to be 94 years old, did observe that 'at six to seven miles high I experienced the limit of our power of breathing in the attenuated atmosphere'.

Mountain sickness in Tibet and South America

One of the first descriptions of mountain sickness comes from Chinese sources between BC 37 and BC 32. A Chinese official counselled against a party going from Pe-Shan, SE of Yarkand, to Afghanistan because they would be passing 'the Great Headache Mountain, the Little Headache Mountain, the Red Land and the Fever Slope, when men's bodies become feverish, they lose colour and are attacked with headache and vomiting'. In addition, a case of mountain sickness (possibly high-altitude pulmonary oedema) was reported in AD 403 by Fa-Hsien, a Chinese traveller whose companion died after foaming at the mouth when they were crossing a pass, probably in Kashmir.

The Tibetans, too, recognised mountain sickness, which they called 'La-Drak', 'the Poison of the Pass' or 'The Poison of the Mountain'. This was thought to

LA

PRESSION BAROMÉTRIQUE

RECHERCHES

DE PHYSIOLOGIE EXPÉRIMENTALE

PAR

PAUL BERT

PROFESSEUR A LA FACULTÉ DES SCIENCES DE PARIS

LAURÉAT DE L'ACADÉMIE DES SCIENCES
(Prix de physiologie expérimentale, 1865)

LAURÉAT DE L'INSTITUT (Grand Prix biennal, 1875)

AVEC 89 FIGURES DANS LE TEXTE

PARIS

G. MASSON, ÉDITEUR

LIBRAIRE DE L'ACADÉMIE DE MÉDECINE

BOULEVARD SAINT-GERMAIN, EN FACE DE L'ÉCOLE DE MÉDECINE

M DCCC LXXVIII

Title page of the first 'textbook' on barometric pressure, 1878.

be due to the exhalations of mischievous gods who also caused earthquakes and landslides. Another long-standing form, 'Tutek', was recognised in Tibetans working at 16-17,000ft in gold mines in western Tibet. The sufferers invariably died. Other causes of mountain sickness were thought to derive from the 'pestilential vapour' given off by rhubarb, which grows in the mountains. Eating garlic, smoking tobacco, and incising the forehead at the hair-line were thought to be suitable alternative treatments.

Christian missionaries entering Tibet in the 16th century described mountain sickness, though cold was often thought to be more lethal; frostbite is depicted in a Tibetan medical text that dates back to BC 889.

In the highlands of South America mountain sickness was well recognised from earliest times, and was thought to be due either to the metal antimony or the vapours of rhubarb, primroses or roses. The government of the Incas clearly recognised its effect and those who normally lived by the sea died in great numbers if transported to mines at 3000m-4000m. These deaths were probably due to a combination of malnutrition, disease, altitude and cold.

The first important description of mountain sickness was given by Father Joseph D'Acosta in 1590, when crossing 'a high pass in the Andes'. He wrote '[I] was surprised with such pangs of straining and casting as though I thought to caste up my heart too, having caste up fleugme and choller both yellow and greene. In the end I caste up blood with the straining of my stomach. To conclude, if this had continued I should undoubtedly have died.' He considered these symptoms were due to the 'thinnesse of the aire'. It was an inspired deduction coming as it did many years before the work of Torricelli in Italy.

Other disorders of altitude

Over the centuries a number of other disorders of altitude became increasingly recognised. One of the most dramatic of these occurred in a physician from Chamonix, Dr Jacottet, who died on Mont Blanc at a height of about 14,500ft from what a post-mortem examination diagnosed as 'waterlogged lungs, the result of pneumonia'. There seems little doubt that this case, first reported in Angelo Mosso's book *Life of Man on the High Alps*, was one of high-altitude pulmonary oedema, or water in the lungs.

The first good modern clinical description of other forms of mountain sickness was given in 1913 by Ravenhill, an English doctor attached to a mining town in South America. He differentiated between a high-altitude cerebral oedema and a cardiac form. But the latter is now regarded as being pulmonary oedema. The condition was described again in 1937 by Alberto Hurtado, a South American physician, and by Lundberg in 1952. It was re-discovered by C S Houston in 1960, and is now recognised as one of a number of clinical conditions of altitude in which there is a disorder of fluid balance brought on by oxygen lack, over-exertion and other factors.

Another dramatic disorder at altitude is a 'stroke', or paralysis of one side of the body. This phenomenon was first reported in Tibet by a Russian traveller, Roborovsky. Further cases were noted on early Everest expeditions.

At altitude control of breathing is disorganised, and on a famous occasion John Tyndall (1820-93), a distinguished scientist and early member of the Alpine Club, was thought to have died on the top of Mont Blanc (15,850ft) because his breathing had stopped for such a long period. This disorder, first described by John Hunter, the father of scientific surgery, in 1781, is well known to occur in terminally ill patients and is referred to as periodic or Cheyne-Stokes respiration. Yet another disorder is the physical and mental deterioration that occurs after spending long periods above 19,000ft. This was first noted in 1909 in the course of the Duke of the Abruzzi's expedition to the Karakoram, and was investigated and confirmed during the Silver Hut expedition to the Everest region in 1960-61.

The other main feature of altitude is cold. It was, however, only relatively recently that specific disorders of cold were recognised, and the mountaineer may suffer from each or all of them simultaneously. These disorders are hypothermia, or general cold injury, when the core temperature of the body falls to 35°C or below (the normal core temperature is 37°C); frostbite, when the tissues freeze at 0°C and may become gangrenous; and non-freezing cold injury, when the tissues are at 0°C–15°C. At extreme altitude the mountaineer, particularly if he is not using supplementary oxygen, may suffer from disorders of both high altitude and cold – a potentially lethal combination. That is why the region over 8,000 metres is often called 'the death zone'.

Oxygen and the *diffusion* versus *secretion* controversy: experiments by Joseph Barcroft and J B S Haldane

At the end of the 19th century the fact that climbers were able to exercise at great altitude amazed many physiologists, since this required greatly increased amounts of oxygen to fuel the muscles. Moreover, it was thought at the time that insufficient oxygen could *diffuse* through the lungs from the air to the blood. The explanation seemed to be that the lungs produced, or secreted, oxygen at great altitude. This was a matter of fundamental importance in understanding the transport of oxygen in the body and in the burgeoning subjects of anaesthetics, lung medicine and surgery. One possible method of testing this was to lower the oxygen pressure in the lungs by going to great altitude and simultaneously measuring the oxygen in the blood and lungs.

Two physiologists, Joseph Barcroft and J B S Haldane, from Cambridge and Oxford Universities respectively, were often in competition; to test their theories they visited the European Alps, Pike's Peak in the United States, Pico de Teide on Tenerife and the Altiplano of South America.

In 1920 a clinching experiment was performed by Barcroft on himself in a specially constructed decompression chamber in the physiology laboratory at Cambridge. This indicated that oxygen was *diffused* and not *secreted* by the lungs. Haldane, however, continued to believe in the secretion theory until his death in 1936.

The estimation of 'blood gases', ie oxygen and carbon dioxide, is now a routine examination in all hospitals and has been of immense benefit in the diagnosis and treatment of heart and lung disease at sea level, for which the fit mountaineer, at altitude, is such a good model.

BIBLIOGRAPHY

Paul Bert, *Barometric Pressure*. 1878. Translation from the French by M A and
    F Hitchcock. College Book Company, Ohio, 1943.

Fa-Hsien, *A record of Buddhistic kingdoms*, being an account by the Chinese monk
    Fa-Hsien of his travels in India and Ceylon (AD 399-414) in search of the
    Buddhist Books of Discipline. Translated and annotated with a Korean recension
    of the Chinese text by J. Legge, Dover Publications, New York, 40-41, 1965.
    (Page 12 of the Korean text.)

J S Milledge, 'The Great Oxygen Secretion Controversy' in *Lancet 2, 1408-1411*. 1985.

Angelo Mosso, *Life of Man on the High Alps*. T Fisher Unwin, 1898.

M P Ward, J S Milledge, J B West, chapter entitled 'History' in *High Altitude Medicine
    and Physiology*. 3rd Edition. Arnold, 2000.

J B West, *High Life. A History of High Altitude Physiology and Medicine*.
    Oxford University Press, 1998.

A Wylie (1881) 'Notes on the Western Regions', translated from the Tseen Han
    Shoo Book 96, Part 1 in *Journal of the Royal Anthropological Institute 10*, 20-73, 1881.

Chapter 4

NORTHERN APPROACHES 1918-21

Introduction

The First World War was hardly over before the subject of Everest was raised at the Royal Geographical Society (RGS), and on 19 December 1918 Sir Thomas Holditch, the President, reopened negotiations with the Secretary of State for India on behalf of his society and the Alpine Club. As Everest was now the world's major unsolved geographical problem, any solution would involve both geographers and mountaineers and he urged that an expedition be mounted the following year.

C K Howard-Bury and Tibet

Early in 1919, and quite independently, Lt Col C K Howard-Bury wrote to A R Hinks, Secretary of the RGS, suggesting that a preliminary reconnaissance of the mountain should be made that summer, followed later by an attempt on the summit. Howard-Bury was a high Tory who had valuable contacts in India. Although he was not a mountaineer, he had made a secret journey into western Tibet in 1905 and had also travelled in the Tien Shan, the Karakoram and Kashmir between 1905 and 1909. He was tenacious, knowledgeable about flowers, and understood the people of India well. His initial plan was to travel to Tingri in southern Tibet to see if this might be a suitable base for the expedition, and he would then return to Gyantse to seek permission for the expedition through the good offices of the British Trade Agent. If possible, he would also visit the Tashi Lumpo monastery at Shigatse to meet the Tashi Lama, who was second only to the Dalai Lama in the priestly hierarchy of Tibet and in whose 'diocese' Everest lay. A visit to Kathmandu to obtain permission to visit Everest from Nepal was also a possibility, and Howard-Bury proposed seeing the Surveyor-General and the Director of Flying in India for the purpose of setting up an aerial reconnaissance of the mountain. All this was to be done at his own expense.

The Government of India objected to these proposals because it feared that they might prejudice a scheme of its own for installing wireless stations at Gyantse and Lhasa to counter possible Japanese activity in Tibet. In 1919 the Japanese were gradually taking control of China's telegraph and wireless communications and it was feared that this action might spread to Tibet.

The choice of Tingri village as a base for an Everest expedition was first suggested by Captain C G Rawling as a result of his survey of western Tibet, carried out following Younghusband's mission to Lhasa in 1903-4. Tingri was an important focal point, being the Tibetan terminus of a main trade route with Nepal via the Nyalam valley. The route through the Himalaya from Khumbu via the Nangpa La also ended here, as did a subsidiary route by the Phuse La and the Rongshar valley. Finally, the Kyetrak glacier leading from the Nangpa La towards Tingri might provide access to Everest from the west.

Despite the refusal of the Government of India, the matter was not allowed to rest. After hearing a lecture at the RGS by Captain J B L Noel on his attempt in 1913 to approach Everest from the east, Sir Francis Younghusband and others at the RGS spoke strongly in favour of a full-scale attempt.

With the backing of the RGS, Howard-Bury visited India in 1920, saw the Viceroy at Simla and also Sir Charles Bell, the Political Officer in Sikkim, who dealt with Tibetan affairs for the Government of India. By this time the fear of Japanese infiltration into Tibet had receded, but Bell frankly admitted that he was opposed to an Everest expedition because of friction between the Tibetan and British governments over a consignment of ammunition being sent to Tibet. The Dalai Lama was friendly towards Britain but his Council (Tsongdu) favoured turning to China for support.

Eventually it was decided that Bell should visit Lhasa that winter (1920) and semi-official instructions were sent to him asking him to sound out the Dalai Lama and the Tibetan Government about a possible expedition to Everest. The inference was that he should explain that, if no reason existed to fear severe objections on Tibet's part, the Government of India would be glad if permission were granted for an expedition to Everest. This was done.

Sir Charles Bell and the Dalai Lama

Sir Charles Bell visited the Dalai Lama in the late autumn of 1920 at his private estate, the Norbu Linka, about a mile ouside Lhasa. Unlike the bleak valley of the Kyi Chu, this was well watered, with many trees, shrubs and flowers. Later a small zoo was added. Within this walled area there were many houses and lodges belonging to the Dalai Lama and his family. His room was furnished partly as an English sitting room and partly as a Tibetan chapel.

After a preliminary visit Bell, who was very highly regarded by the Dalai Lama, put forward the proposal for an Everest expedition, a concept entirely new to the Tibetans and one of which they might well have been suspicious. Bell left a map and returned some days later, to be told that permission had been granted. It is likely that the expedition was viewed by the Tibetans as a pilgrimage, a concept with which they were familiar.

A passport to travel in Tibet was sent to the 1921 reconnaissance expedition by the Government of Lhasa under the seal of the Prime Minister of Tibet. In translation, it read as follows:

To the Jongpens, and headmen of Phari Jons, Ting-Ke, Kamba and Kharta.
You are to bear in mind that a party of Sahibs are coming to see the Chha-mo-lung-ma mountain and they will evince great friendship towards the Tibetans. On the request of the Great Minister Bell a passport has been issued requiring you and all officials and subjects of the Tibetan Government to supply transport, e.g. riding ponies, pack animals and coolies as required by the Sahibs, the rates for which should be fixed to mutual satisfaction. Any other assistance that the Sahibs may require either by day or by night, on the march or during halts, should be faithfully given, and their requirements about transport or anything else should be promptly attended to. All the people of the country, wherever the Sahibs may happen to come, should render all necessary assistance in the best possible way, in order to maintain friendly relations between the British and Tibetan Governments.

Despatched during the Iron-Bird Year.
Seal of the Prime Minister.

The word Chha-mo-lung-ma meant a district or valley where birds are kept and referred to the Rongbuk valley. According to Bell the correct Tibetan name was Kang Chha-mo Lung-ma or 'The Snows of Bird Land'. However, the present Tibetan name, Chomo-lungma, is now in general use.

H T Morshead and A M Kellas test oxygen on Kamet in the Garhwal Himal

In 1920, at Sir Thomas Holditch's suggestion, Kellas, with H T Morshead of the Survey of India, made an attempt on Kamet (Peak 67, 25,447ft) with the aim not only of climbing the mountain but also of testing oxygen equipment for the proposed Everest expedition in 1921. After camping at 22,000ft they reached the saddle, at 23,600ft, between Kamet and Abi Gamin (24,170ft); but since their porters were suffering severely from cold and Morshead's leave had nearly expired, they descended. Both had acclimatised well and their ascent had been made at a rate of 320ft/hour. Since much step-cutting had been necessary, it appeared that in better conditions an ascent of 600ft/hour might be possible. This rate would be comparable to that of T G Longstaff on Trisul (Peak 58) at a similar height in 1907. Kellas calculated that, on Everest, without supplementary oxygen, the 'last thousand feet' could be climbed at between 250ft and 350ft per hour. Although oxygen equipment was taken on

Kamet, neither climber had felt the need to use it. In any event, the oxygen cylinders were too heavy for use at over 18,000ft and below that level they were not required.

A series of further experiments was carried out involving rubber bags containing oxylite (sodium peroxide), which produces oxygen when water is added. Tests were made, firstly, while breathing supplementary oxygen at rest and then climbing without it, when no gain in rate of ascent was noted; the second test was made while climbing using supplementary oxygen, when the rate of ascent increased as a result. This proved that, providing the O_2 cylinders were light enough, their weight would *not* cancel out an increased rate of ascent.

The main complaint, in 1920, was that the stoves did not function well at altitude, so that little or no hot food had been available and it was difficult to melt snow to obtain water; as a result, dehydration could not be countered and had resulted in undue fatigue.

While Kellas was waiting in Darjeeling for the 1921 expedition to assemble, he trained Sherpas and climbed a peak, Narsingh, and made an attempt on Kabru. There is little doubt that the exhaustion brought about by these efforts contributed to his death, aged 53, on the Plateau, at Kampa Dzong, some weeks later.

The Oxford University decompression chamber experiments

Because of malfunctioning stoves on Kamet, sample stoves were tested in a decompression chamber at Oxford by Professor G Dryer, FRS (1873-1934). He was a consultant to the RAF and had done a great deal of altitude work for them. His views on the use of oxygen on Everest were unambiguous: 'I do not think that you will get up [Everest] without, but if you do succeed you may not get down again.' His opinion had impressed J P Farrar, Alpine Club President from 1917 to 1919, and the whole altitude-oxygen problem was taken very seriously.

The stoves were duly altered for use at altitude and on Good Friday, March 1921, George Finch, mountaineer and research chemist, went to Oxford with P J H Unna to take part in further tests. Unna was a civil engineer, an experienced mountaineer and a member of the Alpine Club. Recognised as an expert on mountain equipment, Unna took a great interest in anything mechanical that mountaineers might find useful. Whilst at Oxford, George Finch was easily convinced that the use of supplementary oxygen should receive serious consideration for a summit attempt.

The next day Finch was decompressed to the equivalent of 21,000ft and exercised both with and without oxygen. Obviously this experiment was not conclusive, since it took no account of acclimatisation, but it did indicate the importance of supplementary oxygen in the presence of *acute* oxygen lack.

The Oxford experiments alerted the Everest Committee to the need to take supplementary oxygen in 1922; this was not considered necessary for the 1921 party which was a reconnaissance only. Time was short, as the expedition was due to depart for India in August 1921. Money had to be raised and an example was set when King George V made a donation. Finally, *The Times* agreed to make up the shortfall in return for articles.

Preparations for the 1921 reconnaissance and choice of membership

On 15 December 1920 the Viceroy of India, Lord Chelmsford, telegraphed the India Office in London explaining that Sir Charles Bell had been successful in obtaining permission from the Dalai Lama for an expedition to Everest. This message galvanised the Alpine Club and the RGS into activity. Howard-Bury always considered that the best approach to Everest would be from Tibet. The route from Darjeeling over the ring of peaks forming the Sikkim-Tibet border by the Jelup La to Phari in the Chumbi valley was well known, as it was the main trade route with Lhasa. Thus, grain and fodder could be obtained easily. Moreover, at Gyantse the proposed route joined another trade route leading west to Kampa Dzong and Tingri, with no high passes to cross.

The Nepalese approach was also considered, and here two routes were possible. One, previously used by the Pundit G.S.S., was via the Arun valley and over the Popti La into Tibet on the eastern side of Everest; the other was the western route, followed by Hari Ram, over the Pangu La (Nangpa La) with descent to Tingri. However, the paths in that country were poor, and in any case it was felt that the Nepalese Government was unlikely to give permission for the expedition to pass through Nepal; although a good deal longer, the Tibetan route seemed to be a better choice over all.

The Tibetan route provided a further advantage: communication was easier, there being a daily post to Phari and a telephone and telegraph line between Darjeeling and Gyantse. The use of aeroplanes for reconnaissance, as suggested by A M Kellas, was vetoed as impractical since, once landed at altitude, no plane, it was believed, could take off again because of the 'thinnesse of the aire'. Transport would be provided by yaks and ponies, whilst Sherpas from Khumbu could be recruited at Tingri, together with Bhotia shepherds from the Sikkim-Tibet border region.

The Everest Committee, under the chairmanship of Sir Francis Younghusband, was set up in January 1921 with A R Hinks (Secretary of the RGS), as Secretary, E L Somers-Cock and Colonel E M Jack, also from the RGS, and, as Alpine Club members, Professor J N Collie (the President), C F Meade and J P Farrar.

They passed the following Resolution:

> The main object this year (1921) is reconnaissance. This does not debar the mountain party from climbing as high as possible on a favourable route but attempts on a particular route must not be prolonged to hinder the completion of the reconnaissance.

The RGS was concerned mainly with surveying and exploratory aspects, whilst climbing the mountain was the Alpine Club's main concern. However, as secretary of the larger organisation, with an adequate secretariat, A R Hinks tended to dominate the proceedings. The quip 'What I do not know is not knowledge' could easily have been attributed to him. A formidable and forceful man, he gave unstinting service to the RGS for many years. A Fellow of the Royal Society, a brilliant mathematician and an academic cartographer, he was quite ignorant of field work and took little interest in mountain exploration – both subjects upon which he would cheerfully pontificate – but he helped young travellers in an imaginative way. He detested publicity and was rather unworldly.

Later, with H F Milne, the RGS's chief draughtsman, Hinks produced the first vital map, completed between 1933 and 1945, of both the north and south sides of Everest. This was a *tour de force*, as the drawing of the southern (Nepalese) side of the mountain had to be completed from aerial photographs taken on the 'Flight over Everest' expedition. This map was a crucially important factor in my discovery of a new route up Everest from Nepal early in 1951, which was the *raison d'être* of the 1951 Everest reconnaissance expedition.

The 1921 party was chosen with exploration and mapping as its primary objective, but the Everest Committee had decided that the membership of any expedition should be British – a decision that ruled out one of the most distinguished mountain cartographers in Europe, the Swiss Marcel Kurz. No Europeans had been within fifty miles of the peak and the north, east and west sides still had to be explored and mapped, the southern, Nepalese aspect being out of bounds. The altitude problem was also recognised from the start as being probably the most critical barrier to success, but in 1921 it was not a factor, since the expedition was not expected to go very high and therefore no supplementary oxygen was taken.

Initially the ebullient and gregarious C G Bruce, an officer in the Indian Army, was considered as a possible leader. A legend among the Gurkhas in India, he was not, at the age of 55, expected to go high, but his knowledge of mountain travel in the Himalaya and the Karakoram was unrivalled, as was his *rapport* with the hill people. However, he had just taken up a new post and was not available. As the Committee was in Howard-Bury's debt for all his work on their behalf, and as he also had a formidable record of Central Asian travel, he was chosen as leader in spite of being a non-mountaineer. A rich man, too, he could pay his own way.

The members of the survey party were chosen and paid for by the Survey of India. The Surveyor-General, C H D Ryder, had surveyed southern Tibet in 1904 and he chose Major H T Morshead who, with F M Bailey, had been in SE Tibet in 1913 surveying the Tsangpo river and confirming that it was continuous with the Dihang and Brahmaputra rivers in India. Morshead had recently been on Kamet with Kellas, testing stoves and oxygen equipment. The other member was E O Wheeler, later Surveyor General of India in 1941-46, who made use of photo-theodolite survey techniques recently developed in Canada. Kenneth Mason, later Superintendent, Survey of India, and the first Professor of Geography at Oxford University from 1932 to 1953, was the reserve.

To avoid upsetting the Tibetans they were asked not to go off the beaten track, a flexible request under all the circumstances. The Tibetans were very friendly towards the surveyors and invitations from local Dzong Pens were extended and accepted by this party. Relations remained cordial except in one instance: in the Rongshar valley, west of Everest, their reception was decidedly unfriendly. As late as 1924, F M Bailey, now Political Officer in Sikkim, confirmed that annoyance was still being expressed at their visit by the people of this valley.

Three Indian surveyors, Lalbir Singh Thapa, Gujjar Singh, Turnubaj Singh and photographer Abdul Jalil Khan made up this extremely professional party. They were joined by A M Heron, sent by the Geological Survey of India, who surveyed an area as far north as the Tsangpo river. This resulted in complaints from the local Dzong Pens that the sacred soil of Tibet had been dug up, releasing demons that would destroy local crops. It was later alleged, too, that stones which grew more precious with time had been removed. The Everest Committee had to deny this and pointed out that no precious stones had been removed, and that ice axes were used to cut steps in snow and ice, and were not spades. They explained that this 'work' enhanced the pilgrimage that the climbers were undertaking to this sacred region and mountain.

The climbing party was chosen by the Alpine Club, and Harold Raeburn, an experienced Scottish climber, was chosen to lead it. Mallory commented that he was dictatorial, often wrong and had no sense of humour, traits made worse, no doubt, by constant abdominal pain. Moreover, he did not get on well with Howard-Bury. During the march-in across Tibet Raeburn became ill, probably with a gastric or duodenal ulcer, and had to return to Sikkim with A F R Wollaston, the medical officer. Later he was able to re-join the expedition.

By contrast, Alexander Kellas was loved by all the members of the party. At 53, he had achieved a better altitude record than any other mountaineer. However, he too became ill and was carried for much of the earlier part of the march-in across Tibet, when he should have been left to recover at lower altitudes. Tragically, at Kampa Dzong, just as the party had their first sight of Everest, the mountain that Kellas had done so much to reach and and which had been his life-long goal, he died of heart failure, or possibly of high-altitude pulmonary oedema. Two younger men, George Finch and George Mallory, were chosen for the high-altitude climbing.

GEORGE LEIGH MALLORY

Mallory was a protégé of Geoffrey Winthrop Young, *éminence grise* of the climbing world, who was a former master at Eton and had a career in education. Although he had a deep love of mountains, Mallory lacked the characteristics necessary to be an outstanding mountaineer. He was by nature an uncommitted and indecisive person who appeared to drift through life. He was never at ease during the expedition, disliked Tibet and worried a lot. Mallory's fellow climbers found him to be without an ounce of practicality. As T G Longstaff later put it: 'He was a very good stout-hearted baby, but quite unfit to be placed in charge of anything, including himself.'

However, Everest appealed to his sense of the dramatic and in climbing terms he was the success of the expedition.

From the start, in London, Mallory had Raeburn sized up as an unsuitable leader for the climbing party which, in the event, consisted only of himself and Finch. George Finch had a better climbing record than Mallory. A tall raw-boned Australian with an excellent, enquiring, scientific mind, he later became a Fellow of the Royal Society and a Professor of Physical Chemistry at London University. He was unconventional and did not view the British establishment with any great veneration. He was strongly backed by J P Farrar, an ex-President of the Alpine Club, whom the dominating Hinks did not like. Finch was quite unfairly rejected on medical grounds for this 1921 party by a physician chosen by the Everest Committee, having previously been pronounced fit for the Oxford decompression chamber experiments.

When it was mooted that W N Ling, Raeburn's climbing partner, should replace Finch, Mallory was unhappy because Ling was 48 and another elderly climber. Fortunately Ling refused the invitation and G H Bullock, aged 34, took his place. A consular officer and mathematical scholar at Winchester College, he had already climbed with Mallory. In 1919 he was in Lima and, having joined the expedition at short notice, he had to return to his post immediately afterwards. He was the perfect partner for Mallory. Like many mathematicians, he had a placid temperament and was an efficient organiser. The brunt of the exploration fell on Mallory and Bullock.

A F R Wollaston, medical officer and naturalist, was another competent person. Aged 46, he had qualified at the London Hospital in 1903 and, having sufficient private means, was able to devote himself to scientific exploration in the mountain regions he loved, including the Ruwenzori and Dutch New Guinea, where he climbed to 14,900ft on Carstenz Pyramid. From the 1921 Everest expedition he brought back the wonderful *Primula wollastonii*: 'Every bell of it was as large as a lady's thimble, of a deep azure blue and lined inside with frosted silver.' Later he became a Fellow and Tutor at King's College, Cambridge where, in 1930, he was murdered by a deranged undergraduate.

BIBLIOGRAPHY

T S Blakeney, 'A R Hinks and the First Everest Expedition, 1921' in *Geographical Journal* 136, 333-343, 1970.

T S Blakeney, 'First Steps towards Mount Everest' in *Alpine Journal* 76, 43-69, 1971.

G I Finch, *The Making of a Mountaineer*. F W Arrowsmith, 1924. Reprinted with a memoir by Scott Russell, 1988.

C K Howard-Bury, 'Some Observations on the Approach to Mount Everest' in
    Geographical Journal 57, 121-124, 1921.

C K Howard-Bury, *Mount Everest: The Reconnaissance, 1921*. Arnold, 1922.

A M Kellas, 'The Possibility of Aerial Reconnaissance in the Himalaya' in *Geographical
    Journal 51*, 374-389, 1918.

A M Kellas, 'Expedition to Kamet in 1920' in *Alpine Journal 33*, 312-319, 1921.

A M Kellas, 'Expedition to Kamet' in *Geographical Journal 57*, 124-130, 1921.

H T Morshead, 'Report of the Expedition to Kamet, 1920' in *Geographical Journal 57*,
    213-219, 1921.

I Morshead, *The Life and Murder of Henry Morshead*. Oleander Press, Cambridge, 1982.

C G Rawling, *Military Report on Western Tibet including the Changtang and Rudok*.
    Intelligence Branch of the Quartermaster General's Department, Simla, India,
    1905.

M P Ward, 'Northern Approaches, Everest 1918-1922' in *Alpine Journal 99*, 213-217,
    1994.

Chapter 5

THE ANATOMY OF A MOUNTAIN
The first reconnaissance from Tibet, 1921

Across southern Tibet. The death of A M Kellas.

The expedition assembled in Darjeeling at the beginning of May. The first group to leave for Tibet, on the 13th, comprised Morshead and his survey party; they followed the Teesta valley north and revised and extended the quarter-inch survey of Sikkim.

The main party left in two groups, on 18 and 19 May respectively, and followed the main trade route from Darjeeling to Lhasa, crossing the rim of frontier peaks by the Jelep La (14,390ft). The journey was made in heavy monsoon rain; much of the path formed a steep causeway up a hillside covered with rhododendrons in full flower, the branches of which were swathed with moss and orchids. Clusters of leeches writhed from the tips of the leaves ready to attach themselves to animals and humans. Higher up, near the pass, extensive meadows were carpeted with multi-coloured primulas.

The Jelep La divides not only two countries but two climates – the warm, torrential rain of tropical Sikkim and the cold, windy and harsh climate of Tibet. The Chumbi valley, into which the party descended, stretches southwards between Bhutan to the east and Sikkim to the west. It is one of the most prosperous parts of Tibet, with large well-built houses and fields of potatoes, barley and wheat. Apples and pears grow well and roses flourish, their scent filling the air. The distance from Yatung in the south to Phari, the main village further north, is only 28 miles.

Phari had a reputation for being the filthiest village in Tibet. Human excreta, tipped into narrow streets, mingled with animal dung; in the centre of a beaten brown path were rivulets of filth, liquid in the sun but frozen in the shade. The effect would have been unpleasantly smelly if it were not for the freezing and ever-present Tibetan wind that removed the stench. The village was then, as now, an important trading centre for goods on their way to India from Tibet via the Jelep La to the south, and to Bhutan by the Tremo La to the east. Chomolhari, Peak I of the Survey of India, lies on the Bhutan-Tibet border and forms a spectacular backdrop and signpost to Lhasa.

Leaving Phari on 31 May with a motley collection of baggage animals, donkeys, mules, bullocks, ponies and yaks, the main party followed a route to the east of the most direct way to Kampa, taking six days instead of three and thus expending more money on the transport animals. For two days they followed the route to Gyantse, skirting the west edge of the Bam Tso, a large shallow lake under the spectacular wall formed by peaks of the Bhutan-Tibet frontier north of Chomolhari. The lake was a kaleidoscope of colour, changing from deep blue to purple to green; owing to a particular water weed, it was also in parts red. Terns, Brahminy ducks and bar-headed geese covered its surface and on the plateau roamed vast herds of *Kiang* (wild horses) and *Gor* (Tibetan gazelles).

Crossing two passes at heights of 15–16,000ft, they reached Ka, a large deserted village, and three days later arrived at Kampa Dzong after crossing a 17,200ft pass. Here they met up again with Morshead and his surveyors.

A double blow now hit the expedition. For the last few days A M Kellas, while getting weaker and weaker, had been carried on a stretcher until, just within sight of Everest, he died. Fittingly, he was buried within sight of three great mountains that he had climbed – Pauhunri, Kanchenjau and Chomiomo. It would be difficult to imagine a more poignant end to the life of this pioneer who, despite his outstanding contribution to high-altitude medicine and mountain exploration, remained largely unknown until 60 years later when his work was recalled in a series of articles by Professor John West of the University of California, San Diego.

The other blow was the collapse of Raeburn, the climbing leader, with acute abdominal pain probably caused by a gastric or duodenal ulcer; he had to return to a lower altitude with Wollaston, the medical officer. Thus, at one stroke, the climbing party was halved and everything now depended upon Bullock and Mallory.

From Kampa the route lay west across the swampy valley of the Yaru Chu river – the eastern tributary of the Arun river – covered in small lakes on whose surfaces were flocks of teal, duck and geese. The Dzong Pen of Tinki rode out to meet the party and escorted them to specially pitched tents where tea, sweetmeats and *chang* were produced. He also gave them 100 eggs and four sheep, for this was a prosperous area with many well-founded monasteries and villages.

On 11 June they left Tinki and, crossing the Tinki La, descended into the Yaru valley. For the next few days they marched across a plain full of quicksands and were engulfed by violent winds and sandstorms. Camping at the junction of two tributaries of the Arun – the Yaru Chu and Bhong Chu – they gained another fleeting glimpse of Everest, which the yak herders called by its local name Chomo Uri, 'The Goddess of the Turquoise Peak'.

They now followed the wide valley of the Bhong Chu to Tingri. Wheeler, Morshead and the survey team worked from dawn to dusk, as they were now in unsurveyed country. From a peak north of the Bhong Chu they had views of over 250 miles of the northern flanks of the Himalaya, from the Bhutan Himal and

Chomolhari to Gosainthan. Everest towered over them all; it had no rival. Shekar Dzong, the main village of the area, was reached after a further three days' march. Its white houses clustered around the base of a solitary rock spire jutting up from the plain. Clinging to this enormous spire was a rising series of monastery buildings guarded, at half height, by a wall. Another wall snaked up to the summit on which there was a fort. The greatly venerated Abbot of Shekar, the reincarnation of a former abbot, had spent 65 years in this spectacularly sited monastery.

Two days further on was Tingri, a large village set on a hill in the middle of an extensive plain. No information was available about the country to the south of Tingri or about the peaks of the Everest group which towered above it. However, the broad gap of the Nangpa La – the glacier route to Khumbu in NE Nepal – was visible just west of Cho Oyu. This was the pass crossed by Hari Ram from Nepal to Tibet in 1885.

Tingri was an important centre, being the terminus of a number of routes from Nepal. In the 18th century it had been the site of a battle between Nepal and Tibet. An invading force of Gurkhas had penetrated Tibet as far as Shigatse before Chinese reinforcements checked their advance. As a result, the Tibetans of Tingri still paid tribute to the Nepalese, who kept a headman there and another at Nyalam, the main village in the valley of that name. Today an extremely precipitous road, constantly cut by rockfall and landslides, runs from Tingri to Kathmandu. On the top of the hill of Tingri was an old Chinese fort containing many frescoes, whilst at the bottom, a Chinese rest house had been prepared for the expedition. Some days later Wollaston arrived here from Lachen, where he had left Raeburn to recover.

The expedition now split into several parties. On 23 June Bullock and Mallory went east to explore the Langma La and the north side of Everest. One can imagine their feelings, as the expedition's only experienced climbers, setting out into unknown country to find a route up the world's highest peak. They must have felt a combination of apprehension, anticipation and the sheer joy of walking and climbing into the unknown. They were a well-matched pair – Mallory all fire and enthusiasm, Bullock all competence.

Meanwhile, Howard-Bury, Wheeler and Dr A M Heron carried out a photo-theodolite survey of the Kyetrak glacier leading from the Nangpa La towards Tingri. From a hill behind Tingri they could see the whole Everest range: Everest, Gyachung Kang, Cho Oyu, the Nangpa La and, on its west side, the elegant spire of Jobo Rabzang. To the north of the Tsangpo river was the Gangdise range.

Morshead took his surveyors to the north and west of Tingri and to the lower slopes of Gosainthan, whilst Wollaston stayed in Tingri, seeing patients and collecting birds, lizards and flowers, specimens being identified in London.

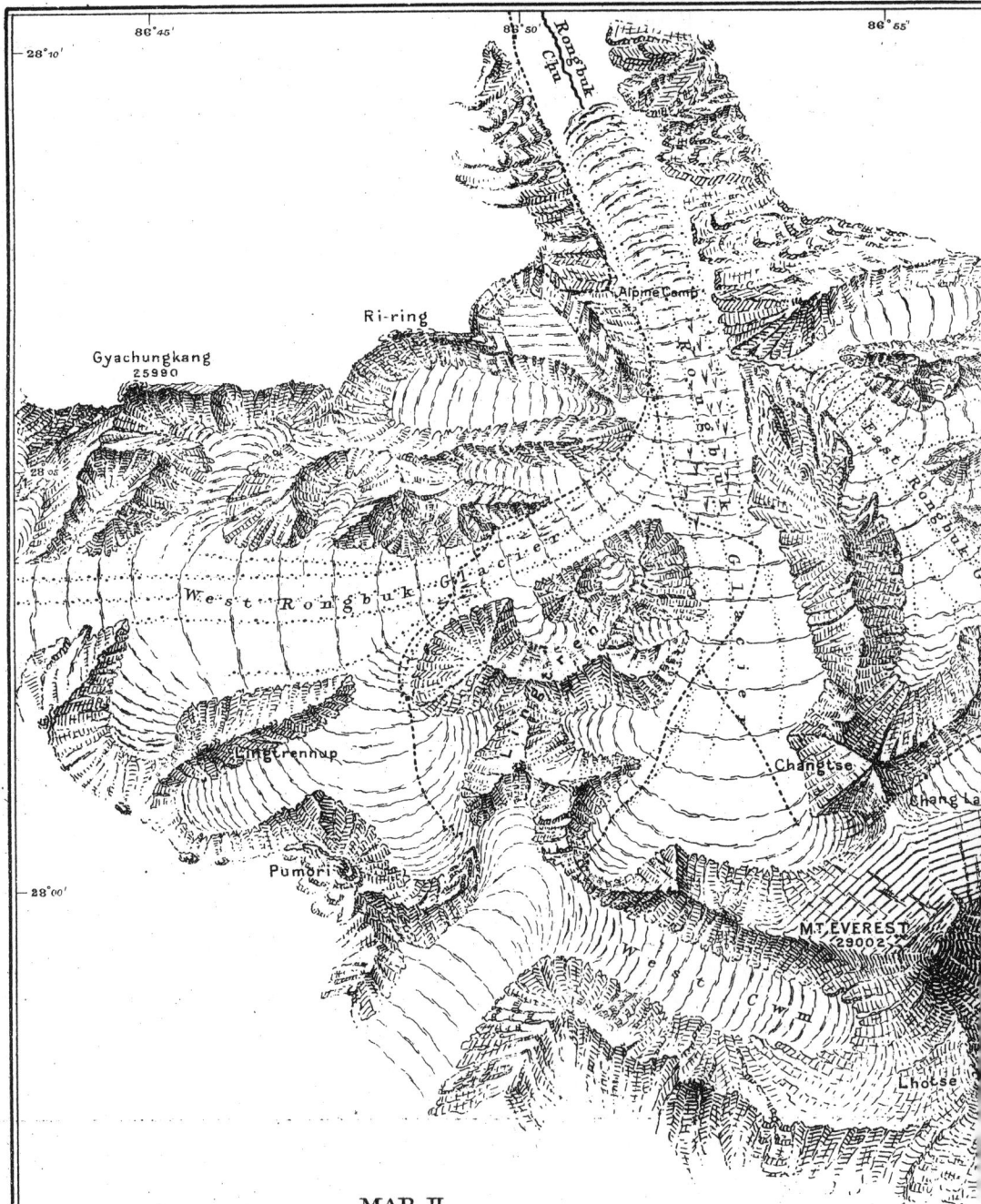

86°45' 86°50' 86°55'

28°10'

Rongbuk
Chu

Alpine Camp

Ri-ring

Gyachungkang
25990

West Rongbuk Glacier

Changtse

Pumori

28°00'

MT. EVEREST
(29002)

Lhotse

27°55'

MAP II
Preliminary Map
of
MOUNT EVEREST
constructed at the R.G.S.
from photographs and sketches
made by the
EXPEDITION of 1921

Scale 1/100,000 or 1 Inch = 1·58 Stat. Miles.

Miles 1 ¾ ½ ¼ 0   1   2   3   4   5 Miles

o = *Panoram Camera Station*

86°45' 86°50' 86°55'

blished by the

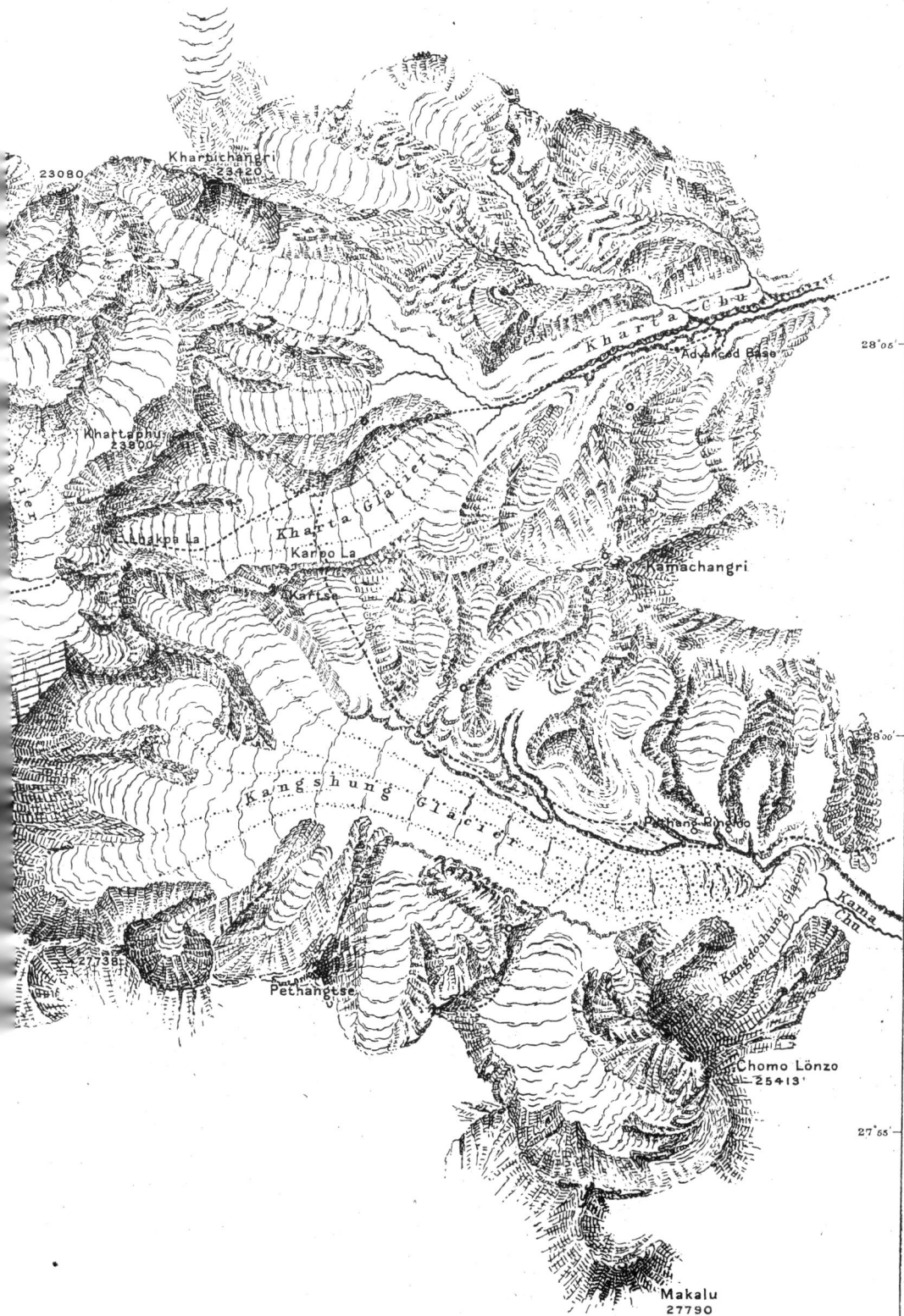

Khartichangri
23080
23420
Khartaphu
23900
Lhakpa La
Karpo La
Kartse
Kamachangri
Kharta Chu
Advanced Base
Kharta Glacier
Kangshung Glacier
Pethang Ringmo
Kama Chu
Kangdoshung Glacier
27738
Pethangtse
Chomo Lönzo
25413
Makalu
27790

Exploration and mapping west of Everest: the Nangpa La

Howard-Bury, Wheeler and Heron decided to explore the glaciers around the Nangpa La to see if there was any possible approach to Everest from the west. Wheeler had brought a set of photo-theodolite survey instruments newly developed in Canada. The advantage of these was that a larger area could be covered more quickly than by using a plane table; moreover the instruments were easily portable and by observing views from different angles a better idea of the country could be obtained. The disadvantages of this method were that more instruments were involved, a 'running' map could not be made in the field and clear weather was necessary.

From Kyetrak, a village at 16,000ft, it was possible to climb to both the Nangpa La and the Phuse La: both passes gave access to Nepal. In between was the peak Jobo Rabzang. On 24 June all three set out for the Nangpa La, which Howard-Bury reached. It was a broad easy glacier pass with good views into Nepal, but there was no access to Everest from the glaciers which fell from the easy northern slopes of Cho Oyu or Gyachung Kang. To get a different view, Wheeler went up a shoulder on Jobo Rabzang, and he confirmed that there was no way to Everest from the west.

Returning to Tingri, Wheeler developed his photographs, while Howard-Bury and Heron crossed the Phuse La at 17,000ft to Tazang, descending the Upper Rongshar valley which was covered with wild roses and gooseberry bushes. Further down the ever-deepening gorge lay the Nepal-Tibet frontier. Returning over the Phuse La to Kyetrak and Tingri, all three explorers decided to follow Mallory and Bullock to the Rongbuk glacier.

For Heron, the geologist, the three great gorges, the Arun, the Rongshar and the Nyalam – which had been formed by rivers rising in Tibet cutting their way through the emerging Himalaya – confirmed that the Himalaya was a 'young' range and still rising. Its formation had been caused by the collision of the Indian tectonic plate with the Eurasian plate, which had in turn resulted in the formation of the Tibetan plateau and the Kun Lun range that separates the plateau from the deserts of Central Asia. Dr Heron's geological map of the Everest region was the first such map to be made, and complemented the Survey of India's topographical work.

The death of Kellas was a great blow to Morshead who had been his companion on Kamet the year before. However, with work as an antidote to depression, Morshead and Lalbir Singh started surveying west of the Tinki La, continuing to Tingri. The monsoon clouds greatly restricted the time at their disposal but they worked furiously whenever the skies were clear.

At Tingri, cloud over the Himalaya made surveying impossible so, with Gujjar Singh, Morshead went north towards the Tsangpo valley to explore the headwaters of the Bhong Chu, the main western tributary of the Arun river, and the lower slopes of Gosainthan (Shisha Pangma, 26,337ft). On this plain they found many deserted and ruined watch towers and villages, remnants of the Gurkha wars, and on 28 June they camped at Menkhap, the highest of these villages. Above this, they went west over a spur of the Lungchen La (17,700ft) where they had excellent views of Gosainthan over the Pekkhu plain with its three glistening lakes. Here Morshead left Gujjar Singh to complete the survey while he himself returned to Tingri.

By the end of June, Lalbir Singh had completed his work between Tinki and Tingri, and after checking all the place names with local officials, he went east of Everest to the Kharta region and Pharuk where he spent three months completing a survey of this extremely difficult country.

Exploration and mapping further west: the Nyalam valley

In the meantime an invitation to visit his village had been received from the Dzong Pen of Nyalam. Although this was outside the area covered by their permission, it was of great strategic and historical importance, being at a key point in the spectacularly steep gorge carved by the Bhote Kosi river linking southern Tibet with Kathmandu. It was along this valley and gorge that Fathers Desideri and Grüber and d'Orville had travelled from Tibet to Nepal some centuries earlier.

It was decided, after consultation with Howard-Bury, that Morshead, Wollaston and Gujjar Singh should accept the Dzong Pen's invitation after the survey north and west of Tingri had been completed. The party set off on 13 July, passing the thousand-year-old monastery in Lankar which contained a sacred stone said to have been hurled across the Himalaya from India. The noise (*ting*) made by the falling stone had given Tingri village its name. After crossing the Tang La (17,800ft) in driving snow and sleet, the party reached the bleak upper Bhote Kosi valley. Continuing south through a massive granite gorge next day, they reached the village of Nyalam (Tibetan name) or Kuti (Nepalese name) where the Nepalese had their own court house and magistrate. Below Nyalam the gorge became even deeper and narrower, while the path crossed the river at least four times in six miles before reaching Choksum and the Nepal frontier at Dram.

From here they retraced their steps and went east over the lower slopes of the Lapche Kang range. The main village, Lapche, is sacred, being the birthplace of Mila Repa, greatly-loved poet-saint of the 11th century, founding father of the Kagya order and one of the founders of Tibetan Buddhism. The village was deserted, since in winter the population migrates south to Nepal, ten miles away along the Rongshar gorge. Morshead's party followed a more adventurous route – a little-used and difficult track which at one place traversed a sheer rock wall by the use of branches attached to the rock by wooden pegs hammered into cracks. After negotiating this dangerous route, allegedly used by smugglers, they descended into the gorge at

Trintang where they enjoyed fine views of Gaurisankar (Jobo Tseringma) and other peaks shown on the Waddell picture map of 1898.

Turning north up the Rongshar valley, they returned to Tazang, passing on their way a path that led east to the Menlung La, a pass over the main Himalayan Range to Solu Khumbu. Finally, an easy day over the Phuse La brought them back to Kyetrak and Tingri.

Exploration and mapping north of Everest. The Nepal-Tibet frontier and the Western Cwm. Mallory's failure to find a route to the summit.

From the mountaineering point of view, nothing was known of Everest before the 1921 expedition, as the only photographs then available had been taken from over 50 miles away. The first clear view of the mountain was taken from Kampa Dzong on the day that Kellas died. As Mallory described it in *Mount Everest: the reconnaissance, 1921*, 'Everest was a prodigious white fang excrescent upon the jaw of the world.'

Later, from 60 miles further west, above Tinki, the long North-East Ridge could be seen, whilst a further ridge appeared to join Everest to the North Peak (Changtse). Between them there was a pass, the North Col (Chang La). From this col a valley seemed to drain east into the Arun river. Another ridge ran south from the summit to a high peak, Lhotse; the east face of Everest and Lhotse seemed to be continuous. None of these features could be found on any map, and though further glimpses were seen on the way to Tingri, none gave a better idea of this complicated mountain than the view from the hills above the Arun gorge.

Bullock and Mallory set out from Tingri on 23 June with 16 porters, a cook and a sirdar, with only one object: to find a route to the summit. It was to prove immensely difficult. Local information suggested that a long straight valley led from the north into the heart of the mountain, and that this valley could be reached by crossing the Langma La – a pass ten miles east of Tingri – and by descending to a monastery, Chobuk.

On 25 June they reached Chobuk, turned south along a river, and entered a limestone gorge between high red cliffs. A thin ribbon of grass, with dwarf rhododendrons and juniper and dotted with yellow asters, edged the stream at the foot of the gorge. Suddenly the path rose steeply between two chortens and the party were brought to a halt by their first sight of Everest. It was a dramatic confrontation, with the Rongbuk valley framing the peak as if in a picture.

The floor of the valley and the main Rongbuk glacier beyond the pass were almost flat for twenty miles, and then suddenly the mountain reared up, with no satellite peaks, in a single overwhelming mass. Its structure was simple: a massive wall of rock and ice, over two miles high, with horizontal strata. To the east, a long ridge rose at a gentle angle to the summit, while to the west a steep ridge plunged to a group of snow mountains on the Nepal-Tibet border. From the gentle east ridge an almost imperceptible broad arête ran north towards the Rongbuk valley, ending at the North Col, and then rose steeply up to the North Peak. The southern, Nepalese side of Everest was hidden.

On 26 June a camp was pitched near Rongbuk monastery in full sight of the mountain which totally dominated the surrounding country. Next day Bullock and Mallory set off at 3.15am to explore the Rongbuk glacier for the first time. Ascending between the glacier and the west moraine, they soon came across a large branch glacier, the West Rongbuk, joining from the west, draining peaks on the Nepal-Tibet border and the Nup La, a high pass first crossed by Westerners in 1952. Bullock and Mallory crossed the West Rongbuk glacier and returned down the east side of the main Rongbuk glacier, crossing the small and seemingly unimportant stream and moraine of the East Rongbuk glacier that drained peaks to the east. Though they did not then realise it, this glacier was the key to the summit route on the north side of Everest. The scale of the glaciers and peaks was immense, and both men were extremely fatigued. As Mallory wrote, 'It was the glacier [sun] that knocked us out.' *

Looking at Everest through field glasses next day they considered that the steeper portion of the east ridge, just below the summit, would be climbable, and they confirmed that, lower down, the east ridge joined up with a broad ridge descending to the North Col and North Peak (Changtse). Opinions on the steeper west arête were divided: Bullock was not hopeful, whilst Mallory was more optimistic. (It was not until 1963 that the first ascent of the West Ridge was made by an American party led by Tom Hornbein.) To get a better idea of the problem they carried a camp further up the Rongbuk valley and then ascended the West Rongbuk glacier to try to find a way over the frontier ridge to look at the south, Nepalese side of the mountain.

One immediate problem was that the Sherpas from Khumbu, although hill men, had to be taught mountaineering skills, the use of rope and ice axe, and how to move safely, so it was several days before Mallory could set out with five Sherpas to reach the great snow basin beneath the North Face. From here, despite the rapidly worsening weather, they had excellent views of the west side of the North Col which, it was becoming apparent, was one of the keys to the gently sloping north ridge and the upper part of the east ridge. The west side of the North Col looked dangerous rather than difficult: naturally Mallory was confident that the other, east side, would

---

* The combination of the direct rays of the sun and the reflected heat from the snow, especially if there is no wind, produces 'glacier lassitude', an early stage of heat exhaustion.

be easier; but the problem was how to get there, as the stream and moraine of the East Rongbuk glacier seemed too small to come from a glacier draining the obviously very large glaciated area east of Everest. Finally, on closer inspection, they concluded that the West Ridge of Everest looked very difficult and they decided only to attempt it as a last resort.

July 3 was spent training Sherpas and on the 5th Mallory and Bullock ascended a peak, Ri-Ring, at the junction of the main and West Rongbuk glaciers. The summit provided an excellent viewpoint. A very long ridge ran east from the summit of the North Peak towards the Arun valley, and Mallory assumed (wrongly) that this was the same ridge, running east from the North Col, that they had seen from the hill above Tinki. They also had a good view of the whole of the upper part of the North Face, which looked not too steep. On the south side of Everest, a peak of 26,000ft to the west (Nuptse) might join up with Lhotse, but the Western Cwm was not visible. They decided to move camp to explore this southern area.

On 12 July large crevasses foiled their attempt to ascend the West Rongbuk glacier. The next day they reached the Nepal frontier ridge but owing to cloud cover there were no views and they were uncertain of their position. On 15 July Bullock managed to ascend the West Rongbuk glacier to the Nup La on the Nepal border. But the mystery remained: did Nuptse join with Lhotse and was there a deep valley between them and the South Face of Everest?

On 16 July they made a determined effort to solve these problems. They reached the frontier ridge and gained their first view of the Western Cwm. It looked a lonely, forbidding valley, untouched by the sun. The narrow entrance was guarded by a 1500ft-high icefall, a maze of crevasses and ice towers; even from a mile away they could hear the groans and crashes of moving ice. As Mallory wrote:

> It was unlikely that the gap [the South Col which they could not see] between Everest and Lhotse could be reached from the west. From what we have seen now I do not much fancy it would be possible even if we could get up the glacier [ie up the Khumbu icefall and into the Western Cwm].

By 19 July no route up Everest had been found and Mallory was despondent. 'So far ... little enough has been accomplished.' he wrote, 'If ever the mountain were to be climbed, the route would lie not along the whole length of any one of its colossal ridges.' He had, in effect, found no route from the south, west or north. The only side that they had not looked at was the east. The North Col seemed to be the key to the mild slopes of the north and east ridges, but how could they get to the mountain's eastern side? Mallory's assumption that the East Rongbuk glacier did not drain the east side of the North Col was false, and if he had gone up it the problem would have been solved in 48 hours. Later the survey team under Wheeler did precisely that and provided the right answer.

In fact Mallory *was* intending to explore the East Rongbuk glacier but first he had to re-photograph the whole of the main and West Rongbuk glaciers as he had previously put his photographic plates into the camera back to front. As a result, his East Rongbuk plan was dropped.

In the meantime Bullock returned to the Lho La on the Nepal-Tibet frontier ridge; he looked down the Khumbu glacier in Nepal and saw its icefall in profile. The Khumbu icefall looked no more inviting when seen from the side than it did end on.

Exploration and mapping east of Everest. Discovery of the correct route via the East Rongbuk glacier by E O Wheeler of the Survey of India.

Following their return from the Nangpa La, Howard-Bury and Wheeler decided to join Mallory and Bullock on the north side of Everest. Rongbuk monastery was cold and bleak. The monks and head lama did not welcome the expedition, fearing that they would disturb the meditation of the twenty permanent lamas who lived there or the 300 or so hermits who lived in caves nearby.

On 4 July they went up to see Mallory and Bullock just before the latter climbed Ri-Ring. Since the possibility of a route from Rongbuk was not very hopeful, it was decided to go east to the Kharta and Kama valleys from where an approach might be made to the east side of the North Col. Next day, 5 July, they descended to the village of Zambuk, and went east by a series of valleys draining glaciers from the north and east sides of Everest. Crossing the Doya La, they descended into the Arun valley. The Doya La is on the border between the harsh upland climate of Tibet to the north and the luxuriant climate of the Arun valley to the south, up which the warm, moisture-laden monsoon winds flow. Peas, mustard and barley grow in the terraced fields and the villages are surrounded by groves of willow and poplar. Descending the Arun for three miles they turned west up a side valley into which a river from Everest flowed. At a village, Kharta Sikha, they rented a house. It was here that Howard-Bury was later joined by Bullock and Mallory after they had left the Rongbuk glacier.

On 2 August the whole party set off up the Kharta valley hoping that this would turn out to be a highway to the east side of the North Col. Delayed by drunken porters, they reached a fork and, taking the southern valley, found themselves by the side of a lake at 17,000ft. Beyond was a pass, the Langma La, which ended under the east face of Everest. Disturbingly, however, they were told that there were 'two Everests'. After crossing the pass in cloud they found no view on the far side.

The west-running Kama valley led to the cliffs of the 'first' Chomolungma which was probably Makalu. The clouds descended again, but next day all was clear and the whole of the East (Kangshung) Face of Everest was revealed, with the east side of the South Col and the east side of Lhotse. But there was no sign of the North Col for which they were looking. They were in the wrong valley.

To confirm their mistake they climbed a peak, Karpo-Ri, hoping to see both the east face of Everest and a glacier draining east from the North Col. Everest's east face was obviously too difficult for them (it was first climbed in 1983). They could also see that the North-East Ridge, with its many spires and towers, was impracticable. Finally they confirmed that the glacier that flowed into the head of the Kharta valley did not come from the North Col. This was a bitter blow, for all that remained between them and miserable failure was to go to the head of this Kharta glacier, where there was a snow col, and see what lay beyond it.

Mallory now became ill and had to stay in camp, so on 13 August Bullock went up the Kharta valley, sending back a note saying that the next day he would be climbing the high snow pass at its head. Joined at the Kharta camp by Morshead, who had completed his survey west of Everest, Mallory, who had recovered, and Morshead went up to join Bullock and prepared to cross the Lhakpa La. On 15 August they received a note from Howard-Bury with a sketch from Wheeler, who had been surveying the main Rongbuk glacier and the East Rongbuk glacier (which Mallory had omitted to investigate). This suggested that the latter might drain the east side of the North Col.

Over the next four days Morshead, Mallory and Bullock climbed to the Lhakpa La, which they called 'Windy Gap', but clouds obscured the view of the far side – a gentle snow slope leading almost certainly to a broad snow basin, the upper part of the East Rongbuk glacier. Because of the very soft snow on their ascent, rackets (snow shoes) had been used, but as Mallory later described it:

> Our greatest enemy as we went on was not, after all, the deep powdery snow. The racket sank slightly below the surface and carried a little snow each step as one lifted it; the work was arduous for the first man. But at a slow pace it was possible to plod on without undue exhaustion. The heat was a different matter. In the glacier-furnace the thin mist became steam, it enveloped us with a clinging garment from which no escape was possible, and far from being protected by it from the sun's fierce heat, we seemed to be scorched all the more because of it. The atmosphere was enervating to the last degree; to halt even for a few minutes was to be almost overwhelmed by inertia, so difficult it seemed, once the machinery had stopped and lost momentum, to heave it into motion again.

Having neither food nor tents, they decided not to attempt to climb to the North Col and returned to Kharta. Now, however, the mood of the party changed dramatically from despair to hope. The key to the upper slopes of Everest was obviously the North Col. This had to be reached and the North Ridge climbed. They believed that this was a gentle round ridge that led to the north-east shoulder and the summit.

The first ascent of the North Col

It was another three weeks before they set out again for the Lhakpa La. In the meantime, Gujjar Singh started a one-inch plane table survey of the north of the Kharta valley, whilst Morshead and Wheeler, who had come round from Rongbuk, carried out a photographic survey of the Kharta valley. Morshead went as far south as the Popti La on the Nepal frontier, thus 'joining up' with the survey from Nepal carried out by the Pundit G.S.S. in the mid-19th century.

On 19 September Howard-Bury, Mallory and Morshead set out to climb Kama Changri, a peak to the south of their camp that overhung the Kama valley. They hoped that from here good views of Makalu and the East (Kangshung) Face of Everest would be obtained. Howard-Bury wrote in *Mount Everest. The Reconnaissance 1921*:

> We left the camp at 2 a.m., by the light of a full moon, which made the going as light as though it were day. We soon reached our view-point of a few days before, where, except for the distant roar of the stream far away below in the valley, there was no other sound, only an intense stillness. Never anywhere have I seen the moon or the stars shine so brightly. To the South, far away from us, there were constant flashes of lightning – the valleys in Tibet, the great gorges of the Arun, the wooded valleys of Nepal all lay buried under a white sea of clouds, out of which emerged the higher mountains like islands out of a fairy sea. In this bright moonlight, mountains like Kanchenjunga – 100 miles away – stood out sharp and distinct. Here on this sharp ridge, at a height of 21,000 feet, with no obstruction to hide the view, sunrise came to us in all its beauty and grandeur. To the West, and close at hand, towered up Mount Everest, still over 8,000 feet above us; at first showing up cold, grey and dead against a sky of deep purple. All of a sudden a ray of sunshine touched the summit, and soon flooded the higher snows and ridges with golden light, while behind, the deep purple of the sky changed to orange. Makalu was the next to catch the first rays of the sun and glowed as though alive; then the white sea of clouds was struck by the gleaming rays of the sun, and all aglow with colour rose slowly and seemed to break against the island peaks in great billows of fleecy white.

On 20 September, joined by Raeburn and Wollaston, they all set out for the Lhakpa La. No one was at his best, for the constant travel and life at high altitude had taken their toll. Neither Bullock nor Mallory was able to call upon the reserves of strength that they had at the start of the expedition and Raeburn was working on will-power alone. They arrived at the pass exhausted, and letting their rucksacks slip from their shoulders as they sat in the snow, they had, for the first time, a clear view of the key to the upper slopes of Everest – the North Col. From the basin under the north-east face it was about 1,000 feet in height, with many large crevasses stretching across its face. Head on, the east side looked steep, and to carry a camp to its crest at 23,000ft would need a strong party.

A camp was pitched on the sheltered side of the Lhakpa La, just below the crest, and a survey station, the world's highest, installed. Next day Bullock, Mallory and Wheeler crossed the basin to the foot of the North Col. For Wheeler this was the last link in the chain of his survey, for he could see the top of the East Rongbuk glacier draining this basin. The thoroughness of his survey of the Rongbuk glacier system was in telling contrast to Mallory's slapdash 'reconnaissance'.

Surprisingly, the climb to the North Col involved little more than putting one foot in front of the other and avoiding crevasses when the slope got too steep. By 11.30am the party, which included three Sherpas, were on the col itself, the first ever to reach this bleak spot. Looking down the east side they could see where, many days before, they had been on the main Rongbuk glacier looking up at the North Col. The rounded slopes of the North Ridge would present no difficulty, they thought. If the climbing looked amenable, the weather was not; the wind, fierce, penetrating and persistent, whistled across the face of the mountain in ever-strengthening gusts, polishing the snow with an unseen hand. Snow eddies boiled in the air, and an unprotected face would quickly have become frostbitten. This settled the question of going higher, and they camped for the night.

Next day, neither Bullock nor Mallory felt strong enough to go higher without any backup. They were at the extreme end of a long line of communication, with the Lhakpa La at 22,470ft and the North Col at 23,000ft, so that if either got ill or had even a minor accident the chances of getting back to safety in the Kharta valley were slim. Equipment and attitudes in 1921 made it impossible for climbers to be self-supporting for several days, as they are nowadays. The wind became a gale and without argument they descended. Re-crossing the Lhakpa La needed an infinite effort of will-power by the three exhausted climbers and only served to underline their correct decision.

Exploration near Makalu

Later, Howard-Bury, Wheeler and Wollaston paid another visit to the Kama valley, crossed the Karpo La and descended to the grassy meadow of Pethang Ringmo where Wheeler made a photo survey, previously omitted, of that part of the valley. Howard-Bury and the Sherpas also climbed to the frontier ridge and looked down a deep, unknown glacier and valley in Nepal. This was the Barun valley, 'discovered' on the 1933 'Flight Over Everest' and explored for the first time in 1952. The Sherpas recognised many peaks in Khumbu and told Howard-Bury that there used to be a route from the Kama valley to Khumbu. (In 1954, Norman Hardie crossed this frontier from Nepal in much the same place, while mapping and exploring, for the first time, the south-east quadrant of Everest.) Following the exploration near Makalu the party returned to Darjeeling and the UK.

The first map of Everest

The 1921 reconnaissance expedition was a triumph for the Survey of India, for their members had been everywhere that the mountaineering party had been, and more than that, had surveyed a vast area of unknown country whilst doing so.

The area mapped was 12,000 square miles at ¼ inch original, 4,000 square miles at ¼ inch revision, and 600 square miles of detailed photo-survey, at an average cost of 3.9 rupees per square mile – a phenomenal result under the prevailing conditions. The survey work was done so quickly and efficiently under its Surveyor-General C H D Ryder that a preliminary map was available in six colours before the last expedition members sailed from Bombay to the UK. It was a thoroughly professional performance.

Identification and naming of the main geographical features of the north, Tibetan side of Everest

The name 'Everest', which appears on the map in this book, had been used worldwide for many years, though the Tibetans knew the mountain as 'Chomolungma'. Some topographical features had more than one name, or had been given a number by the Survey of India. Examples are given below:

Chorabsang, T.42	=	Chorapsang
Cho Oyu, T.45	=	Cho Oyu
Gyachung Kang, T.57	=	Gyachung Kang
Chomolonzo, N.53	=	Chomolonzo
Pk XIII	=	Makalu

Many prominent peaks and other features had no local name, so in consultation
with Howard-Bury and Mallory, the descriptive name for each peak was given its
Tibetan equivalent and the list submitted to Sir Charles Bell, Political Officer of
Sikkim, who dealt with Tibetan affairs, for his approval:

Peak at head of Kharta valley	=	Khartaphu
Isolated peak on watershed between Makalu and Everest and visible from Pethang Ringmo	=	Pethangtse
South Peak of Everest	=	Lhotse
North Peak of Everest	=	Changtse
North Col	=	Chang La
Peak 6	=	Kartichangri
Group of mountains at the head of the Rongbuk valley and glacier lying like an island between the main and the West Rongbuk glacier	=	Lingtren
Small or island peak to the west of above group	=	Lingtren Nup
Peak climbed at head of the Kama valley	=	Kartse
Peak climbed at the junction of the main and West Rongbuk glaciers	=	Ri-Ring
Peak north of Kama valley	=	Kama Changri
Isolated peak west of Everest	=	Pumo Ri
Pass at head of the West Rongbuk glacier	=	Nup La
Pass at head of the main Rongbuk glacier	=	Lho La
West peak of Everest	=	Nuptse

BIBLIOGRAPHY

T S Blakeney, 'First Steps towards Mount Everest' in *Alpine Journal* 76, 43-69, 1971.

G H Bullock, 'The Everest Expedition 1921. Diary' in *Alpine Journal* 67, 130-149, 291-309, 1962.

J N Collie, 'The Mount Everest Expedition' in *Alpine Journal* 34, 114-117, 1922.

A M Heron, 'Geological Results of the Mount Everest Reconnaissance Expedition Records' in *Geological Survey of India* 54, 215-234, 1922.

A R Hinks, 'The Mount Everest Maps and Photographs' in *Alpine Journal* 34, 228-235, 1922.

C K Howard-Bury, 'Some Observations on the Approach to Mount Everest' in *Geographical Journal* 57, 121-124, 1921.

C K Howard-Bury, 'The Mount Everest Expedition' in *Geographical Journal 59*, 81-99, 1922.

C K Howard-Bury, 'The 1921 Mount Everest Expedition' in *Alpine Journal 34*, 195-227, 1922.

C K Howard-Bury, *Mount Everest. The Reconnaissance 1921*. Arnold 1922.

N B Kinnear, 'On the birds collected by Mr A F R Wollaston during the first Mt Everest Expedition' in *The Ibis*, 495-526, July 1922.

G H L Mallory, 'Mount Everest. The Reconnaissance' in *Geographical Journal 59*, 100-112, 1922.

I Morshead, *The Life and Murder of Henry Morshead*. The Oleander Press, Cambridge, 1982.

Unattributed note, 'The Mount Everest Expedition. Organisation and Equipment' in *Geographical Journal 57*, 271-282, 1921.

Unattributed notes, 'The Mount Everest Expedition' in *Geographical Journal 58*, 276-283 & 446-454, 1921.

M P Ward, 'Mapping Everest' in *Cartographic Journal 31*, 33-44, 1994.

J B West, 'Alexander M Kellas and the Physiological Challenge of Mount Everest' in *Journal of Applied Physiology 63*, 3-11, 1987.

J B West, 'A M Kellas. Pioneer Himalayan Physiologist and Mountaineer' in *Alpine Journal 94*, 207-213, 1989/90.

A F R Wollaston, 'The Natural History of South-Western Tibet' in *Geographical Journal 60*, 5-20, 1922.

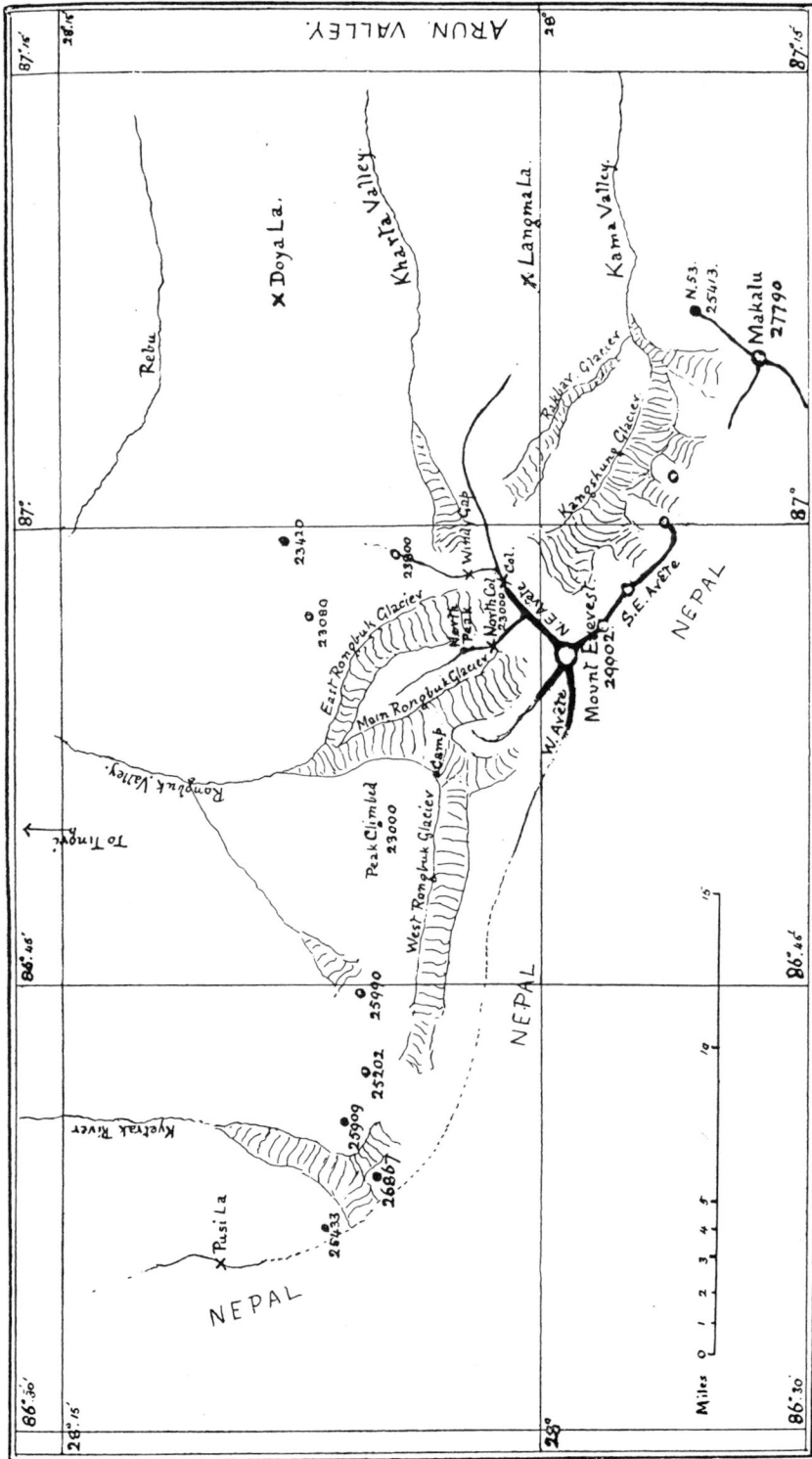

SKETCH MAP OF MOUNT EVEREST, 1921

Chapter 6

INTO THE UNKNOWN
The first attempt on the summit, 1922

Decompression chamber experiments at Oxford

Thanks mainly to the extraordinary efforts of the members of the Survey of India, the 1921 reconnaissance expedition had been an outstanding success. Both the East Rongbuk glacier and the North Col, keys to the summit, had been climbed and, after the initial loss of Kellas through death and Raeburn through illness, the party had acclimatised well and remained vigorous at 23,000ft. In addition, a vast amount of mapping had been accomplished.

The only objective of the 1922 expedition was to climb Everest, and because the returning 1921 party had not reached Darjeeling until 25 October, it was December before organisation in the UK could begin. The 1922 party was scheduled to return to Darjeeling in March so that an attempt could be made before the monsoon in June; the autumn and winter were considered too cold for climbing, using the existing clothing and equipment. At that time the window of opportunity was very small.

In January 1922 another visit was made to the decompression chamber at Oxford, by J P Farrar and P J H Unna, together with G I Finch and T H Somervell who were to be members of the 1922 party. Both climbers were decompressed to 23,000ft and exercised: with no preliminary acclimatisation, it is no surprise that Somervell became unconscious and had to be revived with oxygen.

On their return to London a report was submitted to the Everest Committee stating that supplementary oxygen must be taken to Everest, and the Air Ministry immediately started work. An oxygen flow rate of 2 to 2.4 litres per minute was decided upon. This was a critical factor in the outcome of the 1922 expedition, for it was later discovered that this flow rate was too low to compensate both for the weight of the oxygen set that the climber had to carry and for the enhanced performance necessary at great altitude. Also, the whole question of acclimatisation to extreme oxygen lack at great altitude had yet to be investigated. The oxylite bags used on Kamet by Kellas and Morshead, containing sodium peroxide and added water, could only produce oxygen at rest and not while exercising. Other remedies for mountain sickness were taken. These included morphia, bicarbonate of soda, and garlic. Liquid oxygen was considered too expensive. Most experts supported the view that an ascent of Everest was unlikely to be made without an artificial aid to respiration. How correct they were.

Members of the party

As Brigadier General C G Bruce was now free from military duties he was asked to
lead the expedition, with Lt Col E L Strutt as his second-in-command. T G Longstaff,
one of the most experienced of Himalayan mountaineers, went as doctor and
naturalist. The climbing party consisted of G I Finch, who was in charge of
oxygen, G H L Mallory, Major E F Norton, a soldier with a fine alpine record, T H
Somervell, a surgeon at University College Hospital, London, and A W Wakefield,
a doctor and mountaineer from the north of England. The official photographer
was Captain J B L Noel, whilst Major H T Morshead, of the 1921 survey team,
reinforced the party. Three transport officers were taken: C G Crawford, J G Bruce,
a relation of the leader, and C J Morris, a Gurkha officer and ethnologist.

John Morris had served in the army during the First World War. Frustrated in
his desire to become a doctor, he had joined the Gurkhas where he acquired linguistic
abilities that fitted him to join the 1922 and later the 1936 Everest expeditions as
transport officer. He later became a Professor of English in Japan and finally Director
of the Third Programme of the BBC.

Morris joined the 1922 expedition in Darjeeling, and later, in his book *Hired to
Kill*, wrote in an illuminating manner about the personalities and dynamics of the
group:

> There was no hint of the friendly atmosphere which we later enjoyed. Indeed, for
> the first few weeks we seemed inevitably to divide into two factions: those who had
> considerable experience of climbing in the Alps before the war and those who, like
> myself, had been selected for their knowledge of the local language and conditions.
> Only General Bruce was fully at home in both worlds, and he soon made it clear
> that he would recognise no distinction ... At first the climbers tended to regard
> those few of us who were not climbers rather as their predecessors did their Swiss
> porters, that is as slightly superior servants, but this attitude disappeared as soon as
> the climbers realised that they were dependent on us for their every need; between
> them they had no word of any useful language.

Of General Bruce he gave a thumbnail sketch:

> He had long been known to the men of his own regiment as *Bhalu*, the bear, and
> as he lumbered into the room, almost breaking down the door as he did so, I realised
> that no description could be more apt. It was typical of him that, even before shaking
> hands, he should address me in a stream of fluent Nepali, much of it abusive and
> obscene, after which he broke into roars of schoolboyish laughter. Fortunately

I had the presence of mind to enter into the spirit of the occasion and answered him in the same language. It was lucky that I did so; many years later, after we had become intimate friends, he told me that he was horrified when he first set eyes upon my bespectacled and unmilitary features; he realised he had made a mistake and wondered how he could decently arrange to get rid of me. It was only my knowledge of Nepali that saved the situation. ...

He had the reputation of knowing more about Gurkhas than anybody living ... He was the very finest type of paternal Indian Army officer. ... it was upon men such as he that the high reputation of the old Indian Army had been built. They were splendid regimental officers, but most of them were temperamentally unfitted for higher command. ... He was a great mountain-traveller, but never at any time a great climber. ... his function was to get the party to the scene of action in good order ... in 1922 he was without question the right man for the job.

Of the second in command, Col E L Strutt, Morris made the point that Strutt's view of the sciences was that they were not a respectable occupation for anyone who regarded himself as a gentleman. An aristocrat by birth and possessed of considerable private means, Strutt was the greatest snob that Morris had ever encountered. ' ... he was incapable of understanding that large numbers of acceptable members of society found it necessary to work for their living.'

Morris described Mallory as looking much younger than his thirty-six years, because his body was perfectly proportioned and he moved with effortless grace. He was very absent-minded and as Sherpas did not understand the need for toothbrushes, pyjamas and the like and he left these lying about, they were thrown away. Other members of the expedition took it in turns to see that none of Mallory's kit was left behind.

At one time, before he became a master at Charterhouse, he had considered joining the regular army ... He was as unfitted as I to be a soldier and had moreover no sense of discipline. ... although he had an infectious enthusiasm for his chosen profession he was incapable of keeping order. ... his classes were a riot of disorder.

The official doctor was T G Longstaff who had more practical experience of exploration than any other member. Before the party left Darjeeling he called them together. 'I want to make one thing clear,' he said. 'I am the expedition's official medical officer. I am, as a matter of fact, a qualified doctor but I feel it my duty to remind you that I have never practised in my life. I beg you in no circumstances to seek my professional advice since it would almost certainly turn out to be wrong.

I am, however, willing if necessary to sign a certificate of death.' Fortunately the expedition included Somervell, a distinguished surgeon, and Wakefield, an exper-ienced General Practitioner, so Longstaff's medical expertise (or lack of it) was not called upon.

In an article in the *Alpine Journal*, A W Wakefield made some pertinent observations about the general health of the party as they crossed the Tibetan plateau. With Longstaff and Somervell, he had to take sick parade twice a day and noticed the large amount of upper respiratory infections suffered by the local Tibetans, which also affected members of the Everest party. Without antibiotics, these sapped the strength of the expedition, exacerbated by the all-pervading wind and dust and the unhygienic habits of the cooks.

Somervell, a formidably energetic man, later became a missionary surgeon in South India, and Professor of Surgery at the Christian Medical College, Vellore. He came to be acknowledged as a master surgeon far beyond the confines of India. He was also a talented artist and musician.

G I Finch was born in New South Wales and was given the option of attending an English public school after the family moved to Europe, but Finch preferred the freer environment of Europe. After initially studying medicine in Paris, he switched to physical sciences, studying in Zurich between 1906 and 1911. During this time he became an excellent mountaineer. After fighting in the First World War he joined Imperial College, London, and was elected a Fellow of the Royal Society in 1938. Following his retirement he became Director of the National Chemical Laboratory in India for five years. In 1922 Finch was the key figure in the use of oxygen and he played a major role in the organisation of equipment. Newer, lighter cylinders were obtained, and throughout the expedition he worked hard to ensure that the oxygen was satisfactory. Doubts persisted, however, as to its effectiveness when climbing at altitude.

HIGH PRESSURE OXYGEN APPARATUS
DESIGNED FOR
MOUNT EVEREST COMMITTEE

P_1 = PORT CYLINDER STOP VALVE.
P_2 = PORT   „   UNION.
P_3 = PORT STOP VALVE.
S_1 = STARBOARD CYLINDER STOP VALVE.
S_2 = STAR^{BD} „   UNION.
S_3 = STAR^{BD} STOP VALVE.
B.P. = BYE PASS.
F.M.= FLOW METER.
P.G. = PRESSURE GAUGE.
F.A. = FINE ADJUSTMENT VALVE.
R.V. = REDUCING VALVE.
F.T. = FLEX TUBE.
M. = MASK.

NOTE:- ONLY THE METAL PARTS OF THE CARRIER ARE SHOWN,
THE SHOULDER AND WAIST STRAPS BEING OMITTED.

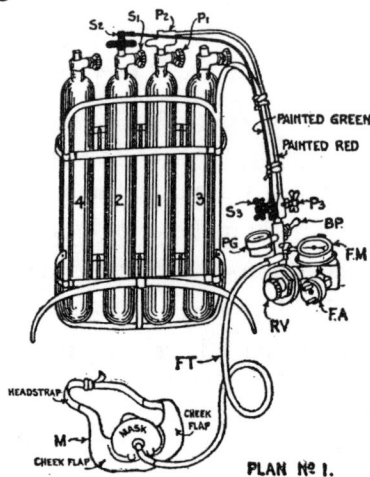

PLAN N° 1.

John Morris's comments on Finch were perceptive:

> He seemed at first ill at ease, probably knowing that his presence was not particularly welcome. But it was at once clear that his whole approach to the problem with which during the next few months we should be confronted was different from that of the rest. His attitude was thoroughly professional, and although this was his first visit to the Himalayas, his scientific training had led him to consider a number of matters the importance of which was barely sensed by some of the others. It was his misfortune to be of the right age to attempt Everest in 1922. His ideas of how such expeditions should be conducted were in advance of his time.*

Darjeeling to Rongbuk

Owing to the haste with which the expedition had had to be organised, the stores arrived in separate batches and General Bruce was in Darjeeling for a month before the main party arrived. The oxygen supplies were also delayed, so Finch and Crawford stayed in Darjeeling after the expedition left on 26 March.

Crossing the Jelep La into Tibet the main party encountered the fierce Tibetan wind that could cut through exposed skin like a whetted knife. From Phari to Kampa Dzong they took a direct route by the Tang La. On 9 April they made the hardest march of the expedition, crossing three spurs running down from the north side of Pauhunri and spending all day above 16,000ft. As Bruce later commented, 'What was brought home to us was the absolute necessity of windproof material to keep out the tremendous cold of the wind [which] blew through and through wool.' On this expedition the climbers wore Norfolk jackets only and had little or no windproof gear – except for Finch who, with typical foresight and thoroughness, had provided himself with windproof garments and an eiderdown jacket. It is not surprising therefore that, except for Finch, the party suffered from severe frostbite and incipient hypothermia when high on Everest.

On the 10th they descended to Kampa Dzong where they inspected the grave of A M Kellas, and here they were joined by Finch and Crawford with the oxygen equipment. From Kampa to Tinki and Shekar they followed the same route as in 1921, and on the way they attempted Sangkar Ri (20,000ft) in the Nyonno Ri range. A wonderful view of Everest could be seen at the junction of the Yaru Chu and Arun river.

---

* Immediately after the successful ascent of Everest in 1953, I lectured, at Finch's invitation, at the National Chemical Laboratory in Delhi. The questions he put to me after the lecture showed how well he understood all the problems, solved by Griffith Pugh of the Medical Research Council in London and myself, which had led to the solution of the medical/scientific problems of the 'last thousand feet' of Everest.

They stayed for three days at Shekar ('shining glass') where the Dzong Pen was an important official; all the country to the south, which included Everest, fell under his jurisdiction. After friendly relations were established and his photograph had been taken, the Dzong Pen arranged for large amounts of grain and transport to be made available.

From Shekar they went due south over the Pang La ('grass pass') and in four days reached Rongbuk monastery, passing on the way a mani wall at Chobuk which marked the start of the upper, sacred, part of the Rongbuk valley. In Tibetan, 'Rongbuk' means 'The Valley of the Precipices'. The monastery is in the same 'diocese' as Thyangboche in Khumbu on the south side of Everest. The head Lama of Rongbuk, the incarnation of the god Chongray Say, asked about the object of the expedition and was happy to be told that it was a pilgrimage – a concept easily understood in Tibet. A site for base camp at 16,500ft was found at the base of the Rongbuk glacier and all the porters were paid off. It was the first of May and the race against the monsoon, only a month away, really began.

The East Rongbuk glacier and the North Col

The map drawn up the previous year (1921) by E O Wheeler of the Survey of India indicated that an approach by the East Rongbuk glacier to the basin beneath the east face of the North Col was likely to be easy, so a reconnaissance party consisting of Norton, Strutt, Longstaff and Morshead set out to find suitable camp sites.

In the meantime, Finch was active in repairing the oxygen sets and in training the other members how to use them; he also experimented with the oxylite bags. In addition, as the Primus stoves tended to blow up if misused, he demonstrated how to use them correctly and safely.

Only 45 of the 90 Tibetans needed to move stores turned up, and they worked for a short period only before returning to their villages to start spring ploughing. However, with the help of the agent of the Dzong Pen, small family groups arrived to help, sleeping at 17,000ft at sub-zero temperatures without demur. Many had relatives in Khumbu, who had crossed the Nangpa La looking for work. Mothers often brought children less than a year old on this, to Western eyes, formidable journey. This was the start of a bond between the Sherpas of Khumbu and European members of Everest expeditions.

Eventually Camp III was established at the foot of the North Col, and on 13 May Mallory and Somervell reached the col. Both had already climbed a small peak on the east bank of the East Rongbuk glacier, and on the 12th Somervell had walked alone up to the Rapiu La where he had made a sketch of Makalu.

MOUNT EVEREST AND THE RONGBUK GLACIERS, 1922

Sketch-map compiled from surveys made by E O Wheeler in 1921,
with route and camps of the 1924 expedition added later by Colonel Strutt.

Their route to the North Col involved a long traverse right and then a reverse traverse left up a steep snow slope leading to an ice shelf just below the col itself. Both men reached this haven suffering severely from 'glacier lassitude'. From here they were able to climb directly, by the lip of a crevasse, to the col. The view was stupendous but, more importantly, the route up the North Ridge towards the summit did not look too difficult, confirming the opinion of Bullock and Mallory a few months earlier. After pitching a tent in a sheltered site, they descended to Camp III at the foot of the col.

On 16 May a large caravan reached Camp III and an assault plan was worked out. Initially Mallory and Somervell were to make the first attempt, but as four climbers were considered safer than two on the unknown upper part of the mountain, Norton and Morshead joined them. However, bad weather now disrupted their plans and a further visit to the Rapiu La revealed monsoon clouds boiling up from Nepal to the south and east. Despite the possible onset of bad weather, Strutt, Morshead, Norton, Somervell and Mallory, with ten porters, carried half their stores to the North Col on the 17th, and the remainder went up on the 19th.

Remarkably, the Primus stoves were not taken and cooking had to be done on spirit stoves using alcohol and meta fuel which took much longer to reach boiling point. Inevitably, the result was that none of the climbers took in enough fluid and became weak through dehydration; also they were partially starved. This was not fully recognised at the time, as lack of oxygen blunts feelings of hunger and thirst.

First attempt to 27,000ft, without supplementary oxygen
On 20 May the start from the North Col was delayed until 7.30am and only four of the nine porters were fit enough to carry loads to a higher camp. The route up the North Ridge was at an easy angle between the rock of the North Face and the snow on the crest of the ridge. The day was clear but the devastating and deadly Tibetan wind began to chill the climbers, none of whom had adequate windproof clothing. The sun then disappeared, cooling them further. Seeking to gain the snow crest of the ridge in order to reach the lee side out of the wind, their pace slowed as steps had to be cut, but by 11.30am they had climbed to 2,000ft above the North Col and had reached nearly 25,000ft, when a further camp site was found. At 3pm the porters descended.

Of the party of four Europeans, three were now suffering from frostbite: Norton had a frostbitten ear, Mallory and Morshead frostbitten fingertips. All four were badly chilled with incipient hypothermia – all due to inadequate oxygen uptake and poor clothing, plus the potent effect of wind-chill. After only one day of easy climbing above the North Col, the party was already in poor physical shape.

That night the temperature fell to 7°F and next day, 21 May, Morshead was too exhausted to move more than a few feet from the tent. Norton, Somervell and Mallory continued. The climbing was not difficult, and they could climb continuously for about 20 minutes without halting. Not counting their halts, which became more frequent and lasted longer as they gained height, their rate of ascent was 400ft per hour, and it soon became clear that despite the ease of the climbing they would not be able to reach the summit and return in daylight. Hypothermia would have killed them if they had spent a night in the open.

At 2.15pm, therefore, they stopped at 27,000ft, not owing to any technical climbing difficulty but because they were ascending too slowly. Their senses were so dulled by oxygen lack and cold that they hardly noticed the view, and felt no elation at having reached a point 2,000ft higher than any previous mountaineer. They ate chocolate, raisins and Kendal Mint Cake and, as Mallory put it, 'their tongues were hanging out after so much exercise of breathing'. At 4.0pm they reached Camp V at 25,000ft; here they collected Morshead, reaching the North Col camp after dark at 11.30pm. All were quite exhausted. Their main complaint was a terrible thirst, but having no cooking pans in which to melt snow, they ate a mixture of tinned strawberry jam, frozen ideal milk and snow. Next day, on arrival at Camp III, Somervell drank 17 cups of tea (3 litres) and all recovered quickly.

Their attempt on the summit had been defeated not by any climbing difficulty but by oxygen lack, cold and exhaustion which had *not* been countered by adequate clothing, food and fluid intake, or by adequate oxygen uptake.

This combination was destined to be repeated time and time again on subsequent Everest expeditions in the 1920s and 1930s until all these problems were solved in the first six months of 1951 at the Medical Research Council in London.

Second attempt to 27,400ft, using supplementary oxygen

On 10 May, when Mallory and Somervell set out from Camp III, Finch had expected to be able to make a second attempt with Norton, using supplementary oxygen. Unfortunately, Finch developed diarrhoea so, instead, Norton and Morshead had joined the first attempt.

By 15 May Finch had recovered and he left base camp with J G Bruce and Tejbir, a Gurkha NCO. On 18 May he had to give his two companions lessons in mountain craft as neither were mountaineers. At Camp III, at the foot of the North Col, they overhauled their oxygen equipment and found that, though the cylinders were in good shape, the valves and masks were inadequate. Four days, from the 19th onwards, were spent, in freezing wind, repairing these with a soldering iron, hacksaw and pliers. As the masks were quite useless, they improvised a satisfactory alternative by putting tubes in their mouths and biting when breathing out – a solution which, after a little practice, worked well. A number of 'trial runs' were made to the Rapiu La (22,340ft) and on these Finch and Bruce, using supplementary oxygen, easily out-distanced those who were not using it

On 22 May Finch, Bruce and Wakefield met the first assault party on their way down from the North Col. Leaving Wakefield to help the exhausted party back to Camp III, the rest continued up to the North Col, taking three hours on the ascent and 50 minutes only on the descent. Two days later, on the 24th, using supplementary oxygen, Finch, Bruce and Tejbir climbed to the North Col again. Next day, with three porters, they set off carrying loads to a high camp, while Captain Noel was left at camp to take photographs. Using oxygen, Bruce, Finch and Tejbir carried 40lbs each, which was more than the porters were carrying, yet, despite starting later, they overtook them at 24,500ft. The porters called oxygen 'English air' and were most impressed by it. As the weather worsened, camp was made at 25,500ft and not 26,000ft, as planned, and the porters descended to the North Col camp.

After dark a gale blew up and the three climbers had to hold on to the poles of the tent to stop it from being blown down to the East Rongbuk glacier thousands of feet below. Reaching its zenith at 1.0am, the gale continued next day and pinned the party in their tent. At noon a stone blown by the wind cut a hole in the canvas, but luckily an hour later the wind dropped as suddenly as it had started. At 6.0pm some porters arrived from the North Col bringing hot beef tea in thermos flasks, an amazing and thoughtful gesture.

The night of the 26th began critically; all were stressed and very tired and Finch felt a numbing cold creeping up from his hands and feet. Recognising the onset of hypothermia he knew that coma and death were not too far off. In his book *The Making of a Mountaineer* Finch described what happened next:

> ... Like a heaven-sent inspiration came the idea of trying the effect of oxygen. ... Now hauling in one apparatus together with a supply of cylinders, we took doses [of oxygen] all round, giving the action the air of a joke. Tejbir took his medicine without much interest; but as he inhaled, I saw with relief that his face brightened up. The effect of the oxygen on Geoffrey Bruce was particularly visible in his rapid change of expression; the hitherto drawn, anxious look on his face gave place to a more normal one. The result on myself was no less marvellous; almost at once I felt the painful, prickling, tingling sensation, due to the returning circulation of the blood, as the lost warmth slowly came back to my limbs. We connected up the apparatus so that all could breathe a small quantity throughout the night. There is no doubt whatsoever that oxygen saved our lives that night; without it, in our well-nigh exhausted and famished condition, we would have succumbed to the cold.

Next day, the 27th, they left camp at 6.30am soon after the sun had warmed their tent. Bruce and Finch carried 40lbs each, whilst Tejbir took the two extra oxygen bottles; in all, his load was 50lbs. The day was clear but the pervading wind gradually increased in strength. Tejbir stopped at about 26,000ft and could go no further. Finch and Bruce took his oxygen cylinders and let him return over easy ground to their tent, which was plainly visible.

Ascending another 500ft to 26,500ft the wind forced them to leave the North Ridge and traverse to the right across the North Face. Suddenly the angle steepened and the direction of the strata meant that the rocks overlapped and sloped outwards like the tiles of a roof. Even so, the climbing was not difficult enough to require a rope and Finch led through a mixture of snow, ice, scree and rock. At 27,000ft they stopped traversing and started to climb directly upwards, but at 27,400ft a trivial accident put Bruce's oxygen apparatus out of action. Finch connected him up to his own apparatus, traced the fault and rectified it.

They were now standing on an insecure rock ledge by an inverted V of snow just below a red-yellow rock cliff that ran through the green-black slabs of the North Face. Within half a mile of the summit they could distinguish the individual stones on a little patch of scree just underneath the highest point, but weakened by hunger and thirst they knew that if they continued for another 500ft, they would not return alive. It was midday when they stopped and from their camp at 25,500ft to their highest point at 27,400ft they had taken 5½ hours including halts, at an overall climbing rate of 320ft per hour, carrying a total weight, including oxygen set, of 40-50lbs. Their rate of climb had been a little faster than that of the first party, which reached 27,000ft without using supplementary oxygen, but Finch's party had got closer to the summit.

Returning, they reached camp at 25,500ft at 2.30pm, where they found Tejbir asleep and also some porters who had come up from the North Col to help them carry their gear down. All reached the North Col at 4.0pm. After some food they descended from the North Col to Camp III in the basin at the foot of the col which they reached at 5.30pm. They had descended from their highest point, 6,000ft above, at an average rate of 1,000ft per hour, three times faster than their previous rate of ascent. Neither Finch nor Bruce was particularly thirsty because, unlike the first party, their rate of breathing when using oxygen was slower, and they therefore lost less water from their lungs. Both had mildly frostbitten feet but their general physical condition was good. This was in marked contrast to the first party who were totally exhausted, and Norton had even cut off part of his frostbitten ear with scissors. Their overall performance and condition, therefore, was better than that of the first party, all of whom were good mountaineers. By contrast, Bruce and Tejbir had no previous mountaineering experience.

Finch made a number of comments about this expedition. He pointed out that windproof clothing was essential, and that the greatly increased rate of breathing led to loss of both heat and water from the lungs. He also pointed out that both attempts had failed not because of climbing difficulties but from the effects of oxygen lack and cold; 'sleeping' oxygen had saved the lives of his party. Finch was of course quite right, but the Everest Committee in London made little attempt to act upon his suggestions, and he was dropped from the 1924 expedition.

Third attempt and fatal avalanche

After these two unsuccessful attempts only Somervell was really fit, so on 3 June he, with Mallory and Finch and using supplementary oxygen, set out for the North Col. Unfortunately Finch, exhausted by his efforts a few days previously, had to stand down, but Crawford and Wakefield joined them. The weather remained poor, and at Camp III it became obvious that because of repeated snowfall, the slopes of the North Col were dangerous. In spite of this, Somervell, Mallory and Crawford set off with fourteen porters to establish Camp IV, once again on the col itself.

At 21,800ft the slope on which they were climbing avalanched, the fault line being just above the line of their steps. All were swept down over an ice cliff sixty feet high, and seven porters were fatally buried under the snow. This tragedy emphasised how treacherous these snow slopes were, for the combined experience of the climbers was considerable and the slope had been ascended and descended without incident only a few days previously. This episode ended the expedition.

Exploration east of Everest. The Nepalese frontier.

The full force of the monsoon now arrived, with deep snowfalls and persistent bad weather; the tents on the upper slopes of Everest had to be abandoned. Before the expedition left England, its planned itinerary included some exploration of the Cho Oyu and Gyachung Kang group of peaks, west of Everest. It now became clear, however, that the original plan would have to be abandoned, since the physical state of the party was so poor that they had to descend to lower levels as soon as possible.

A service for the dead porters was held by the Lama of Rongbuk. All the porters were Buddhists whose belief was that if their time had come they would die. The individual deaths were a sacrifice to the gods, in particular the god of Everest. By contrast, the Hindu population of Nepal had a different concept, believing that the porters' deaths were retribution for invading the privacy of the gods Shiva and Parvati who lived on the peaks of the Himalaya.

On 14 June yak transport arrived at base camp and the party decided, when fully recovered, to cross into the Kharta valley, extend the exploration of the Kama valley and descend the Arun valley to the Nepal border. Crossing the climatic border at the Doya La (17,000ft) between Dzakar Chu and the Kharta valley, a profusion of alpine flowers greeted them at the village of Teng on the southern side of the pass. Soon they dropped down steeply into the Kharta district and the Arun valley.

At a lower altitude, the health of the party improved rapidly and on 19 June they set off from Kharta Sikha to explore the Kharta valley. Crossing the Samchung La, and Chog La (16,280ft) they descended to Sakyetang (11,000ft), a charming grassy glade deep in alpine flowers. Unfortunately, they could not see into the Arun valley owing to cloud cover, but next morning they caught a fleeting glimpse of the peak, Chomo Lonzo, at the head of the Karma Chu. In the woods a group of Gurung (Nepali) shepherds were camped, their sheep being larger than Tibetan sheep. Milk and butter from these were sold to Nepali inhabitants in the foothills. Most of the party returned north to the Tibetan plateau, but Morris and Noel decided to descend the Karma Chu to the Arun gorge and the Nepal border.

The actual border was at Kyamathang, where the Karma Chu flowed into the Arun. This was a typical Nepali village but so inaccessible that the cultural life of the inhabitants was independent of either Tibet or Nepal. Here Morris and Noel were told that a seldom-used path led up to the Popti La,* a pass which crossed the frontier ridge between the Karma Chu and the Barun Khola coming from the south-east side of Everest and Makalu.

Morris and Noel were also told that, up a side valley to the east of the Arun, a path connected with Tashirak, which Noel had visited in 1913. That path, however, had been partially destroyed. Instead, they turned north up the Arun gorge and after a difficult four days' travel they found a path used by Tibetans coming from the Kharta valley to get wood. They followed this up a side valley to the west, crossed a pass of 16,000ft, crossed the Yulok La and thus reached Kharta.

Going north again up the side of the Arun gorge, they reached the foot of the Chey La and finally Shekar Dzong. From Shekar to Kampa Dzong they followed a route along a tributary of the Arun, passing Solpo where they met a lama from Urga in northern Mongolia. A true devotee of Buddhism, he was progressing from Lhasa to Kathmandu by way of the Nyalam valley in the time-honoured method of prostration. He had left Lhasa a year previously and now relied on the generosity of local villagers for food; he believed that it would take him another year to reach Kathmandu. Within the next few days the party crossed the Pharmogadora La to Tinki and two days later reached Kampa Dzong and then Darjeeling.

* The first recorded visit to this pass was made by the Pundit G.S.S. in 1880 and it was later explored by the Cho Oyu party in 1952.

George Finch's comments on equipment and other matters

Following the 1922 expedition George Finch made a number of recommendations about the equipment used during the expedition and other matters. These show how prescient he was. They may be summarised as follows:

1 **Snow conditions and climate**
   Above 22,000ft snow conditions change and resemble those found in mid-winter in the European Alps. At this height the climate changes radically, with cold more severe and associated with loss of heat from the lungs. Climbing efficiency is reduced as a result.

2 **High-altitude deterioration**
   Deterioration starts at about 23,000ft.

3 **Oxygen**
   Supplementary oxygen should be used from about 21,500ft upwards. Sleeping oxygen improves sleep. As supplementary oxygen increases appetite, there should be adequate food and fluid intake.

4 **Sources of oxygen**
   Compressed oxygen in cylinders should be taken. Water and sodium peroxide to produce oxygen is not effective and neither is the use of garlic. Subcutaneous oxygen has no scientific rationale; neither does potassium chlorate. With hydrogen peroxide, the rate of oxygen production could not be controlled.

5 **Tobacco**
   Smoking cigarettes at great altitude seemed to stimulate respiration.

6 **Clothing**
   Warm and windproof clothing should be worn. The following is suggested: thin silk underwear, light woollen underwear, heavy woollen underwear, woollen sweater and trousers, warm and windproof clothing.
   [Finch himself wore a padded down windproof jacket that he had had specially made. This type of jacket did not become standard wear until the Second World War.]

7 **Gloves**
   Thin wool, lambskin, and over-gauntlets of canvas with a flannel lining.

8 **Headgear**
   RNAS helmet which covers most of the face and ears, with Crookes goggles. [These were specially tinted glass goggles incorporated in the helmet – presumably to counter snow blindness at altitude.]

9 **Boots**
   As leather conducts heat away from the foot, the uppers should be of felt covered with canvas. The sole should be thin leather underneath hinged plywood. Tricouni nails should penetrate only the leather. Puttees should be worn.

BIBLIOGRAPHY

C G Bruce, *The Assault on Mount Everest 1922*. Arnold, 1923.

G I Finch, 'The Second Attempt on Mt Everest' in *Alpine Journal 34*, 439-450, 1922.

G I Finch, Report: 'Equipment for High Altitude Mountaineering with special reference to climbing Mt Everest'. 1923.

G I Finch, *The Making of a Mountaineer*. Arrowsmith, 1924.

G I Finch, *Der Kampf um den Everest*. F A Brockhaus, Leipzig, 1925.

G H L Mallory, 'The Second Mount Everest Expedition' in *Alpine Journal 34*, 425-439, 1922.

C J Morris, 'The Gorge of the Arun' in *Geographical Journal 62*, 161-173, 1923.

C J Morris, *Hired to Kill*. R Hart-Davis and Cresset Press, 1960.

H T Morshead, 'Mount Everest' in *The Royal Engineers' Journal 37*, 353-368, 1923.

Ian Morshead, *The Life and Murder of Henry Morshead*. Oleander Press, 1982.

Scott Russell, a memoir of G I Finch included in a new edition of *The Making of a Mountaineer*. Arrowsmith, 1988.

Unattributed Note, 'The Mount Everest Expedition' in *Geographical Journal 60*, 141-144, 1922.

Unattributed Note, 'Photographs' in *Geographical Journal 60*, 288-291, 1922.

Unattributed Note, 'The Mount Everest Expedition of 1922' in *Geographical Journal 60*, 385-424, 1922.

Unattributed Notes: on Illustrations and Conclusions in respect of the 1922 Everest Expedition, in *Alpine Journal 34*, 450-456, 1922.

P J H Unna, 'The oxygen equipment of the 1922 Everest expedition' in *Alpine Journal 34*, 235-250, 1922.

A W Wakefield, 'The Health of the Everest Expedition 1922' in *Alpine Journal 46*, 449-451, 1934.

M P Ward, 'Northern Approaches: Everest 1918-22' in *Alpine Journal 99*, 213-217, 1994.

Chapter 7

ROUTS AND DISCOMFITURES
The second attempt on the summit, 1924

High-altitude meeting at the Royal Society of Medicine, December 1922
Mountaineers and scientists were amazed that members of the 1922 party had managed to climb to over 27,000ft without the use of supplementary oxygen, for at that height, without its help, balloonists and pilots of aeroplanes had become unconscious and some had died.

In addition, there was a fierce academic debate, which had been running for some years, as to whether at altitude the lungs produce (secrete) oxygen or whether oxygen diffuses through the walls of the lungs from the air to the blood. If oxygen was *produced* by the lungs, Everest could be climbed without the help of supplementary oxygen. More importantly, a resolution of this debate would be a critical step towards finding out how oxygen is transported around the body, from the air to the cells. Although Barcroft had demonstrated in 1920 that oxygen *diffused* through the lungs, it would be some time before his findings were generally accepted.

As a result of this medical and physiological interest in Everest, a meeting was arranged at the Royal Society of Medicine in London on 15 December 1922. Both Longstaff and Barcroft (Professor of Physiology at Cambridge University) considered that Everest could be climbed without the use of supplementary oxygen *provided* that a long enough period of acclimatisation preceded the summit attempt; and Longstaff was the first to observe that those climbers on Everest who *had* used supplementary oxygen, ie Finch and Bruce, did not suffer so severely from frostbite as the 'non-oxygen' party. The use of supplementary oxygen seemed to have increased climbing rate and therefore heat output and seemed also to promote dilatation of the peripheral blood vessels, so that warm blood went to the extremities, preventing frostbite. The use of oxygen while sleeping had probably saved Finch's party from hypothermia.

The outcome of this meeting was inconclusive so far as the use of supplementary oxygen on Everest was concerned, though it seemed that there were some obvious advantages in its use. However, the key practical question was not considered. This was to determine what flow rate of supplementary oxygen would be sufficient to allow climbers to move fast enough to reach the summit from a high camp and to return in daylight.

Selection of the party

A series of lectures about the 1922 expedition was given at home and abroad mainly by Finch and Mallory, so that by the spring of 1923 about eighty had been delivered. From the proceeds of the expedition book, enough money was available for the proposed 1924 expedition.

When members of the 1924 party were chosen it might be thought that Finch, who had worked tirelessly to make the oxygen sets function properly and who had climbed higher than anyone else in 1922, would automatically be chosen, but this was not the case. Possibly his meticulous preparations and preoccupation with oxygen may have irritated his fellow climbers, though there is no evidence that they made their feelings known. Another factor may have been his unwillingness to contribute a percentage of the proceeds of his lectures towards the next expedition, as had been previously agreed. It was unfortunate, too, that Hinks was on the selection committee; he could not abide Finch, a professional among amateurs, and amateur attitudes to climbing Everest still prevailed in the Alpine Club and Royal Geographical Society at that time.

Finch did have his supporters, though, including Professor J B S Haldane who considered that it would be safer to use supplementary oxygen; but some influential climbers, such as Somervell, were doubtful about its use for 'moral' as well as practical reasons. To counter such views, Douglas Freshfield wrote robustly 'So long as the summit is reached, who cares whether it is with or without supplementary oxygen.'

The final party consisted of Brigadier General C G Bruce, Lt Col E F Norton, J G Bruce (General Bruce's cousin), N E Odell, G H L Mallory, Dr T H Somervell, A C Irvine, E O Shebbeare, Major R W G Hingston (the expedition doctor), Bentley Beetham and J de V Hazard. Captain J B L Noel accompanied the team in order to make a film and it was largely through him that funds were made available to finance the expedition. In addition, C G Bruce invited Micky Weatherall to help Noel. John Macdonald, who spoke Tibetan and knew Tibet well, also joined the party.

To the mountains

Leaving Darjeeling on 25 March, they crossed the Sikkim-Tibet border by the Jelep La again, descended into the Chumbi valley and climbed slowly to Phari and the southern plains of Tibet. From Phari, after two days spent haggling over the price of yaks, the main party continued to Kampa Dzong. Unfortunately, at Tuna (15,000ft), General Bruce ran a high temperature, caused by a recurrence of malaria, and this forced him to go with Hingston to a lower altitude at Gangtok in Sikkim, where he recuperated with F M Bailey, the Political Officer, and his wife.

This was a great blow to the party because General Bruce was a charismatic leader. However, Norton, who took over, was a more than adequate substitute. Also an army officer, Norton was a modest man, an excellent mountaineer and organiser, and easily the most talented of those who had previously led British Everest expeditions. Moreover, he was able to write lucid, simple and descriptive prose and was a good amateur water-colour painter who made many delightful sketches during the 1922 and 1924 expeditions.

Noel Odell became one of the outstanding high-altitude mountaineers of his generation. By profession a geologist, he was a Fellow of the Royal Society of Edinburgh. It was on an expedition to Spitsbergen that the talents of A C Irvine, both as an expedition member and as a repairer of instruments, impressed Odell so much that he recommended him for the 1924 expedition.

Initially, in 1924, Odell did not acclimatise well but it soon became clear that he was one of the fittest members of the team. He was put in charge of the oxygen apparatus and many thought that he, rather than Irvine, should have been chosen to accompany Mallory on their summit attempt using supplementary oxygen. However, it was quite clear that Odell was not impressed by the use of oxygen, for reasons that are explained later. In 1924 he climbed twice to about 28,000ft without oxygen and carried out a geological survey on the upper slopes of Everest.

Later, Odell was asked to take part in the 1933 Everest expedition, but pressure of work prevented this. However, in 1936 he made the first ascent, with H W Tilman, of Nanda Devi (25,645ft), the highest peak yet climbed at that time. He was also a member of the 1938 Everest expedition when he climbed very high. He lived to be nearly 100 years old.*

On 8 April a note from Hingston informed the party that it was unlikely that Bruce would be fit enough to join them. On the 10th they continued across the vast gravel plain of Tibet, 'the very abomination of desolation'. Though seemingly devoid of vegetation, large herds of *Kyang* (gazelle) were seen and the blunt snow-capped peaks of the Sikkim–Tibet border made an exhilarating backdrop.

Next day they descended from this inhospitable plain to Kampa Dzong, tucked away in a fold in the ground, and being sheltered from the biting Tibetan wind, a sun-trap. As Norton wrote in *The Fight for Everest: 1924*:

> The scenery as you descend on the village is striking; the great flat plain of Kampa stretches 10 miles to the west, and from this point of view has an irridescent quality which a closer acquaintance scarcely explains. The variegated foothills which border it look as if they were composed of knife-powder, rust and wood ashes, and the

---

* I operated on him when he was in his mid-90s. The condition of his muscles were those of a man over 20 years younger.

horizon is bounded on three sides by what appear at this season to be all snow mountains. On the south stretch the great peaks of the main range of the Himalayas, where Tibet borders on Sikkim and Nepal, and on the north is a range [the Gangdise], snow-capped except for two summer months, which borders the valley of the Brahmaputra. Eastward [sic], the fine shapes of the Gyankar [Nyonno Ri] range merge into the giants of the Mount Everest system, though these, tinted golden by 100 miles of atmosphere, still seem to dominate the nearer ranges less than half as distant. This morning the familiar shapes of Everest and Makalu remained almost clear of cloud until the foothills shut them from our view, and only as we were losing them did they begin to fly the cloud banner which in this region always marks the master peak.

Prevarication and delay, so beloved of the Tibetan authorities, was provided by the Dzong Pen of Kampa during the change of transport animals – but this afforded the team an opportunity for a rest after their high-level trek from Sikkim, and time to discuss future plans. General Bruce had left a very efficient organisation, a strong element of which was a party of four Gurkha NCOs 'lent' by the 2nd/6th Gurkha Rifles, who had also 'lent' Geoffrey Bruce. On the 1922 expedition J G Bruce had taken part in all the interviews with Tibetan officials, which Norton had not, so the latter found him invaluable. In addition, Bruce was highly efficient and a very pleasant person, and his presence on the expedition allowed it to continue with no disruption from the loss of its leader.

On 15 April the party left Kampa Dzong and continued over the plain of southern Tibet to Tinki Dzong, whose Dzong Pen rode out to greet them. A day spent changing yaks enabled them to discuss plans for the mountain. The health of Mallory and Beetham, who had both been ill, was improving. From Tinki they crossed a pass into the basin of the eastern (Phung Chu) branch of the Arun river, which they descended to Shiling. Climbing a hill above camp they had a striking view of Everest, 60 miles away, and the 6,000ft high, snow-covered East (Kangchung) Face. Following the Phung Chu river, they arrived at Shekar Dzong on 23 April. Here Odell and Irvine checked the oxygen sets, repaired many leaking valves and tested the sets on a nearby hill. Here, too, Norton revealed his plans for the summit attempts, one with supplementary oxygen, the other without. Each attempt would be made independently, one supporting the other. Four climbers would be held in reserve, but so confident was the party, that all felt that a second attempt would not be necessary. The provisional make-up of each party was as follows:

First attempt: Mallory and Irvine, using supplementary oxygen. Somervell and Norton, without oxygen. *Second attempt*: Bruce and Odell, using supplementary oxygen. Beetham and Hazard without oxygen.

Leaving Shekar on 25 April they went due south towards Everest, crossing the Pang La, from where they had another striking view of Everest only 35 miles away. From a small hill beside the pass, six of the world's highest peaks were visible: Everest, Makalu, Kangchenjunga, Gosainthan, Gyachung Kang and Cho Oyu. All were snow-covered except for Everest, the top 6,000 feet of which consisted of black rock, the ferocious wind having cleared it of snow. On the pass, however, the climate was mild, with many early flowers, butterflies and lizards.

That night they camped at Tashidzom in the valley of the Dzakar Chu, which they followed to its source in the Rongbuk valley. The village of Chodzong lay at the start of this narrow, cheerless and desolate passage. The hills on each side were ugly limestone lumps devoid of beauty of form or colour. A large river draining the glaciers on the north side of Gyachung Kang and Cho Oyu flowed into the east side of the Dzakar Chu. Then suddenly, as the valley took a turn towards Everest, the massive form of the mountain came into view at the valley's end, together with the familiar sight of the Rongbuk monastery.

A survey of the West Rongbuk glacier

On 29 April the party reached the site of Base Camp, four miles beyond Rongbuk, and spent the rest of the day sorting stores. Next day loads were carried up to establish Camps I and II on the East Rongbuk glacier and, in appalling weather, Camp III at the foot of the North Col was also set up and provisioned. But high winds and freezing temperatures played havoc with the poorly-equipped Tibetan porters who retreated to Base Camp, leaving Odell, Hazard and Irvine at Camp III. In poor weather, they made an attempt to reach the North Col, and left a dump of ropes and equipment at their highest point.

After they had retreated to Camp III, the temperature fell to minus 3°F which, with gale force winds, meant freezing the exposed skin and causing frostbite. An attempt on the North Col became impossible and a melancholy procession of climbers and porters, snow blind and frostbitten, retreated to Base Camp. One porter had both feet severely frostbitten to the ankles, another had pneumonia, and one of the Gurkhas suffered a stroke. Luckily, Hingston, the medical officer, who had accompanied General Bruce to Gangtok, opportunely arrived back in camp, where his expertise was badly needed. Thus ended the first attempt by the 1924 party, if attempt it can be called, for little climbing had been done. A combination of cold, altitude and wind had defeated them.

At this stage, the only successful work had been by the surveyor, Hari Singh Thapa, who had been working on the West Rongbuk glacier. This large glacier ran from the Nup La under Gyachung Kang to join the main Rongbuk glacier under the North Face of Everest, draining the northern Tibetan aspect of many peaks on the Nepal-Tibet watershed.

This setback emphasised the inadequacy of the personal protective clothing worn by expedition members in 1924, as windproof outer garments were still rare at that time and the padded jackets used by the Chinese for centuries were not available. Finch's windproof padded jacket, used in 1922, had been ignored.

The death of Manbahadur from a combination of frostbite and pneumonia and of Shamsher from a stroke (caused by the increase in red blood cells and dehydration normally found at altitude) served to lower the morale of the party still further. So Karma Paul, the interpreter, was sent to the Abbot of Rongbuk to ask if he would bless the porters, and it was hoped that this ceremony, together with the benefits of a spell at lower altitude, would restore the spirits of the party. On 15 May the Abbot blessed the whole party – Europeans, Gurkhas, Sherpas and Tibetans alike – and each was given two rupees to donate to the monastery. To conclude the ceremony, after a short address, the Abbot promised that he would pray for each member.

On their return to Base Camp, the mood of the porters changed, and they were nearly their cheerful selves again. Even the weather improved and 16 May was a brilliantly fine, cloudless day with sun that was warm to the skin. All seemed set for a fresh start, when Bentley Beetham had an attack of acute sciatica that put him out of action. However, Camp III at the foot of the North Col was soon reoccupied, and the decisive phase, the establishment of Camp IV on the North Col, was about to begin.

North Col crisis

The race was now on to climb Everest before the start of the monsoon in about two weeks' time at the beginning of June. In 1922 the monsoon had arrived on June 1st when an avalanche had killed seven porters on the slopes of the North Col. Once Camp IV was established, only a few days would be needed for a summit attempt but the weather was consistently poor.

Norton, Somervell, Mallory and Odell, with Lhakpa Tsering, made the first attempt. Paradoxically, Somervell suffered from mild heat exhaustion contracted in the bowl of snow beneath the North Col. In similar circumstances, air temperatures of 180°F have been measured, caused by the reflection of the sun from the snow combined with the direct heat from the sun, and resulting in a high body temperature. Somervell became ill and had to return to Camp III, but the others reached the crest of the col at 3.30pm after an exhausting but not technically difficult climb.

The slopes on the east side of the North Col had changed considerably since 1922 and the obvious route up a shallow scoop, down which the fatal 1922 avalanche had fallen, was avoided. In 1924 a long crescent-shaped crevasse crossed the whole face, its left end reaching the scoop. The lower edge of this crevasse was followed and, where it was broken, the depths of the crevasse were visited from which an ice chimney led back to the surface. Finally, a 200ft ice slope, overhanging an ice cliff, led to a shelf just below the crest of the North Col, and here Camp IV was placed in a sheltered position. Starting down at 3.45pm they reached Camp III at the foot of the col, tired but satisfied. Despite the intense cold (minus 24°F), the next few days were spent carrying loads to Camp IV at about 22,200ft.

On 23 May a crisis overtook the party. Four porters from a group of twelve led by Hazard were left behind on the North Col, two of them in order to prepare a meal for a relieving party which had, in the event, turned back, and the other two because, on the descent, they baulked at crossing an unpleasant-looking snow slope and returned to the North Col. At Camp IV the four porters found themselves isolated, and being prey to superstitions, they could easily have given up hope and succumbed to cold, exhaustion and fear.

Though their own general physical condition was not good, Norton, Somervell and Mallory set out next day for the North Col, with only a fifty-fifty chance, they believed, of success in rescuing the stranded porters. They found two porters badly frostbitten, one with both hands affected and the other with both feet. Somervell had to take each man individually down to the safety of the crevasse while Norton and Mallory were safely anchored. In the course of this laborious exercise, two porters slid out of the steps cut in the ice, but miraculously stopped thirty feet short of an overhanging cliff. Somervell then had to cut steps down to them and haul them up into the safety of the crevasse. Although all the porters had been trained in mountaineering techniques, fear rendered them incapable of applying what they had learned.

At 4.30pm they all started down, with Norton bringing up the rear. For the first time on the expedition he was using crampons and stopped many slips made by the exhausted and demoralised men. Three hours later, at 7.30pm, they reached Camp III to be met by Odell and Noel with hot soup. Next day they all retreated to Camp I to recuperate.

The final effort
On the North Col there was now enough equipment for the summit attempt but not enough food and fuel. Only 15 porters could be counted on to carry loads to the North Col, but fortunately most of these were willing to continue as far as the top camp at 27,000ft. Despite Finch's climb to 27,400ft in 1922, using supplementary oxygen, there was still no consensus of view that its use improved climbing rate.

After a long discussion it was decided to use it, but the rather complicated original plan was scrapped and instead it was arranged that consecutive parties of just two members with support from the North Col would make the summit attempts. The pairs were to be Mallory and Bruce followed by Somervell and Norton, with Odell and Irvine at Camp IV on the North Col in support.

At the lower altitude of Camp I the improvement in the health of the party was so marked that they remained there an extra day, leaving on 21 May. For a change, too, the sun came out and they basked in it. On 1st June the North Col camp was occupied, and Camp V on the North Ridge at 25,000ft was established the next day by Mallory and Bruce. Returning to the North Col they met Odell and Irvine in support. These two were to spend the next week based on the North Col; on three separate occasions during the next few days Odell descended to Camp III and reascended, either escorting porters or bringing up supplies. Though usually slow to acclimatise, Odell was now reaching the peak of his fitness.

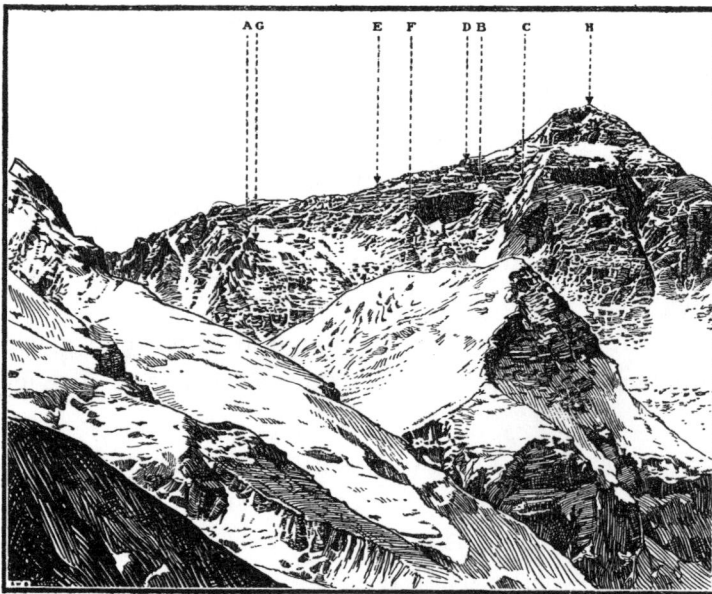

THE NORTH FACE OF EVEREST SHOWING HEIGHTS REACHED ON THE 1922 AND 1924 EXPEDITIONS

    A. Camp VI, 26,700 feet.
    B. The point reached by Somervell in 1924.
    C. The point reached by Norton in 1924.
    D. 'The Second Step' where Mallory and Irvine were last seen.
    E. 'The First Step'
    F. The point reached by Finch and Geoffrey Bruce in 1922.
    G. The point reached by Mallory, Norton and Somervell in 1922.
    H. The summit, 29,002 feet.

The first attempt, by E F Norton and T H Somervell, without supplementary oxygen, to 28,000ft

On 1st June, following in the footsteps of Mallory and Bruce, Norton and Somervell left Camp III with six porters, reaching the North Col at 3.0pm. The next day was fine: it was assumed that Mallory and Bruce had occupied Camp V and were on their way up to Camp VI. So, carrying 20lbs each, Norton and Somervell left the shelter of the North Col camp with the six porters, only to be exposed to the full force of the west wind on their way up to Camp V. Norton wrote in *The Fight for Everest*:

> ... that was a bad moment, its memory is still fresh. The wind, even at this early hour, took our breath away like a plunge into the icy waters of a mountain lake, and in a minute or two our well-protected hands lost all sensation as they grasped the frozen rocks to steady us.

The wind cut through their supposedly 'windproof' outer gaberdine suits as if they did not exist, and as they followed the easy North Ridge, between the rocks at its crest and a snow bed below the crest, they became increasingly chilled. Halfway up they met Mallory, Bruce and four porters descending. Having sent down two of their own porters with Mallory, they continued with the remaining four porters, reaching Camp V at 1pm. So exhausted were they that it took 45 minutes before they felt able to start the relentless chore of collecting snow for melting over a meta burner, with added pemmican. It was a most distasteful duty to have to prepare and eat the necessary quantities of food and fluid.

On 3 June they were up at 5.0am. Norton went to the porters' tent to persuade them to start. Overnight, to keep warm, the porters had kept their stoves alight and, with the tent closely sealed, were suffering from a mild degree of carbon monoxide poisoning. Finally they were persuaded to move. Meanwhile, Somervell's dry hacking cough, the result of breathing the extremely cold, dry air at altitude, had worsened, but by midday they had passed the highest point of the 1922 attempt, and as a camp was to be placed above this point, hopes were high that the summit could be reached next day.

At 1.30pm the porters could go no further, and after scraping a platform for one tent at 26,800ft, they left for Camp IV, an easy descent of 4,000ft, arriving just before dark. Norton and Somervell spent the rest of the day eating, drinking and preparing for the next day's climb.

On 4 June it was a fine, windless day when they left at 6.40am – yet bitterly cold. Norton, not wearing snow goggles, began to see double at 27,500ft. He wrote in *The Fight for Everest*:

Our pace was wretched. My ambition was to do twenty consecutive paces uphill without a pause to rest and pant, elbow on bent knee; yet I never remember achieving it – thirteen was nearer the mark. The process of breathing in the intensely cold dry air, which caught the back of the larynx, had a disastrous effect on poor Somervell's already very bad sore throat and he had constantly to stop and cough. Every five or ten minutes he had to sit down for a minute or two, and we must have looked a sorry couple.

Because they were so high, the view was disappointing, the peaks flattened and any beauty of outline lost, yet their imagination was fired by partly-seen mountains over the horizon.

At noon they were just below the top edge of a band of limestone that ran through the North Face and near a gully that cut through the base of the final pyramid. Climbing horizontally, on a line some 100 feet below the crest of the North-East Ridge, Somervell was forced to stop at midday because his infected throat was making it difficult for him to breathe. Norton went on alone, following the top edge of the limestone band, which led in a rising traverse to the Great Gully. The angle steepened gradually and the rocks resembled the overhanging tiles of a roof, so steep in some places that they brushed his shoulder; when loosened, they clattered straight down the North Face: it was no place to slip, for a fall could not be stopped. Eventually Norton entered the Great Gully, and sank to his knees and then to his waist in powder snow which, like the rocks, would not support a slip.

Beyond the couloir the rock tiles steepened, and the strain of being alone and dependent upon the friction of his boot nails, with few good holds for his hands, began to tell. In addition, his sight was getting worse. Suffering from extreme breathlessness, feelings of exhaustion and the insecurity of the rocks and snow, Norton stopped within 200 feet of an overhang which guarded the exit of the rocks onto the easier summit pyramid beyond. It was 1.0pm and at his very slow rate of climbing, Norton knew that he had no chance of reaching the summit and returning to camp in daylight. His highest point was 28,126ft, as fixed later by theodolite measurement.

He descended, relieved that the strain and extreme effort had ended. So exhausted was he that, nearing Somervell, he waited for the psychological help of a rope to cross an easy snow slope. Retracing their steps, they looked in at Camp VI and sunset found them at Camp V, where Norton unroped and glissaded down towards Camp IV on the North Col. Halfway down he realised that Somervell was not with him. Somervell, meanwhile, was fighting for his life. The lining of his throat had become gangrenous and had detached itself, blocking his larynx. Somervell wrote a graphic account of what followed in his book *After Everest*:

... when darkness was gathering, I had one of my fits of coughing and dislodged something in my throat which stuck so that I could breathe neither in nor out. I could not, of course, make a sign to Norton, or stop him, for the rope was off now; so I sat in the snow to die whilst he walked on, little knowing that his companion was awaiting the end only a few yards behind him. I made one or two attempts to breathe, but nothing happened. Finally, I pressed my chest with both hands, gave one last almighty push – and the obstruction came up.

This modified Heimlich Manœuvre saved Somervell's life, and he caught up with Norton as they approached Camp IV where, parched but with little appetite, they were plied with fluid and oxygen. Both had lost an enormous amount of weight but could eat little. Later, as Norton and Mallory lay in their tent, Mallory explained that, as the first attempt had failed, he was determined that one more attempt should be made using oxygen, and Norton agreed.

Norton, who was very sympathetic towards Mallory despite the latter's personal disorganisation, was happy with his choice of Irvine as his companion, for two reasons. Firstly, Irvine was not suffering from the prevailing altitude throat which had nearly killed Somervell and, secondly, he was a wizard at repairing the oxygen sets. As Odell commented:

Nothing would have amused him [Irvine] more ... than to have spent the previous evening on a job of work of some kind or other in connection with the oxygen apparatus, or to have invented some problem to be solved even if it never really had turned up! He ... was never happier than when up against some mechanical difficulty.

Irvine, too, had great faith in the efficacy of supplementary oxygen. Odell was not so sure, for when using oxygen he had climbed more slowly than a Sherpa without it. The reason, as Pugh and I discovered in 1951, was that the flow rate used by Odell was only one litre per minute – not enough to compensate for the weight of the set. He had therefore ascended *more slowly* than the Sherpa who was carrying no extra weight. If Odell had used a flow rate of two litres per minute he could have climbed at approximately the *same* rate as the Sherpa, but if he had used four litres a minute (as members of the 1953 expedition did), he would have climbed *faster* than the Sherpa.

Later that night Norton became snow blind and remained so for the next three days. This did not stop him from encouraging the porters who were to support Mallory and Irvine. On that day, too, Hazard came up to join Odell in support.

On 6 June at 7.30am they said goodbye to Mallory and Irvine. Norton's last impression, for he was snow blind, was of a handshake and some words of encouragement, after which he could only imagine the two climbers and four porters slowly climbing the North Ridge. Later that day Hingston, the medical officer, arrived from Camp III and confirmed that Norton's snow blindness would cure itself, given time. As Norton was useless on the col, he descended, blind as he was. With the help of two porters and Hazard guiding every step, and with Hingston leading, he made the long descent to the glacier moraine where he had to be carried, as he could not walk blind across the irregular frozen boulders and shifting scree and ice. So sure-footed were the Sherpas that Camp III was reached with no slips.

The second attempt, using supplementary oxygen, by G H L Mallory and A D Irvine with N E Odell in support. The loss of Mallory and Irvine.
Mallory and Irvine left Camp IV on the North Col at 8.30am. Each carried two oxygen cylinders, making a total weight, with their own personal gear, of 25lbs. The porters who accompanied them without using supplementary oxygen carried loads of 20-25lbs. At Camp V, reached at 5.0pm, Mallory sent down a note 'There is no wind here and things look hopeful'.

The next day, 7 June, Mallory's party went up to Camp VI, whilst Odell, carrying a spare oxygen apparatus, went up to Camp V with a Sherpa, Nima. Soon after they arrived, the porters who had carried to Camp VI brought down notes for Odell and John Noel:

Dear Odell,

We're awfully sorry to have left things in such a mess – our Unna cooker rolled down the slope at the last moment. Be sure of getting back to IV tomorrow in time to evacuate before dark, as I hope to. In the tent I must have left a compass – for the Lord's sake rescue it; we are without. To here on 90 atmospheres for the two days – so we'll probably go on two cylinders – but it's a bloody load for climbing. Perfect weather for the job!

Yours ever,
G. Mallory

Dear Noel,

We'll probably start early tomorrow (8th) in order to have clear weather. It won't be too early to start looking for us either crossing the rock band under the pyramid or going up skyline at 8.00 p.m. [sic]

Yours ever,
G. Mallory

As Nima Sherpa was not well he left with the other porters for Camp IV, leaving Odell alone at Camp V. He found the compass and that evening the weather was clear for a change. For a meal he had Force, jam, macaroni and tomatoes and was able to use two sleeping bags and sleep diagonally across the tent – a luxury for a man of over six foot. He slept very well and the night was windless.

Up at 6.0am on the 8th, he left at 8.0am and climbed a steep snow and rock slope above and behind the camp, reaching the crest of the North Ridge. Clouds started to roll across the mountain but the wind was mild. His plan was to make a circuitous route onto the North Face and make the first geological examination of the upper part of the mountain. Above 25,000ft the general slope was 40°- 45° and the overlapping rock was covered in debris, with loose and uncertain footholds.

NOEL ODELL

Later, Odell wrote in Norton's book *The Fight for Everest: 1924*:

At about 26,000 feet I climbed a little crag which could possibly have been circum-vented, but which I decided to tackle direct, more perhaps as a test of my condition than for any other reason. There was scarcely 100 feet of it, and as I reached the top

there was a sudden clearing of the atmosphere above me and I saw the whole summit ridge and final peak of Everest unveiled. I noticed far away on a snow slope
leading up to what seemed to me to be the last step but one from the base of the
final pyramid, a tiny object moving and approaching the rock step. A second object
followed, and then the first climbed to the top of the step. As I stood intently watch-
ing this dramatic appearance, the scene became enveloped in cloud once more, and
I could not actually be certain that I saw the second figure join the first. It was of
course none other than Mallory and Irvine, and I was surprised above all to see
them so late as this, namely 12.50, at a point which, if the "second rock step," they
should have reached according to Mallory's schedule by 8 a.m. at latest, and if the
"first rock step" proportionately earlier. ... Owing to the small portion of the summit ridge uncovered I could not be precisely certain at which of these two "steps"
they were, as in profile and from below they are very similar, but at the time I took
it for the upper "second step." However, I am a little doubtful now whether the
latter would not be hidden by the projecting nearer ground from my position below
on the face. I could see that they were moving expeditiously as if endeavouring to
make up for lost time. ... I had seen that there was a considerable quantity of new
snow covering some of the upper rocks near the summit ridge, and this may well
have caused delay in the ascent. Burdened as they undoubtedly would be with the
oxygen apparatus, these snow-covered débris-sprinkled slabs may have given much
trouble. The oxygen apparatus itself may have needed repair or readjustment either
before or after they left Camp VI, and so have delayed them. Though rather unlikely,
it is just conceivable that the zone of mist and clouds I had experienced below may
have extended up to their level and so have somewhat impeded their progress. Any
or all of these factors may have hindered them and prevented their getting higher in
the time.

At the time, Odell placed them below the Second Step, a position just above the
point where Norton had left Somervell on his first attempt a few days before, but his
view was fleeting. Controversy has dogged this sighting ever since, but as an excellent
field geologist, Odell's powers of perception and description of objects in the field
would have been of an order and accuracy superior to the normal observer. Also, he
was an entirely truthful person who would only describe what he saw – not what he
thought he saw or would like to have seen – and he never played to the gallery.
Continuing up to Camp VI Odell arrived at 2.0pm and decided to stay. Snow
soon began to fall and he scrambled up 200 feet or so, collecting some rock, but saw
no sign of his two friends, even when the snow squall passed and the North Face
became bathed in sunshine. At 4.30pm, as there was no room in the solitary tent
for a third person, he left Mallory's compass and descended to Camp V, which he

passed and, hurrying on down, glissaded the last few hundred feet to Camp IV on the North Col, arriving at 6.45pm. The ascent from Camp IV to V took 3½ hours, whilst the descent took 35 minutes. Here Odell was welcomed by Hazard with soup, but unlike others, he did not suffer from extreme thirst and was clearly in good physical shape.

Next day, 9 June, no movement could be seen either at Camp V or VI and at noon Odell decided to search for the two climbers. Before he left he arranged a code of signals and at 12.15pm he left the North Col camp yet again. In spite of increasing wind, he reached Camp V in 3¼ hours, expecting to find some sign of Mallory and Irvine. There was nothing. Using the oxygen apparatus he had left at Camp V he continued alone to Camp VI and found everything as he had left it two days previously. Dumping the set, he continued up along the line they might have descended. For two hours, alone in an increasing gale in one of the cruellest and least hospitable places on earth, he found no sign of them.

Returning to the tent, he got out the two sleeping bags and placed them in the form of a T, to signal that no trace of the missing climbers could be found. This was seen by Hazard 4,000 feet below on the North Col. Before he left Camp VI, Odell took the prismatic compass that he had brought up for Mallory and Irvine's oxygen set; then, closing the tent, he left.

Descending to the North Col he had to shelter from the gale in the lee of a convenient cliff. At Camp IV there was a note from Norton saying that, as the monsoon was about to start, a prolonged search should not be carried out. Next day Odell descended from the North Col to Camp III and, after a meal, continued down to Camp II. After a night there, he joined the others gathered at Base Camp.

Devastated by the loss of their two companions, they constructed a 19ft-high monument on a prominent moraine overlooking Base Camp. Beetham cut the following inscription on the large flat slabs of blue slate:

IN MEMORY OF THREE
EVEREST EXPEDITIONS

The stones also recorded the death of Kellas in 1921, the deaths of the seven porters killed in an avalanche on the North Col in 1922, and finally:

1924 Mallory, Irvine,
Shamshar, Manbahadur.

Twelve people had died on just three expeditions to Everest. It was far too high a death rate.

The discovery of Mallory's body, 1999

In 1980 I was in Beijing as leader of the Mt Kongur Scientific and Mountaineering Expedition that was to carry out a reconnaissance of this peak in the Pamir. I also gave a paper at the Tibet symposium organised by the Chinese Academy of Sciences. I was told that the Chinese Everest expedition of 1975 had found a body, possibly Mallory's, at about 27,000ft on the north side of Everest: I could get no further details.

In 1999 an American party found a body in roughly the same position. It was Mallory's, being identified by name tags on his collar. A broken rope was evidence of a fall, as was a double fracture of one of his legs. The position was about 1,000 feet below where an ice axe, belonging to either Mallory or Irvine, was found in 1933. There was no sign of Irvine's body.

There has been much speculation, but no firm evidence as yet, as to whether Mallory and Irvine actually made the first ascent of Everest in 1924. I am inclined to believe that they did not, for three reasons. Firstly, though they were using supplementary oxygen, their flow rate was too low – only two litres per minute – which would not have compensated for the weight of their sets nor given them the necessary boost to climbing rate. Secondly, it was likely that they were suffering from severe dehydration, since the fluid intake by all those who went high on Everest in the 1920s and '30s was too low. This would have led to exhaustion. However, the loss of fluid from excessive panting at great altitude would have been countered to some extent by the use of supplementary oxygen even at two litres per minute. Thirdly, their clothing was not adequate to counter the cold and wind-chill effect high on Everest. As far as I can gather, no member of the three expeditions in 1921, 1922 and 1924 had windproof or adequate clothing. The one exception was G I Finch in 1922, who wore a windproof jacket lined with down – an extremely warm and 'modern' combination. The use of supplementary oxygen by Mallory and Irvine would, to some extent, have countered the effects of cold by allowing them to move relatively fast and therefore to generate more heat. However, the sets in the 1920s were unreliable and kept on breaking down. In any event, the oxygen flow rate they used was probably too low to yield its full benefit.

Exploration west of Everest: the Rongshar valley

On 15 June Base Camp was evacuated and the party divided. Hari Singh continued his survey of the West Rongbuk glacier, which he completed within the next week or so. Noel left for the Chumbi valley where he met his wife and an artist helper. The main group went to explore the Rongshar valley, west of Everest.

Before they left Rongbuk a service was held in the monastery, and as they descended the Dzakar Chu, signs of both plant and animal life were starting to show in the dead landscape. After crossing the river draining the glaciers falling from Cho Oyu and Gyachung Kang, for the first time in many weeks they camped on grass sprinkled with primulas. The air was soft and moist and being at only 15,000ft they started to gain weight again as their appetites increased.

On the 18th they could see Jobo Rabzang, a conical peak that marked the west side of the Nangpa La, and descended to Kyetrak village. It was a forlorn and miserable place surrounded by heaps of stones from the nearby moraine. Despite its filthy hovels, the village was an important staging centre and crossroads, with extensive pastures for grazing yaks. To the north was Tingri, whilst to the south was the Nangpa La and Khumbu in Nepal: east was the Langma La, and to the west was the Phuse La at the head of the Rongshar valley. Wool, salt and cloth came from Tibet; rice, sugar, grain and sheet copper came from Nepal.

Leaving next day at 8.0am, they crossed the Phuse La (17,000ft), an easy grass pass, and had gorgeous views of the Tibetan side of Cho Oyu and Gyachung Kang. Beyond the pass they entered a narrow and serpentine gorge, lichen was succeeded by azaleas, junipers by birch and mountain ash, and that night they slept below the treeline and had a wood fire, the first for months.

On the 23rd they continued down the gorge, through rain and mist. At a small grass clearing, covered with flowering shrubs and blue irises, Norton and Somervell camped by the thundering river. Next day, 24 June, Bruce, Hingston, Shebbeare, Odell and Beetham set off towards the Nepal border. The Rongshar gorge became steeper and narrower, with sheer granite walls rising thousands of feet. The path crossed and re-crossed the river and early in the day they passed over the Nepal-Tibet border, which was marked by a stone structure. It looked like a shrine – a stepped plinth surmounted by a well-dressed slab shaped like a gothic tombstone. On it were inscriptions in Nepalese and Tibetan to the effect that Tibetans were forbidden to descend the gorge, whilst Nepalese were forbidden to ascend it. Below the boundary stone the gorge narrowed and steepened, with the path often reduced to rickety bamboo ladders secured by lengths of vine.

Eventually, on 25 June, the party was stopped by an impassable cliff; the bamboo ladders had been washed away, and there was no way across the river. Retreating, they camped on a small sand spit in torrential rain, and next morning were attacked by a large swarm of bees, disturbed by the smoke from their fire. From this camp they had a glimpse of a snow peak that they had seen and sketched from a point 15,000 feet above the gorge. They returned to the same spot but the clouds obscured any view. It is difficult to be sure whether the peak was Gaurisankar or Menlungtse (which in 1924 had not been identified). Somervell's sketch is now held by the Royal Geographical Society with the title 'Gaurisankar'. Having seen both this mountain and Menlungtse I would think it was more likely that the mountain they saw and sketched was Menlungtse.

On 3 July, returning over the Phuse La, they reached Tingri, crossed the plateau and entered Sikkim by the Natu La, finally arriving in Darjeeling and the long journey home to face the after-shock from these tragic events.

LIEUT. COL. E. F. NORTON, D.S.O.

Mr. T. H. Somervell

BIBLIOGRAPHY

H R C Carr, *The Irvine diaries: Andrew Irvine and the enigma of Everest 1924.*
    Gastons-West Col, 1979.

J Hemmleb, L A Johnson, E R Simonson, *Ghosts of Everest.* Macmillan 1999.

R W G Hingston, 'Physiological difficulties in the ascent of Mount Everest' in
    Geographical Journal 65, 4-23, 1925.

R W G Hingston, 'Physiological difficulties in the ascent of Mount Everest' in
    Alpine Journal 37, 22-38, 1925.

R W G Hingston, 'Bird notes from the Mount Everest expedition of 1924' in
    Journal of Bombay National History Society 32, 320-329, 1927.

T Holzel, A Salkeld, *The Mystery of Mallory and Irvine*. Jonathan Cape, 1986.

E F Norton, *The Fight for Everest: 1924*, Arnold, 1925.

E F Norton 'The Problem of Mount Everest' in *Alpine Journal 37*, 1-22, 1925.

E F Norton, 'Mount Everest: the last lap' in *Alpine Journal 57*, 255-292, 1949-50.

N E Odell, 'Observations on the Rocks and Glaciers of Mount Everest' in
    Geographical Journal 66, 289-314, 1925.

N E Odell, 'High Altitude and Oxygen' in *Himalayan Journal 4*, 91-95, 1932.

N E Odell, 'The Ice Axe found on Everest' in *Alpine Journal 46*, 447-449, 1934.

N E Odell, 'Everest 1924. The disappearance of Mallory and Irvine' in *Alpine Journal
    59*, 495-496, 1953-54.

D Robertson, *George Mallory*. Faber & Faber, 1969.

T H Somervell, 'Note on the composition of alveolar air at extreme altitude' in
    Journal of Physiology 60, 282-285, 1925.

T H Somervell, *After Everest*. Hodder & Stoughton, 1936.

Unattributed note, 'Experiences with the Everest Expedition' in *Proceedings of the
    Royal Society of Medicine 16*, 57-62, 1922-23.

Unattributed note, 'The Mount Everest Despatches' in *Geographical Journal 64*,
    145-165, 1924.

Unattributed note, 'The Mount Everest Expedition of 1924' in *Geographical Journal
    64*, 433-469, 1924.

Unattributed note, 'The Mount Everest Despatches' in *Alpine Journal 36*, 196-281,
    1924.

M P Ward, 'Cold, Hypoxia, and Dehydration' in *Hypoxia and Cold*, ed. J R Sutton,
    C S Houston, G Coates. Praeger, New York/London, 1987.

M P Ward, 'The Everest Sketches of Lt Col E F Norton' in *Alpine Journal 98*, 82, 1993.

Chapter 8

AFTER SHOCK 1924-1933

Aeroplanes and new ideas

Following the 1924 expedition, the photographer Captain J B L Noel, a man of many original ideas who had tried to get to Everest from the east in 1913, proposed a novel way of climbing Everest. He suggested that an aeroplane should be flown into the fierce wind that scoured the top of Everest, hoping that, as a result, it might be able to hover. A climber, suitably protected by windproof clothing, would descend by rope to the summit. With the aid of liquid oxygen and previous acclimatisation, he would descend the mountain in two days to the East Rongbuk glacier, using dumps of food and tents previously dropped by aeroplane. On the glacier he would join another aeroplane which could land easily and fly him back to India.

Another of his suggestions was more conventional. Both Noel and the physiologists had been impressed by the remarkable degree of acclimatisation attained by members of the 1922 and 1924 expeditions who had successfully climbed to, and descended safely from, altitudes of 27,400ft and 28,000ft respectively, heights which had formerly been considered lethal. The consensus of opinion before the 1922 expedition had held that a limit existed above which human beings could not survive owing to mental and physical deterioration. Noel believed that, if countered by good food and shelter, no such limit existed and that, in theory, mountaineers could live on the top of Everest. Many years later, in 1960-61, it was shown that, despite good living conditions, men born and bred at sea level did deteriorate at 19,000ft. However, those born and bred at altitude could live comfortably at 20,000ft.

Noel's proposals for climbing Everest were as follows:

1   Base camp should be established at the foot of the North Col. The site of Camp III should be at 21,000ft and weatherproof tents or a hut should be provided. Above the North Col very lightweight huts rather than tents should be used. These would be warmer and provide better protection from the wind.
2   To ensure a long period of acclimatisation, the expedition should spend the spring and autumn on the mountain.
3   Supplementary oxygen should be used from an altitude of 25,000ft to the summit.
4   A path should be made for yak transport from Rongbuk monastery to Base Camp at the foot of the North Col.
5   An aerial ropeway should be installed from this Base Camp to the North Col.

In this way, transport to 21,000ft would be by animal, and from 21,000ft to the North Col (23,000ft) by mechanical means; thus exhaustion in the climbers would be prevented. But it was not appreciated, at the time, that exercise played an important part in altitude acclimatisation.

The hut at Base Camp would be similar to those used in polar regions, with bunks and a stove.* At 25,000ft, on the North Ridge, a hut made of plywood on a duralumin frame, and held down by wire and telescopic supports, would be used. The last camp before the summit would be a tent. As the weather in the autumn was better, though colder, than in the spring, an ascent in the autumn might be easier than a spring ascent.

All these ideas were an extension of those of A M Kellas, who had already considered the use of a high-altitude hut on the top of Kamet before the First World War. They also pre-dated many technical advances made in high-altitude mountaineering and medical investigations from 1960 onwards. It is likely that Kellas and Noel discussed all these options when they were planning to approach Everest from the east, a project which never took place for political reasons.

F M Bailey, the Everest Committee and the Dancing Lamas

The first three Everest expeditions had, perhaps inevitably, upset the local Dzong Pens of southern Tibet. Their objections were first conveyed to Sir Charles Bell, formerly Political Officer in Sikkim, by the Prime Minister of Tibet as early as September 1921. Bell had been recalled from retirement to act as a locum for F M Bailey, the incumbent Political Officer in Sikkim, who was on leave following an extremely hazardous mission to Tashkent in Central Asia from which he was lucky to escape with his life.

F M Bailey became a legendary figure in his own lifetime as a result of his explorations and political expertise in Central Asia, a fact which did not endear him to his seniors in the Indian Civil Service (ICS). Trained as a sapper, he had begun his active service in India in 1900. In 1903-4 he was with Younghusband's mission to Lhasa during which he had become fluent in Tibetan – so fluent that for many years he was the only person in the ICS able to converse with the Dalai Lama without using an interpreter. During the Younghusband mission he took part, with Rawling, Wood and Ryder, in an expedition which surveyed southern Tibet, identified Everest for the first time from the north, and confirmed that no higher peak could be found.

In 1911, while on leave, Bailey travelled through Russia to China by the trans-Siberian railway, and explored the then almost unknown gorge country of south-eastern Tibet. Two years later, in 1913, he returned to this region as Intelligence

* The same method was used 40 years later by the Silver Hut expedition to the Everest region in 1960-61.

Officer of the Abor Expeditionary Force, in a survey team that finally solved one of the major geographical problems of Central Asia. The team confirmed that the Tsangpo river, after rising in the region of Mt Kailas (Kangrinboche, the holiest peak in Tibet), changed direction in the eastern Himalaya and passed between two of the highest peaks of the area, Gyala Peri and Namche Barwa. Turning south, it became continuous with the Dihang and changed its name to the Brahmaputra. Its extremely steep fall in altitude led to the conclusion that a high waterfall must surely exist in the 'bend' of the river. Bailey and his companion Henry Morshead, the surveyor who was with Kellas on Kamet in 1920 and on the 1921 and 1922 Everest expeditions, failed to confirm this but found instead a series of steep rapids which accounted for the fall in height of the river. This exploration proved of great value in demarcating and delineating the frontier with China which was being discussed at Simla and which became known as the Macmahon Line.

During the First World War Bailey was wounded in France and Gallipoli and was then posted back to India as one of the few available Tibetan speakers. In 1918 he was sent on a mission to Tashkent in Russian Turkestan to obtain accurate inform- ation about the extent of the Russian revolution and its influence in Central Asia. Escaping capture and assassination, Bailey returned after two years for debriefing in Delhi and was given leave in the UK.

In 1921 he was appointed Political Officer in Sikkim, where he stayed for seven years looking after British interests in Tibet, Sikkim and Bhutan. It was during this period that Bailey, with the surveyor Captain H R C Meade, measured the height of the highest peak in Bhutan (named Kangri, Rinchita or Gangkar Puensum) at 24,742ft. A lifelong naturalist, his name was given by Frank Kingdon Ward to the blue poppy *Meconopsis Baileyi*.

The Prime Minister of Tibet, in a letter to Bell, accused members of the 1921 reconnaissance party of digging up rubies and turquoise and claimed that this 'mining' in the sacred soil of Tibet, which was inhabited by demons, would cause epidemics in both cattle and inhabitants, and serious loss of life would ensue. He referred in particular to the activities of Dr A M Heron, the geologist on the 1921 expedition. In his verbal reply, Bell had reassured the Prime Minister that no mining had in fact taken place. At this stage no formal written reply had been made and this was done by Bailey when he returned to his post. As a result of this reassurance, H H Hayden had carried out a geological survey of Central Tibet, north and west of Lhasa, in 1922 which included the Nyenchen Tanglha range. In addition, permission had been granted for an attempt on Everest in 1922.

Despite the death on this expedition of seven porters on the North Col, talks with the Tibetans had resulted in permission for a further attempt in 1924. After this expedition a film taken by J B L Noel on both the 1922 and 1924 expeditions was exhibited in the UK. A film company was set up with Sir Francis Younghusband on the board, but the Everest Committee, while giving the film its blessing, had no financial stake or control. In addition, Noel brought to England some Tibetan monks from a monastery near Gyantse to perform ritual dances on the cinema stage. The dances had no religious significance and had been performed on public occasions in Tibet. However, when the news of these London performances reached Lhasa it caused consternation and A R Hinks, Secretary of the Everest Committee, was asked by Bailey to investigate. In his reply Hinks confirmed that the dances were not religious in content but that he would nevertheless approach Younghusband and Noel for clarification. In January 1925 Bailey wrote again to Hinks warning him that the Tibetan Government might refuse permission for a further Everest expedition, as they had been upset by these and several other incidents, including an allegedly unauthorised journey by Hazard, of the 1924 party, to Lhatse, which was well away from the expedition's permitted route. Some cuts in the film, requested by Lhasa, had not been made; and finally, the enticing away of the monks for monetary gain gave cause for concern.

Bailey also pointed out to the Everest Committee that permission for Everest was only gained as a result of the friendliness of the Tibetan Government towards the United Kingdom, and that, although they had made no *official* complaint, the Tibetans were most unhappy about the whole episode.

The Abbot of Palkor Chode monastery at Gyantse, who had agreed that the monks should leave and who had supplied costumes and musical instruments, was summoned to Lhasa for questioning and there was every likelihood that he would be severely punished. By this time a further request had been despatched for an Everest expedition in 1925 and this was summarily refused.

In due course Hinks wrote to Bailey on behalf of the Everest Committee acknowledging the Tibetan refusal and agreeing that the monks should return. But Hinks implied that, if Bailey had not approved of the monks leaving Tibet, he should have stopped them, and he gave the impression that Bailey was the main culprit in the whole affair. Hinks further maintained that the visit of Everest expeditions would be of such benefit to the Tibetans that they should be allowed to go ahead. In this Hinks showed that he was both arrogant and ignorant, for the exact opposite was the truth, that the advent of each Everest expedition disrupted the fragile subsistence economy of the region, taking Tibetans away from the fields to act as porters and using yaks as baggage animals rather than for ploughing or trade. Hinks also implied that Bailey had allied himself with conservative elements in Lhasa, possibly in order to prevent such expeditions taking place.

The row hotted up and the British Foreign Secretary became involved; after an investigation it became clear what had really happened. The passport application for the monks had been made in Darjeeling by John Macdonald, son of David Macdonald, the trade agent at Gyantse and Yatung. John Macdonald then went to Calcutta where he persuaded the Commissioner of Police to give exit permits, but without disclosing that 'official' exit permits had already been refused. This fact was unknown to Noel when he made the arrangements for the lamas' visit and his main fault was not to have checked that 'official' permits had been obtained for them.

In October the Under-Secretary of State for India wrote to the Everest Committee:

> Finally I am directed by Lord Birkenhead [Secretary of State for India] to say that he must take the strongest exception to the tone of your remarks in regard to Lt .-Colonel F. M. Bailey ... the criticisms and insinuations in your letters regarding Lt.-Colonel Bailey appear to his lordship to be misplaced and uncalled for.

Hinks had to make a grovelling apology on behalf of the Everest Committee for his and their conduct; but his apology concerning Bailey was unsatisfactory – a fact that did not go unnoticed. The credit of Hinks and the Mount Everest Committee suffered accordingly, and it was to be nine years before another British Everest expedition was allowed to return to Tibet.

BIBLIOGRAPHY

H H Hayden, C Cosson, *Sport and Travel in the Highlands of Tibet*. Cobden-Sanderson, 1927.

J B L Noel, Appendix 'Science versus Nature' in *Through Tibet to Everest*. Arnold, 1927.

A Salkeld, 'The Scapegoat' in *Alpine Journal 101*, 224-226, 1996.

A Swinson, *Beyond the Frontiers. The Biography of Colonel F M Bailey. Explorer and Secret Agent*. Hutchinson, 1971.

M P Ward, 'The Exploration of the Tsangpo River and its Mountains' in *Alpine Journal 105*, 124-130, 2000.

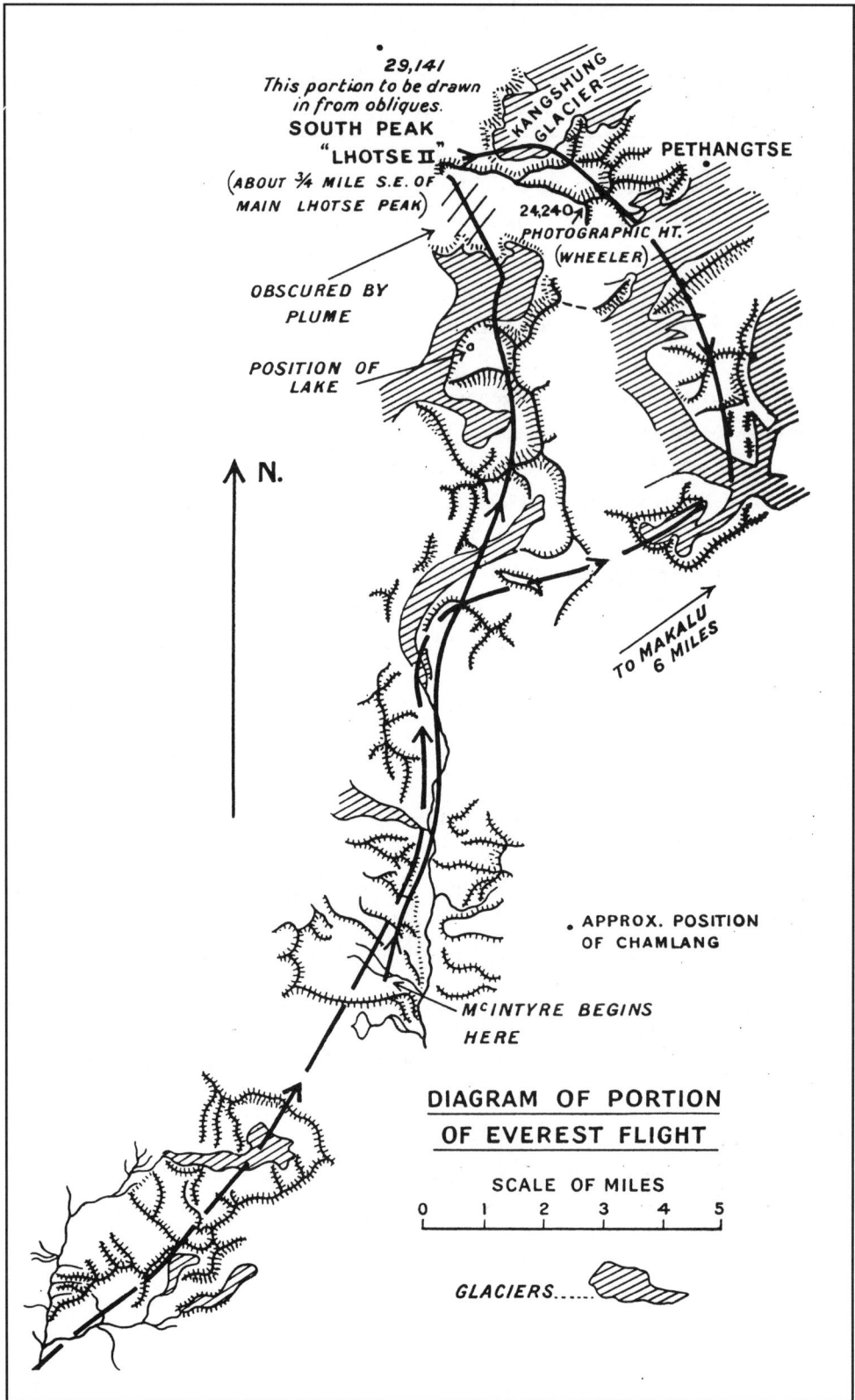

29,141
*This portion to be drawn
in from obliques.*
**SOUTH PEAK
"LHOTSE II"**
(ABOUT ¾ MILE S.E. OF
MAIN LHOTSE PEAK)

KANGSHUNG
GLACIER

PETHANGTSE

24,240
PHOTOGRAPHIC HT.
(WHEELER)

OBSCURED BY
PLUME

POSITION OF
LAKE

N.

TO MAKALU
6 MILES

• APPROX. POSITION
OF CHAMLANG

M^cINTYRE BEGINS
HERE

DIAGRAM OF PORTION
OF EVEREST FLIGHT

SCALE OF MILES

0   1   2   3   4   5

GLACIERS.....

A PORTION OF THE ROUTE OF THE 'FLIGHT OVER EVEREST', 1933

112

Chapter 9

THE SECOND COMING OF KRISHNA

The first flight over Everest
and the first aerial survey of the Nepalese side of Everest, 1933

Objectives

In 1933 an aerial survey produced the first topographical information about the southern, Nepalese, side of Everest which was then virtually unknown; at the same time, a mountaineering expedition from Tibet got no higher than in 1924 – 1000 feet from the summit.

The Houston-Westland expedition of 1933 had two principal objectives. The first was to make an aerial map of the unexplored southern side of the mountain. Between 1924 and 1927 native surveyors of the Nepal detachment of the Survey of India had mapped up to Dingboche in the Imja Khola, but the glaciated regions of the Nepalese side of Everest, together with those of the rest of the Nepal Himalaya, remained unsurveyed.

The second objective was meteorological. Given that a west wind at over 120mph was encountered at 30,000ft, how much dust from the plains of India would be found at these altitudes?

Organisation

The originator of this expedition was L V S Blacker, a major in the regular Army who, in 1932, seized on the fact that the Bristol Pegasus engine, with supercharger, might be able to gain enough height to fly over Everest. He submitted a plan to the Royal Geographical Society and in April 1932 a letter was sent to the Secretary of State for India for onward transmission to Nepal, still forbidden to Europeans.

In August the flight was sanctioned by the Nepalese Government, as it might resemble 'the second coming of Krishna', the Hindu god said to have constructed a silver chariot and flown around the southern face of Everest. Tibetan airspace was forbidden. Later, Lady Houston, who had helped fund the Schneider Trophy races which led eventually to the development of the Spitfire fighter, was approached for financial support, which she was happy to give.

The organisation was part civilian and part Air Force. Owing to injuries sustained during the First World War, Blacker was unable to be a pilot himself and he delegated the organisation of the project to Air Commodore P F M Fellowes; he himself acted as Chief Observer on both flights over Everest.

A suitable engine was vital to the success of the project, and only the Bristol Pegasus had the necessary qualities. It was being developed to make an attempt on the world height record, then held by the US Army Air Corps. Later in 1932 this record was indeed captured by Captain C F Unwins, who flew to 44,000ft using a supercharged Pegasus engine of the same type as that later used by the 1933 expedition.

Two aircraft were chosen: a Westland PV3, an experimental plane built for general military purposes, and a Westland Wallace. Both were ideal, being bi-planes with a huge wing surface, high under-carriage and a broad fuselage with a roomy cockpit. An airfield, Lalbalu, 10 miles east of Purnea and 206 miles north of Calcutta, was provided by the Indian Army.

On 16 February three light aircraft left Heston in the UK for India, while the two Westlands left by sea in packing cases. P T Etherton of the expedition travelled to Kathmandu to inform the Nepalese, whilst in March the Viceroy of India inspected the aircraft and members of the expedition in Delhi.

Flights

The first flight took place on 3 April, the pilot of the Houston-Westland being the Marquess of Clydesdale, with L V S Blacker as Observer. The Westland Wallace was piloted by Flight Lieutenant D F McIntyre with S P Bonnett, aerial photographer of the Gaumont-British Corporation, as Observer.

The Clydesdale / Blacker flight crossed the Nepal border just east of Jogbani and followed the Arun river north, flying over Dhankuta and Bhojpur. Approaching Everest, they saw an immense plume of white ice particles streaming from the summit, blown by the west wind almost as far as Makalu, 30 miles to the east. Over Lhotse, five miles south of Everest, there was a sudden down-draught and the plane dropped like a stone for 1,500ft. At 10.15am, after regaining height and flying over Everest, which they cleared by only 100ft, they turned east towards Makalu. After 15 minutes spent in the vicinity of Everest, they turned south following the gorge of the Arun river to return to Lalbalu airfield, which they reached at 11.25am.

Meanwhile, McIntyre and Bonnett in the Westland Wallace were flying east of the others. Blown towards Makalu, they just managed to scrape over the lowest point of the frontier ridge between the two mountains. The North-East Ridge of Everest swept up above them, as did the North Face, as they tried to gain height. Finally, they flew over the summit, having taken some photographs of the north side. At this point Bonnett, the Observer, inadvertently fractured his oxygen pipe, and became unconscious until they descended to 8,000ft. Many of the vertical photos taken on these two flights turned out to have been spoilt by the dust haze, but luckily those taken by the oblique cameras were good.

Before arrangements could be made for a second flight over Everest, a flight over Kangchenjunga was undertaken. Air Commodore Fellowes piloted the Houston-Westland with Fisher as Observer, and Ellison piloted the Westland Wallace with Bonnett as Observer. Unfortunately, the top 1,500ft of the mountain was enveloped in cloud so they were unable to get good photographs. On his return, Fellowes ran out of fuel and had to land at Dinajpur, some way short of Lalbalu.

The second flight over Everest approached from further west. Both planes took off on 19 April and circled around Everest and Makalu at 31,000ft. All their photos were free from distortion and dust and an unbroken strip for survey was made. The photographic results of this second expedition were excellent and two new glaciers were identified. One was the Barun, draining the east side of Everest and the south and west sides of Makalu. Also, large numbers of spot heights were estimated; the upper slopes of Lhotse were photographed but the Western Cwm was not photographed at all. The summit of Everest and the upper part of the North Face were well depicted. Some oblique photos showed the country to the west of Everest as far as Gosainthan (Shisha Pangma). Owing to some sort of mix-up after the photographs were developed, the frontispiece of *The Times* Supplement of the Expedition showed an excellent photo of the South-East Ridge of Makalu, wrongly labelled as Everest.

The calculations necessary to convert the vertical and horizontal photographs into a map were done mainly by A R Hinks, Secretary of the Royal Geographical Society, between 1935 and 1950. In early 1951, I used this Hinks-Milne map as evidence of a new route up Everest from Nepal, a route that was to be confirmed on our reconnaissance expedition in the autumn of the same year.

BIBLIOGRAPHY

L V S Blacker, 'The Mount Everest Flights' in *Himalayan Journal 6*, 54-60, 1934.

The Marquis of Clydesdale, D F McIntyre, *The Pilots' Book of Everest*. Hodge, 1936.

P F M Fellowes, L V Stewart Blacker, P T Etherton, The Marquess of Douglas and Clydesdale, *First Over Everest. The Houston-Mount Everest Expedition 1933*. John Lane, The Bodley Head Limited, 1933.

A R Hinks, 'Photographs from the Mount Everest Flight' in *Geographical Journal 82*, 54-60, 1933.

J S A Salt, 'Plotting the Vertical Photographs of the Second Mount Everest Flight' in *Geographical Journal 83*, 101-110, 1934.

The Times: photographs in special supplement, 24 April 1933.

Unattributed note, 'Everest. Houston flight' in Alpine Notes in *Alpine Journal 46*, 405-406, 1934.

M P Ward, P K Clark, 'Everest 1951: Cartographic and photographic evidence of a new route from Nepal' in *Geographical Journal 158*, 47-56, 1992.

Chapter 10

BLIND TO REASON
The third attempt, 1933

The episode of the Dancing Lamas set back Everest expeditions by nine years, and it was not until August 1932 that permission was obtained for another attempt.

The first task of the Everest Committee, presided over by Admiral Sir William Goodenough, President of the Royal Geographical Society, was to choose a leader. Unfortunately, General Bruce, who had led the 1922 and 1924 parties, was not available; nor was General Norton, probably the best of all Everest leaders, who had assumed that role in 1924 when Bruce became ill.

The Committee's choice fell on Hugh Ruttledge of the Indian Civil Service, who had trekked extensively in the Himalaya, had circumnavigated Mount Kailas, and who got on well with the hill tribes. He was not, however, a mountaineer, and the feeling among party members was that a mountaineer should have been chosen. As a result, relations between the Committee and the climbers were strained from the start, though this feeling was never directed at Ruttledge himself; in fact he performed a difficult balancing task with skill and was well liked by all.

HUGH RUTTLEDGE

The core of the party came from the group which had climbed Kamet (25,447ft) in the Garhwal Himal in 1931, and whose leader, F S Smythe, was the outstanding British mountaineer of the period. He had been invalided out of the RAF with an 'innocent' heart murmur which had no effect on heart function, and he earned his living by mountain writing and photography.

In 1928 Smythe had taken part in a major breakthrough in British rock climbing by being a member of the party that made the first ascent of the West Buttress of Clogwyn du'r Arddu in Snowdonia, led by Jack Longland, then a lecturer in English at Durham University. In the European Alps, Smythe, with Professor T Graham Brown, had made new and important routes on the Italian, Brenva, face of Mont Blanc; in 1930 he had taken part in an international attempt on Kangchenjunga, the world's third highest peak.

Dr Raymond Greene, a friend of Smythe's since childhood, wrote in his book *Moments of Being* :

> At great altitude a new force seemed to enter Frank. His body, still apparently frail as it had been in boyhood, was capable of astonishing feats of sudden strength and prolonged endurance. His mind, too, took on a different colour. At sea-level the mistaken sense of inferiority, so unfairly planted by his early experiences, rendered him sometimes irritable, a little tactless and rather easily offended. At high levels that self-confidence which flowed into his mind and body, the emanation, as it were, of the mountains whose strength he loved, changed him almost beyond recognition. It seemed impossible, above 20,000ft, to disturb his composure or his essential quietism. I remember the Kamet expedition as a period of calm, unbroken by no more than a rare ripple of disagreement, and the calm was the result of Frank's confident but always modest and unassuming leadership.

Though he never led an Everest expedition, Smythe was throughout the 1930s a powerful influence on decision-making; more than one Everest expedition member told me that Smythe was adamantly opposed to the use of supplementary oxygen at that period.

Jack Longland, another member of the 1933 Everest expedition, was at the time one of the best rock climbers in the UK. He was not only an all-round athlete but was also outstandingly clever, having gained a first class degree in History at Cambridge, followed by a starred first in English. He spent his professional life in education, his own idealism being his primary motivation. Longland had a devastating wit, and could suffer neither fools nor pomposity gladly. On the 1933 expedition he could never understand why the supplementary oxygen sets, designed with great care by the medical officer Raymond Greene, were discarded and never used. He thought that those who made that decision were blind to reason.

Eric Shipton, who climbed Kamet with Frank Smythe in 1931, was to become one of the best-known Himalayan explorers. Following in the footsteps of T G Longstaff by using small two to four-man expeditions, he and H W Tilman, with the Sherpa Angtharkay, explored and helped to map large areas of the unexplored ranges of the Himalaya and Central Asia. His most important contribution, for which he gained the Patron's Medal of the Royal Geographical Society, was in 1937 when he worked in an extremely difficult area north of K2 and the main Karakoram watershed on the undemarcated frontiers of Chinese Turkestan, Hunza and Kashmir. In 1951 and 1952 he took expeditions to the Nepalese side of Everest. Accounts of these are given later in this monograph and can also be found in *Eric Shipton. Everest and Beyond* by Peter Steele.

Raymond Greene, the medical officer on the 1933 expedition, was, at the time, a General Practitioner in Oxford. In the Second World War he carried out research on frostbite and suggested that oxygen might be used at altitude as a treatment. After the war he became a consultant physician in the new and expanding subject of endocrinology, and worked in a world-famous unit at New End Hospital, Hampstead on disorders of the thyroid and thymus. With E St J Birnie, an Indian Army officer, also a member of the 1933 expedition, he too had climbed Kamet in 1931. Dr W McLean, the second medical officer, had a good Alpine record.

Percy Wyn Harris had gained a blue at Cambridge for cross-country running. While a member of the Kenya Civil Service he had made a number of new routes on Mount Kenya with Eric Shipton.

Lawrence Wager was an academic geologist who in 1933 had just returned from Greenland. A lecturer at Reading University, he became Professor of Geology at Durham and then Oxford, being a Fellow of the Royal Society and a Fellow of University College Oxford. He had previously climbed with both Longland and Wyn Harris.

The youngest member of the 1933 expedition, at 24 years old, T A Brocklebank was an old Etonian who had already stroked Cambridge to victory in the boat race for three successive years. Since his schooldays he had climbed without guides and later became a housemaster at Eton.

Hugh Boustead had long cherished an ambition to go to Everest. In 1933 he was Commandant of the Sudan Camel Corps, having had an extraordinarily varied career. Starting in the navy, he transferred to the army and served throughout the First World War. He captained the British pentathlon team in the 1920 Olympic Games, had a good all-round record as a mountaineer and in 1927 visited the Sikkim Himal.

A tea planter in Darjeeling, George Wood-Johnson knew the Himalayan hill tribes intimately and spoke fluent Nepali. In 1930 he had been with Frank Smythe on the International Kangchenjunga Expedition, and had climbed high on Jonsong Peak.

C G Crawford had climbed on Kangchenjunga with Harold Raeburn in 1920 and was a member of the 1922 Everest party. With Mallory and Somervell, he had been on the slopes of the North Col when an avalanche swept away a number of porters.

At 49, E O Shebbeare was the transport officer, a post he had also held in 1924. While working in the Indian Forestry Service he had gained a natural affinity with the people of the Himalayan foothills. He later became head of the Bengal Forestry Service and then chief game warden in Malaya where he knew my father who was in the Malayan Civil Service. During the Second World War both were interned in Changi Jail in Singapore by the Japanese.

Two other outstanding Himalayan mountaineers were invited to join this expedition: N E Odell had to refuse for personal academic reasons, while Howard Somervell considered that he was too tired by his unremitting surgical work as a medical missionary in South India to give as good an account of himself at extreme altitude as he would have wished.

Preparations

Before the expedition left the UK there was considerable debate among mountaineers about the use of supplementary oxygen. Both Smythe and Shipton were against its use, preferring to rely on acclimatisation alone. In theory supplementary oxygen should have improved performance at extreme altitude, but in practice it did not appear to do so. The reason for this was not immediately clear.

Oxygen equipment was, however, provided by Siebe-Gorman and developed with the help of Raymond Greene. The set weighed only 12¾lbs but still provided only a 2 litres/minute flow rate. Although this rate was too low to make a significant improvement to performance at altitude, it might have helped to alleviate the sore throats from which most mountaineers suffer at high altitudes. Unfortunately, however, even this amount of supplementary oxygen was never used on the expedition while climbing, but only for the treatment of frostbite.

Climbers on previous expeditions had complained bitterly of sore throats; Somervell in 1924 had nearly choked to death when the lining of his naso-pharynx sloughed. Despite good clothing, cold was another major factor and both these were related to heat loss through the lungs resulting from the rapid respiration necessary at extreme altitude.

Bryan Mathews, a lecturer in physiology at Cambridge who had worked with Joseph Barcroft and who was to play a major part in the scientific preparations for the successful 1953 expedition, made some excellent suggestions. To help combat heat and water loss from the lungs, he designed a mask consisting of several layers of copper gauze. This worked well at rest, when the rate of breathing was low, but not so well with the extremely high rate of breathing necessary during exercise, when it caused a feeling of suffocation. The mask was therefore not popular.

All equipment left the UK before Christmas 1932, and the expedition members gathered in Darjeeling at the end of February 1933. Here their porters were selected with help from an excellent middleman, Karma Paul. A local man, first employed by the 1922 party, he spoke almost perfect English, as well as being at home in Tibetan, Nepali, Urdu, Bengali, Sikkimese and the local language of the Lepchas. He also understood Tibetan social and diplomatic etiquette, and knew about local rates of pay in different parts of Tibet. He was an excellent negotiator, with common sense and a good sense of humour, and was the agent and lynchpin of many expeditions passing through Tibet.

To obtain weather reports, an up-to-date wireless was taken which was run by a signal detachment from the Indian Army. A station was set up at Base Camp to provide information about the monsoon from meteorological stations in India.

Across Tibet

The original intention was to go to Kampa Dzong by the most direct route over the watershed peaks dividing Sikkim from Tibet. The Sebu La (17,000ft) was, however, still closed by winter snow, so the Natu La, a more circuitous route to the east that ended in the Chumbi valley, had to be taken.

From the top of the Natu La, the flagpost peak Chomolhari pointed the way to Lhasa. An easy track descended to a village where a convicted murderer lay recovering from 150 lashes. With no death penalty, since life is sacred in Tibet, punishment was simple, stark and rigorous. A suspected murderer might be beaten on alternate days until he confessed. Punishment for theft varied from beating to amputation of an ear, hand or foot, according to the severity of the offence. Raymond Greene described such a beating and added an interesting comment:

> To the Westerner this beating was brutal and unjust, and so it was. But there is another side. At the expense of ten minutes pain which he obviously did not regard as unbearable, the muleteers of Tibet, amongst whom the news undoubtedly spread fast, had been taught a salutary lesson. The foreigner brought much money to Tibet and he should therefore be protected from brigandage.

The country now changed to an open, wide valley with a single surreal line of telegraph poles striding along the road connecting India and Lhasa. Phari, the next village, consisted of one-storey houses built with rough stones and no mortar. They were roofed with turf. Some members rode up to the Tremo La, which was probably the route by which George Bogle entered Tibet from Bhutan for the first time in 1774. Despite its squalid state, Phari, when seen from this pass, had a mystic dreamlike quality far removed from the brutal facts of its existence.

At Kampa Dzong, the expedition members visited the grave of A M Kellas, but only a few fragments of his memorial survived. Many stones had been taken away by the villagers, so a very large stone was hauled into place and local lamas were asked to inscribe it. A few marches further on, one of the Sherpas broke his collar bone and Raymond Greene, an experienced anaesthetist, gave a general anaesthetic for it to be set. In 1933 it was not known that general anaesthetics diminish the ability of the body to respond to oxygen lack and can therefore be dangerous at altitude. The Sherpa stopped breathing, turned blue and nearly died, but luckily the effects of the anaesthetic wore off quickly, he started breathing again and was none the worse.

On the mountain

The expedition reached Rongbuk on 16 April. Camps were set up in the narrow East Rongbuk glacier and the broad snow basin at the foot of the North Col and the North-East Face was reached. As usual, the summit was flying a pennant of cloud that streamed to the east almost as far as Makalu. To the east were the slopes of the Lhakpa La, crossed by Mallory, Bullock and others in 1921 from Kharta in their search for the North Col. In 1933, however, the route to the North Col was not an easy snow plod as it had been in 1921. Instead, much of it was ice and Smythe had to cut steps up a steep ice wall down which a ladder was hung.

Finally, on 11 May, Camp IV at 22,400ft was established just below the crest of the North Col. Immediately a series of storms immobilised the party and over the radio they heard that the monsoon was already in the Bay of Bengal, many weeks earlier than usual. By 20 May the storms had blown themselves out. Unfortunately Wood-Johnson then had a recurrence of a gastric ulcer and had to return to Base Camp. In good weather, camps above the North Col on the North Ridge were established, and on 22 May Camp V at 25,700ft, 500 feet higher than in 1924, was pitched. Here Greene took samples of alveolar air from the depths of the lungs, the highest altitude at which this procedure had been carried out. From the samples taken he was able to calculate the pressure at which oxygen was being driven through the walls of the lungs. Unfortunately, he himself began to suffer from high-altitude deterioration and his place in the first assault party was taken by Lawrence Wager. That night, the 23rd, the wind at Camp V was ferocious, but in a lull during the afternoon Smythe and Shipton came up and it was decided that they should make the first attempt. Next day, however, the weather worsened and on the 25th all descended to the North Col. One porter lost two fingers from frostbite and another porter lost one finger.

On 28 May Camp V was re-established, and Camp VI established a day later by Longland, Wyn Harris, Wager and eight Sherpas. Up to 27,000ft they maintained an average climbing rate of 400 feet per hour, but above that height the angle steepened, due to a band of yellow limestone, a conspicuous feature about 1,000 feet high, running across the North Face. The overlapping strata of this limestone band also became more prominent and to find even a small level area on which to pitch a tent was extremely difficult. However, halfway up the band they found a place at 27,400ft, which was 600 feet higher and 400 yards nearer to the summit than Norton's highest camp of 1924. After pitching camp at 1.30pm, Longland left with the porters. It was a nightmare descent, for just as they reached the North Ridge his party were hit by a ferocious storm. Wind swept unhindered across the North Face, the horizon vanished, and only by clinging to the rocks were they able to stay upright. Slowly, roped together, on easy ground to stay in touch, it took them over two hours to reach Camp V, and then on down to the North Col camp, reaching it just before dark. This epic descent prevented them from being benighted which would have meant certain death in those conditions.

The first assault, to 28,000ft, without supplementary oxygen
At Camp VI, Wyn Harris and Wager had a disturbed night; the wind blew in furious noisy gusts that kept them awake. Both were thirsty but could not bear the thought of food. After a sketchy meal they left at 5.40am, but until the sun came up they felt bitterly cold. At about 60 feet below the crest of the North-East Ridge and 250 yards from their tent, they found an ice axe lying on the smooth brown 'boiler plate' slabs on which they were climbing. It looked new and was stamped with the name of its maker, Willisch of Täsch, from the Zermatt district of Switzerland, who had supplied a number of axes to the 1924 expedition. It could only have belonged to Mallory or Irvine. Whether or not it was the site of a fatal accident was unclear. They left it in place and climbed slowly up to have a look at the 'First Step' on the ridge. If it could be climbed they could continue along the ridge to the summit pyramid. If not, they would have to traverse to the right along the face on the top of the limestone band, about 300 feet below the crest, towards a gully partly filled with snow, cross this gully, climb the slabs on the far side and then ascend directly to the summit.

It was now about 7.0am and it soon became obvious that the ridge itself would be unclimbable, so they decided to traverse, as Norton had done in 1924. They followed the line between the top of the limestone band and the dark rocks above it which formed the First Step. They were still unroped, as at this stage the climbing was easy. Continuing, they reached the foot of the Second Step on the ridge. As it was smooth and without holds they did not think it would be possible to climb it directly and so reach the summit ridge. Instead, they continued traversing until they reached a small gully that might, they thought, lead to the North-East Ridge beyond the Second Step. But unfortunately the 'gully' was an optical illusion and only a shallow scoop. However, they now roped up and attempted to climb it. The attempt failed, so again they continued traversing to the right. After about 150 yards they came upon another snow-filled gully ascending to the final pyramid. As they approached it, the angle steepened but, more importantly, the rocks, which overlapped each other due to the type of strata, became snow-covered with patches of ice holding them in place. In the sun this 'glue of ice' melted and the rocks tended to slide under their feet. With few sound holds or places to belay, a slip by one climber could cause both to fall out of control down the North Face. As they continued into the floor of the gully, the rocks above began to overhang. They managed to cross the gully on powdery unstable snow, but found the rocks on the far side even steeper, looser, and more unstable owing to the overlapping strata.

At 28,100ft they stopped at more or less the same place at which Norton had turned back nine years earlier, which was still a thousand feet below the summit. The climbing was more dangerous than difficult, depending largely on balance. If the rocks had been dry and free from snow it might have been easier, but they were not. They calculated that it would take a minimum of four hours and probably longer to reach the summit and at least another two hours to descend. But that would have meant a descent in the dark and the possibility of a bivouac – when they might freeze to death. Very sensibly they decided to return, hoping, on the way, to make another attempt at the Second Step so that Shipton and Smythe, the second pair, could be told with certainty whether or not it was climbable. However, they were both too exhausted to attempt that project.

When they got back to the place on the rocks where Wyn Harris had found the ice axe, he took it and left his own in its place. Wager managed to drag himself up to the North-East Ridge, below the First Step and became the first European to look down the East (Kangshung) Face. They reached Camp VI at 4.0pm and after an hour's rest, descended to the North Col. On the way down Wyn Harris started to glissade down a snow slope, lost control, but managed to stop before falling several thousand feet to the East Rongbuk glacier. On 31 May they recovered at the North Col camp and on 1st June descended to Camp III at its foot.

The second assault, to 28,000ft.
No supplementary oxygen used.

In the meantime, Shipton and Smythe had occupied Camp VI, but had to spend a day stormbound in the tiny tent. Both felt hungry, with a craving for fresh food rather than the tinned soup and jellies that they were forced to eat. Inevitably both spent an uncomfortable night. The floor of the tent sloped, and Smythe, who slept in the upper berth, spent the night rolling down towards Shipton. In sheer self-preservation, Shipton kept jabbing him with his knee or elbow, so that neither slept much. Hours before dawn they started to prepare for their attempt. Just before it became properly light the wind rose and snow started to fall.

ERIC SHIPTON

It was impossible to climb in a storm and falling snow would inevitably make the rocks more difficult; on the other hand, they knew that an extra day at this height would rapidly increase their physical deterioration, due to oxygen lack, exhaustion, and insufficient food, fluid and sleep. How long could they survive at this height?

When the wind dropped they could see the summit. It was only 1,600 feet above and, at sea-level, would have taken no more than an hour or two to climb. Yet every hour that they remained tent-bound sapped their strength still further.

FRANK S SMYTHE

The next night was a repetition of the night before: kneeing, elbowing and panting. At 3.0am they started melting snow, and after an age were able to drink it. Their boots, which they had imprudently left outside their sleeping-bags, were now lumps of ice. It was only by holding them over a candle so that the leather uppers eventually became pliable, that they were able, with a great effort, to force in their feet, encased in four pairs of socks. Under a windproof suit with a hood and a balaclava, they each wore two sets of long thick wool underpants and seven sweaters. They also wore thick wool mitts covered by sheepskin gauntlets. As Shipton observed, 'I felt about as suitably equipped for delicate rock-climbing as a fully rigged sea-diver for dancing a tango.' Even so, it was so cold that they waited an hour before leaving at 7.30am. Shipton started with a stomach ache which got worse, and after two hours he began to feel sick and had to stop, for to go on until he literally collapsed would have put Smythe, his companion, in a dangerous position. Smythe therefore continued alone and Shipton returned to camp. If it had not been for the oxygen lack at altitude, which dulls all senses, he would have felt keenly disappointed, but as it was he just accepted it.

Smythe continued to traverse right across the face, following more or less the same route as the first pair, between the yellow limestone band and the black rock above: powder snow from the storm of the day before lay on the outward-sloping rocks. Starting at an easy angle, these gradually steepened; then, turning a corner of rock, he could see into the gully rising to the summit. This was filled with snow, but higher up the rock overhung in a series of overlaps. 200 feet below, the gully steepened to a vertical drop 10,000 feet down the North Face. Edging along a wide snow ledge, Smythe found himself on the edge of the gully. The snow in the bed of the gully was compacted, which was a surprise because at over 23,000ft snow did not usually consolidate but remained like powder. After the exhausting process of cutting steps to the far side, which he reached at 10am, he climbed upwards as the snow turned to powder. It was like climbing on the tiles of a roof covered in soft snow which could not hold a foot firmly enough to prevent a slip which, once started, would end many thousands of feet below. By 11am, having reached much the same place as Wyn Harris, Wager and Norton, Smythe could go no higher and turned back.

Returning at a lower level on the limestone band, he found the going easier; yet it was exhausting because, although not difficult, it was still very dangerous, with every step needing care to prevent a slip and an uncontrollable, unstoppable slide. Suddenly a mist came down, all landmarks disappeared and Smythe felt very much alone. Then suddenly he recognised the rocks of a gully just above Camp VI and, in a few minutes, he reached the tent with Shipton inside.

Smythe later described two hallucinations, undoubtedly caused by oxygen lack and fatigue, that he had experienced during his climb to 28,000ft. The first was the 'third man' effect. He felt as though he were accompanied by another man on his rope, and so powerful was this presence that he had offered it some food. The 'presence' was entirely benign and peaceful and similar hallucinations have appeared at sea-level to many, including myself, when exhausted and over-stressed.

The second hallucination experienced by Smythe was of a pulsating balloon in the sky, which gradually faded. At 2.30pm Shipton left Camp VI, alone, and in spite of a storm, reached Camp V safely. Smythe was too tired to accompany him, so after supper, using both sleeping-bags, he slept from 6.0pm to 7.0am and had his best night's sleep of the expedition.

After breakfast Smythe started down but was soon engulfed in yet another storm, with a wind so violent that he felt his whole body cooling to a 'deadening numbness' – in other words, incipient hypothermia. Keeping out of the wind, he warmed up and then continued down to the North Col camp, where he was met, 1,000ft above the camp, by Longland with a flask of hot tea. The whole party now descended to Base Camp where Smythe found that he had lost so much weight that he could almost encircle his thigh with the fingers of one hand. This indicated how much muscle-wasting had occurred at altitude: in a starvation situation fat is the first to go, followed by the protein of muscle.

Originally the plan was for the whole party to recuperate in the Kharta valley some five marches away, which was lower than Base Camp and where green grass and shrubs would be more refreshing for both body and spirit. But the psychological effect of losing touch with the mountain so soon would have been considerable. As the party were recovering well at Base Camp, which was not so dreary as it had been in April and, at 16,000ft, had some green grass and flowers struggling through, they decided to recuperate nearer to Everest. But though the mountain remained white and blanketed with snow, there were to be no more attempts on the summit that season. Birnie, suffering from frostbite, and Wood-Johnson, from an exacerbation of his gastric ulcer, were both out of contention for a summit bid. As a gesture, however, Camp III at the foot of the North Col was reoccupied and the Rapiu La, 22,340ft, revisited. It was then that the oxygen apparatus was successfully tried for the first time.

On their return from the Rapiu La, snow again began to fall and by morning another six inches had been deposited. The sun was so weak that it was not melting the snow after it had fallen, and frequent avalanches were falling down the North-East Face into the basin in which Camp III lay. The west wind, which normally blows the snow from the upper slopes of Everest, had died down, to be replaced by a gentle southern breeze. It looked as though the monsoon had started, and this was confirmed over the wireless and later by the Abbot at Rongbuk who was familiar with the local weather.

Although there was still the possibility that a few members might stay to study conditions during the monsoon, funds were short and the Tibetan Government, after the affair of the Dancing Lamas, was still unhappy. The Abbot of Rongbuk was ambivalent, saying that while he could not recommend to his goverment that permission should be given for an attempt in 1934, he would place no obstacle in the way. The party left Rongbuk on 2nd July, arriving in Darjeeling a month later on 1st August.

Visit to the Arun valley and exploration of the Nyonno Ri range

On their way back to Darjeeling, Shipton and Wager left the main group at Rungkang, two marches west of Tinki Dzong, to carry out some geological and mountain exploration between the Arun river and the Sikkim Himalaya. The Arun rises in southern Tibet and carves one of the world's steepest and deepest gorges through the Himalaya. The great depth and steepness of this feature are caused by the Arun river having pre-dated the Himalaya, which are still rising by about a centimetre a year.

On 13 July Shipton and Wager headed almost due south along the eastern side of Sangkar Ri, the main northern peak of the Nyonno Ri range, reaching Phuru the same night. Next day they climbed a peak of 20,000ft in the Nyonno Ri to get their bearings, and had good views of Sangkar Ri and the rest of the Nyonno Ri range before returning to Phuru. They then moved south through Chang Mo, coming to a valley leading to the Lashar plain (south of Tinki Dzong) and saw an immense tangle of peaks up to 24,000ft which they had no time to investigate.

On 18 July they went up a large glacier heading north from the Jonsong and Lhonak peaks which form the boundary mountain rim of Sikkim. While Wager went to explore a col north of the main peak, Shipton and Aila, one of the porters, ascended the main Lhonak Peak. After meeting on the col between this peak and the mountain known as Kellas Peak on the International Kangchenjunga Expedition, they both set out next day to climb Kellas Peak, but heavy snow during the night forced them to abandon that project.

On the 20th they descended into Sikkim, eventually reaching the Lhonak glacier. Finally they reached Tangu in the Lachen valley by crossing the Lungnak La, and were once again 'on the map'. Later, Wager wrote a short paper on the geological aspects of the Arun gorge. It was the first time that this important feature of the Himalaya had been properly described.

Aftermath: H Ruttledge versus C G Crawford

The 1933 expedition was yet another failure, having got no higher than the 1924 expedition. One of the many questions now being asked was why supplementary oxygen had not been used, particularly as a lightweight set had been specially designed for the expedition with the help of Raymond Greene, the medical officer. There seemed to be no good reason for this omission, especially as Greene had actually used oxygen during the expedition for the successful treatment of frostbite.

Inevitably, this latest failure caused a good deal of discontent and widened the potential gap between members of the Alpine Club, whose main interest was in the climbing, and the members of the Royal Geographical Society, with their broader perspective. The general discontent inevitably focused on the leader, Hugh Ruttledge, a pleasant man who knew the Himalaya well but who was not a mountaineer in the strict sense – he had never, for instance, climbed difficult routes on challenging peaks. Was he the correct type of person to lead further Everest expeditions? The younger climbers knew that Everest was not a technically difficult peak and, looking at the Everest Committee, they did not like what they saw. There seemed little point in having representatives from the Royal Geographical Society, since Everest was seen solely as a mountaineering problem. They did not like the Alpine Club members either, as few had been on a serious climb for years and were considered long past their sell-by date. Although no voices had been raised against Ruttledge during the 1933 expedition, a number of members now felt that they could not support him as a future expedition leader. Knowing this, and to avoid controversy, Ruttledge resigned.

A new Everest Committee was now convened and in May 1934 confidential statements were taken from 1933 party members as to their views about the leadership. At about the same time the Tibetans gave permission for another expedition and, as time was short, the Committee decided to send out a lightweight reconnaissance party, to be led by Shipton, in 1935, prior to a full-scale attempt in 1936. Ruttledge was invited to lead the later party purely as a matter of courtesy, but, to everyone's surprise, he withdrew his resignation and accepted!

All hell now broke loose and two opposing factions emerged – the anti-Ruttledge group, led by Crawford and supported by Longland, Wager and Brocklebank; and, on the opposite side, the Ruttledge supporters – Wyn Harris, Shipton and Smythe. With no stomach for a fight, Ruttledge resigned again. However, the Committee did not altogether approve of Crawford either, so, once again, they cast around for a new leader. Approaches were made to Norton, Geoffrey Bruce, General R C Wilson, C J Morris, and two members of the Commitee, E L Strutt and Kenneth Mason, the geographer. All refused. Finally, Jack Longland was invited to lead the party. He replied that he would accept only if he was acceptable to *all* the members of the 1933 party. This demonstration of loyalty and democracy affronted the Committee and Longland was promptly dropped.

Finally, the Committee was forced to choose between Crawford and Ruttledge and, by a casting vote of the Chairman Sir Percy Cox, Ruttledge was reappointed leader. Two 'rebels' from the opposing faction were not included in the 1936 team: L R Wager, who was unable to go anyway because of academic commitments, and Longland himself who, principled to the last, declined on the grounds that he could not fully support Ruttledge.

This was a distasteful episode, but the frustration felt by the 'young Turks' was directed at the wrong target; in 1933 it was not the organisation and leadership that had been at fault. The correct target was the failure to understand and investigate the medical/scientific problem of 'the last thousand feet' of Everest. That approach had to wait for another twenty years to be adopted.

BIBLIOGRAPHY

H Boustead, *Wind of Morning*. Chatto & Windus, 1971.

R Greene, 'The Everest Oxygen Apparatus 1933' in *Lancet 2*, 1122, 1934.

R Greene, 'Observations on the composition of alveolar air on Everest' in *Journal of Physiology 32*, 481-485, 1934.

R Greene, 'Oxygen and Everest' in *Nature,* November 28th, 3-7, 1934.

R Greene, 'Mental performance in chronic anoxia' *British Medical Journal 1*, 1028-1031, 1957.

R Greene, *Moments of Being*. Heinemann, 1974.

H Ruttledge, *Everest 1933*. Hodder & Stoughton, 1934.

H Ruttledge, 'The Mount Everest Expedition 1933' in *Geographical Journal 83*, 1-17, 1934.

H Ruttledge, 'The Mount Everest Expedition 1933' in *Alpine Journal 45*, 216-231, 1933.

E E Shipton, 'Lashar Plain (Nyonno Ri Range)' in *Alpine Journal 46*, 129-131, 1934.

F S Smythe, 'Everest. The Final Problem' in *Alpine Journal 46*, 442-446, 1934.

F S Smythe, *Camp Six*. Hodder & Stoughton 1937.

Peter Steele, *Eric Shipton. Everest and Beyond*. Constable, 1998.

L R Wager, 'Mount Everest's weather in 1933' in *Himalayan Journal 6*, 47-50, 1934.

L R Wager, 'The Lhonak La' in *Himalayan Journal 6*, 51-53, 1934.

L R Wager, 'The Arun River drainage pattern and the rise of the Himalaya' in *Geographical Journal 89*, 239-250, 1937.

Chapter 11

A PLETHORA OF PEAKS
The Everest Reconnaissance Expedition (Tibetan side), 1935

Objectives and membership

In the early spring of 1935, Hugh Ruttledge was told by J C Walton, a friend in the India Office in London, that the Tibetan Government was prepared to allow another attempt on Everest. Soon afterwards, at a lunch in London with Eric Shipton, who had just returned from his and Tilman's outstanding reconnaissance of the Nanda Devi basin, they both realised that there would not be enough time to organise a full-scale Everest attempt in 1935. However, if a small reconnaissance party were to go in May, much could be done in preparation for an attempt in 1936.

By contrast, the news from Nepal was bad. C J Morris, a member of the 1922 expedition who was later to join the 1936 party, had just paid a visit to Kathmandu. The Royal Geographical Society had made the Maharajah an Honorary Fellow and Morris had been asked to present the diploma. At the same time he was to enquire about an approach to Everest from the south. The Maharajah accepted the scroll, threw it on the desk without looking at it, and was obviously displeased when the subject of Everest was raised. The British Ambassador added his voice in support, but both were dismissed with the words 'No, certainly not'.

In London Ruttledge suggested to a meeting of the Everest Committee that Shipton should be invited to lead a small party from Tibet in 1935, and that the Tibetans should be asked to extend permission from June 1935 to June 1936 to allow for a full-scale attempt in 1936. These suggestions were agreed by the Committee

The objectives of the 1935 reconnaissance expedition were to collect data about monsoon snow conditions at great altitude on Everest and to investigate the possibility of an attempt either during or after the monsoon. It appeared that, once the monsoon had taken hold, the ferocious winds usually died down and there followed a period of relative calm. With warmer weather, there might be a chance of climbing Everest if the snow conditions were less dangerous than they had been in 1922.

Alternative routes would also be examined, notably the North-West Ridge; and an attempt would be made to examine the Western Cwm on the south side of Everest, from which a route might be made to the summit from the South Col, which had not yet been seen. Ice and snow conditions on the North Col would also be examined, and new climbers tried out as, in general, 'first timers' do not acclimatise well at altitude. Finally, a stereo-grammetric map of the North-East Face would be made, and a photo-theodolite survey of the north side of the whole region would extend the 1921 survey. Most of these objectives were achieved during the 1935 expedition, which was one of the more successful expeditions of the 1930s; moreover, it was carried out at a fraction of the usual cost of a large party. The budget was £200 for each climber. More peaks over 20,000ft were climbed than had so far been ascended worldwide.

Shipton was given a free hand in the choice of members. H W Tilman was one of his first choices, as he had climbed with him in East Africa and on the highly successful reconnaissance of the Nanda Devi sanctuary in 1934.

After serving in the First World War, where he gained a Military Cross, Tilman went to Kenya to grow coffee. With Shipton, he pioneered the lightweight exploratory type of expedition, building on the efforts of Tom Longstaff. With Angtharkay, they became famous for their exploits in the Himalaya and Central Asia. During the Second World War Tilman served with the Special Operations Executive in Italy, gaining a DSO. A highly intelligent man with a quirky sense of humour, Tilman later took up deep-water sailing and wrote a series of highly readable and informative books on both mountaineering and sailing.

L V Bryant was a New Zealand mountaineer and a schoolmaster. E G H Kempson, a Cambridge mathematical wrangler at Marlborough College, was a formidable walker known by the Sherpas as 'the walking Sahib'. He had had twelve years' experience of summer and winter climbing in the European Alps and it was he who had first introduced me to climbing during my school holidays. The medical officer, Dr Charles Warren, was trained at St Bartholomew's Hospital and in 1933 had been to the Garhwal Himal where he climbed the central Satopanth Peak (Bhagirathi III) with Colin Kirkus. E H L Wigram was a medical student at St Thomas's Hospital.

Finally, Michael Spender was taken as surveyor. Spender had been working in Denmark on his results from a recent expedition to Greenland. He took with him to Everest a Wild photo-theodolite used by Kenneth Mason in the Karakoram in 1926, a lighter Zeiss photo-theodolite used in Greenland, and the Watts-Leica photo-theodolite, an instrument of great simplicity. Later, in 1937, Spender joined Shipton, Tilman and Auden on their exploration of the north side of the Karakoram watershed. Frank Smythe, a prospective member of the 1936 expedition, could not join for business reasons.

Colin Kirkus, one of the two outstanding rock climbers in the UK (the other being Menlove Edwards), who had been with Charles Warren to the Himalaya in 1933, was not chosen for 1935 on the grounds that he lacked the necessary Alpine experience. This was a mistake, and was repeated in 1953 with Tony Streather, for much the same reason.

After gathering in Darjeeling on 22 May, the party left on the 24th. Karma Paul, who had been on every previous Everest expedition except that of 1921, went as interpreter. Fifteen Sherpas were employed, including the young Tenzing Norgay who was Charles Warren's Sherpa, with Angtharkay as sirdar. So keen was the party to leave that, despite no official Passport, Rai Bahadur, the assistant to the Political Officer of Sikkim, felt able to give them a temporary pass, as he was so well regarded in Lhasa.

Exploration of the Nyonno Ri range

The party crossed into Tibet by the Kongra La and Sebu La at the head of the Lachen valley, and once in Tibet, turned immediately west through one of the poorest parts of that country, south of the main east-west track from Kampa Dzong to Tingri. Their aim was to explore further the beautiful Nyonno Ri range that had so much impressed Shipton and Wager in 1933.

On 8 June they reached Sar on the east side of the range. The village consisted of a few houses and the ruins of an old fort with fine stone walls which had been destroyed by Nepalese invaders a century earlier. The setting of these walls and ruined houses was magnificent, indicating an instinct for design among Tibetans in stark contrast to the 'imported' Chinese buildings now so prevalent in Tibet.

The Nyonno Ri range ran for about fifty miles north and south, forming the east side of the Arun gorge. The route from Kampa to Tingri Dzong skirts the northern end of the range, whilst the route that Noel took in 1913 to Tashirak went round the southern end.

At Sar the party split into three groups. Michael Spender carried out a photographic survey from five separate stations, whilst Shipton, Bryant and Wigram crossed a high pass and explored a basin on the west side of the range. Here they found extensive yak and sheep pastures used by the inhabitants of Kharta and the Arun valleys. From this basin they climbed a number of peaks and had extensive views over the Arun gorge towards Everest and Makalu to the west. Recrossing the range by a different pass, they returned to Sar.

The third party, Tilman, Warren and Kempson, left Sar for an attempt on Ama Drime, the main peak of the range. Leaving at 10.0am on 10 June, they made for the snout of the main glacier and bought yak milk at a monastery in a lovely pasture; a few hours later they camped by the side of the glacier at 18,000ft. Next day, they reached a small lake where they separated, with Tilman and Angtharkay trying to climb the glacier's icefall while Kempson and Warren went up a peak of 19,700ft to get an idea of the topography of the region. Returning in the afternoon, they learned that the icefall was impracticable.

Next day Kempson and Warren tried another glacier falling from a col between the main peak of Ama Drime and a subsidiary. After camping on lateral moraine, they continued next day with Tilman suffering badly from the altitude. Snow conditions worsened and after falling into a crevasse on the slopes leading to the col, Kempson and Warren finally reached the col by a different route, where they took a round of photo-theodolite photographs.

On 17 June, Tilman having recovered from his altitude sickness, they started for the south peak of the Nyonno Ri and reached 21,600ft on a ridge of mixed rock and ice. Here the ridge became more difficult, and though the summit was only 200 feet further on, they were so exhausted through lack of acclimatisation that they returned to camp. The following day they explored the next valley to the south but as the weather was breaking, they only got poor theodolite positions. Leaving the Nyonno Ri, the party then continued directly to Rongbuk, using the normal route.

E G H Kempson

Finding the body of Maurice Wilson

Reaching Rongbuk on 4 July, they were greeted with great warmth by the Abbot, and were allowed to use for storage a house owned by the headman of Sar. Then the whole party, which now included forty porters, left for Camp III at the foot of the North Col, which they reached on 8 July. The route up the East Rongbuk glacier was a strip of moraine running like an alley between 25 to 30ft-high ice pinnacles. Camp III was on rock-covered moraine just where the glacier broadened into a snow basin.

After establishing camp, Shipton, Warren and Kempson went up towards the slopes of the North Col. Warren was a little ahead of the other two when he saw a boot sticking out of the snow. He saw that the maker was Robert Lawrie, a well-known bootmaker from the Midlands, who supplied equipment to many Himalayan expeditions. Nearby were the tattered remains of a green tent which Warren at first thought must have been left by the 1933 expedition. He recorded in his diary what happened next:

> I shouted to Eric as I advanced – 'Hullo! here is a perfectly good pair of boots and a tent; must be a dump. Then on approaching the green heap I got a bit of a shock to see that it was the body of a man lying huddled in the snow. At once the thought flashed into my mind – Maurice Wilson. I shouted to Eric – I say it's this fellow Wilson. ...

Maurice Wilson had disappeared on Everest in 1934.

> The body was lying on its left side with the knees drawn up in an attitude of flexion. The first boot I had found some 10 yards down the slope, the second was lying near the man's feet. He was wearing a mauve pullover, grey flannel trousers with woollen vest and pants underneath. There was a stone near his left hand to which a guyline of a tent was attached. The torn remains of the tent was pulled out of the snow some few feet down the slope from him.

Most of the porters, who had come up to see what was happening, took a matter-of-fact view of the discovery. Before disturbing the body Warren and the other members of the party searched the snow for Wilson's diary and other belongings. Eventually a lightweight rucksack was found, with a small Union Jack on which his girlfriends had signed their names; also his diary with a gold pencil and elephant hair ring. The diary told of his clandestine journey through southern Tibet from Darjeeling and was 'an extraordinary documentary revelation of monomania and determination of purpose'. The diary entries ended with the statement that he was off to the North Col for the second time. From his position he appeared to have died in his sleep from a combination of exhaustion and hypothermia, and the tent may have been blown away at a later date. Warren recorded in his diary that no sleeping-bag was found and that Wilson was within 200 yards of the 1933 expedition food dump, of which he had previously made use. Also, he was within hailing distance of Camp III, where his accompanying Sherpas were camped.

This was one of the more bizarre attempts on Everest. Maurice Wilson was aged 37 when he went to Everest. He had formed the idea that if a man were to go without food for long enough his mind would reach a state of semi-consciousness enabling it to communicate directly with his soul. These powers of self-hypnosis would give him greatly increased spiritual and bodily strength. He also believed that he had received instructions to preach this doctrine to mankind and that

Everest was the ideal place to do it. If he were to succeed in reaching the summit by himself, the resulting publicity would give credence to his cause. But how to implement this daring plan?

After the Houston 'Flight over Everest' expedition in 1933, which had received wide press coverage, Wilson, who knew nothing about mountaineering, conceived the idea that if he were to fly a plane as high as possible on the mountain and then crash it, he could climb from that point to the summit and descend on foot. He therefore bought a plane in the UK, learned to fly it and set off for India. Eventually he reached Purnea, where the Houston party had set out on their flight over the mountain, but here his plane was confiscated. Refusing to abandon his plan, he continued to Darjeeling where he stayed for four months, both training and making secret preparations. He got in touch with three Tibetans who agreed to smuggle him through Sikkim to Everest. They were, according to Tenzing Norgay who met them in Darjeeling after their return, Tewang Bhotia, Rinzing Bhotia and Tshering Bhotia. Wilson wore a disguise and the party travelled by the normal route to Everest, avoiding Tibetan officials and patrols by travelling mainly at night. Reaching Rongbuk, they rested there for 15 days, Wilson telling the Abbot that he was a former member of the 1933 expedition. As a result, he was given some items of equipment left behind by the earlier expedition.

From Rongbuk they continued up the East Rongbuk glacier, and reached Camp III at the foot of the North Col at 21,000ft. Here his three Tibetan companions had been unwilling to go any further. However, they found a dump of food left by the 1933 expedition consisting of chocolate, Ovaltine, sardines, biscuits and other food, which was eaten.

Maurice Wilson continued alone, expecting to find and use the fixed ropes and the steps which had been cut nearly a year previously in the snow and ice slopes leading to the North Col. He was shattered to find bare windswept slopes with no ropes and no steps. Though he had an ice axe, he did not know how to use it and made little progress. For many days he set out each day on his fruitless quest, and though he had plenty of food, he became weaker and weaker and the entries in his diary less and less coherent. The last entry was on 31 May 1934.

After some discussion it was decided to bury Wilson in a crevasse, to which he was carried in the remains of his tent. Hats were raised in salute as the body disappeared. As Charles Warren, a paediatrician, commented:

> I thought that I had grown immune to the sight of dead bodies, but somehow or other the circumstances and the fact that he was after all doing almost the same as ourselves seemed to bring his tragedy a little too near home.

The North Col and the North Ridge up to 24,000ft

Not surprisingly, the slopes to the North Col had changed markedly since 1933, and now they were a series of ice walls and dangerously tottering séracs. After three days Shipton, Kempson and Warren and nine Sherpas placed a camp on the North Col with enough food for fifteen days.

During the night of 15 July a large snowfall covered their tents, inside and out. The mountain was white and no black rocks were showing. As the sun touched the snow, avalanches started to fall off the face. The North Ridge was safe, so they set off for Camp V, but soon Kempson got a pain in his chest and looked very blue, Warren's feet started to lose sensation and Shipton complained of the excessive cold. All were in the early stages of hypothermia and frostbite because lack of oxygen prevented them from going fast enough to generate enough heat to counteract these symptoms. At 24,000ft they stopped and returned to their camp on the col.

By the next day it was obvious that the mountain would remain out of condition for several days, so they decided to leave food and tents on the North Col and start their exploration and mapping, returning when the peak was in better condition.

On the 16th, while descending from the North Col, they came across the brink of an avalanche 'cut off'. It stretched for 100 yards in each direction to a depth of six feet. Although they had camped only a few yards away, they had not heard the roar of an avalanche. After a long discussion, they descended on the snow and ice laid bare by the avalanche. Both Warren and Kempson thought this was very dangerous, and considered that they should have returned to camp to await better weather.

This episode illustrated that, despite the experience of each of the party, most of whom had climbed in the Himalaya and Alps in all seasons, none was able to gauge the avalanche risk, so by mutual consent the North Col was abandoned. In Shipton's opinion the only safe period to climb to the North Col was between the end of winter and the approach of the monsoon, and to be successful, speed was essential.

According to Warren, to whom I spoke later, they had intended to make a push for the summit even though they were reduced to only three climbers. It was the heavy snow on the North Face and the unexpected finding of the track of an avalanche that had persuaded Shipton that at over 22,000ft, snow conditions on Everest were too unpredictable and dangerous to justify taking risks. Ruttledge in similar conditions in 1936 was also perhaps over-cautious.

On their return to Camp III at the foot of the North Col, they found a note from Tilman and Wigram saying that they had gone down to Camp II for more food and that they had climbed two peaks to the north of Changtse, and had visited both the Lhakpa La and the Rapiu La. When they came back, Warren had to remove one of Wigram's teeth as he had an apical abscess.

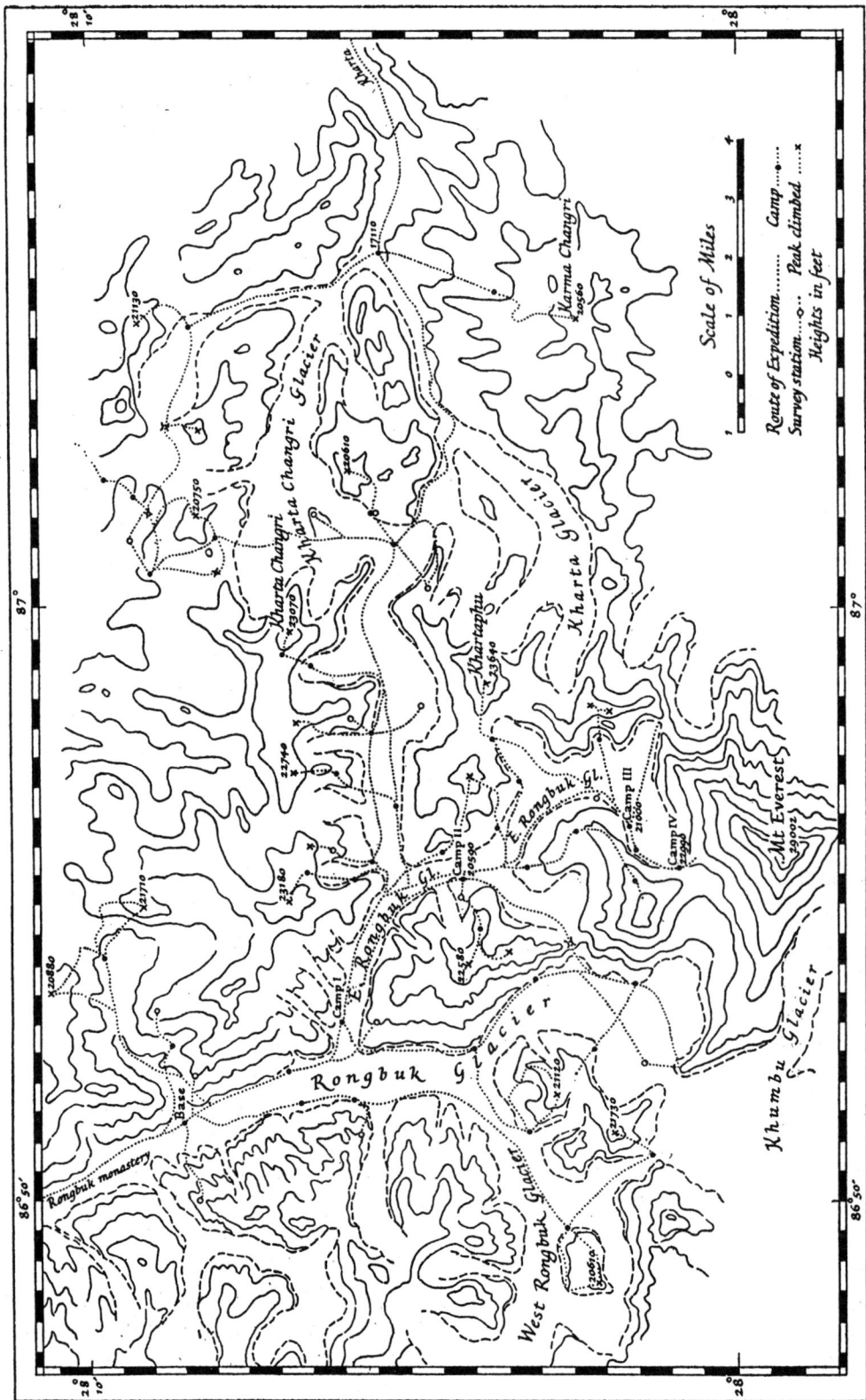

ROUTES TAKEN BY EVEREST RECONNAISSANCE PARTIES IN 1935

Exploration and survey, north and east of Everest

On 17 July camp was moved to a big unnamed glacier that flowed into the East Rongbuk glacier from the east. At its head was a peak, Khartaphu (23,400ft), which was climbed in the next few days. Though they took the light photo-theodolite to the summit, cloud obscured any views of Everest. However, good views were obtained of the country to the east and north which helped later exploration.

On their descent, at Camp III they had met Michael Spender who had been surveying on both sides of the main Rongbuk glacier. From these results he was able to construct a large-scale photogrammetric map of the North Face of Everest showing the precise altitude of many important features. This was extremely useful in planning further attempts on Everest from the north and in the production of the Milne-Hinks map in 1952.

CHARLES WARREN

The party now split. Spender, Kempson and Warren, all scientists, were to explore and map the country between the East Rongbuk and the Doya La, that is to the east and north. The remainder were to stay in the vicinity of Camp III on the East Rongbuk glacier and climb a number of peaks.

Tilman, Wigram and Bryant managed to climb 'Kellas Rock Peak' or Lixin Peak (23,000ft) close to Camp III. There, as on Khartaphu, they found a sudden and marked change in the consistency of the snow at 22-23,000ft; above this level it did not consolidate and had a tendency to avalanche; below it, the snow consolidated well and was safe. Later, they climbed another peak of about 22,800ft descending to the main Rongbuk glacier. They then went up another glacier coming in from the east and climbed two more peaks, and to supplement Spender's survey, they took photo-theodolite readings. This party returned to Rongbuk on 31 July.

E H L WIGRAM

The other group (Kempson, Spender and Warren) went up the glacier that flowed into the East Rongbuk from the east. Two peaks of 22,000ft on the south side were climbed, followed by Kharta Changri (23,000ft); and on each the survey was continued. They then returned to Rongbuk where some sick Sherpas were discharged and Kempson returned home to his teaching post at Marlborough College. His leave was nearly finished and he was 'homesick for school', according to Warren.

West of Everest

The next project was to explore to the west and south in order to have a look at the Western Cwm, first seen by Mallory and Bullock in 1921, and the West Ridge of Everest. On 3 August Tilman, Shipton, Wigram and Bryant left Rongbuk and went up the main Rongbuk glacier. Warren stayed at Rongbuk with Spender who was recovering from an attack of influenza, and when he was better they followed and were able to complete the survey to the west of Everest.

Tilman and Wigram tried to cross the Lho La with the idea of getting into the Western Cwm via the Khumbu icefall, whilst Shipton and Bryant went up the West Rongbuk glacier. Here they climbed two outstanding peaks in the Lingtren group. On Lingtren Nup they were able to get a good round of photos with the photo-theodolite and then camped for two days on the Nepal-Tibet watershed in very bad weather. On 10 August they climbed a third peak, at 21,730ft, on which Bryant broke through a cornice, was held by Shipton and had to cut his way back to the ridge. Next day they put the photo-theodolite on the crest of the watershed and took a series of photographs of the upper part of the Khumbu glacier and the entrance to the Western Cwm. Unfortunately many of these photos were spoilt by the camera jamming. It was, however, obvious that a descent into Nepal to the foot of the Khumbu icefall was out of the question. As they had agreed to be in Rongbuk by 14 August, an excursion up the West Rongbuk glacier to the Nup La was also ruled out.

Wigram and Tilman had been to the Lho La and found no route into Nepal; they also thought there was no chance of success on the West Ridge. On their return to Rongbuk they had crossed a pass to the north of Changtse and descended directly to Camp II on the East Rongbuk glacier, from which they climbed two more peaks.

Changtse (24,500ft) and north-east of Everest

The whole party reassembled at Rongbuk and told Karma Paul to meet them at Kharta in three weeks' time. Their first objective was to climb Changtse, to get good photos of the North Ridge of Everest and to collect further evidence of monsoon snow over 23,000ft.

From Camp II on the East Rongbuk glacier they attempted Changtse (North Peak) by its horseshoe-shaped north and east ridges, but the higher they climbed the worse became the snow. At the highest camp, at 23,200ft, the powder snow was a bottomless pit into which they sank further and further until they had to give up 500 metres from the summit. From this point they could look down on the tents on the North Col which they had left some weeks before.

The next two weeks were spent making a high-level route and mapping east towards the Doya La, and from there to Kharta. First they had to cross the Kharta Changri pass to what Spender called the 'ice cap station'. Here the upper glacier was flat for miles, exactly like the Greenland ice cap, whilst the lower glacier was Himalayan in complexity.

At the camp on the 'ice cap' the party divided; Warren and Bryant, the latter by now better acclimatised, climbed a peak of 22,470ft. They then rejoined the main party, went north-east and crossed the head of the Kharta Chu glacier. On the way, a peak of 20,750ft was climbed which gave excellent views of the surrounding country. Now in almost totally unmapped country, they called the most outstanding peak the 'Dent Blanche' because it resembled the peak of that name in the Swiss Pennine Alps. One evening a strike by the Sherpas took place because their loads were too heavy and they had had to jettison some tsampa. As a result Tilman, Bryant and Wigram descended to the Kharta valley to get more food, while Shipton and Warren stayed to tackle the 'Dent Blanche'. Spender, in the meantime, started surveying in the Lang Chu valley. After camping that night at 20,000ft, Shipton and Warren failed to reach the summit next day and descended to the Lang Chu.

The next few days were spent in reaching the Doya La where the pleasure of seeing grass, shrubs and flowers more than compensated for having to leave behind the dead land of high peaks and glaciers. On 6 September they reached Kharta. From there they had hoped to expand their exploration of the Nyonno Ri range, but the Tibetan authorities were not in favour. So Tilman, Wigram, Bryant and Shipton left Tibet by the Chorten Nyima La and climbed in the Dodang Nyima range. The monsoon, too, was so fierce and snowfall so great that Spender was prevented from surveying north of Kanchenjau. Finally all returned to Darjeeling, and began preparations for the attempt on Everest in 1936.

This expedition demonstrated how much useful work could be carried out by lightweight parties, at a fraction of the cost of the large, juggernaut expeditions.

BIBLIOGRAPHY

E G H Kempson, *Diary of Mt Everest Reconnaissance Expedition 1935.* Alpine Club Library.

H Ruttledge, *Everest. The Unfinished Adventure.* Hodder & Stoughton, 1937.

A Salkeld, 'The Mad Yorkshireman'. Chapter in P Gillman's *Everest.* Little Brown, 47-48, 1993.

E E Shipton, 'The Mount Everest Reconnaissance 1935' in *Himalayan Journal 8,* 1-13, 1936.

E E Shipton, 'The Mount Everest Reconnaissance' in *Geographical Journal 87,* 98-112, 1936.

E E Shipton, *Upon That Mountain.* Hodder and Stoughton, 1943.

E E Shipton, 'Note on Michael Spender' in *Alpine Journal 55,* 318-320, 1945-6.

M Spender, 'Photographic surveys in the Mount Everest region' in *Geographical Journal 88,* 289--303, 1936.

M Spender, 'Survey on the Mount Everest Reconnaissance 1935' in *Himalayan Journal 9,* 14-20, 1937.

M Spender, 'Notes on the photo-surveyed maps of the Mount Everest region and Nyonno Ri' in *Himalayan Journal 11,* 176-179, 1939.

C B M Warren, *Diary of Mt Everest Reconnaissance Expedition 1935.* Alpine Club Library

C B M Warren, 'Everest 1935: The Forgotten Adventure' in *Alpine Journal 100,* 3-14, 1995.

E H L Wigram, Diary of Mt Everest Reconnaissance Expedition 1935. Alpine Club Library.

Chapter 12

WEATHER WASHOUT
The Fourth Attempt, 1936

The march through Tibet

Members of this party were chosen from those who had acclimatised well on the 1935 reconnaissance expedition and from other experienced high-altitude climbers, such as F S Smythe and P Wyn Harris, who had not been available in 1935. Hugh Ruttledge was again asked to act as leader. The 1936 expedition was one of the best equipped and well organised of all the Everest expeditions, yet atrocious weather and snow conditions precluded success, and they got no higher than the North Col (23,000ft), a thousand feet lower than the highest point reached by the more lightly equipped 1935 party.

The team members were H Ruttledge, F S Smythe, E E Shipton, Dr C B M Warren, E H L Wigram, E G H Kempson, J M L Gavin, a sapper officer who had climbed with Smythe in the Alps, G N Humphreys, a widely travelled doctor, P Wyn Harris from 1933, W R Smijth-Windham; Peter Oliver, an army officer and gifted amateur artist, and John Morris made up the party. Two members of the highly successful 1935 group, H W Tilman and the New Zealander L V Bryant, were not taken, as they did not acclimatise well.

Before the 1936 Everest party left the UK, the open-circuit oxygen sets were tested on Box Hill, south-east of London. At sea-level no extra boost was expected, but the sets worked well and did not interfere with climbing. Warren and Shipton climbed five times up and down the steep 350ft-high chalk slope in just over an hour. But the attitude of climbers on this expedition to supplementary oxygen was still equivocal. It did not appear to increase climbing rate and many felt that they were better off without it. On the other hand, scientists thought that for reasons of safety on the last thousand feet of Everest, improved oxygen sets ought to be developed. It is interesting that, in a letter from Argyll Campbell, a well-known physiologist, to Professor Leonard Hill, Campbell discussed the possible use of nine litres per minute of oxygen. At the time, the standard flow rate on Everest was only two litres per minute in the open-circuit sets, which was not enough to increase performance because any possible benefits were nullified by the weight of the set.

The expedition left the UK on 1st February and gathered in Darjeeling on the 26th, but did not leave until 19th March. On 1st April they crossed into Tibet by the Kongra La and the Sebu La.

At Kampa Dzong yak transport was once again organised by Karma Paul. During the march across Tibet, Warren was able to test the oxygen apparatus on a number of steep hills up to 18,000ft. He felt that supplementary oxygen at this altitude and flow rate (two litres per minute) maintained a reasonable rate of ascent with less effort, and wearing a set weighing 35lbs he was able to climb twice as fast as his less fit companion who relied on acclimatisation alone.

The party became and remained extremely fit but the weather in the Everest region was particularly vile that year, with thick cloud and high winds.

At Shekar Dzong a number of Sherpas who had crossed the Nangpa La from Khumbu joined the expedition. On 23 April the party crossed the Pangu Pass (18,000ft) but their hopes of a fine view of Everest were blotted out by black clouds boiling around the mountain. However, a good view was obtained in the next few days from a position between Chodzong and Tashidzom. The upper slopes were black, having been blown clear of snow by the ferocious west wind.

On the 25th they went up the valley from Chodzong, passing on the way the defile down which the Sherpas had come from the Nangpa La. Soon they turned due south and Everest now dominated the end of the valley; the scale changed dramatically, with other peaks being dwarfed by its immense mass.

At Rongbuk it was sunny, and the monks remained absorbed by their religious exercises and indifferent to expeditions and the outside world. The head lama was now aware that Everest was the world's highest peak, and he had seen many expeditions come and go. But whereas in 1933 he had appeared to disapprove of the whole project, by 1936 his manner had changed and the members of this latest expedition were welcomed as friends rather than merely accepted on sufferance. In a ceremony performed with the scent of burning juniper filling the air, the head lama blessed the whole expedition individually. While the porters prostrated themselves before him, the European members advanced towards him in turn, repeating the formula 'Om Mani Padme Hum', and were touched on the forehead by a silver dorje (thunderbolt). Since Thyangboche in Khumbu is within the 'diocese' of Rongbuk, the porters were all parishioners of the Abbot and he asked them to do their duty by the expedition and themselves, not to kill any wildlife since the valley was sacred, and not to cut brushwood, which was needed by the many hermits who lived in caves around the monastery. Since he wished Rongbuk to remain peaceful and isolated, he asked the party not to go to the Kharta and Kama valleys to the east, which might encourage their use as established routes. Finally he gave Karma Paul and Hugh Ruttledge a pamphlet he had written about Mount Everest, recounting the history of its local name Chomolungma. This was the first local document on the subject. Such an unsolicited blessing from the Abbot was unparalleled and the whole party left at midday, elated by such a good omen.

The East Rongbuk glacier and the North Col

Within a few days base camp was established – a task of no small size and complexity for this full-scale expedition. For instance, 58 loads of 80lbs each were needed to transport the wireless equipment alone, which was about the same as the total amount of baggage required for a lightweight expedition.

The weather forecasts were good at first, and the local weather was also fine. Then, on 30 April, a report from Calcutta warned of approaching bad weather, and that afternoon a heavy snowfall covered the upper slopes. Locally, however, the weather remained reasonable and the organisation was so good that plans for establishing Camp IV on the North Col were advanced by a week to 15 May.

The medical officer, Noel Humphreys, in a letter to a friend written on 3 May, commented that the first attempt, by Smythe and Shipton, would be made without supplementary oxygen. If that failed, the second attempt, probably by Wyn Harris and Kempson, would be made using supplementary oxygen. He added that, though the oxygen sets were clumsy, it was probable that the mountain could not be climbed without supplementary oxygen; if the oxygen ran out, however, the climber would suddenly feel very exhausted and vulnerable.

Camp III (21,500ft) at the foot of the slopes leading to the North Col was established on 7 May and the general condition of these slopes looked good. However, the condition of different parts of the slope varied throughout the day, as the wind blew vast amounts of powder snow over the crest of the col from its west side, to be deposited as spindrift on the upper portion of its east side. On 9 May the first 500 feet were reconnoitred. The party was very fit but, ominously, the weather remained warm and the north-west wind, which would normally clear snow from the upper part of the mountain, was absent. Next day snow fell. At this point Morris developed malaria and was sent down to Rongbuk with Humphreys to recuperate.

The 11th and 12th were fine, so on the 13th Smythe, Gavin, Wigram and Oliver set off with three Sherpas for the North Col. They were followed by Kempson, Warren and Ruttledge. Five and a half hours later, at 3.30pm, the first party reached the North Col (23,000ft) followed soon afterwards by the second. A few days later, Kempson and Wyn Harris took up 46 porters and established Camp IV on the col itself, and on the 15th, in only two hours, another 50 porters, led by Smythe and Shipton, took more loads to the col. The plan now was for 36 porters to stay and help to establish the higher camps. Over the next few days, though, snow started to fall heavily on the upper slopes of the mountain. On the 18th Smythe phoned down to say that up to two feet of snow were lying on the col, with more on the upper slopes, and that any attempt now was out of the question. He thought that if they stayed much longer, high-altitude deterioration would weaken the party, and that they should descend to Camp III until conditions improved.

Retreat

Everest now lay under so much snow that even the more prominent rock pinnacles were white, and there was no north-west wind to clear it. Instead, the wind blew gently from the east. In these conditions no climbing could be done on the upper slopes and to stay even at Camp III would cause physical deterioration, so the whole party retreated to Camp I. The mood of frustration was summed up by one of the Sherpa sirdars, Nursing:

> I can't understand the way things are going this year: you have the most competent mountaineering party I have seen, and by far the best porters. The latter only ask for an opportunity – they will carry anywhere you like, and go to the summit if you want them to. But Everest is not willing. She has lured us on with false encouragement, and now closes the door. Always hitherto we have been beaten by wind and cold, never by this warmth and vile snow. I don't like it at all – we shan't get up unless the north wind comes.

How right he was. The effect of retreat to a lower altitude was immediate. The whole party started to look better and their appetites improved, but a nasty shock, in the form of a telegram, awaited them. It said that conditions favourable for an early monsoon had been observed off the coast of Ceylon (Sri Lanka).

On 23 May they received even worse weather news – the monsoon had reached Darjeeling, taking only four days to travel the length of India. Frustrated, the party returned to Camp III; the snow lay thick on the ground and avalanches fell continuously from the slopes of the North Col.

To wile away the time, Shipton, Oliver and Gavin went across the basin of the East Rongbuk glacier to the Rapiu La to look at the North-East Ridge. Another possible route of ascent was the west side of the North Col, despite unpromising reports by Mallory in 1921 and others on the 1935 expedition.

A further weather report indicated that the monsoon had arrived and severe storms on 27 and 28 May confirmed this. But on the 29th the mood of the party changed dramatically for the better. They awoke to find a fierce north-west wind blowing, while snow clouds enveloped the North Face and it was colder. The weather report indicated that the monsoon was gathering strength towards the east in Assam, but the local weather had flattered only to deceive, and on the night of 30 May the north-west wind hesitated and died. Snow began to fall heavily again and continued to do so for four days until 3 June.

Despite this, Smythe, Shipton and Kempson once again went up to Camp III at the foot of the North Col, returning with a moderately favourable report. If the wind continued, it might be justifiable to try to occupy Camp IV on the North Col again. Next day a very early start was made by the whole climbing party with 42 porters; the plan was for Smythe and Shipton to remain at Camp IV and continue up the North Ridge next day.

On 5 June, after a cold, clear night, the whole party left at 6.0am, and soon came across an avalanche that had fallen from the North Peak. A long traverse had to be made to the crest of the col. But soon it became obvious that avalanche danger would make it suicidal to continue the traverse, and Smythe started cutting steps in steep ice straight up to the col. This soon became too difficult and he retreated. In the meantime Shipton had started to descend with some of the porters. The weather now got worse again; it became very warm and the wind veered to the south and east. The effect on the snow was immediate – it became unstable and rotten instead of firm and crisp. The porters were only allowed to move one at a time, for if all moved together the whole slope could easily avalanche. But at last, in very dangerous conditions, they all reached Camp III safely.

Avalanche on the North Col

On 6 June a full gale from the north was raging, and Shipton and Wyn Harris examined the North Col slopes yet again. They moved very quickly and the first 500 feet were in good condition. Continuing along the traverse once more, they reached a large crevasse where they roped up. Then, on a slope of only moderate steepness, there was a sudden crack and the whole surface of the slope on which Shipton was standing started to slide downwards. Wyn Harris just managed to jump away from the moving slope, rammed his ice axe into the snow and coiled his rope around it. The rope tightened, and Shipton was pulled slowly sideways away from the sliding snow. Although the whole of Wyn Harris's weight was on the ice axe, it was being slowly wrenched from the snow, when the avalanche hesitated and stopped on the lip of a 400ft ice cliff. Shipton was winded and immobile, so Wyn Harris climbed down to him and together they managed, very gingerly, to edge their way back to the line of steps by which they had ascended. After a rest they returned to Camp III. It had been a narrow escape, and it was decisive. Under prevailing conditions, the eastern slopes of the North Col were far too dangerous; so they prepared to leave.

The west side of the North Col. The Lho La on the Nepal-Tibet frontier ridge.

As transport would take some days to arrange, they considered it would be worthwhile to inspect once again the western slopes of the North Col. To do this they had to go up the main Rongbuk glacier which they did on 8 June. In the afternoon they found a glorious camp site – a lake in a side moraine with a green circle of grass containing a lark's nest and some flowers. In this oasis of fertility two eggs were hatched in the next few days. Around the corner was one of Spender's survey sites of the previous year.

Across the main Rongbuk glacier rose the enormous West Ridge of Everest, called 'Hazard's Folly' after the climber on the 1924 expedition who had been keen to attempt it. As a route, it had been turned down by the 1935 reconnaissance party as too difficult for porters on its steeper sections. The upper part was eventually climbed by an American party in 1963.

The morning of 10 June was fine, so parties set out for the Lho La on the Nepal-Tibet frontier ridge, hoping, *en route*, to be able to get a good view of the west side of the North Col. This possible alternative route began with an obvious and easy glacier, with an icefall and a partially filled-in *bergschrund*, above which rose an 800ft-high snow couloir which could be followed to the North Col itself. It looked encouraging, so Smythe and Wyn Harris made their way to the foot of the couloir; but then the clouds came down.

Next day Kempson and Gavin crossed the main Rongbuk glacier to the Lho La and, on the way, had another good look at the final 700 feet of the slopes leading to the west side of the North Col, which appeared to be perfectly feasible. From the Lho La they could see the Khumbu icefall in profile. The previous year, 1935, this had been seen and photographed face-on by both Bryant and Shipton from the Lingtren peaks.*

Meanwhile, Smythe and Wyn Harris had not tried to ascend the west slopes of the North Col as they considered that the avalanche risk was too great. Although, in general terms, snow conditions seemed more stable on the west side of the North Col, the technical difficulties were greater. Smythe's opinion was that, unless monsoon conditions precluded this approach, the east side of the the North Col was the better option.

Whilst the Lho La and the North Col were being examined, another party tried the North Peak (Changtse). However, having put a camp at 22,500ft, they were forced to turn back at 23,400ft because at that altitude snow became like unconsolidated powder with the maximum likelihood of avalanche.

Although Warren and Shipton and some of the others would have liked to make another attempt on Everest, possibly via the west side of the North Col, both Ruttledge and Smythe decided that enough was enough; so on 17 June the expedition left Everest and the Sherpas went home to Khumbu over the Nangpa La.

---

* These were among the photographs that I discovered in 1951 in the archives of the Royal Geographical Society. At about the same time, Kempson passed on to me a profile view of the Khumbu icefall which he had taken on the 1936 expedition.

On their way back to Darjeeling, Kempson, Wigram, Warren and Shipton left the main party on 1 July and crossed the Kongra La from Tibet into Sikkim. They followed a valley that ran from the foot of the north face of Kangchenjunga from the south shore of Gordamah Lake and put a camp at 18,500ft on the col between Kanchenjau and Gordamah Peak (22,200ft). Kempson and Shipton reached the summit of this peak at about 1.0pm, returning to Gordamah the same evening.

Rejoining the main party, they returned to Darjeeling after an expedition frustrated by appalling weather. However, a positive result was a report by Charles Warren containing some excellent basic medical observations on the effects of high altitude.

P WYN HARRIS

BIBLIOGRAPHY

H Ruttledge, 'The Mount Everest Expedition of 1936' in *Geographical Journal 88*, 491-523, 1936.

H Ruttledge, 'Mount Everest: the Sixth Expedition' in *Alpine Journal 48*, 221-233, 1936.

H Ruttledge, *Everest: The Unfinished Adventure*. Hodder & Stoughton, 1937.

E E Shipton, 'Ascent of Gordamah Peak, North Sikkim' in *Alpine Journal 49*, 103, 1937.

C B M Warren, 'The Medical and Physiological Aspects of the Mount Everest Expedition' in *Geographical Journal 90*, 126-147, 1937.

Chapter 13

ADVANCE AND RETREAT
The Fifth Attempt, 1938

'Only essential equipment and not much of that'

Appalling weather had turned the 1936 expedition into an expensive fiasco, which was the fault of neither the climbers nor the organisation. However, some progress had been made by Charles Warren who carried out a number of medical investigations, adding basic knowledge to the fledgling subject of high-altitude medicine. In addition, a good look had been taken at the west side of the North Col; and the icefall at the entrance to the Western Cwm on the south side of Everest had been inspected visually, though from a distance. Against this, the highest point reached had been only 23,000ft, and a large amount of expensive equipment had been abandoned on the North Col.

The cost of the 1936 expedition was around £10,000, with little to show for it. The comparative costs of successive expeditions can be seen from the following table:

Expedition	Cost
	£
1921	5,000
1922	10,000
1924	10,000+
1933	10,000+
1935	1,500
1936	10,000+
1938	2,360

It was now felt that a small party consisting only of experienced mountaineers would have as good a chance of reaching the summit as a larger, more cumbersome one. Not only would this cut the cost but, importantly, it would not disrupt the fragile local economy. It was decided that individual members of the expedition should make a contribution.

These principles had worked well on successful expeditions to Kamet in 1931 and to Nanda Devi in 1936. Both peaks were over 25,000ft. Nanda Devi, 25,645ft, in the Garhwal Himal, the highest peak in the British Empire, had been explored by

Shipton and Tilman in 1934 and its first ascent, in 1936, by an Anglo-American party, was an important milestone. Also, the small, exploratory parties pioneered by Longstaff in the 1920s and by Shipton and Tilman in the 1930s had provided excellent results with a modest financial outlay. The 1935 Everest reconnaissance party, too, had been both cheap and successful.

It was decided that the 1938 party should be led by either Shipton or Tilman; Longstaff, who contributed a considerable amount of money, was adamant about this. In the event, Tilman took over as leader. In 1937, with Shipton, J B Auden, a geologist, and Michael Spender (surveyor in the 1935 Everest expedition), Tilman had taken part in a very bold and successful exploration and mapping party in the Shaksgam region on the north side of the Karakoram watershed on the boundary of Chinese Turkestan.

In 1938 Tilman wished to include C S Houston, one of the Americans from the 1936 Nanda Devi party, but the Everest Committee vetoed that suggestion on the grounds that he was not a UK national. Tilman also wished to dispense with both a medical officer and the use of supplementary oxygen. Neither of these ideas was acceptable to the Everest Committee and, in the event, the amount of illness on the 1938 expedition amply justified the presence of a doctor. Charles Warren, the medical officer in 1935 and 1936, was also taken in 1938. As he commented to me later: he did not know whether he would be a saviour or a scapegoat.

Tilman chose a highly experienced party which included N E Odell who, as well as to going to 28,000ft on Everest in 1924, had climbed Nanda Devi with Tilman in 1936. As Tilman commented, Odell's age at 47 years seemed immaterial. Frank Smythe had been to the Himalaya five times, and Shipton had been every year since 1932. Peter Lloyd, a chemist with an excellent Alpine record, had been high on Nanda Devi in 1936. Peter Oliver had climbed Trisul in 1933, had been on Everest in 1936 and in the Garhwal in 1937. The talented young climber Jack Longland unfortunately could not go, as he had just taken up a new post. But this was a formidable group with good experience of high-altitude climbing.

The equipment for the party had been ordered by Shipton at the end of the 1936 expedition, just before he left, with Tilman, for the Karakoram in 1937. As Tilman commented wryly: 'The sole innovation in the matter of equipment was that we took only essentials and not too much of those.'

A stringent look was also taken at food, and a figure of 2lbs per man per day was considered adequate, with local food being eaten in preference to tinned food. The vital importance of sugar at great altitude was recognised and ½lb per man/day was catered for.

The question of oxygen equipment remained unresolved, for there was still no concrete evidence from field tests that its use had any advantage over acclimatisation.

In April 1937 Dr Charles Warren, Dr Raymond Greene of the 1933 expedition and Dr C G Douglas FRS, a well-known respiratory physiologist at Oxford, had discussed the whole problem. They concluded that supplementary oxygen should be used on the 'last lap' to the summit, ie approximately the last 1,000 feet, with reliance on acclimatisation to reach the final camp. It was also recognised that if the closed-circuit apparatus broke down, the result of suddenly going from the equivalent of 'sea-level' to great altitude, with resulting oxygen deprivation, in a few minutes could be disastrous. Such an event was less likely to happen with the open-circuit sets, where the climber was at the equivalent of a higher altitude in his lungs, so that any sudden oxygen loss would be less dangerous. Open-circuit sets were taken in 1938, based on the 'Greene' set from the 1933 expedition, which had never been used.

In addition to its use when climbing, oxygen could be used for medical purposes, particularly chest infections and in the treatment of frostbite. Greene had used it for this latter purpose during the 1933 expedition, and several years later a number of surgeons, myself included, used hyperbaric oxygen (oxygen at a high atmospheric pressure) on frostbite cases at sea-level. However, it seemed to be no more effective than the standard rapid re-warming therapy, and because of its potential dangers has now been discarded.

In July 1937 Charles Warren and Harold Wager (brother of Lawrence Wager who had climbed to 28,000ft on Everest in 1933) tested the closed-circuit oxygen apparatus in the European Alps – on the Matterhorn and the Wellenkuppe. They found no trouble from overheating, which had occurred when the apparatus was previously tested at sea-level on Box Hill in Surrey and on the Berkshire Downs. These sets were based on Siebe Gorman mine rescue equipment and the flow rate of oxygen was half a litre per minute.

In September 1937 Charles Warren wrote to Professor George Finch, then teaching at Imperial College London, asking for his assistance. He was very willing to give it despite the fact that he was superintending laboratories in both South Kensington and Brussels. Although Warren initially was much in favour of the closed-circuit apparatus, which he later used above the North Col in 1938, in the field it did not function as well as the open-circuit set which, by the end of the 1938 expedition, Warren preferred as being more practical.

The party assembled in Darjeeling and left Gangtok on 4 March. Following the Teesta river they climbed up through sub-tropical jungle infested with leeches, entering Tibet by the Kongra La. Here, as they crossed onto the Tibetan plateau, the scenery changed abruptly from tropical valley to undulating brown hills dotted with the black tents of yak herders stretching into the distance. The early mornings were cold and calm, but towards midday a cold wind blew up from the north-west until some hours after sunset. Great clouds of dust were swept across the plain, which made the afternoon marches extremely uncomfortable. The dust also caused more sore throats, coughs and colds than was usual. By the time the party arrived at Rongbuk, most team members were affected and three had influenza. The high incidence of illness on this expedition was attributed to their diet, which was plain but perfectly adequate. Tilman, in his own defence and with his tongue firmly in his cheek, commented that it was well known that coughs and colds were the result of overeating!

At Rongbuk they were joined by a group of Sherpas from Khumbu who, having crossed the Nangpa La, told them that its guardian spirit was in the form of a horse. This was unusual, as Sherpa legend has it that any fourfooted animal was bound to be struck dead on crossing the pass. Despite this, yaks and their herders crossed it regularly in both directions without incident.

Rongbuk and retreat to Kharta

The Abbot of Rongbuk was once again pleased to see them and entertained them to a large meal. To a query about overeating he replied that the greedy receive their punishment in this world, and sooner rather than later.

Base camp was established by 10 April, and as there were too many Sherpas, a number had to be sent back to Khumbu. Finally Camp I was occupied on 13 April and from then on the party was self-sufficient. Despite being a 'small' party by Everest standards, and despite Tilman's aim to keep things simple, they had 31 porters and an amazing amount of gear.

Although there was no wind on the East Rongbuk glacier, a cloud banner could be seen streaming from the summit, showing clearly that at 29,000ft the wind was ferocious. Night temperatures were around 46 degrees of frost and illness continued to dog the party, with Tilman developing laryngitis followed by influenza. The plan was for Shipton and Smythe, the two most experienced climbers, to have a look at the North Col and then to go down to the lush vegetation of the Kharta valley at 11,000ft, whilst the remainder established a camp on the North Col. The intention was that Shipton and Smythe should save their energy for a summit bid. An attempt would be made at the end of May or in the first few days of June.

By 26 April the health of the party was still poor, and all except Shipton had some minor complaint, cough, cold, sore throat, or influenza. The weather remained very cold indeed and got worse over the next few days, so it was decided that, as it was useless to try to recuperate at Rongbuk, which at 16,500ft was too high, dirty and dusty, the whole party should descend to Kharta, rather than just Smythe and Shipton. They left on 29 April, crossed the upper basin of the East Rongbuk and went over the Rapiu La at the foot of the North-East Ridge of Everest. On the far, eastern side was an easy glacier explored for the first time in 1921. Two days later they reached the first village and yak pasture of Kharta and here Tilman, whose 'flu was very bad, had to stay for 48 hours. The main party continued and camped on the south side of the Kharta Chu just above the gorge of the Arun river.

The camp in the Kharta valley was beautiful, with grass, rhododendrons, birdsong and the pale green shoots of birch just starting to show. However, even in this idyllic spot the wind rushed up the Arun gorge from Nepal bringing rain, clouds and, higher up, snow. The party remained here for six days. On 10 May, leaving Shipton and Smythe to go directly over the Lhakpa La to Camp III on the East Rongbuk glacier, the rest of the party took the long way round by the Doya La to Rongbuk. Their first stop was at a village in the Chongphu valley leading to the Doya La; the weather remained mild, whilst the vegetation was subtropical. Crossing the Doya La at 17,000ft in a snowstorm, they reached Chodzong, and on the Tibetan, north side of the pass the country immediately became bleak and uninviting again.

The North Col, east and west sides

Going up the East Rongbuk glacier once again, they found that winter had changed to spring, most of the snow had melted and there was a stream in the floor of the glacier trough. At Camp III there was enough food to last for five weeks, but next day clouds boiled up from the south, pouring over the Rapiu La into the basin of the East Rongbuk. Tilman's 'flu returned and Lloyd too developed a high fever. The temperature that night dropped to 30 degrees of frost – only a little warmer than a month previously.

Going up to the North Col next day, they found the climbing easy until 300 feet from the crest. Here a small avalanche occurred. After midday it became so hot that they had to clear surface powder to reach a depth of 3-4 feet of firm snow. Wooden stakes were hammered in to provide a handrail. Returning to camp, they found Shipton and Smythe who had come over the Rapiu La; unfortunately Shipton had developed a sore throat and cough.

That night it snowed heavily and avalanches could be heard roaring off Everest and the North Peak. Next morning it was very muggy, and the east slopes of the North Col became avalanche prone. Snow was again being blown over the crest of the col and being deposited on the upper few hundred feet on the east side, forming very dangerous and avalanche-prone windslab. As a result, the party discussed the possibility of ascending to the North Col from the west which, though steeper, would be less dangerous.

It was decided that Smythe and Shipton, with a number of porters, would leave Camp III and attempt this route to the North Col, and on 27 May they left in a sun

Everest 1938: routes on the east and west sides of the North Col temperature of 117°F . In the meantime, more loads were ferried to the North Col camp by the eastern route. Snow was knee deep as they went up the North Ridge and Warren, who was using the closed-circuit oxygen apparatus, found that it produced a feeling of suffocation. With Tenzing and Tilman leading, they reached 23,000ft, where the snow deepened. Then more snow fell. Realising that it was not going to be possible to put in a high camp, they descended and returned to Camp III. Attempts on the east side of the North Col were now abandoned.

The west side of the North Col

On 1 June the weather changed; a ferocious wind blew snow off the North Face and the whole party moved round to the west side of the North Col. On 3 June the wind died down and a camp on the North Face was occupied where the short glacier from the west side of the North Col joins the main Rongbuk glacier. It was so warm that in the afternoon they sat around on boulders in their shirt-sleeves until the sun disappeared at 5.0pm and the temperature suddenly dropped.

Leaving on 5 June at 9.30am they climbed easily on good snow up to and then through the icefall guarding the western slopes of the North Col, and put in a camp at 21,000ft. After a good night, Shipton, Smythe and Lloyd left before dawn, crossing a vast avalanche cone, a few days old, that had fallen from the North Col. The result was that the first 500 feet was now bare ice, the snow having been swept off. Cutting steps in this slowed them down considerably. By now the sun had appeared over the crest of the col and was heating up the snow, which rapidly acquired the consistency of porridge. Had it not been for the haze that filtered the sun's heat, the slopes would have avalanched again and it was with great relief that the crest of the col was reached at 11am. Here they re-pitched the tents at Camp IV, abandoned on 30 May, and cleared out the spindrift. Once again they could start on the upper slopes of Everest.

6 June started fine and 15 porters, carrying loads of up to 30lbs each, left to establish two high camps. The snow on the North Ridge required a good kick to make a step, but higher up the snow was loose and soft. Lloyd used the open-circuit apparatus for this ascent. As the set did not have a mask, an open tube was used to feed oxygen into the mouth and this had to be bitten when breathing out and released when breathing in. On stopping, oxygen accumulated in a bag mounted above the cylinders. The problem was that the rubber mouthpiece was so stiff that after only a few minutes Lloyd's jaw became stiff, but he remedied this by using the softer rubber of the connecting tube instead. As they trudged up the snow, he found that he was moving more easily and comfortably, but no faster, than Smythe who was not using supplementary oxygen. The main difference between them was that, at the end of the day, after climbing from 22,400ft to 25,700ft, Lloyd still felt comparatively fresh.

This was the first time ever that a direct comparison had been made, under the same conditions and at the same altitude, between a climber using supplementary oxygen at two litres per minute (Lloyd) and a climber relying on acclimatisation alone (Smythe). Even at the low flow rate of only two litres/minute and at a comparatively 'low' altitude, supplementary oxygen had seemed to provide Lloyd with some benefit. It was obvious that the weight of the set prohibited faster movement, yet, despite its weight, Lloyd felt less fatigued. Whenever he stopped, he turned off the apparatus, both to economise and to test the effect of suddenly removing the stimulus of oxygen. While at rest, and therefore requiring less oxygen, Lloyd experienced no adverse effect, but when the cylinder began running out while he was climbing, and he needed more oxygen than was available in order to keep moving, not surprisingly he felt dreadful. The porters, led by Shipton, were carrying loads similar in weight to the oxygen sets, and without the help of supplementary oxygen they struggled to keep up.

It was a classic 'experiment'. Lloyd, using two litres per minute of supplementary oxygen, was only climbing as fast as Smythe who was not using supplementary oxygen and relying on acclimatisation alone. The use of two litres/minute of oxygen was thus cancelled out by the weight of the set. The porters, carrying loads and not using supplementary oxygen, struggled and went even more slowly. This went a long way towards clinching the argument for Pugh and myself in 1951 – that extra flow rates, in the event four litres per minute, *must* be used on the upper slopes of Everest to improve performance and to give a reasonable chance of reaching the summit and returning in daylight.

A storm blew up in the afternoon, sapping the resolution of all the porters except for Tenzing, but by 4.0pm Camp V at 25,700ft was established. Unfortunately a load had been abandoned containing a necessary pyramid tent, and later in the afternoon Tenzing and Pasang, two of the strongest Sherpas, descended and brought it up – an astonishing example of strength and vitality. Leaving Shipton and Smythe in residence, Tilman and Lloyd descended to the North Col camp.

To 27,400ft, with and without supplementary oxygen

Next day, 7 June, a storm prevented any movement, but the 8th was better, and despite the upper part of the mountain being white with snow, Smythe and Shipton started at 8.0am. On the ridge above the camp the snow was firm, consolidated and safer than below the camp, but about 500 feet higher it became powdery and unconsolidated. Progress was slow but the porters needed no driving, though Pasang was ill and Ongdi exhausted. Finally, however, Camp VI was placed at 27,200ft on a gentle slope below the yellow band, and the porters descended.

The weather was fine and the setting sun glowed red and gold on the monsoon clouds far below. It was a big effort to cook supper and drink cocoa and sugar, and Smythe and Shipton consumed far too little food and drink to counter the day's exertion. At 3.50am next day they started to cook, and left the tent before the sun had reached it. Immediately, they lost all feeling in their hands and feet and returned to the tent to wait until the sun had warmed up the day a little. Then, slowly, they climbed over steepening, outward-sloping rock, flogging their way through waist-deep deposits of loose, powdery snow, with an hour's climbing yielding less than 100 feet in height. As the rocks steepened, the danger from possible snow slides increased. As on previous expeditions, it was as if they were edging their way along the tiles of a snow-covered roof, with a 5,000ft drop below. It was not technically difficult, but extremely dangerous, with no good holds or belays. If the snow had consolidated they might have had a chance, but it had not done so, and despite the fact that they were both far fitter than the climbers had been in 1933, they had to give up. As Shipton wrote in the chapter he contributed to Tilman's book of the expedition:

> It is difficult to give the layman much idea of the actual physical difficulties of the last 2000 ft. of Everest. The Alpine mountaineer can visualize them when he is told that the slabs which we are trying to climb are very similar to those on the Tiefenmatten face of the Matterhorn, and he will know that though these slabs are easy enough when clear of ice and snow they can be desperately difficult when covered in deep powder snow. He should also remember that [without adequate supplementary oxygen] a climber on the upper part of Everest is like a sick man climbing in a dream.

Lower down, at Camp IV on the North Col, Tilman and Lloyd were as inactive on 7 June as Shipton and Smythe had been higher up. However, Lloyd wanted to test the closed-circuit oxygen set so, in the company of a Sherpa, he set out up the North Ridge, intending to go as far as the top of the snow slope, to compare and contrast the open-circuit and closed-circuit sets. It soon became evident that something was wrong with the closed-circuit set. While everything appeared to be working perfectly and the valves were opening and closing properly, inside the mask the feeling of suffocation was intolerable. Lloyd was climbing far more slowly than the Sherpa, who was scornful of the performance of the 'oxy', as he called it, the term 'English air' being no longer used. After half-an-hour they had to return to camp.

The following day, the 8th, was spent escorting Sherpas down the west side of the North Col, and on the next, the 9th, Tilman and Lloyd went up to Camp V. It was decided that, since the closed-circuit set had proved so unsatisfactory, Lloyd should use the open-circuit set and that Tilman should not use any supplementary oxygen at all. Six Sherpas carried their kit and extra oxygen bottles, and before long they met another group of Sherpas, on their way down, who had carried to Camp VI for Shipton and Smythe.

Soon they reached the top of the snow slope and started up the rocks leading to Camp V. Lloyd got into camp at 3.0pm and started making tea for Shipton and Smythe, who soon appeared. After telling of their failure to reach the North-East Ridge, Smythe and Shipton suggested that an attempt should be made on the steeper rocks above Camp VI, as they were relatively free from snow, being too steep for it to settle. After tea they descended while Tilman and Lloyd settled in for the night during which the temperature fell to minus 1°F. Starting next day at 8.0am, Lloyd used the open-circuit oxygen set. He led through deepening snow yet, despite the extra work, he was actually going faster than the others and arrived at Camp VI (27,200ft) at 12.30pm, feeling fairly fresh, thirty minutes before Tilman or any of the porters.

As expected, the higher Lloyd got, the greater the benefit that he received from the supplementary oxygen. Using a flow rate of only two litres per minute, he had ascended a little faster and with less effort than Tilman who was relying on acclimatisation alone. This was another 'experiment' which indicated that under exactly the same climatic conditions, supplementary oxygen, even at this relatively low flow rate, was able to increase climbing rate; and if the flow rate were improved, an even faster rate of ascent might be possible.

The site of the camp was about 250 yards east of the site chosen for Camp VI in 1933, and being just under a steep rock wall was free from snow. It was magnificently situated on a gently inclined scree slope at the top of the North-East Ridge. The scree was cemented together with ice, showing that sometimes the snow *did* melt and then refreeze. The tent had been collapsed by Smythe and Shipton and weighted down with stones, and it was soon erected again. The summit was clear of cloud and the final pyramid could be seen. But the snow-covered rocks of Norton's traverse looked very steep. The ridge, their next day's objective, was liberally decorated with snow and looked formidable.

After sending the Sherpas down, they heated up the best part of a pint of hot pemmican soup. Tilman remarked that this represented about half their total food intake for the day but was equivalent, in fact, to only a quarter, which was less than the amount required by men doing hard physical work.

Next morning, the 11th, they started early with a mug of tea containing a quarter of a pound of sugar – again not nearly enough food or fluid for a hard day's work. By 8.0am they thought it was warm enough to start but, like Shipton and Smythe, they returned to their tents because of the danger of frostbite. Finally, after a second cup of tea, they left at 10am. The cold was now tolerable. They made for an obvious broad snow gully running up to the right of the rocks and were looking for a belt of firm, compacted snow which would give an easy line of ascent. But such a line did not exist. Again and again they sank thigh-deep in the new snow and were forced back to the rocks. These offered two possible alternatives – a chimney, or a slanting traverse leading to a series of sloping ledges. But since holds on the outward-dipping strata of these ledges were absent or sloping, and covered with ice, it was all balance climbing on ice-covered rock and very dangerous. They found it a humiliating experience to start on a pitch that looked easy, only to be unable to make any head-way. Their failure was complete, so they returned to Camp VI and, in the afternoon, continued down to Camp V and the North Col.

Odell and Oliver, with seven porters, were at the col, for Warren had descended with the Sherpa Ongdi who had pneumonia. Ongdi had suffered a similar condition on Everest in 1933, and it is likely that he was suffering from high-altitude pulmon-ary oedema, for he recovered quickly at lower levels. In addition, Pasang, who had carried to Camp VI, developed a stroke* on the North Col which affected his speech and the right side of his body. It was the second case recorded at high altitude on Everest, the first having been in 1924. Pasang was part carried and part dragged down the east side of the North Col, by Angtharkay and Kusang whose immediate attitude was that the mountain gods had claimed a sacrificial victim and that he should be left to die. They were quickly disabused of that idea. Later, Pasang was admitted to the Victoria Hospital at Darjeeling on 8 July, by which time his speech had returned to normal. There was some slight facial weakness and his right arm was practically useless; however, he could walk, with some difficulty but without aid. He was discharged on 4 August. The rest of the party reached Rongbuk on 14 June but had to wait until the 20th for yaks to accompany them and transport their baggage back to Darjeeling.

Some members of the party wished to stay until the autumn but only Shipton and Tilman could afford to do so. Conditions could only worsen. The days would be shorter and the wind and cold would increase. The sun's warmth had been so vital at the top camp that they thought the intense cold high on Everest would probably stop any ascent made with their present clothing and equipment.

Exploration of the Nyonno Ri range

The Nyonno Ri range, which forms the eastern bank of the Tibetan part of the

---

* Stroke is now recognised as being the result of a combination, normally found at altitude, of dehydration and an increase in the number of red blood cells. This causes the blood to become very thick, and spasm or thrombosis can occur.

Arun river, is one of the few ranges in Central Asia that runs north-south. The majority run east-west. In 1913 Captain J B L Noel, during his attempt to reach Everest from the east, skirted the southern tip of the Nyonno Ri range on his way from the Chorten Nyima La over the Sikkim Himalaya to Tashirak and Qodo. During the 1921 reconnaissance, the five main peaks of the range were fixed by the survey party, but no exploration was carried out. In 1922 Mallory, Somervell, Finch and Wakefield attempted to climb Sangkar Ri, the most northerly peak of the range, from two directions; whilst in 1933 Wager and Shipton climbed a small peak on its eastern flank and Wager carried out geological work.

In planning the 1935 reconnaissance expedition, a visit to the range formed part of the programme and Tilman, Kempson and Warren attempted the highest peak, Nyonno Ri (22,142ft), but without success. Shipton and Wigram crossed a pass and entered an isolated basin of pastureland on its western side, and returned to Sar by a pass between Nyonno Ri and Ama Drime to the south. Also, Michael Spender carried out some survey work.

In 1938 Shipton, with some Sherpas, spent a short time in the area. Initially the weather was bad and they were unable to fix their position in the northern valleys. Later, however, on the western side, it improved and they were able to use the Watts theodolite extensively. The whole range is of granite, each valley containing a deep lake. Crossing by the same pass as the one he had crossed with Wigram in 1935, Shipton and the Sherpas camped by a lake on the eastern side, five miles from the Nye La, before returning to Sar.

BIBLIOGRAPHY

G I Finch, 'Oxygen and Mount Everest' in *Alpine Journal 51*, 89-90, 1939.

P Lloyd, 'Oxygen on Mt Everest 1938' in *Alpine Journal 51*, 85-89, 1939.

N E Odell, P Lloyd, 'The Chorten Nyima La from the Tibetan side' in *Himalayan Journal 12*, 107-116, 1940.

H W Tilman, 'Mount Everest 1938' in *Alpine Journal 51*, 3-17, 1939.

H W Tilman, 'Mount Everest 1938' in *Himalayan Journal 11*, 1-14, 1939.

H W Tilman, *Mount Everest 1938*, Cambridge University Press, 1948

H W Tilman, 'The Mount Everest Expedition of 1938' in *Geographical Journal 92*, 481-498, 1938.

C B M Warren, 'Alveolar Air on Mount Everest' in *Journal of Physiology 96*, 34-35, 1939.

Chapter 14

THE SECOND WORLD WAR
Interlude, 1939-1947

Introduction

Although the Second World War prevented any further attempts on Everest, some of the techniques of mountain warfare, developed during the war, were subsequently applied to the successful assault on Everest in 1953.

At the start of the war Germany had at least twelve mountain divisions. The British had none, their only previous experience of mountain warfare having been on the north-west frontier of India. Between 1939 and 1940, when the Russians invaded Finland, a unit was formed, the 1st Scots Guards Ski Battalion, consisting of a number of mountaineers and skiers. This battalion first went into action in Norway after the German invasion, when British county battalions, which were only able to advance along the roads in the valleys, were outflanked and decimated by the enemy.

One British lowland division, the 52nd, was therefore earmarked for training in the Scottish Highlands for service as mountain troops, and a training school was set up at Lochailort on the west coast of Scotland. Among the instructors were F Spencer Chapman, who had made the first ascent of Chomolhari in 1936, J M L Gavin, a member of the 1936 Everest expedition, and Ashley Greenwood. All these mount-aineers later achieved distinguished war records. Eventually the 52nd Division went into action, but owing to the vagaries of war it first saw active service at or below sea-level, clearing the estuary of the River Scheldt following the capture of Antwerp later in the war.

Compared with the ample training provided for desert and jungle warfare, training for mountain warfare was virtually non-existent before 1942, when Major-General R L Laycock, commanding the Special Service Brigade, asked F S Smythe, Britain's most experienced mountaineer, to open a training school for commandos, in order to teach them the necessary rock-climbing skills to mount raiding parties on the European coastline. Laycock's dictum was that 'commandos must do anything and go anywhere'. The school was set up in the Cairngorms of Scotland, with John Hunt, then a regular army officer, as Chief Instructor and David Cox, an Oxford academic and an outstanding rock-climber, also involved. In May 1943 the school moved to North Wales and some groups were trained on the Cornish cliffs for assault landings on D-Day.

In July 1943 F S Smythe accompanied a military mission to Canada and the USA. Its objectives were to order American and Canadian equipment and to select a training area for the Lovat Scouts – the only other unit to be trained specifically for mountain warfare. Jasper in Alberta was chosen as the most suitable venue and 86 instructors from the UK, USA and Canada were posted there and a training programme completed. This bore fruit in the Italian campaign in the Apennines, proving beyond doubt the superiority of mountain troops over those trained only in flat country.

Other centres were set up, including a recreation centre in Kashmir, but the most important, from the point of view of its influence on post-war mountaineering, was the ski and mountain warfare centre at the Cedars of Lebanon in the Middle East.

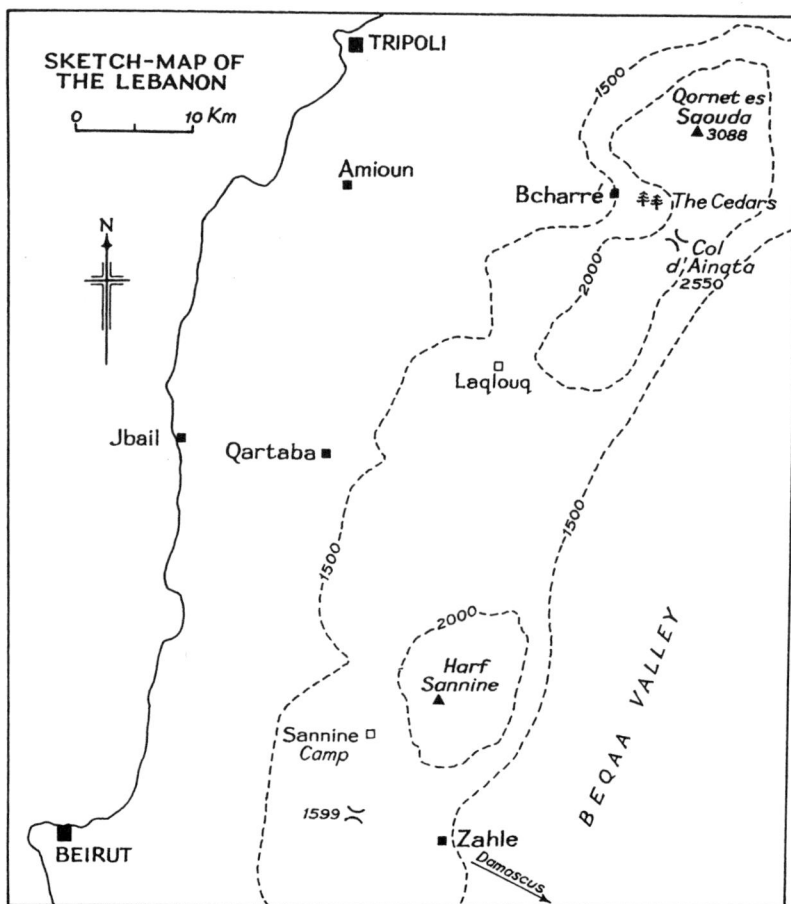

1943-1945 The Lebanon: site of the Ski and Mountain Warfare School

Ski and mountain warfare school, Cedars of Lebanon, 1943-1945

The ski and mountain warfare school was the brain-child of W J Riddell, a former Olympic downhill skier and Political Officer in the Middle East during the early part of the war. It was his imagination and persistence that persuaded the military authorities in Cairo that such a centre was needed, despite the current emphasis on training for desert warfare. However, Churchill anticipated that, after the projected invasion of Europe, mountains of South Germany would become a theatre of war for which mountain troops might well be needed.

The limestone mountains of Lebanon lie on the west side of the Beqaa valley, 30km from the Mediterranean. A series of deep *wadis,* or dry ravines, run up from the sea to the range, and the rock-climbing centre was sited on a friendly cliff at Laqlouq in the north, some 70kms from the highest point, Qornet es Souda, at 3,088m. Fifty kilometres to the south, in the Sannine area, was the site of a snow training centre at 1750m, just below Harf Sannine (2,628m).

Although in summer it was possible to ski in the morning and, two hours later, swim in the Mediterranean, in winter a vast amount of snow fell, sometimes as much as four feet in 24 hours. Storms could be ferocious, and one February at Sannine a sergeant instructor left his hut at 7.0pm to go to another hut only half a minute away, got lost and was not found until 48 hours later, with incipient hypothermia, but still alive. The centre was opened in December 1941, and all equipment had to be manufactured locally: skis, ski-sticks, bindings, windproof clothing and much else. Fortunately, the main sports shops in Beirut stocked Swiss and Scandinavian cross-country skis, and these were used as models for Lebanese craftsmen to copy. The best wood for skis came from the Turkish border north of Aleppo, and ski wax had to be improvised from a brew of Stockholm tar, beeswax, resin, paraffin, and graphite from melted down gramophone records!

The commander of the mountain warfare school was Col H M Head, with W J Riddell as Chief Instructor. John Carryer, a New Zealander, was 'Chief Instructor, Snow'. In mid-November 1943 David Cox was transferred to Sannine as 'Chief Instructor, Rock'. The centre was a great success and had many functions. Ostensibly it was a leave centre, but it trained over 20,000 soldiers to climb and ski; it also trained members of the Special Operations Executive in survival techniques before they entered southern Europe.

To find suitable instructors, W J Riddell combed the army lists and found, amongst others, a contemporary of his at Harrow, Dr L G C E Pugh. They had started school on the same day and had both skied in the Olympic team before the war. Knowing of Pugh's interest in the behaviour of the human body in extreme climatic conditions, Riddell arranged for him to be transferred from Tehran to the centre as a human exercise physiologist – one of the very few such experts in the armed forces. His job was to choose and train an elite group of men who possessed the special qualities necessary for mountain warfare. The Cedars, a more or less private mountain range, provided a vast natural training ground.

Although Pugh had to work without medical or scientific equipment, his idiosyncratic knowledge and experience as a clinician, skier and mountaineer made him an ideal person for the task. The library at the American University in Beirut provided him with useful specialist journals, in particular those covering work at the Fatigue Laboratory at Harvard run by D B Dill.

To establish what was the best type of mental and physical make-up for mountain troops, Pugh took as models the characteristics of the various instructors. He also meticulously investigated all aspects of mountain warfare, including methods of training, physical fitness, diet, safety measures, and the best ski-bindings, lightweight tents, stoves and cooking utensils. This was the first time that a comprehensive investigation of this type had been carried out and it proved of great importance in providing guidelines to the choice of individuals for specific tasks and in the understanding of cold and altitude. Later, Pugh's wartime researches were to prove invaluable on Everest.

Pugh trawled the Middle East for suitable candidates, and these were sent to him from every unit, including the Long Range Desert Group, now the Special Air Service. Only about a third of those sent proved suitable for training. Pugh himself had been chosen for the 18 kilometre cross-country event in the 1936 Winter Olympics, but owing to illness he had been unable to take part. However, during the constant training at the Cedars, he became accustomed to climbing an average of some 4,000ft a day on skins, and this helped to make him a formidable performer. For example, he organised a special unit which could be self-sufficient for up to 6-8 days, covering 20 miles a day, each man carrying military and other equipment weighing up to 100lbs. Throughout this period Pugh wrote many papers for the War Office, and after being recalled to London, he helped to produce a series of army training manuals on mountain warfare. It was these scientific investigations by Pugh that formed the basic framework for his subsequent work at the Medical Research Council in 1951-52, which, in turn, led to the first successful ascent of Everest in 1953.

The war also brought a change in the way that clinical medicine and surgery were carried out. Before the war many diagnoses and treatments had evolved on a purely anecdotal basis, rather than from the much more precise scientific methods which afterwards became the norm. Because the transfer of oxygen in the body involves mainly the heart, lungs and blood vessels, where measurement is relatively easy, scientific experiments in survival at altitude could be conducted in the field and not just in the laboratory. This was another area of research, pioneered by Pugh in the Lebanon, which he later applied to the conquest of Everest.

'Operation Everest' at Pensacola Naval Air Base, Florida

An important contribution to the post-war exploration and ascent of Everest came from the United States and, in particular, from the American physician Dr C S Houston who had made many first ascents in Alaska. He had also been a member of the successful Anglo-American expedition to Nanda Devi in 1936, during which his friend T Graham Brown developed symptoms of what was later recognised as high-altitude cerebral oedema, with personality change. This traumatic event may have been a factor in prompting Houston's initial interest in high-altitude medicine.

Prior to that expedition, Houston had met Ross McFarland, a pioneer in the then new science of aviation medicine, and had been taken to the equivalent of 28,000ft in a small decompression chamber. Immediately he foresaw its potential as a research tool. At the outbreak of the war, he joined the Naval Air Force, obtained his 'Wings' and became a Flight Surgeon. His altitude experience was then put to good use in a job at Pensacola Naval Air Base in Florida, training air crew in high-altitude flying.

In 1945 Houston began to wonder whether an experiment could be conducted in a decompression chamber to demonstrate that a man could reach the altitude equivalent of the summit of Everest without the help of supplementary oxygen. Bearing in mind that a height of 28,000ft had already been reached on Everest by eight climbers, it should be possible, he believed, and not too dangerous, to surmount 'the last thousand feet' under the controlled conditions of a chamber experiment. It so happened that there was a decompression chamber at the air base, and after much lobbying, he and Richard Riley, a distinguished respiratory physiologist and physician, obtained permission in April 1946 to start this work. He recruited two workers, Frank Consolazio and George Selden, from the well-known and highly respected Harvard Fatigue Laboratory. With Walter Jervis, a physician, and Richard Riley, they would carry out the necessary biochemical analyses. The same laboratory had previously provided help in the form of scientific articles for Pugh's work in the Lebanon.

Because so little was known about man at extreme altitude, stringent safety precautions were taken in carrying out the research programme. In particular, each of the four volunteers was medically checked each day when in the chamber. The four were carefully chosen from ten applicants, one being rejected because his arteries were too small to be easily entered by the large bore steel arterial needles then available, for obtaining arterial blood to measure oxygen content.

Fourteen technicians operated the chamber, each standing four-hour watches around the clock, and, as an additional safeguard, one of the operating crew, breathing oxygen, stood two-hour watches inside the chamber over night, whilst a student Flight Surgeon did the same outside the chamber. The experiment was visited by and discussed with John Fulton, Professor of Physiology, and Leslie Nims, both of

Yale, and Bruce Dill of the Harvard Fatigue Laboratory and a member of the high-altitude expedition to Chile in 1935.

For three days the chamber was kept at the equivalent of sea-level for base-line studies. One problem was condensation within the chamber, with water dripping from the roof and walls. This was partially corrected by air-conditioning and a drying agent. Each evening the 'altitude' was raised in the hope that a night's sleep would make the next day's testing less arduous – a fallacy, for we now know that periodic respiration (ie disordered breathing) whilst sleeping at altitude can result from extreme cerebral oxygen lack.

By 27 July the subjects had reached the equivalent of 21,000ft and had become very lethargic. To demonstrate the effects of acclimatisation, two of them bicycled on a stationary bicycle at this height without ill effect. By contrast, a third was taken from sea-level to 22,000ft, breathing oxygen. He then rode on the bicycle ergometer at this height *without* supplementary oxygen and lost consciousness in just over a minute, still denying the need for oxygen, as victims have no insight into their condition. On the night of 29 July the chamber was 'lowered' to 21,000ft for better sleep and on 30 July the 'dash for the summit' at 29,000ft was made.

The height of the chamber was first raised to 25,500ft and, an hour later, to 26,500ft. At 26,700ft one of the volunteers reached his ceiling and was given supplementary oxygen. Another gave up at 27,600ft. At a height of 28,000ft the remaining two volunteers were both mentally alert but not capable of strenuous exercise. At the 'top of Everest', the two remained for 21 minutes without exercising. It was to be another 32 years, in 1978, before the summit would be reached on the ground, by Habeler and Messner, without the use of supplementary oxygen.

At this stage, in 1946, the experimenters wondered if, when breathing oxygen, this degree of acclimatisation could increase man's tolerance to even greater heights. To test this theory, the subjects were fitted with standard oxygen masks, and decompressed further to the equivalent of 50,225ft, where both were alert but dizzy. Next, the height at which they could do physical work using supplementary oxygen was determined. At 46,000ft they felt that they could do light work indefinitely, at 47,000ft for a few hours and at 48,500ft for 30 minutes. On 1st August the subjects 'descended' to sea-level, 34 days and 8 hours after entering the chamber, and they appeared to suffer no adverse after-effects.

This experiment was a landmark and a considerable step forward into the unknown world of extreme altitude. It showed that man *could* survive, by acclimatisation alone, at an altitude equivalent to the summit of Everest. However, it remained uncertain whether this would still be possible with all the added climatic and other problems that climbers would face in a real-life situation.

Charles Houston explained the thinking behind Operation Everest in a Special Article in the US Naval Medical Bulletin for December 1946:

If man is suddenly exposed to severe oxygen lack, such as may occur at high altitudes, in asphyxia, or in numerous types of disease or injury of the pulmonary system, symptoms appear rapidly. Impairment of cerebral function, muscular incoordination, cardiovascular changes, and loss of consciousness are the most prominent of these. If, however, the oxygen deprivation develops gradually over a period of weeks or months, certain physiological changes, known as acclimatization, protect the organism from anoxia. The effectiveness of acclimatization is most dramatically demonstrated by the mountaineer who can live and work as high as 28,000 feet, an altitude which produces unconsciousness in less than 5 minutes in unacclimatized man. Clinical conditions in which anoxia may develop slowly enough to give rise to acclimatization are represented by chronic pulmonary fibrosis, emphysema, and cardiac decompensation. It may be seen that adaptation to anoxia is important to mountaineers and also clinically, and furthermore that some of the functional changes involved may be of service to the aviator.

1945-47 Proposed Alpine Club expedition to Mount Everest

After the Second World War, on 22 October 1945, the Alpine Club considered a letter from Eric Shipton outlining proposals for an Everest expedition from Tibet in 1947. An informal letter was sent to Lord Wavell, the Viceroy of India, who replied that it was unlikely that the Tibetan authorities would accede to such a request. The Royal Geographical Society was also consulted, to establish whether they would, as in the past, co-operate in such a venture.

Later, however, a second letter from the Viceroy made it clear that there was no possibility of sending an expedition to Tibet, and the project was abandoned.

Expedition to the north side of Everest by Earl Denman and Tenzing, 1947

Earl Denman was a Canadian living in Johannesburg who wanted to climb Everest – alone. In 1947 he went to Darjeeling and there met Karma Paul, the interpreter and middle-man for many British expeditions in the 1930s, who put him in touch with two Sherpas, Tenzing Norgay and Ang Dawa. Denman had very little equipment or money and had signed a paper promising not to approach the Tibetan border, but Tenzing, who spoke Tibetan and had been to 27,000ft on Everest in 1938, found the pull of Everest so strong that he agreed to accompany Denman in spite of the obvious difficulties involved.

Secrecy was essential so, leaving Darjeeling on 22 March, they met at a prearranged point outside the town. They crossed the Sikkim-Tibet border by a little-used pass and immediately turned west, avoiding all the larger Tibetan villages. Eventually they were stopped by a Tibetan patrol, but avoided arrest by turning back and making a long detour. Passing through Sar and Tranak, they arrived at Rongbuk during the first week in April.

Their equipment was minimal, their clothes scarcely windproof, and they were perpetually cold; but they ventured up the East Rongbuk glacier as far as the foot of the North Col. After a brief sortie up the lower slopes, they returned exhausted and defeated, but Denman, although extremely determined, was no fanatic. To continue would have been impossible, for their clothes were in rags and their boots so worn that Denman had to walk barefoot. Thus they fled across Tibet, arriving in Darjeeling on 28 April. The whole expedition had taken five weeks and cost £250.

The next year, 1948, Denman was back in Darjeeling with better equipment, but still without permission. Tenzing, who had been criticised for their illegal trip in 1947, refused to go with him again, so Denman, unable to find anyone else, finally gave up his attempt, abandoned his equipment and returned to South Africa.

When Tenzing stood on the summit of Everest on 29 May 1953, he wore the woollen balaclava given to him by Denman in 1947.

BIBLIOGRAPHY

L S Amery, 'Mountaineering as Training for War' in *Royal Engineers Journal 45*, 52-56, 1931.

A D M Cox, 'The Lebanon. Some Memories of Mountain Warfare Training in World War II' in *Alpine Journal 97*, 191-197, 1992/93.

E Denman, *Alone to Everest*. Collins, 1954.

C S Houston, 'Operation Everest' in *US Naval Medical Bulletin 46*, 1783-1792, 1946.

C S Houston, A Cymerman, J R Sutton, 'Operation Everest (O.E.I.) 1946' in *Operation Everest II. 1985*. US Army Research Institute of Environmental Medicine. Natick, Massachusetts, USA, 100-166, 1991.

T A H Peacocke, 'Training in the Canadian Rockies' in *Alpine Journal 55*, 32-45, 1945/46.

A D B Side, 'Mountaineering with the Army in the Middle East' in *Alpine Journal 57*, 66-75, 1949/50.

F S Smythe, 'Some Experiences in Mountain Warfare Training' in *Alpine Journal 55*, 233-240 and 345-351, 1945/46.

Unattributed note, 'A Projected Mount Everest Expedition' in *Alpine Journal 55*, 314-315, 1945/1946.

M P Ward, 'Griffith Pugh: An Eightieth Birthday Tribute' in *Alpine Journal 95*, 188-190, 1990/91.

M P Ward, W J Riddell, obituary of Lewis Griffith Cresswell Evans Pugh in *Alpine Journal 100*, 326-329, 1995.

M P Ward, J S Milledge, 'Griffith Pugh – Pioneer Everest Physiologist' in *High Altitude Medicine and Biology Vol 3, Number 1*, 77-87, 2002.

Chapter 15

LONDON TRIUMPH AND FIRST STEPS IN NEPAL
1949-1951

Immediately after the Second World War all official attempts to visit Everest foundered on the implacable opposition to foreigners evinced by both the Tibetan and the Nepalese governments. All the pre-war Everest expeditions had been restricted to the north, Tibetan, side of the mountain, since an approach through Nepal was forbidden at that time. However, in 1949 the Rana family, hereditary Prime Ministers of Nepal, had been overthrown in a bloodless revolution by King Tribhuvan Shah of the rival Shah dynasty, and replaced by a constitutional monarchy. This led to the gradual opening up of Nepal and, with it, access to the southern side of Everest. When, in 1950, Tibet closed her borders, all access to Everest would have been impossible had it not been for the opening up of Nepal a few months earlier.

Topographical knowledge of Nepal up to 1949
Before 1949 topographical information about the mountains of Nepal was almost non-existent and relied largely upon reports by the Pundits compiled at the end of the 19th century. However, between 1924 and 1927 native surveyors of the Nepal detachment of the Survey of India were allowed to survey 55,000 square miles of the country and produced a quarter-inch map which extended as far as Dingboche, 12 miles from Everest. Unfortunately, the mountain areas were the least accurately surveyed, often depicting only spot heights. Although the maps showed fair detail up to glacier level, it was not until 1929 that representation of the glaciated regions of the Himalaya was considered necessary in order to meet the requirements of glaciology. However, this did not apply to the Nepal sheets, as the Survey there had ended in 1927.

An early visitor to Solu Khumbu was Major Lal Dhwoj, a retired Nepalese army officer who, in 1930, made an extensive botanical survey. His work was continued in 1933 by another Nepali, K N Sharma. In addition, an Indian, M L Banerji, made five visits to east Nepal between 1948 and 1955, but his routes are uncertain.

In 1930 the Survey of India published a quarter-inch map covering both the Tibetan and Nepalese sides of Everest and its immediate region. The detail was, however, very poor and of little use to mountaineers. The map showed the main topographical features, the main peaks and the exploratory routes of the 1921, 1922 and 1924 expeditions on the Tibetan side of the mountain. On the southern,

Nepalese, side the map showed only the marked tracks in the valleys which converged on Namche Bazar, the main village of Khumbu. These included the track up the Bhote Kosi valley to the Nangpa La (Pangu La). There was also a marked track leading up the Dudh Kosi valley to its head at the Nup La, a pass between the Ngozumpa and the West Rongbuk glaciers. The Nup La was first visited from the Tibetan side by G H Bullock in 1921, and crossed by Hillary and Lowe in 1952. Finally, there was a marked path along the Imja Khola on the south side of the Lhotse-Nuptse ridge. However, no detail of Everest itself was included, nor of the Western Cwm, nor the Khumbu or other glaciers. The map was adequate only as an approach map to Everest, but for glaciologists or mountaineers it was inadequate. The Milne-Hinkes map, published by the Royal Geographical Society in 1952, was the first to provide these details.

H W Tilman, Peter Lloyd, Oleg Polunin, a well-known botanist, and J S Scott, a geologist, visited central Nepal in 1949. Originally this group had asked to go to the south side of Everest but their request had been refused and they went instead to the Langtang Himal. Theirs was the first party of Westerners to carry out any mountain exploration in the Nepal Himalaya.

Anglo-American Trekking Party to Solu Khumbu, 1950

The first party of Westerners to visit the Nepalese side of Everest was an Anglo-American trekking group which included several mountaineers. In May 1950 Charles S Houston, who had left the US Air Force after his work on Operation Everest I in 1946, had been asked by the American journalist Lowell Thomas to accompany him on a second visit to Lhasa. Thomas had visited Tibet the previous year to interview Heinrich Harrer, the Austrian mountaineer who had been living in Lhasa for six years after escaping from an allied prisoner-of-war camp in northern India. As Thomas had broken a leg on the journey he felt that a doctor should accompany the party. Houston was also asked to convey the new medication, cortisone, to Reginald Fox, a clandestine wireless operator in northern Tibet, who had developed severe rheumatoid arthritis. Unfortunately, word came that the Chinese had occupied Lhasa and the visit had to be cancelled.

Meanwhile, Charles Houston's father Oscar Houston, a New York lawyer, who had been with his son on the first ascent of Mount Foraker in Alaska, had obtained permission to visit the Nepalese side of Everest. He asked his son to accompany him, together with Elizabeth Cowles and an American teacher Anderson Bakewell, then studying at a Jesuit College near Darjeeling. While in Kathmandu they met, by chance, H W Tilman who had just returned from climbing in the Annapurna and Langtang Himal of Central Nepal with, amongst others, Charles Evans.

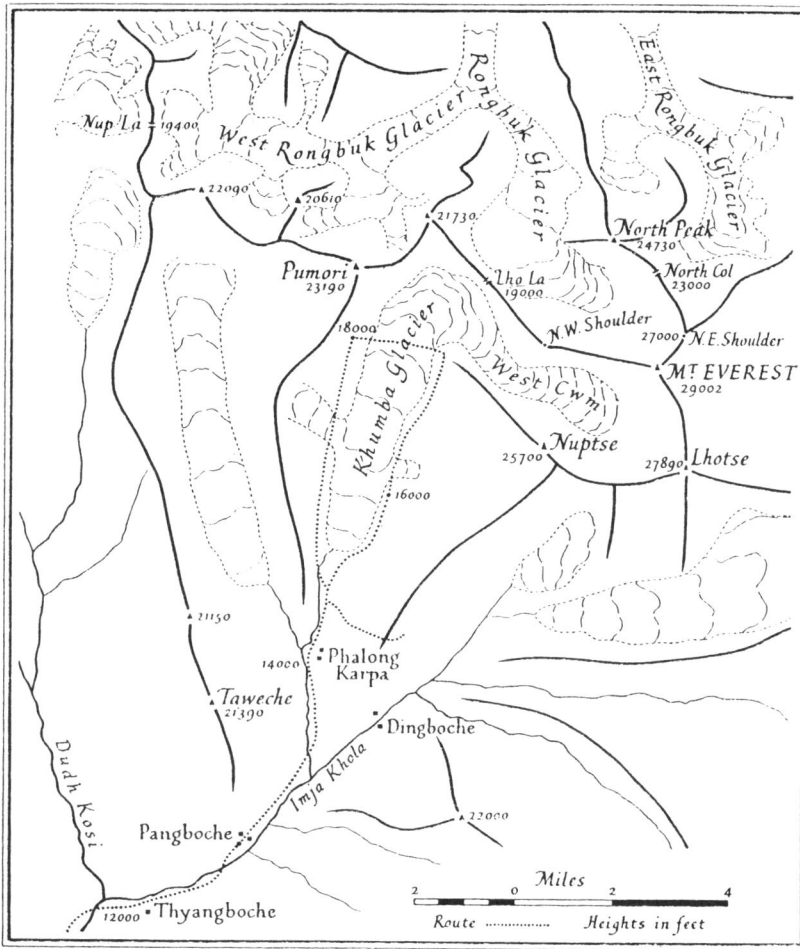

The southern approach to Everest.
The route taken by H W Tilman and C S Houston in 1950

Tilman was invited to join the Houston party to visit the Khumbu. Approaching Everest from Jogbani on the Nepal-Indian border, due south of the mountain, they arrived at Namche Bazar and, having no map, had difficulty in finding the correct approach to the Khumbu glacier. Ascending Kala Pattar, Tilman took the first photograph of the south side of Everest. Unfortunately, their viewpoint, at 18,000ft, yielded neither a good view of the mountain nor, more importantly, a view into the Western Cwm. Most importantly of all, they were not high enough to be able to see the slopes leading from the end of the Western Cwm to the South Col. Far better views would be obtained in 1951 from 20,000ft on Pumori. Both Tilman and Houston were mountaineers experienced in exploration and it was unfortunate that they were unable to go higher on this expedition. However, Houston was suffering from mountain sickness, a mild form of cerebral oedema, and was insufficiently acclimatised. They were also running out of time. Neither followed up this tantalising glimpse of the route by which Everest would eventually be climbed, Houston because he was deeply involved in organising an American expedition to K2, the world's second highest peak, and Tilman because he felt that the Himalaya had become, for him, 'too high and too large'. Another factor may have been that in 1951 icefalls were regarded by mountaineers as posing an unacceptably dangerous risk, and the Khumbu icefall looked both dangerous and unavoidable.

On their return from Nepal both men were pessimistic about a feasible route up Everest by this southern approach because of the dangers of what they had seen of the Khumbu icefall and the unlikelihood of finding a safe way around it. In his book *Nepal Himalaya* Tilman wrote: 'We could see at most the upper 3,000 ft. of the south ridge which looked so steep that we dismissed at once any idea of there being a route, even supposing the col could be reached.' Their reservations no doubt contributed to the initial refusal by the newly-formed Joint Himalayan Committee of the Alpine Club and the the Royal Geographical Society (generally referred to as the 'Himalayan Committee') which had replaced the Everest Committee of pre-war days, to support the reconnaissance of the southern approach proposed by Bill Murray, Tom Bourdillon and myself, despite the many photographs I had found in the archives of the Royal Geographical Society (RGS) showing a route to the summit. Eventually Campbell Secord persuaded them to reverse their decision.

Discovery of a new route on the Nepalese side of Everest, from photographs and maps in the RGS archives

Quite independently of the Houston-Tilman party, I had come to the conclusion that there must be a feasible route up the southern, Nepalese, side of Everest. Every other mountain seemed to have more than one climbable route on it, and there was no reason why Everest should be an exception. At the time, early in 1951, I was doing my National Service in the Royal Army Medical Corps, and as I was based in London I had both the time and the opportunity to make a thorough search of the photographic archives of the RGS.

I examined about 3,000 photographs and obtained a large amount of topographical information which showed a possible route to the summit of Everest from the Western Cwm – the first time that this approach had been seriously considered. Information came from photographs taken on the 1921, 1935 and 1936 expeditions, on the 1933 Houston–Westland 'Flight over Everest', on clandestine flights over Everest in 1945 and 1947, and from a photo taken by Tilman in 1950. Some of these photos had been wrongly labelled, but I was able to identify them. At about the same time, I met Ian Mumford who happened to be working temporarily in the map room of the RGS and who told me that a hitherto unknown working drawing of both the north and south sides of Everest existed. It had been drawn by H F Milne, chief draughtsman of the RGS, and its existence was only known to one or two people. The drawing had been compiled with the help of A R Hinks, former Secretary of the RGS, from vertical and oblique photos taken during the 'Flight over Everest' in 1933; they had combined these with the 1935 photogrammetric survey by Michael Spender on the the north side of the mountain. At a scale of 1:50,000, with numerous spot heights, it was a drawing of great historic and topographical importance, as it depicted with accuracy both the Nepalese and Tibetan sides of the mountain for the first time. A photostat copy of the original compilation accompanied us on the 1951 reconnaissance expedition. This map was lithographed in 1952 and very few copies exist today.

The first photo of the Khumbu icefall had been taken by Mallory in 1921 from the frontier ridge on the col between Pumori and the Lingtren peaks. It showed the icefall end on, but was a bad photograph with poor delineation of detail. It did indicate, however, that the Khumbu icefall would be a formidable obstacle.

The photo taken by Tilman in 1950 from near Kala Pattar showed the Lho La with the North Peak (Changtse) behind. To the left of the Lho La was the peak Khumbu Tse, whilst to the right was the West Ridge and Summit of Everest. Tilman believed that the steep skyline ridge from the South Summit of Everest fell directly to the South Col, which was invisible from his viewpoint. In fact, other photographs showed clearly that this ridge, the South-West Ridge, ended in a buttress that fell vertically into the Western Cwm. The South Ridge itself, which was hidden and out of sight, was an easy-looking ridge falling to the South Col. This was the obvious line of ascent to the summit from the South Col.

A photograph taken by L V Bryant on the 1935 reconnaissance expedition from the col between Pumori and Lingtren peak was taken from the same position as Mallory's 1921 photo but showed greater detail. It looked straight into the Western Cwm but it did not show the South Col. The height of the icefall was approximately 400 metres and although little could be seen of the floor of the Western Cwm, it did appear to be relatively level, though with crevasses.

Remembering that E G H Kempson had been to Everest before the war, I wrote and asked him for any photographs he might have taken on the 1936 expedition. With J M L Gavin he had visited the Lho La on 11 June 1936 and he sent me a good photograph of the icefall in profile, as well as the upper part of the Khumbu glacier. It appeared that the buttress of Nuptse (West Peak) that bounded the icefall to the south, would be a difficult and dangerous option if the icefall had to be avoided. This was confirmed on the 1951 reconnaissance, when a good and close view of this face of Nuptse was obtained from a buttress on Pumori.

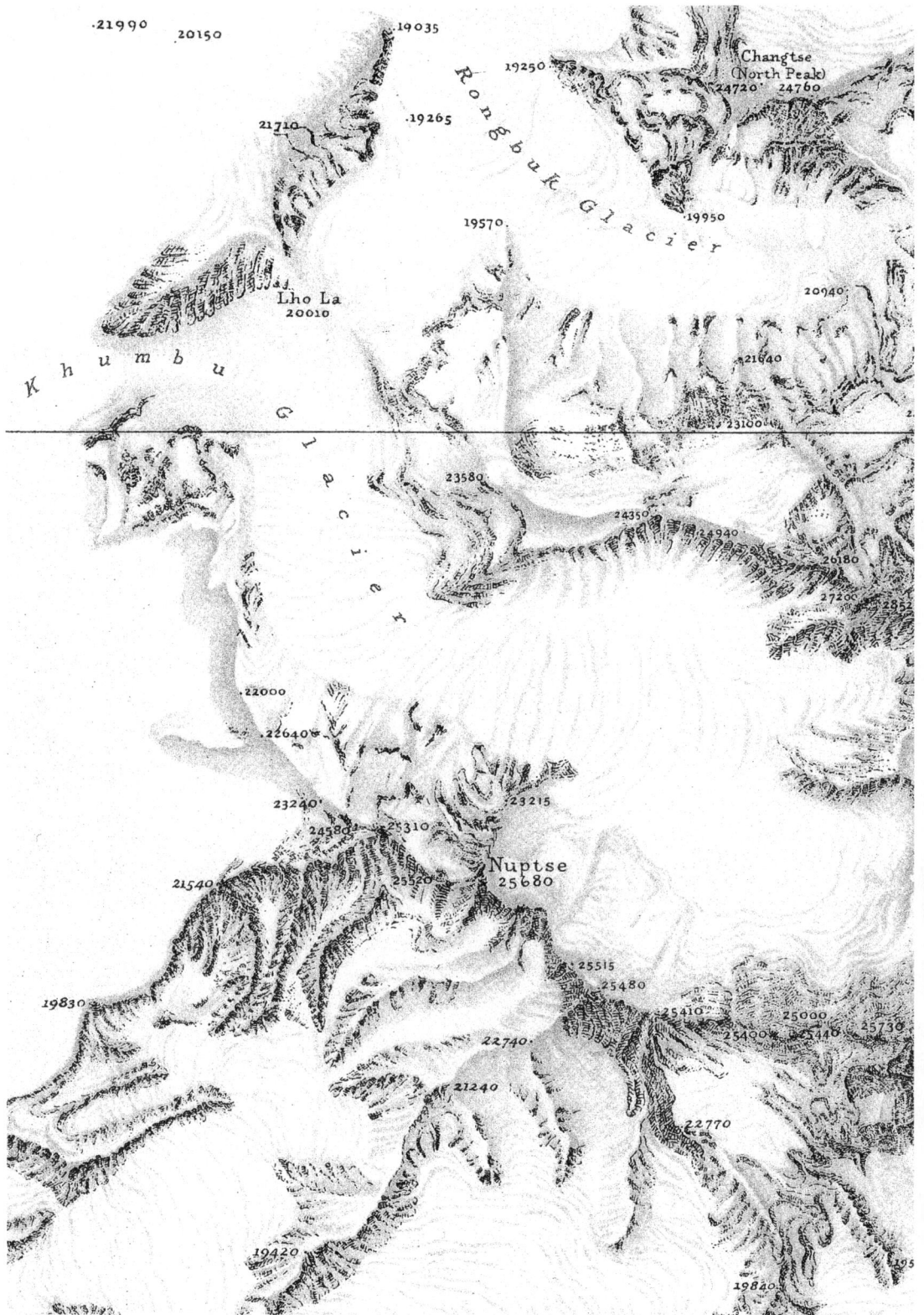

The Milne-Hinks map showing, for the first time, topographical details of the south, Nepalese, side of Everest. The map was compiled from photographs taken on the 1933 'Flight Over Everest', combined

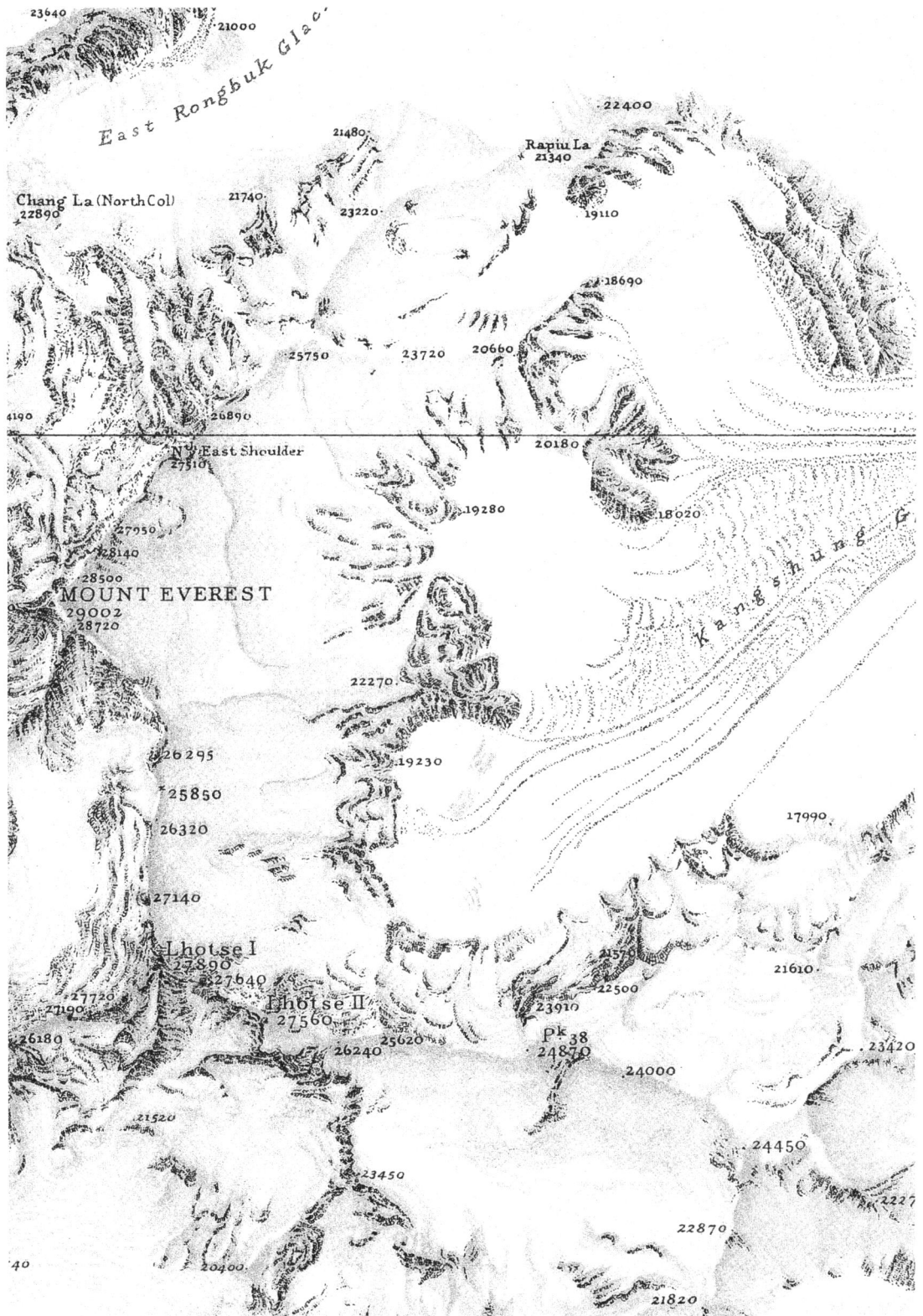

with the 1935 photogrammetric survey by Michael Spender. Many spot heights are shown. The map's existence had been forgotten until it was discovered by M P Ward in the archives of the RGS in 1951.

Also in the RGS archives I came across a number of photographs in two un-marked brown envelopes taken on secret and unrecorded flights over Everest in 1945 and 1947. Those taken in 1945 were the more important and were from a series I later found out had been presented to the photographic archives of the RGS in early 1951 by B H Farmer, an Air Survey Liaison Officer with the Army in India. Taken from a Mosquito XIX aircraft of No 684 Squadron, one showed the slopes from the head of the Western Cwm to the South Col. This photograph was a vital link in the chain of evidence about a new route and was composed of three photos joined together to form a panorama. It showed almost the whole of the north face of Lhotse, from the summit to the Western Cwm. The South Col, Geneva Spur (unnamed at the time) and summit of Lhotse were clearly visible in excellent detail. A line of ascent could be seen to the South Col up what became known as the 'Geneva Spur', together with an alternative line traversing from the upper part of the Lhotse Face to the South Col. Both these lines were confirmed during the 1951 reconnaissance expedition, when a good view of this face was obtained from a but-tress at about 6,100m on Pumori. Another photo from 1945 showed the whole of the South Ridge of Everest from the summit to the South Col in excellent detail, including what became known as the 'Hillary Step'. It showed that there was no unsurmountable difficulty along the whole route, which was entirely on snow.

The other series of aerial photographs was taken in 1947 by Flight-Lieutenant K D Neame of No 34 Squadron on an unofficial flight over Everest. They too were discovered in the photographic archives of the RGS to which they had been given by Neame in 1948. They showed the South Ridge and South Col clearly and also the upper part of the North-East Ridge. Neither the 1945 nor the 1947 photos had been catalogued and their existence, like that of the Milne-Hinks map, was unknown to the staff of the RGS.

Finally, two photographs from the 1933 'Flight Over Everest' expedition, which were not in the RGS archives, were of great use because they clearly indicated that the South-West Ridge (as opposed to the South Ridge) extended from the South Summit of Everest and confirmed that it ended in a precipice falling vertically to the Western Cwm. This was the ridge, seen in profile in Tilman's 1950 photo, which he thought, wrongly, might descend to the South Col.

Much of the country to the north and west of Everest was shown for the first time in two aerial photos from the 1945 and 1947 series. Milne intended to use these to draw a more accurate map of the whole Everest region, not just Everest itself, but he never achieved this. The combined evidence of all these photos and the map showed a climbable 'line' to the summit of Everest once the icefall, the most dangerous part of the route, had been overcome.

For further details of this episode, including reproductions of all the photos, see 'Everest, 1951: cartographic and photographic evidence of a new route from Nepal' by M P Ward and P K Clark in *The Geographical Journal, Vol. 158, No 1*, March 1992, pp. 47-56. This article is reproduced as an Appendix on pages 297-307 of this volume.

The newly formed Himalayan Committee seemed to be disinterested in this photographic and cartographic evidence of a climbable route up the south side of Everest, so I enlisted the support of W H Murray, a writer from Lochgoilhead in Argyll, who had just returned from leading an expedition to the peaks north of Nanda Devi. He was one of the pioneers of Scottish winter climbing. Though there are no glaciers in Scotland, the often polar conditions of high winds, intense cold and ample snowfall result in deep snow and ice-covered ridges and faces, and snow-filled gullies. These conditions provide challenging climbing, often in daunting and extreme weather.

I invited a third member to join our party. This was T D Bourdillon, a rocket physicist, who lived in Buckinghamshire. He was one of the best British climbers of his generation. With Hamish Nicol, he had just completed a major breakthrough in the European Alps by climbing the North Face of the Aiguille du Dru. In 1950 the standard of British climbing had fallen below that of our European counterparts and this was the first major Alpine route to demonstrate that British climbers had at last recovered from the effects of the war and a resulting loss of performance.

Campbell Secord, a Canadian economist who, independently, had been pressing for a reconnaissance expedition, told the Himalayan Committee of our plans, and Alfred Tissières, a Swiss biochemist working at King's College Cambridge, was also initially involved. Unfortunately, Charles Evans, who had been with Tilman in Central Nepal in 1950, was unable to join our party as he had already agreed to take part in an expedition with Tony Trower to Deo Tibba in Kulu.

Although we were excited by the evidence I had uncovered in my researches, the Himalayan Committee initially remained deeply sceptical. However, we continued to organise our own expedition, with W H Murray as leader. When Eric Shipton returned from a diplomatic appointment at Kunming in SW China, we asked him to lead the party, while Bill Murray continued with the active organisation. Shipton's reputation was such that Murray was happy to stand down as leader. Eventually, the Himalayan Committee, under pressure from Secord, decided to back us, and the Nepalese Government gave us permission to take an expedition to Everest in the autumn of 1951. It was later agreed that *The Times* should be asked to sponsor the expedition.

The medical-scientific solution to the problem of 'the last thousand feet' of Everest

In 1951, while examining the photographs in the RGS archive, it became obvious to me as a doctor that the major problem frustrating success on all the pre-war Everest expeditions had been the medical-scientific one of 'the last thousand feet'. This problem was solved, in theory, at the the Medical Research Council (MRC) laboratories in London in the next few months. Their conclusions would be confirmed in the field in 1952.

The Division of Human Physiology at Hampstead had been set up in 1950 to carry out research into all aspects of extreme environments and their effects on man, with cold having priority. This was to meet the requirements of the Falkland Islands Dependency Survey (later British Antarctic Survey) and also because, during the Korean War, casualties due to cold were approaching 10% of the total. The Director of this MRC unit was Otto Edholm, previously Professor of Physiology at the University of Western Ontario in Canada where he had written, with A C Burton, a classical monograph entitled *Man in a Cold Environment*. My introduction to this department in early 1951 came through Dr R B Bourdillon, Tom Bourdillon's father.

Dr Bourdillon was a member of the MRC's electro-medical unit at Stoke Mandeville Hospital, where pioneering work was being carried out on paraplegia. As a former test pilot, he was naturally very interested in the altitude problem of Everest and a meeting was arranged between us in mid-1951. Hearing that our party was definitely going to Everest for a reconnaissance and that high-altitude studies would be crucial to any successful attempt later, Dr Bourdillon suggested that I contact Griffith Pugh who was working at the newly-formed MRC unit in Hampstead. This I did within a few days. Pugh looked at the photographs of our proposed route up Everest and commented that, except for the icefall, he believed that, as an Olympic class skier, he could ski down it.* If he could *ski* Everest, any competent mountaineer could surely *climb* it. The Khumbu icefall did indeed look technically difficult and dangerous, but Tom Bourdillon and I were competent on both rock and ice and considered that, given time, we could crack any difficulties presented by the icefall.

We now turned our attention to more complicated matters concerning cold and high altitude. The main problem was that Everest appeared, technically, to be about as difficult as Mont Blanc, which had been climbed many thousands of times since its first ascent in 1786. Yet even though, on Everest, climbers had used supplementary oxygen at extreme altitude, why had they consistently failed to reach the summit during the last thirty years?

---

* This has since been done. In 2000 Davo Karnicar, from Slovenia, skied down Everest from Summit to Base Camp in less than five hours. *The Sunday Times*, 8 October 2000.

Underlying all our discussions was the feeling that all previous Everest attempts had been much too amateurish in their approach and that we did not want their failures to be repeated yet again in any new attempt. Our initial discussions highlighted the fact that, despite the use of supplementary oxygen on many pre-war expeditions, mountaineers had been climbing so slowly that they were unable to reach the summit and return to a high camp during daylight on the same day. Moreover, the intense cold high on Everest appeared to be another serious problem, for despite seemingly adequate clothing, and temperatures often higher than in polar regions where they were known to drop to minus 50°C, frostbite was reported regularly. Other problems, concerning dehydration and weight loss, which led to undue fatigue and loss of performance, were also very important. Finally, from the purely medical point of view, there had been far too much illness on pre-war Everest expeditions, including chest conditions, strokes, personality disorders, hallucinations, together with a considerable mortality.

A lot of these problems had been identified during my close study and analysis of the many accounts of the Everest expeditions of the 1920s and 1930s. The American work on 'Operation Everest' in 1946 was also a great help. As no textbooks on high-altitude medicine or physiology existed at that time, we had to use primary sources to build up an overall picture of 'high-altitude disease'.

At lower altitudes, as in the European Alps, 'the last thousand feet' on any mountain would take only an hour or two to climb. Yet on Everest, though 25 mountaineers had reached 27,000ft and eight had reached 28,000ft, none had reached the summit. Moreover, it was not at all clear whether supplementary oxygen was as effective as acclimatisation in producing a performance adequate to reach the summit. The history of the use of supplementary oxygen on Everest was a chequered one. The only time that it had appeared to increase climbing rate was in 1938 – though the use of oxygen while asleep had prevented Finch's 1922 party from suffering hypothermia, and probably saved their lives.

Oxygen sets had been developed in connection with high-altitude flying during the Second World War and were discussed by Roxburgh of the Institute of Aviation Medicine at Farnborough in 1947. Even so, by 1951 there was no consistent evidence that supplementary oxygen had given a significant boost to climbing rates on Everest. Because pre-war climbers, using supplementary oxygen, had only ascended as fast, but no faster, than those relying on acclimatisation alone, Pugh wondered whether it was the weight of the oxygen set that had slowed them down. A simple series of tests on a bicycle ergometer, with myself as a subject carrying weights of up to 40lbs (equivalent to the weight of an oxygen set), showed conclusively that a higher flow rate of oxygen was needed both to compensate for the weight of the set and to increase climbing rate. This conclusion was critical to our later success on Everest.

Two types of set had been developed for mountaineers. In the open-circuit set, oxygen was added at different flow rates to the air that the mountaineer breathed. The equivalent 'altitude' in the depths of his lungs was determined by this flow rate. A high flow rate meant that the equivalent 'altitude' in his lungs was lower than the altitude at which he was actually climbing. His exhaled breath was vented to the atmosphere. The apparatus was simple and rugged, but several cylinders needed to be carried on any extended trip at altitude. With the closed-circuit set, pure oxygen was breathed rather than air enriched with oxygen, and this was exhaled into a soda-lime cannister where CO_2 was absorbed and the oxygen recycled. Hence the term 'closed-circuit'. Obviously a much lower flow rate of oxygen was needed for this type of set, since the mountaineer, when climbing at altitude, would be climbing at the equivalent of 'sea-level' in the depths of his lungs. The addition of the soda-lime cannister made the apparatus heavy, and if it broke down, the sudden exposure from the equivalent of sea-level to the altitude at which the mountaineer was actually climbing, had the potential to cause coma or death.

Another important observation was made by Bryan Mathews FRS (Director of the Institute of Aviation Medicine at Farnborough and later Professor of Physiology at Cambridge) who emphasised that the increased respiration required at altitude would result in heat loss through the lungs, followed by general body cooling. This could account for the relatively high incidence of frostbite at altitude, compared with similar temperatures in polar regions.

The major part played by dehydration at extreme altitude had been documented on early Everest expeditions, and was discussed at an informal seminar in 1947 by Peter Lloyd, a member of the 1938 expedition. He described how, at great altitude, his urine output decreased markedly, and also how dark and concentrated it became. Professor Rudolf Peters FRS, of the Biochemistry Department of Oxford University, suggested that this phenomenon was the result of fluid loss, due to the high rate of respiration at altitude.

Throughout the 1920s and 1930s opinion about the use of supplementary oxygen had been divided, with arguments both for and against. Early in 1951 Griffith Pugh and I came to the conclusion that the flow rates of supplementary oxygen used on pre-war expeditions had not been high enough to give a boost to climbing rate. We recommended that the rate should be doubled, from two litres per minute to four litres per minute, and, as a result, mountaineers in 1953 were able to climb faster at altitude, and generate enough heat, to prevent hypothermia and frostbite. The increased flow rate transformed climbing performance on Everest and was the main reason for our success in 1953. No longer were climbers at great altitude like 'sick men climbing in a dream'.

Other potential problems of altitude were fatigue and muscle wasting which were severe, as was loss of weight and appetite. Moreover, two cases of 'stroke' due to vascular episodes had been reported. In all, there had been fifteen deaths on Everest expeditions – an unacceptable mortality rate of five per cent. It was decided, therefore, that all attempts on the summit should be made with adequate supplementary oxygen. There was no evidence that contemporary mountaineers were fit enough to climb the peak relying on acclimatisation alone. That achievement had to wait for 25 years until 1978.

This immediate and 'unofficial' interest by the Medical Research Council in the Everest problem, from early 1951 onwards, meant that, unlike on previous expeditions, the thrust of the 1953 expedition was based from the start on sound medical-scientific principles, and not on climbers' 'hunches'.

Solitary attempt by R B Larsen, 1951

In 1951 a solitary attempt on Everest was made by a Dane, R B Larsen. He left Darjeeling on 31 March with four Sherpas. At Sandakphu, near the Sikkim-Nepal border, three more Sherpas joined him, and they travelled swiftly across Nepal by the shortest route to the Dudh Kosi river. Turning north, Larsen reached Namche Bazar on 22 April, but after continuing up the Lobuje Khola he was stopped from reaching the foot of the Khumbu icefall by deep spring snow. Returning to Namche Bazar he moved west and north up the Bhote Kosi valley to the Nangpa La (18,750ft) which he was the first European to cross. Arriving at Kyetrak village (15,300ft) in Tibet, he continued but avoided the fort at Tingri and headed east to Rongbuk on the north side of Everest. Here the Abbot protected him from the Tibetan police, and he continued up the East Rongbuk glacier to the foot of the North Col.

On 7 May he climbed the lower slopes of the North Col but his equipment was defective, with poor quality sleeping-bags and no primus stove for cooking. His Sherpas refused to go any further and they all retreated to Rongbuk. Returning over the Nangpa La they reached Namche Bazar some days later.

BIBLIOGRAPHY

C G Andrews, *Flight Over Everest*, 6-10, 1947. Wellington Tramping Club, Tararua, New Zealand.

C S Houston, 'Operation Everest' in *US Naval Medical Bulletin 46*, 1783-1792, 1946.

C S Houston, 'Towards Everest' in *Himalayan Journal 17*, 9-18, 1952.

M Jeffries, M Clarbrough, *Sagarmatha, Mother of the Universe. The Story of the Mount Everest National Park*. Cobb/Horwood Publications, Auckland, New Zealand, 1985.

P Lloyd, 'Valedictory Address' in *Alpine Journal 85*, 3-15, 1980.

K Mason, 'The representation of glaciated regions on maps of the Survey of India'. Professional paper No 25, Dehra Dun, India. 1929.

B Mathews, 'Loss of Heat at High Altitudes' in *Journal of Physiology 77*, 28-29, 1932.

W H Murray, *The Evidence of Things Not Seen*. Bâton Wicks, 2002.

K Neame, 'Alone over Everest' in *The Mountain World*, 133-142. Allen and Unwin, 1955.

H W Tilman, *Nepal Himalaya*. Cambridge University Press, 1952.

H W Tilman, 'Exploration in the Nepal Himalaya' in *Geographical Journal 117*, 263-274, 1951.

H W Tilman, 'The Annapurna Himal and the South Side of Everest' in *Alpine Journal 58*, 101-110, 1951/52.

M P Ward, P K Clark, 'Everest 1951: cartographic and photographic evidence of a new route from Nepal' in *Geographical Journal 158*, 47-56, 1992.

M P Ward, 'The Exploration of the Nepalese side of Everest' in *Alpine Journal 97*, 213-221, 1992/93.

M P Ward, 'The Contribution of Medical Science to the First Ascent of Mount Everest' in *Alpine Journal 98*, 37-51, 1993.

Chapter 16

THE GREAT DAYS
Reconnaissance of Everest from Nepal, 1951

Introduction

Despite the initial disinterest of the Himalayan Committee, the British group of Murray, Bourdillon and myself had continued our plans for a reconnaissance expedition in the autumn of 1951. Unfortunately, Campbell Secord and Alfred Tissières had to drop out, but in June, when Eric Shipton returned from his post in south-west China, Secord, who was still taking an active part in the preparations, suggested that he might be invited to join our party. But having so recently returned from the claustrophobic atmosphere of Chinese communism, and relishing the freedom of the UK, Shipton took about a month to make up his mind. The deciding factor appears to have been his unfulfilled wish to visit Solu Khumbu, a mecca of Himalayan exploration and home of the Sherpas, rather than any conviction that Everest could be climbed from Nepal.

Following representations from the New Zealand Alpine Club, Shipton decided to strengthen the party by inviting two members of a New Zealand expedition who were currently climbing on Mukut Parbat in the Garhwal Himal. He did this for two reasons. Firstly, experience had shown that newcomers to the Himalaya, in this instance Bourdillon and myself, were less likely to perform well on their first expedition than those who had been more than once; secondly, he had been greatly impressed by L V Bryant, a New Zealand member of the 1935 Everest reconnaissance expedition, despite the great difficulty that the latter had had with acclimatisation. The skills acquired by New Zealand climbers were particularly suitable for Himalayan exploration: in the Southern Alps they were accustomed to being entirely self-supporting as they travelled through steep, forested country with glaciers falling to sea-level. This kind of experience resulted in an extensive knowledge of snow and ice conditions.

The decision by Shipton to include New Zealanders caused him much soul searching, for other British aspirants had been told that a party of four was considered adequate for this reconnaissance; in fact it had now become a party of six.

Edmund Hillary and Earle Riddiford joined our group in Nepal. Their presence was a great asset, for not only were they extremely fit and mountain hardened, but the skills that they had acquired and honed in the New Zealand Alps proved, as expected, ideal for mountain exploration in the Himalaya.

Since the expedition was concerned with exploration only, no attempt was made to take supplementary oxygen, as we would not be climbing above about 22,000ft. We thought, at most, that the icefall could be overcome and that a good view might be obtained of the slopes leading to the South Col. Possibly, too, a start could be made on these, but an attempt on Everest itself was provisionally scheduled in all our minds for the spring of 1952. Before we left the UK the Himalayan Committee undertook to request permission from the Nepalese Government for a 1952 expedition. It later became clear that the Swiss had applied in May 1951 for permission for an attempt on Everest in 1952. When plans for a joint Anglo-Swiss party for 1952 fell through, the Himalayan Committee applied instead for permission for Cho Oyu in the spring of 1952, and also for an attempt on Everest in 1953, and put down a marker for a further attempt on Everest in 1955. The French, having been refused permission to visit Everest in 1951, wished to make an attempt in 1954.

After consultation with the British Embassy in Kathmandu, it was decided that the best approach to Everest would be from the Indian border directly to the south, at Jogbani, the route used by Houston and Tilman in 1950. This was also the route, along the Arun river, traditionally taken by traders from Khumbu to the Nepalese foothills and the Indian border.

Bill Murray and I left the UK by boat on 2 August, arriving at Jogbani on the 22nd, whilst Shipton and Bourdillon, travelling by air to India, arrived two days later on the 24th. We were joined, as liaison officer, by Lieut Chandra Bahadur, an officer of the Nepalese Army, and by Dr Dutt, an Indian geologist.

On 25 August the Sherpa sirdar Angtharkay joined us from Darjeeling. He was a legendary figure and the most experienced of all the climbing Sherpas, having been on eight expeditions with Shipton. These included the Everest 1933 expedition, when he carried a load to 27,000ft; the exploration of Nanda Devi in 1934; Everest again in 1935, 1936 and 1938; and the Karakoram in 1937 and 1939. He had set up a trekking business in Sikkim in 1950, and in that year had been sirdar to the French expedition that climbed Annapurna – the first ascent of an 8,000-metre peak. After this he had been to Paris, received the *Legion d'Honneur* and had even visited the Folies Bergère, three Sherpa 'firsts'.

Both Shipton and Tilman had the highest regard for Angtharkay. Shipton later wrote of him in *Upon That Mountain*:

We soon learned to value his rare qualities, qualities which made him outstandingly the best of all the Sherpas I have known. He had a shrewd judgment both of men and of situations, and was absolutely steady in any crisis. He was a most lovable person, modest, unselfish and completely sincere, with an infectious gaiety of spirit.

When I first met Angtharkay at Jogbani he was neatly dressed in European clothes and with a normal European haircut at a time when most Sherpas still wore pigtails. Despite having been with Europeans a great deal he spoke very little English. Just above five feet tall, he was slightly knock-kneed and had a rather impassive expression illuminated by highly intelligent eyes that missed nothing.

Angtharkay

With him from Darjeeling he brought twelve Sherpas, all of whom were on their way to Solu Khumbu. Four signed up specifically with the expedition as climbing Sherpas, whilst the others were employed at the same rate as the local porters.

The party left Jogbani on 27 August in heavy monsoon rain and went by lorry along an appalling track across the flat terai. After a few miles the foothills rose suddenly for 5,000 feet into rain-sodden clouds. Climbing into these, we reached Dhankuta, the seat of the local governor, where the party was held up by lack of porters, as few wished to travel during the monsoon. Here we found epidemics of cholera and smallpox, though malaria, common in the terai, was almost absent at this higher altitude. We discovered that information about the route ahead was either lacking or unreliable, and that beyond Dingla, the next major village, all was uncertain. Between heavy monsoon showers we searched for beetles and caught magnificently-coloured butterflies in a cardboard box for the Natural History Museum in London.

As we later discovered, we were making for the lower valley of the Arun river which rises in southern Tibet and forms the eastern boundary of the Everest region. On the ¼-inch Survey of India map these mountains, east of Everest, were shown as part of the Mahalangur Himal. The northern reaches of the Arun river, in Tibet, had been surveyed during the 1921 reconnaissance, whilst some members of the 1933 party had travelled south down the Arun gorge on their way back from Everest. We crossed the Arun river, about 100 yards wide, at Legua Ghat. The ferry was a hollowed-out tree-trunk that took seven passengers and their loads. The two ferry men paddled into the current sweeping us downstream and with a few deft strokes of their paddles guided us towards the calm water by the opposite bank. After letting us disembark, they had to drag the ferry further up stream in order to repeat the process in the reverse direction. We followed the west bank of the Arun for eight miles and then took a path which climbed steeply across the grain of the country to the small village of Dingla. For a few exhilarating minutes we had our first view of the Himalaya. Makalu and Chamlang rose clearly above the clouds, and then suddenly we had a glimpse of Everest. But as quickly as they had lifted, the clouds returned, a black sullen mass of cumulus. It rained almost continuously for the next three weeks.

On 8 September the two New Zealanders, Hillary and Riddiford, came surging up the hill brandishing enormous Victorian-style ice-axes. It was good to see them. They were very fit, very hungry and exuded energy. Expecting to meet a group of well-dressed Englishmen, they were surprised and perhaps a little disconcerted to find that, if anything, we were scruffier than they were.

Our next objective was a 12,000ft pass, the Salpa Bhanyang, which crossed the ridge between the Arun river and the next valley west, the Hongu. As the monsoon took hold, leeches appeared on the end of every leaf. Black, pin-thin and about one or two inches long, they writhed around in clusters looking for blood. The faces of all domestic animals were covered with leeches and with the flies that clustered around their puncture wounds. Some leeches, gorged with blood, became as thick and as long as a thumb. They were to be found mainly on our ankles until brushed or burnt off with a cigarette stub, and the sores which they left behind did not heal until the monsoon ended and our legs became dry again. (Today, far from being banished from medicine, leeches are still used by plastic surgeons to reduce the engorgement by blood that sometimes occurs when flaps of skin are transposed.)

On 15 September we crossed the 12,000ft Salpa Bhanyang pass in a thick, cold mist, and joined the route traditionally used by Sherpas when travelling from Darjeeling to Khumbu. Angtharkay was now on familiar ground. The previous year several Sherpas had died from hypothermia on this pass when caught in a blizzard. We descended steeply to the Hongu river 7,000 feet below, where we learned that the bridge over the next river, the Inukhu Khola, had been destroyed. When we reached the makeshift replacement, we found it to be so flimsy that a sudden surge of water destroyed it, leaving half our porters stranded on the eastern side of the river. The main party scrambled up the very steep western side of the gorge, only to find themselves walking straight into a hornets' nest. One porter was so badly stung that he flung his load down and jumped off the path, fortunately landing safely in the branches of a 15-foot tree below. Another porter developed a very high temperature, with a racing pulse at over 130 beats per minute. Most of us were stung and had swollen hands, legs and faces. As we crawled up the hill towards some abandoned sheds, the wind became a gale and the rain suddenly increased so much that it was as though buckets of water were being thrown over us. Rarely had we felt so miserable, half our baggage was probably lost and most of the porters were shivering violently with high temperatures and cold.

To add to our troubles we had somehow deviated from the main route; it seemed that we were lost and even the battle-hardened New Zealanders looked pretty glum. Our morale, however, was strengthened by the sudden appearance of a wizened crone carrying part of a bamboo trunk. Angtharkay brightened immediately and money swiftly changed hands with, unusually, no pretence at bargaining. From the inside of the trunk there issued a fluid that looked like diluted vomit with the faint green tinge of bile and small solid particles. Angtharkay got some cups and poured out about half a pint for each of us. We drank it rapidly, trying not to see or smell it, because, if anything, it tasted even worse than it looked. But as the benificent effects of the nearly-neat alcohol took hold, the disgusted expressions on our faces changed to a mixture of pleasure and stupefaction – and we all, porters included, pressed on up the hill with renewed vigour. By about 2.0pm, however, we could go no further. We found some sheds covered in leaves and went to sleep in a quagmire of mud with rain still pouring down on us through the roof. Unaccountably we woke next day feeling better, yet still cold and wet. The rain was coming down in torrents as we made our way along a ridge, asking the way from one group of huts to another, until at last we found the traditional route again. Then, quite suddenly, on 20 September, the rain stopped. The monsoon had ended.

We now descended to the Dudh Kosi river and followed it north to Namche Bazar. At each village we were welcomed with *chang* and food, and after the rigours of the monsoon, the sun dried our clothes, healed our leech ulcers and put us in good spirits. Some of the villagers had been suffering from abdominal pain and nose-bleeds – these also disappeared with the sun. But chronic eye infections were common, as were goitres, some of an enormous size, though none appeared to be malignant. Chronic chest disease, too, was not unknown, probably caused by sitting for hours during the winter in rooms full of smoke from the open yak-dung fires.

Climbing up the path to Namche Bazar (Namche means 'shaded by forest', though there were no trees in 1951), tucked in a fold on the hillside underneath the sacred peak of Khumbilia, we felt very much at home and the Sherpas were delighted to see us; they were particularly pleased to see Shipton who had employed some of them on previous expeditions. The night after we arrived, the village threw a mammoth party for us and line dancing continued until dawn.

Exploration of the Khumbu icefall and confirmation of the route to the summit
We now entered a critically important phase of the expedition. Would we be able to confirm the evidence of the photographs, and find a feasible route up Everest? The photographs and map had given us a good idea of the problems, but there was no substitute for seeing the real thing. We knew that the icefall would be dangerous and difficult but what really worried us most was the route from the end of the Western Cwm up to the South Col. From the photos alone, it was not easy to judge the steepness of these snow slopes or whether they were avalanche-prone. The photos taken by 684 Squadron made them look very steep indeed, but this could be a false perspective, and we hoped that they might turn out to be easier.

Full of hope but rather apprehensive, we left Namche Bazar on 25 September. The early morning sun rapidly cleared the mists from the surrounding peaks, which glistened against the deep blue sky. It was one of the most memorable days that I have ever experienced in the mountains. Each corner of the path opened up a new and fascinating vista of unknown country, unclimbed peaks, unvisited valleys and glaciers.

The most spectacular of an extraordinary variety of gothic spires was an immensely steep obelisk, sheathed in glittering ice, which dominated the end of the valley. Hanging glaciers clung to its black cliffs and guarded the steep upper flutings below the summit. This impressive peak, often referred to as 'the Matterhorn of the Himalaya', overhung the monastery of Thyangboche, which we reached in the afternoon. From the local Sherpas we learned that it was called Ama Dablam – 'Ama' meaning a mother, and 'Dablam' meaning the locket in which Sherpa women keep their valuables.

On the way to Thyangboche we met a Sherpa, Sen Tensing, who, like Angtharkay, had climbed with Shipton on Nanda Devi in the Karakoram and on Everest. He had been herding yaks three days' march away in a remote valley when he heard of our arrival and immediately came to greet us. Sen Tensing was a considerable character who was first employed as a Sherpa on the 1935 Everest reconnaissance expedition. As Tilman wrote in his contribution to Shipton's book *Blank on the Map*:

> Sen Tensing ... had attached himself to the Everest reconnaissance party in 1935 on the East Rongbuk glacier at Camp II, having turned up, un-announced, from Solu Khumbu in Nepal. He was so pleased with the clothes we gave him, or rather his appearance in them, that he never again took them off. Down in the valley under a blazing sun, miles from any snow, Sen Tensing could be seen fully attired in a windproof suit, gloves, glasses, boots, puttees and Balaclava helmet, ready apparently to battle with some imminent and terrific blizzard. So fond was he of dressing the part of the complete mountaineer that I dubbed him the Foreign Sportsman, and the name stuck. He is as broad as long, and somewhat stout, very willing, cheerful, and talkative ... He reads and writes Tibetan characters, and manages to do rather less than his share of the menial work without protest from the others; this, taken in conjunction with the prayer-chanting, leads us to suppose him an unfrocked Lama.

In Namche Bazar we had already engaged as one of our Sherpas Ang Phuter, the brother of Angtharkay. He had been with Shipton on the 1938 Everest expedition, aged 14 years. On that occasion he had crossed the Nangpa La to join the expedition at Rongbuk, and had carried a load to 21,000ft.

Late that afternoon we climbed the 2,000ft path from the valley of the Dudh Kosi through a pine forest to the monastery, gaining the meadow on which it was placed through a ceremonial arch. A black and white Tibetan tent had been pitched

for us and that night we slept in one of the world's most beautiful mountain settings. Next morning at dawn the valley up which we had come lay dark, mysterious and cloud-covered to the south. It formed a trough, cutting through a range south of Namche Bazar which would be explored in the autumn of 1953 by Charles Evans and Jimmy Roberts. The range separated Khumbu from the rest of Nepal. To the north, the valley was blocked by a monstrous wall of rock and ice – the ridge joining Lhotse, the south peak of Everest, with Nuptse, the west peak. About halfway along, peeping over this two-mile-high rock and ice curtain, was a small lump, the summit of Everest, looking so insignificant that it could easily be missed (*Plate 13*). No wonder the Pundit Hari Ram failed to recognise Everest from Nepal.

The meadow on which we were camped was surrounded by a forest of juniper, birch, rhododendron and firs with branches festooned with beards of moss. Gentians were scattered across the turf, which glistened in the early-morning frost. After a leisurely breakfast we left at noon and followed the path gently down to the Imja Khola, crossing this by a small wooden bridge. Soon we entered country of shrubs, heather and coarse grass, camping that night at a small group of houses, Pheriche, and, next day, following the valley of the Lobuje Khola into which the Khumbu glacier flowed. At the head of the valley were the peaks and passes of the Nepal-Tibet watershed, so familiar to Shipton from his four previous Everest expeditions. For him, as for the Sherpas, it seemed like a home-coming, for he had often looked down into Nepal from the Lho La and the watershed peaks. We could easily make out Pumori, Changtse and the Lho La, yet Angtharkay, who knew the peaks well from the northern, Tibetan side, had not recognised them from Nepal despite many years of grazing yaks in the upper valleys of Khumbu. This was a curious blindness in someone who could pick up and follow an animal track invisible to Western eyes.

We were now starting to feel the effects of altitude and to suffer from light-headedness, fatigue, failure to sleep well, poor appetite and headache. Over the next few days we moved slowly up the valley and on 30 September split into two parties. Bourdillon, Riddiford and myself, with some Sherpas, crossed the Khumbu glacier to look at the lower part of the icefall, while Shipton and Hillary climbed to a height of about 20,000ft on a buttress of Pumori and gained a breathtakingly clear view into the Western Cwm. More importantly, they were able to see the northern slopes of Lhotse that led to the South Col. These were not as steep as we had feared, and a route to the South Col looked feasible, especially as it did not appear to be swept by avalanches. On the back of the Milne-Hinks map that I had taken with me, Shipton made a drawing of his impressions of the Western Cwm and he showed it to us that evening.

The icefall was the first problem for us to tackle, as it twisted through 90° on its descent and good views of its whole length were difficult to obtain. Any chances of avoiding it by climbing the cliffs and hanging glaciers of the West Buttress of Nuptse or by creeping round onto the West Ridge of Everest were deemed impracticable: both would be too difficult and dangerous. A route would have to be made straight through the icefall and its dangers confronted. This was a new concept in Himalayan mountaineering, where the vast scale, combined with an inability to move quickly because of altitude, made it sensible to avoid the most dangerous areas.

However, the view into the Western Cwm removed all our doubts. The icefall, though difficult and dangerous, could be overcome, a route to the South Col was indeed feasible and we believed that Everest *could* be climbed. It was a great relief to me, since I had cajoled this expedition into existence. However, the icefall party had so far had no success, for we had tried a route too near to the unstable hanging glaciers of Nuptse.

On 1st October Shipton and Hillary went closer to the Lho La and climbed to about 20,000ft on a small peak which gave them a good view of the upper, more difficult part of the icefall. On 2nd October a determined effort was made on the icefall and a camp was carried through to the steep middle section. The weather was bad on the 3rd but on the 4th most of the icefall was climbed. However, in the upper part an avalanche nearly swept Riddiford into a crevasse. Luckily he was roped, so disaster was narrowly averted, but the party returned shaken by the atrocious snow conditions and the sheer complexity and danger of the route.

With avalanches continuously coming off the cliffs of Nuptse and Everest into the Western Cwm, it was decided to leave the icefall for two weeks to let the monsoon snow stabilise and for the party to get really well acclimatised. After an exploratory journey around Ama Dablam, Shipton and Hillary returned on 19 October and established a large 12-man base tent borrowed from the British Army.

On the 22nd a good and fairly safe route was established up the lower portion of the icefall. On the 23rd, Shipton and Hillary, with Angtharkay, set off confidently, only to find that the upper part of the icefall had changed and was even more dangerous than before. Towers of fragile ice fell without warning and crevasses continually opened and closed. The icefall had become an immense, unstable ruin, as though an earthquake had shaken the entire glacier. On the 24th another route close to the Lho La was tried, but again without success.

That evening the rest of the party, Murray, Bourdillon, Riddiford and myself, joined Shipton and Hillary at Base Camp, after having explored west towards the Nup La and the glaciers falling from Gyachung Kang. On the 27th another excursion was made to 20,000ft on the Pumori buttress to look once again at the full extent of the unstable cataract of ice that made up the icefall. The 28th saw the whole party, with three Sherpas, set out at dawn. By the time the sun had risen the 'earthquake zone' had been crossed, but beyond it we found a steep snow slope in a dangerous condition. Eventually Tom Bourdillon cut steps up this and we stood on the edge of the Cwm, but from one side to the other, from the West Ridge of Everest to the West Buttress of Nuptse, an immensely wide and deep crevasse barred the entrance to the flat and level valley beyond.

We searched for a snow bridge or some way by which we could descend on the valley side and climb the cliff of ice on the mountain side. I started down one or two places where we thought it might just be possible to descend to the bottom of the snow-choked crevasses many feet below; but even if we could have reached these 'bridges', they might have collapsed, or we might have found that the near-vertical ice on the far side needed artificial climbing and the use of our small stock of suitable hardware. After one or two tentative attempts to descend we decided that to have any chance of success we would have to pitch a camp on the lower lip of the crevasse and spend a whole day trying to cross it. Eventually we gave up. I felt very frustrated by this decision, for here was a good piece of technical climbing which, as I was getting fitter, I would have liked to try. Bourdillon felt the same but both our sirdars, Angtharkay and Pasang, were adamant that to ask Sherpas to carry loads through the icefall in such bad conditions would be asking too much; so, with deep reluctance, we descended.

The day after this we tried another route near Nuptse, but to no avail and the attempt was abandoned. It was a bitter disappointment but, at the time, it seemed the only sensible thing to do. We hoped that snow conditions in the spring would be better. Meanwhile, we had shown that the icefall could be climbed and that the snow slopes leading to the South Col looked quite feasible. We had completed what we had set out to do. As Bill Murray put it in his autobiography *The Evidence of Things Not Seen*: "We had climbed up and we had climbed down the impossible! Gainsaying the pundits we had found the route up Everest. This route would 'go'."

Exploration east and south of Everest around the 'inaccessible' Ama Dablam

Before our final attempt on the icefall, and with the advantage of the Milne-Hinks map, Shipton and Hillary explored the peaks south and east of Everest. Their objective was to find a pass into the Kangshung glacier which drained east from the north side of Everest into the Kama valley. This, they hoped, would establish a link with the explorations of the 1921 reconnaissance expedition.

Following the Imja Khola along the south side of the Lhotse-Nuptse wall, it soon became clear that no obvious pass existed leading from the Imja into the Kama valley, thus confirming the accuracy of the Milne-Hinks map. Our attitude towards other existing maps of the Everest region was distinctly sceptical, for the closer one got to the glaciated regions, the greater were the errors to be found on the ¼-inch Survey of India map. Conversely, we found that the Milne-Hinks map was usually correct.

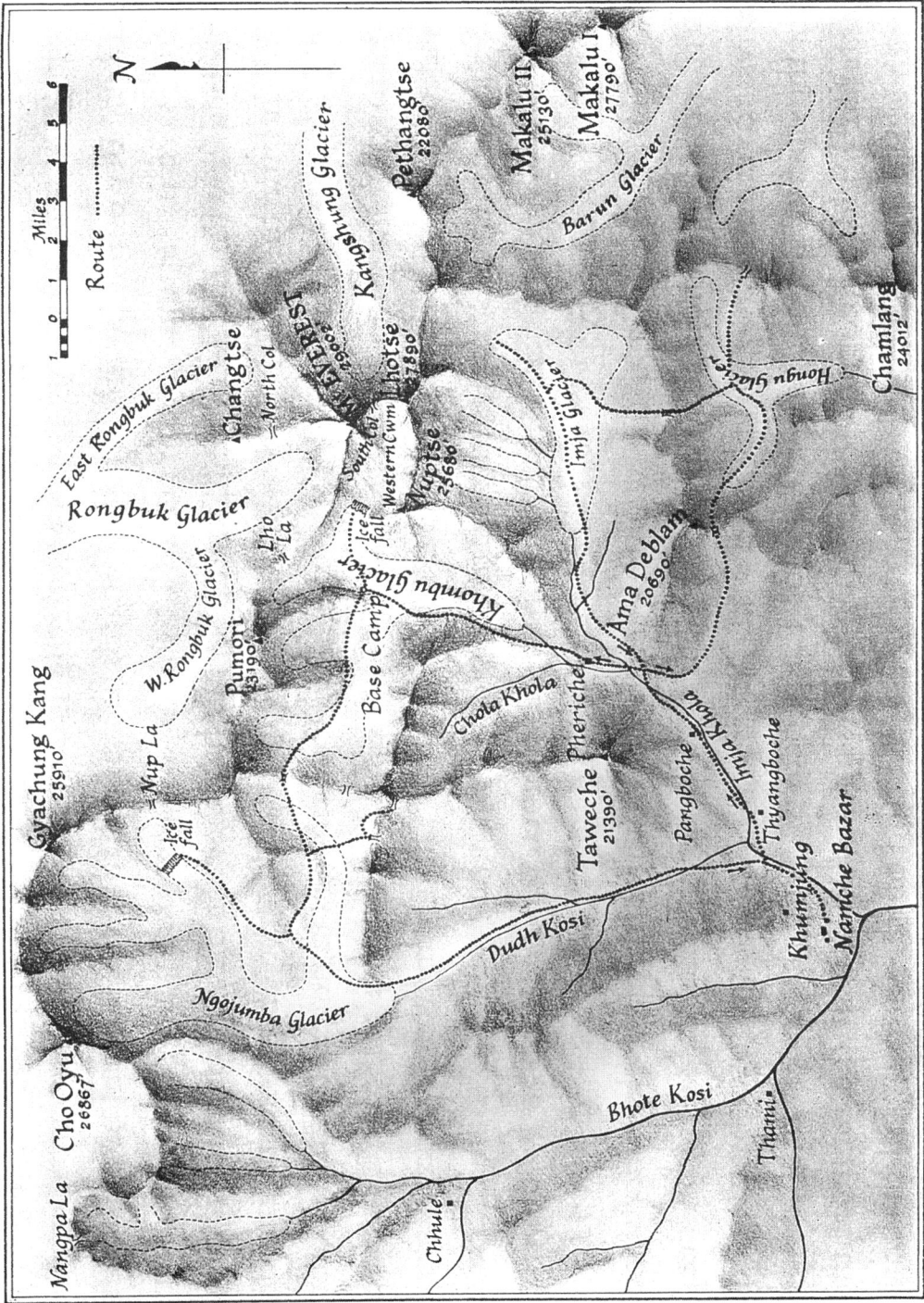

Exploratory journeys to the west and south of Everest, 1951

The party was able to break out of the Imja valley by a 19,000ft pass to the south – the Amphu Labtsa, east of Ama Dablam. This pass led into the upper part of the Hongu glacier system where there were five lakes, the Panch Pokhari. A ridge with a number of peaks and passes separated the Hongu from the next large glacier system to the east, the Barun. This drained not only the west face of Makalu, but also the Tibet-Nepal watershed on either side of the peak Pethangtse and the east side of the Hongu-Barun watershed. The Barun glacier system had been identified during the 1933 'Flight Over Everest'. From a pass on the Hongu-Barun watershed, Shipton and Hillary were able to see a clear route down to the Barun glacier; they also saw a pass leading over the Tibet-Nepal watershed ridge to the west of Pethangtse, which they felt certain would lead onto the Kangshung glacier. They had a clear view of the south and west sides of Makalu and in the distance they could recognise the lower part of the Barun glacier; the descent of this glacier did not look difficult. But any further exploration would have to wait, as the party only had enough food to return to Base Camp. This they did by crossing a col, the Mingbo La, to the south of Ama Dablam and entering the Mingbo valley. Descending this, they crossed to Pheriche and ascended to Base Camp.

This circumnavigation of Ama Dablam opened up a vast unexplored area south and east of Everest. It was fully explored and mapped in 1954 and 1955 by Norman Hardie, and linked up the exploration carried out during the 1921 and 1951 expeditions. It also led to my own first ascent of the peak with Barry Bishop, Mike Gill and Wally Romanes in the winter of 1960-61 during the Silver Hut expedition. At that time it was considered one of the hardest routes in the Himalaya; now it is one of the most sought-after ascents in the Everest region.

Exploration west of Everest and an attempt to reach the Nup La
Bourdillon, Murray, Riddiford and myself travelled due west from Base Camp, making a compass traverse, along a glacier running parallel with the Tibet-Nepal watershed. The Sherpas had told us to look out for a possible pass to the north into Tibet, but none existed. Instead, we crossed a pass westwards from the head of this glacier into a big glacier system falling from the Cho Oyu-Gyachung Kang group. At the head of the Guanara glacier into which we dropped it was possible also to go south, and this we did by another pass looking into the head of the Chola Khola valley which led down to Pheriche and another valley leading to Thyangboche monastery. Returning to the Guanara glacier we descended westwards until it joined the Ngozumpa* glacier which drained the vast and tangled ice fields of the Tibetan border peaks. At the bottom of the east ridge of Gyachung Kang lay the Nup La at the head of the West Rongbuk glacier, which was first visited from the Tibetan side by Bullock in 1921.

* Shown on some maps as Ngojamba.

Gyanchung Kang
7897
8153 Cho Oyu
WEST RONGBUK GLACIER
RONGBUK GLACIER
CHO OYU
EVEREST:
South Side
Nup La
ICE FALL
Changtse
△7538
North Col
Pumori 6623
△
7068
Lho La
NGOJAMBA GLACIER
N
Camp
Camp
Base Camp
KHUMBU GLACIER
EVEREST
South Col
WESTERN CWM
8501
Nuptse 7827
Lhotse
IMJA GLACIER
0 1 2 3 4 5 6 7 8 9 10 km
Namche

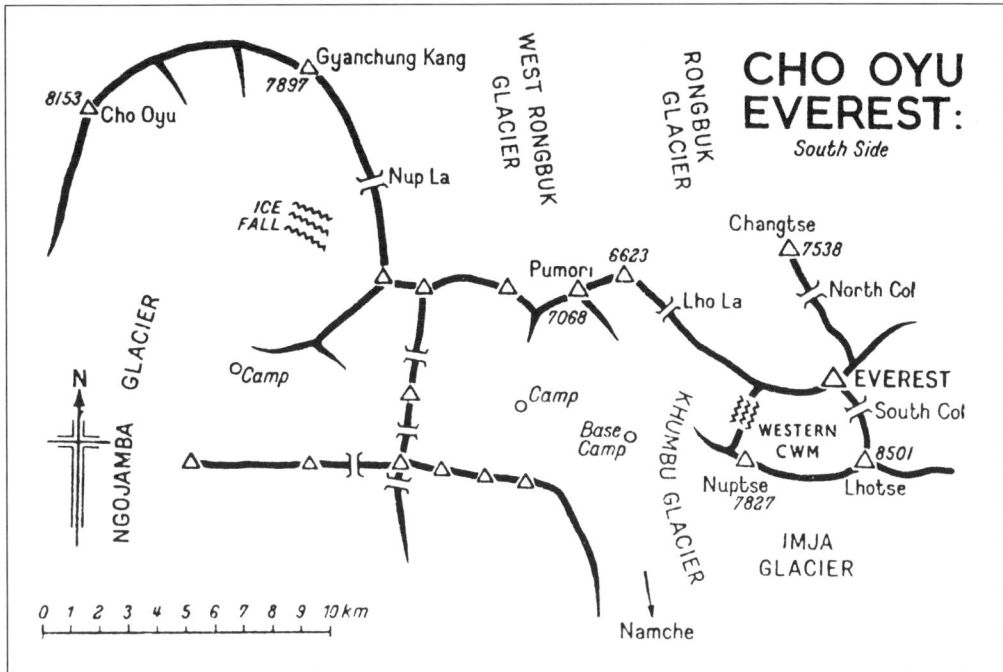

We tried to reach the Nup La, but the lower icefall on the Tibetan side was so technically difficult, even more so than the Khumbu icefall, that after four days we gave up and descended the Ngozumpa glacier to Thyangboche and ascended to Base Camp on the Khumbu glacier.

This exploration to the west of Everest visually linked the 1921 and 1951 expeditions and was complementary to that of Shipton and Hillary around Ama Dablam to the east. Our compass traverse also linked the Khumbu glacier with the Bhote Kosi and eventually with the Menlung basin and the Rongshar.

Exploration further west of Everest: the Nangpa La, Gaurisankar and the Menlungtse group. The yeti footprints.

At the end of October, after we had left the icefall, we returned to Kathmandu by a different route from the one by which we had approached Solu Khumbu. We decided to explore the country to the west of the Bhote Kosi valley. The reasons for this were partly historical and partly geographical.

The Bhote Kosi valley led to the Nangpa La, a glacier pass of nearly 20,000ft on the main trade route between Khumbu and southern Tibet. To the west was the Gaurisankar group of peaks. For many years Guarisankar, which can be seen from Kathmandu, was confused with Everest, yet surprisingly, on the Survey of India ¼-inch sheet, we saw that there was another peak about five miles to the east that was higher than Gaurisankar and yet had no name. This group had spot heights,

EXPLORATION OF
THE MENLUNG AREA
1951

N

Cho Oyu
8188 ▲

Nangpa La

Dudh Kosi

Namche
Bazar

Peak climbed
to see into
Menlung

Bhote Kosi

PANGBUK

MenlungLa

Chhule

Tesi Lapcha

Area of
footprints

Menlungtse
7181 ▲

MenlungChu

Rongshar Chu

Topte

Menlung

Gaurisankar
7135 ▲

Shoktra

Lamobagar

Rolwaling Khola

Bhote Kosi

0   2   4   6   8 Km

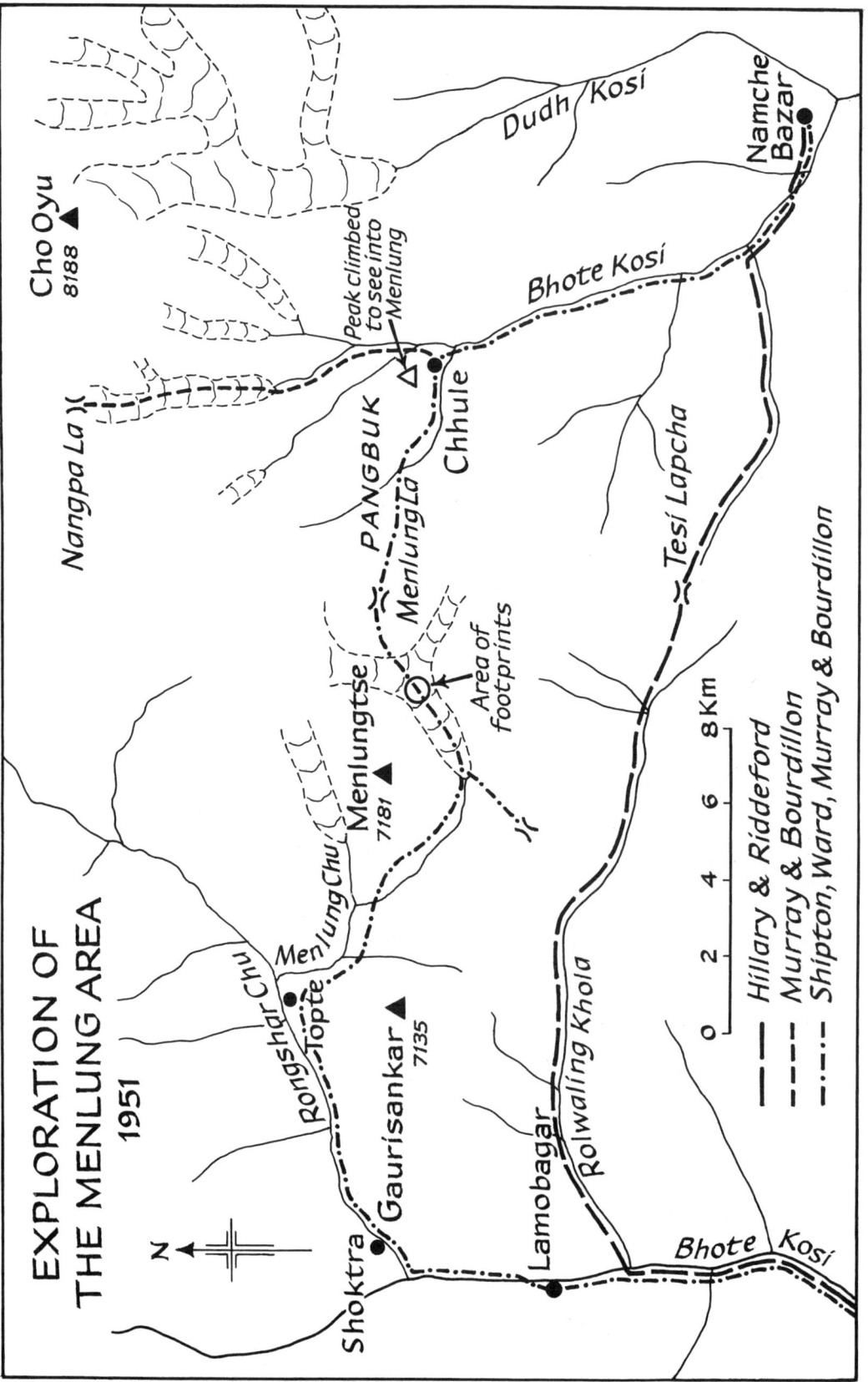

——— Hillary & Riddeford
- - - Murray & Bourdillon
-·-·- Shipton, Ward, Murray & Bourdillon

measured from the plains of India in the 1860s. It seemed highly unlikely that there existed two peaks so close together, and we were inclined to think that a mistake had been made by the Survey. The boundary marked on the map also looked odd as it did not seem to follow a watershed, as demarcated frontiers in the Himalaya tended to do. We wanted, therefore, to solve both these problems, and I made a compass traverse of our exploration to correct the existing map.

Hillary and Riddiford wanted to get back to New Zealand as quickly as they could, as they had been away for six months; so, with Dr Dutt the geologist, they set out for the Tesi Lapcha pass on 4 November. Seldom used by the Khumbu inhabitants, this difficult pass provided access to Khumbu from the west. It led into the Rolwaling valley which ran south of the Gaurisankar group. The rest of us decided to look at the north side of Gaurisankar and an unexplored 'blank on the map' – the Menlung basin.

After saying goodbye to the two New Zealanders, Shipton, Bourdillon, Murray and I went north up the Bhote Kosi towards the Nangpa La, stopping at a grazing site, Chhule. From here Bourdillon and Murray reached the Nangpa La on 7 November, thus creating a visual link with the exploration carried out on the 1921 expedition. To the north, on the Tibetan side of the pass, they had a clear view down the Kyetrak glacier and saw a possible route up Cho Oyu from Tibet. Returning down the Bhote Kosi valley to Chhule, they crossed the Menlung La with Angtharkay on 10 November and joined up with Shipton and myself in the Menlung basin a day or so later.

In the meantime, Shipton and I climbed an 18,000ft peak above Chhule in order to see if there was a pass into the Menlung basin. This climb also provided us with an opportunity to take bearings to the east – to Everest, Cho Oyu and other familiar peaks – and to extend my compass traverse. This would help to supplement the Milne-Hinks map, which lacked detail of the area west of Everest. From 'our' peak we had what we thought was a good view of the south side of Cho Oyu, and what appeared to us to be a possible route up it. To the west, on the frontier ridge that ran north from the Tesi Lapcha to the Nangpa La, we saw a pass and, beyond it, a fine steep peak which did not appear to be in the right position for Gaurisankar. Perhaps the Survey of India was correct after all and this was the 'extra peak' marked on their map.

Leaving Angtharkay behind, Shipton and I, with Sen Tensing, crossed the Menlung La after dawn. A glorious spire of pale pink granite, capped by snow, stood out immediately in front of us in Tibet. This was the unnamed mountain which, on the map, was higher than Gaurisankar. To its north stretched the endless brown bare plains of Tibet, with the Lapche Kang range in the distance and, on the far skyline, Gosainthan (Shisha Pangma). We named our granite peak 'Menlungtse'

The Meh-Teh, the Dzu-Teh and the Chu-Teh,

Drawings of yeti made in 1954 by the lama, Kapa Kalden of Khumjung

after the stream that meandered through green meadows round its foot – a vast amphitheatre of pastureland glacier. It reminded Shipton of the sanctuary from which Nanda Devi springs. The glacier falling from the Menlung La on which we stood swept around Menlungtse to the south and west, separating it from a giant rim of mountains to the south, whose highest peak was Gaurisankar. This rim was on the north side of the Rolwaling valley down which Hillary and Riddiford had gone some days before. It was also the Nepal-Tibet frontier, and we had inadvertently crossed it into Tibet.

For our crossing of the Menlung La, the three of us were carrying loads of 45lbs or more; this enabled us to be self-supporting for up to ten days. It was at about midday that we came across some tracks on the snow of the glacier. We were travelling together, unroped, at about 16-17,000ft. This was a dry glacier and not dangerous, with only very small, easily-seen crevasses. We stopped and examined the tracks.

Sen Tensing had no doubt in his mind as to what they were – yeti tracks.*
Questioned closely, he was quite adamant that he had seen similar tracks in Tibet
and other parts of the Himalaya. Here there seemed to be two distinct sorts of
track. One set was well defined in that individual prints had recognisable features
such as toes; a second group was less well defined, with few if any individual features.

The more interesting were the well-defined tracks, most of which were on a thin
covering of snow over hard glacier snow-ice. Many, but not all, of the imprints were
clear-cut, and there were a great many of them. As we had no means of immediate
measurement, the only way to assess their dimensions was to photograph them
against an object of known length and breadth, so two photographs were taken
with my foot and ice axe for comparison. I take size 42, or 8½ shoes, so I suppose
the tracks were about 10-12 inches long, but broader than a normal 4½-inch wide
boot. We chose one particular print for the photograph, as it seemed a good and
clear impression. It had what looked like a big toe, being broader than the others
but not so long. This feature is, in fact, quite common in human feet. The smaller
toes were less distinct. There may have been four or five, but it was hard to tell. The
print was clearly etched in about an inch of softish snow on a hard, almost icy base.
We were just underneath Pangbuk, a peak climbed by Tom Bourdillon and Ray
Colledge a year later in 1952. These distinct tracks went down the glacier and we
followed them for about half an hour before they turned off onto a side moraine;
we continued down the valley. The tracks went straight down the glacier, which
was almost level but with some very narrow and shallow crevasses, perhaps about a
foot or less wide. Where those crevasses had been crossed by a line of prints, it
seemed as if a 'claw' had protruded beyond the imprint of each of the toes. About 30
minutes further down we saw herds of wild sheep near the side of the glacier. These
could not possibly have made the distinct tracks that I have described but it is just
possible that the less distinct tracks could have been made by an animal running,
though I am unsure about this.

About 48 hours later, on 11 November, Bourdillon and Murray followed the line
of the yeti tracks further down the glacier, and both men noted in their diaries that,
though deformed by wind and sun, the tracks took an excellent line down the glacier.
In his autobiography, published posthumously in 2002 by Bâton Wicks under the
title *The Evidence of Things Not Seen*, Murray wrote as follows:

> Almost at once we found the tracks made three days earlier by Shipton's party
> of three. All these were distinct. We had followed them only a few hundred yards

* The word *yeti* or *yeh-teh* is a mutation of *meh-teh* used in Solu Khumbu. The epithet 'Abominable
Snowman' probably dates from the 1921 Everest expedition and was used as a translation of *mehteh
kangmi* – the creature that made the tracks found on the Lhakpa La on that expedition.

when I was surprised to see a fourth line of footprints descending from the base of a rock buttress close above to our right (west) and joining the three others on the glacier. Sun had obliterated all but the broad imprints ... I pointed out the fourth set of tracks to Bourdillon, who on impulse snapped them with our colour camera.

We followed the tracks for the better part of two miles, for they had taken the best route through the crevasse system until the ice became excessively riven, when they diverged on to the stony moraine, where we lost them. ...

Shortly afterwards, we spotted Shipton's camp just a quarter of a mile lower down. He and Ward came up to join us. ... Then came their most astonishing news – the discovery of clear yeti tracks two days earlier. ...

I repeat this old story because in recent years it has been questioned and Shipton not alive to defend. In a *Sunday Times* article, it was suggested that Shipton might have been a practical joker. I can refute that. Michael Ward and Sen Tensing were there too. Eric Shipton, like us all, had a sense of humour, but we are not practical jokers or party to public deceit. When Bourdillon and I met Shipton, Ward and Sen Tensing, we found all three in a state of subdued excitement, recognisably genuine as they described the detail. Moreover, when they told us of the yeti tracks converging on their own, we knew it to be true. We had not only seen the convergence ourselves, but Tom had photographed it (he later sent me the colour transparency), and I had recorded the incident in my diary, which I still have.

It is to be hoped that this account by Bill Murray, a universally respected figure, will finally put an end to unworthy speculation that the story of the yeti tracks reflected some sort of tasteless joke conducted by Shipton, with the connivance of myself. As Murray succinctly put it 'We are not practical jokers or party to public deceit.'

We camped a good way down the Menlung glacier which ended in a valley curving north and west between Gaurisankar and the solitary spire of Menlungtse. To the south, and fairly close to our present position, we could reach the rim by an easy pass from which we would be able to look into the Rolwaling valley, and perhaps descend into it. Next day we climbed to the pass,* but the descent would have involved over 6,000 feet of cliffs, forest and steep grass with no obvious track, so we decided to continue down the Menlung valley.

We could not see the Tesi Lapcha pass going from Khumbu into the Rolwaling valley – it was tucked away to the east – but the Lumding peaks south of Namche Bazar stood out clearly and the east ridge of Gaurisankar reared up to the west in a series of towers and buttresses. As we followed 'our' glacier down we gradually

---

* This pass, the Hadengi La, was crossed in 1954 by Raymond Lambert's party from the village of Beding in the Rolwaling valley. They then crossed the Menlung La, descended to Chhule and went north over the Nangpa La to attempt Cho Oyu from its north side.

realised that we were in Tibet, and this was confirmed when one of our Sherpas, who had climbed a small hill to see the way ahead, suddenly recognised the steep gorge into which we were descending. It was the Rongshar, he said, and a few years ago he had smuggled horses along it across the frontier. We now knew where we were, for the 1921 expedition had followed the Rongshar gorge from the north to the Nepalese border. In 1924 Somervell had followed the same route after crossing the Phuse La, west of the Kyetrak glacier. He had made a watercolour drawing of 'Gaurisankar', but it is possible that he was mistaken and that the peak he actually painted was Menlungtse which, at that time, was still undiscovered.

The Menlung river which we were descending ended in the Rongshar gorge several miles inside Tibet; this meant that we were in a potentially serious position. Eric Shipton was a former Consul in Kunming who had 'escaped' down the Yangtze Kiang river a few months previously. Moreover, Tom Bourdillon worked for the British Government and I was a member of the Armed Forces. As we did not have permission to be in Tibet, we feared that an ugly diplomatic incident, or worse, was looming. We discussed returning over the Menlung La or descending into the Rolwaling valley but dismissed both ideas as impractical. Lower down we found a path with overhanging bushes that obviously joined the Rongshar, and we descended it to a place some way short of the gorge path. Here we waited for several hours until night fell and our eyes became accustomed to the dark. At about 10.30pm we set off at a good pace for the Nepal border. The full moon lit our steps but as we got deeper into the gorge great pools of black shadow hid the path. Like the Arun river, the Rongshar had carved a massively deep and narrow gorge through the Himalaya. The thunder of the torrent beside the path reverberated against the canyon walls, drowning the noise of our footsteps as we passed quickly through Topte village, hoping that the Tibetan mastiffs, let off their chains at night, would not hear or smell us. In the dark we stumbled over roots and rocks – in places a tree ladder had to be climbed and in one fearsome place the path was only a few branches wide, balanced on a cliff face thirty feet above the boiling river and held into cracks in the rock by small twigs. This particular section must have been the 'impassable' area mentioned in the book of the 1921 Everest expedition. Horses had to be blind-folded before being brought along this path, with riders at front and rear holding onto their heads and tails.

Just before dawn we passed a few huts at the village of Shoktra. At about 4.0am our 'smuggling' Sherpa reckoned we were past the frontier and so we stopped and slept at the side of the path, for we had been travelling hard for six hours in the dark. An hour later the sun came up and we were surprised by a group of six wild-looking Tibetans with long pigtails, armed with swords and muzzle-loaders with antelope-horn rests, who erupted onto the scene with much shouting. We could not escape since a vertical rock cliff of over 2,000ft towered behind us, and the boiling Rongshar river was only a few feet away. Evidently these Tibetan levies, when they had woken at dawn, had seen our boot prints in the sand and had come to investigate. Immediately a noisy and furious argument started, with much gesticulating and shouting. Angtharkay, all of five feet tall, seemed incandescent with fury. He continually shouted at the Tibetans, and as soon as things became quiet he started again. As the whole argument was conducted in Tibetan, we had no idea what it was about.

After ten minutes of this Angtharkay came over to us and suggested that we four Europeans should retire a suitable distance away while he and the other Sherpas sorted things out. After a further twenty minutes he returned with a broad grin. 'Everything is settled,' he said, 'but I'm afraid it will cost you seven rupees to buy them off.' Ten rupees had been demanded but Angtharkay had considered this exorbitant. The shouting had been the negotiations.

At the time, we treated this incident light-heartedly but it could have had serious consequences, and it did indeed influence events in 1952. Later, in Kathmandu, Christopher Summerhayes, the British Ambassador, discussed the incident with the King of Nepal and no further action was taken, but it certainly played an important part in Shipton's decision, the following year, not to go deliberately into Tibet again to attempt Cho Oyu.

When we arrived in Kathmandu I was surprised and deeply disappointed to learn that the Swiss had obtained permission to attempt Everest in 1952. As later became clear, they had applied for permission as early as May 1951.

Some theories about the yeti
Since our sighting of the yeti footprints in the Menlung basin there has been endless speculation about them. Yet after extensive exploration of the Himalaya, Tibet, Central Asia and Western China, no convincing evidence has emerged of any such creature, and no sign of a skeleton, fur, carcass, bones or faeces has ever been found. There must, therefore, be some other explanation and it is possible that, though a bear or monkey cannot be completely discounted, the possibility that 'our' tracks might be human should not be dismissed either.

The Menlung basin, although remote, was only two or three hours away from two small villages – Topte and Shoktra – in the Rongshar gorge, in which there was a path connecting Nepal and Tibet. There was also a well-worn path leading into the gorge from the Menlung basin. It is therefore possible that the grass-covered lower basin was grazed by herds of yak. Though we saw no yaks, we did later disturb a yak herder who fled from us.

Abnormally-shaped prints could be the result of congenital or acquired enlarge-ment of one or more toes, or of part of the whole of a foot. In primitive communities, many miles from basic medical and surgical facilities, any abnormality would remain untreated from birth onwards. Polydactyl births, with up to ten toes on each foot, occur from time to time, as does the fusion of one or more toes. Deformities due to club foot are frequently described and I have seen a Himalayan highlander at 14,000ft who had both his big toes pointing inwards at right angles to the rest of the foot. This congenital deformity made it impossible for him to wear any form of footwear and produced bizarre footprints. Abnormally-shaped feet may also occur as a result of chronic, untreated infections such as leprosy.

The 'claw marks' observed in the Menlung prints could be explained by the presence of *Onychogriffosis* or ram's-horn nail. Though more common in the big toe, when the deformed nail may curve around and puncture the skin of the undersurface, this condition can occur in any of the nails, some of which may stick out like claws an inch or more beyond the toe. It results from minor trauma and infection in unhygienic conditions. Normal treatment is by surgical removal under anaesthetic – a facility not available in remote Himalayan valleys.

Though neither Shipton nor I realised it at the time, the inhabitants of the Himalaya and Tibet can and do walk in the snow for long periods in bare feet with-out frostbite, and I was later to see this also in Bhutan and Tibet. Confirmation came in January 1961, during the Silver Hut expedition in the Everest region, when a Nepalese pilgrim who normally lived at 6,000ft visited our research sites and lived for fourteen days at 15,300ft and above. Throughout this period he wore neither shoes nor gloves and walked in the snow and on rocks in bare feet with no evidence of frostbite. Moreover, he slept outside with no shelter, at measured temperatures of minus 13°C, and managed to avoid hypothermia by controlled light shivering. At no time did the temperature of his bare feet drop to freezing, probably because a certain degree of controlled reflex dilation of the blood vessels to the skin of his feet enabled warm blood to circulate. Eventually he developed deep fissures in his toes, the result of drying and splitting of the skin, which became infected. Because of this he returned home to a lower altitude and warmer climate. Later, an investigation of Buddhist practitioners of G-Tum-Mo yoga confirmed that it was possible to 'warm without fire' under experimental conditions; these practitioners had the capacity to raise the temperature of their fingers and toes by as much as 8.3 per cent. If a non-cold-tolerant person were to follow the example of these individuals he would become severely frostbitten, hypothermic and possibly die.

Following the expedition's return to London, the Natural History Museum put on an exhibition in which they seemed to suggest that the 'yeti footprints' might belong to an as yet unknown animal. The then recent discovery of the Coelacanth and the Chinese Fossil Tree served to encourage this belief. However, despite many expeditions in the Himalaya and Central Asia the existence of the yeti remains a matter of speculation.

BIBLIOGRAPHY

H Benson, J H Lehmann, M S Malhotra, R F Goldman, J Hopkins, M D Epstein, 'Body temperature changes during the practice of G Tum-Mo Yoga' in *Nature 295*, 234-236, 1982.

T D Bourdillon, *Diaries of the Everest Reconnaissance Expedition 1951* from M P Ward archive.

J Jackson, 'The Elusive Snowman' in *Alpine Journal 104*, 71-80, 1999.

W H Murray, 'The Reconnaissance of Mount Everest 1951' in *Alpine Journal 58*, 433-452, 1952.

W H Murray, 'The Reconnaissance of Mount Everest 1951' in *Himalayan Journal 17*, 19-41, 1952.

W H Murray, *The Evidence of Things Not Seen*. Bâton Wicks, 2002.

Letter, dated 10 January 1952, from Basil Goodfellow to Lucien Devies of the Fédération Française de la Montagne. Everest archive, RGS.

L G C E Pugh, 'Tolerance to extreme cold at altitude in a Nepalese pilgrim' in *Journal of Applied Physiology 18*, 1234-1238, 1963.

E E Shipton, *The Mount Everest Reconnaissance Expedition 1951*. Hodder & Stoughton, 1952.

E E Shipton, 'Everest. The 1951 Reconnaissance of the Southern Route' in *Geographical Journal 118*, 117-141, 1952.

Unattributed note, 'Mount Everest Reconnaissance Expedition' in *Geographical Journal 117*, 3633, 1951.

M P Ward, 'The Exploration of the Nepalese side of Everest' in *Alpine Journal 97*, 213-221, 1992/93.

M P Ward, 'The Great Angtharkay' in *Alpine Journal 101*, 182-186, 1996.

M P Ward, 'The Yeti Footprints. Myth and Reality' in *Alpine Journal 104*, 81-87, 1999.

M P Ward, 'Everest 1951: The footprints attributed to the yeti – myth and reality' in *Wilderness and Environmental Medicine 8*, 29-32, 1997.

Chapter 17

JUST A LITTLE FURTHER
The Swiss Expeditions. Spring and Autumn, 1952

Introduction

For many years Swiss mountaineers had wanted to climb Everest, on which the British appeared to have a monopoly. In 1949 René Dittert, a well-known and highly respected Swiss mountaineer, discussed with Dr E Wyss-Dunant, a physician, the idea of a combined mountaineering and scientific party to Everest composed mainly of climbers from Geneva. The recently formed Swiss Foundation for Alpine Research took up this idea with enthusiasm. In August of the same year Ella Maillart, the well-known Swiss Central Asian traveller, and Arnold Heim, a Swiss geologist who had worked in south-west China and southern Tibet, visited Kathmandu and subsequently suggested to their friends that an attempt be made on Everest. Finally, in May 1951, the Swiss applied for permission for an attempt on Everest in 1952. This was granted by the Nepalese Government in November. The Nepalese would have been happy to give permission for a joint Anglo-Swiss expedition but, not surprisingly, negotiations between the two countries broke down. In his auto-biography *That Untravelled World* Eric Shipton describes what happened:

> [The Swiss] suggested that we should unite with them in a combined effort under the joint leadership of Dr Wyss-Dunant and myself. After careful consideration, however, the Himalayan Committee decided to decline this generous offer. The main reason was our belief that neither joint leadership nor a team of mixed nationalities, however idealistic in theory, was likely to work smoothly under the physical and psychological stresses peculiar to an attempt on Everest.

Although this outcome caused despair among the members of the British recon-naissance expedition of 1951, it proved a blessing in disguise, since it allowed the British more time for preparation. In particular, it enabled Griffith Pugh to test his theories about the Everest altitude problem in the field at 20,000ft during the 1952 Cho Oyu expedition, and to confirm that they were correct.

The Swiss party came from a group of extremely active and very able climbers based in Geneva who called themselves l'Androsace. Their numbers were limited to about forty and all were mountaineering fanatics who had completed some of the hardest routes in the Alps. They were sponsored by the Swiss Foundation for Alpine Research, and the City and Canton of Geneva supported their expedition by promising money and equipment. Their physiological advice came from Dr Oskar Wyss of the Medical Faculty of the University of Zurich.

Spring expedition

The strong and talented Swiss team consisted of Dr E Wyss-Dunant (leader), J-J Asper, R Aubert, G Chevalley, R Dittert, L Flory, E Hofstetter, R Lambert, A Roch. The scientific members were Mme Lobsiger, an ethnologist, Dr Lombard, a geologist, and Dr Zimmerman, a botanist.

Arriving in Kathmandu on 26 March 1952 they were able to leave for Everest within three days, as all their equipment had been pre-packed in Switzerland into porter loads. Their sirdar was Tenzing Norgay who had been with a Swiss Himalayan party in 1947 and who, with Angtharkay, was one of the most experienced of the Sherpas. His first Everest expedition had been in 1935, when he was attached to Charles Warren, the medical officer. Another Sherpa on the Swiss expedition was Da Namgyal who in 1950 had been with the French party that climbed Annapurna, thus making the first ascent of an 8,000-metre peak.

The approach march from Kathmandu went east across the grain of the country, by the Chyubas ridge and then by a number of easy passes until the Dudh Kosi river was reached at Jubing. Here the route turned north along the river until the party reached Namche Bazar on 13 April. They left again on the 15th, a day before the arrival of the British Cho Oyu party. By contrast with the latter, the Swiss remained very fit throughout the march-in and free from any serious illness – they probably owed this to their meticulous attention to details of hygiene; to avoid infection they slept away from local houses and outside villages.

Base Camp was established on 20 April but had to be moved closer to the foot of the icefall. The weather remained bleak, with snow falling every afternoon and evening.

Success in the Khumbu icefall

On 25 April a first attempt was made on the icefall by Dittert, Aubert, Chevalley and Lambert, and after six hours they reached 18,400ft. Two days later they took only two hours to reach the flag marking their highest point, but because of the complexity of the climbing, they had only gained 300 feet four hours later. Next day, the 28th, they put a camp in the icefall and on the 29th Roch, Asper, Flory and Hofstetter reached the rim of the Western Cwm. As in 1951, a monstrous crevasse stretched from one side to the other, barring the entrance to the cwm proper.

Next day they returned and Asper tried to pendulum across the crevasse, without success. He then descended 65 feet into the crevasse and managed with great difficulty to climb an ice chimney on the far side of it. In doing so, he became the first man to enter the Western Cwm. A rope was stretched across the crevasse, fixed at both ends; one by one, secured by a karabiner, the party crossed it, hand over hand, with their knees hooked over the rope. This hidden valley, with sides rising 10,000ft to the summits of Everest, Nuptse and Lhotse, was at last giving up its secrets. But having overcome one obstacle, they were now faced with the next one: the slopes leading to the South Col.

With a month left to climb Everest before the start of the monsoon, a stream of porters now carried supplies into the cwm. The route was marked with flags, and tree-trunks were used for bridges across the many crevasses. While this was going on, a party pressed on to the end of the cwm and, on 6 May, they had their first good view of the slopes leading directly up to the South Col. They were confronted by a steep, snow and rock buttress which they called l'Éperon Genevois (Geneva Spur), the height of which was 3,500ft at an average angle of 40°–45°; in other words it was comparable in length and steepness with the Brenva Face of Mont Blanc. To the right was an ice gully separating the buttress from the glacier, which reached up the north face of Lhotse from the head of the Western Cwm. This consisted of a series of ice walls with flat areas in between, and some crevasses and snow slopes. Its overall angle was less, however, than that of the Geneva Spur.

Tenzing was quite happy for the Sherpas to carry loads up the Geneva Spur. 'Just like the North Col,' he commented, remembering his experiences in the 1930s. Camp V was placed at the foot of the Lhotse Face (21,000ft). Here a Sherpa developed malaria, was treated with Paludrine and descended. This was an isolated incidence, as the health of the party remained good throughout the expedition.

Fight for the South Col

The first attempt to reach the South Col (25,850ft) was made on 15 May by Dittert, Roch, Lambert and Tenzing. The route chosen was the gully to the left of the Lhotse Face, and then up the Geneva Spur. At 24,200ft they tried to move left from the crest of the buttress in order to take a more direct line to the South Col, but they found this too difficult and descended again to Camp V. On their return all the climbers complained bitterly of thirst. On 17 May, at 6.0am, there was 30° of frost in camp. As Roch had a fever, Aubert, Chevalley, Dittert, Lambert and Tenzing set out. By 3.0pm they reached their highest point, 25,000ft, and Tenzing was now certain that Sherpas could carry loads up the route. But there was no camp site nor even a good place to bivouac, which meant that the whole 'carry' would have to be done in one day – a Herculean task at that height, with the dangers of exhaustion, hypothermia, frostbite and altitude deterioration.

On 19 May Chevalley, Asper and Da Namgyal tried again and by 5.0pm had reached 25,500ft, but they were too tired and too late to cross to the South Col. Abandoning the buttress, they traversed across to the top of the Lhotse glacier face and descended this without danger or difficulty. On the same day, Flory and Aubert tried another route up the Lhotse Face but they found it too difficult and had to abandon it. Five hundred feet of rope was now fixed to the Geneva Spur to help overcome the difficult places, and a depôt was placed 1,500ft below the South Col at 24,280ft. This was done so that the Sherpas could carry their loads to the South Col in one day and return. As some of them might not be able to achieve this, a bivouac platform was made at 24,000ft.

First attempt: to 28,220 feet

The decision was made that there should be two summit parties, the first with Lambert, Tenzing, Aubert, Flory and six Sherpas, and the second with Dittert, Roch, Asper, Hofstetter, Chevalley and five Sherpas.

On 25 May, after 48 hours of storm, the wind died down and the sun reappeared. A very late start by the first assault team meant that the South Col was not reached before dark, resulting in an enforced bivouac on the upper part of the Geneva Spur. On 26 May, tents were pitched for the first time on the South Col – a white, wind-polished waste land of hard ice. Not all the Sherpas had been able to leave the bivouac site, and Tenzing returned to help them carry their loads to the South Col.

On the 27th, three Sherpas had to leave the South Col exhausted and suffering from altitude deterioration. At the same time, Aubert, Flory, Lambert and Tenzing set off to pitch the final camp as high on the South Ridge as possible. Climbing a couloir from the col to the ridge, the temperature out of the wind was pleasant, but, owing to a design fault, they were unable to use their oxygen sets while climbing; the sets, which were based on mine rescue apparatus, were hopelessly inadequate. They were based on the principle that the expired air, containing moisture, would generate oxygen from chemicals; but the resistance to breathing became prohibitively high at the extremely high rates of ventilation necessary at extreme altitude – so high, in fact, that the climbers felt suffocated and could only make use of the sets while they were at rest. This was useless because extra oxygen is always needed when climbing and it is physiologically impossible to build up reserves when at rest. Another obvious fault was that the oxygen equipment employed a rigid plastic mouthpiece, so that the climber, with his head position fixed, was unable to look

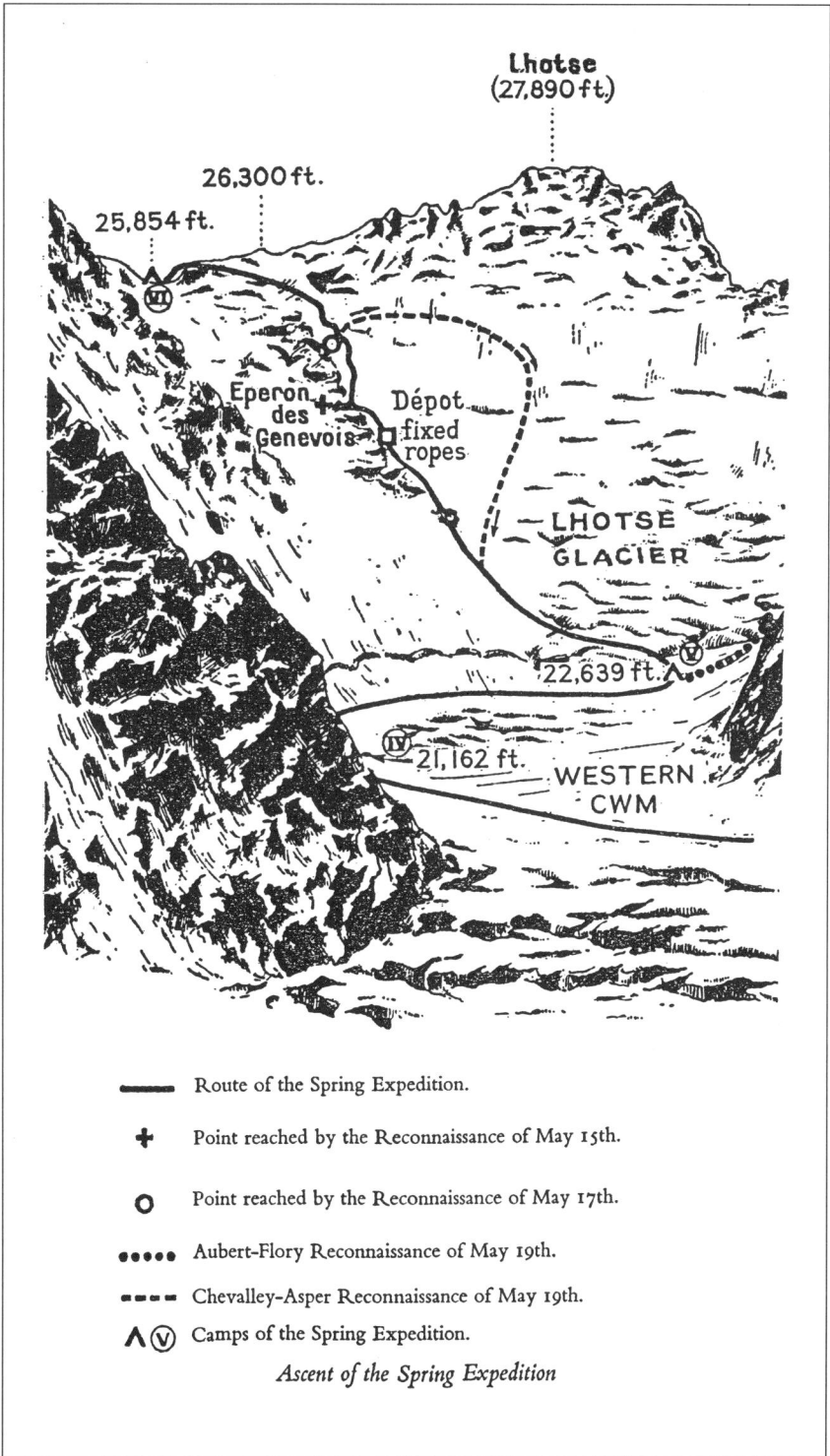

Lhotse
(27,890 ft.)

26,300 ft.

25,854 ft.

Eperon
des
Genevois

Dépot
fixed
ropes

LHOTSE
GLACIER

22,639 ft.

21,162 ft.

WESTERN
CWM

———   Route of the Spring Expedition.

✛   Point reached by the Reconnaissance of May 15th.

O   Point reached by the Reconnaissance of May 17th.

•••••   Aubert-Flory Reconnaissance of May 19th.

- - - -   Chevalley-Asper Reconnaissance of May 19th.

Λ Ⓥ   Camps of the Spring Expedition.

Ascent of the Spring Expedition

The route of the Swiss expedition. Spring 1952.

South Peak

Swiss Camp VII

Couloir

S O U T H   C O L

25,850'

Spring 1952: X = 28,220ft, the highest point reached by the Swiss,
500 feet below the South Summit (South Peak)

for the best holds for his hands and feet. This made the equipment virtually impossible to use while climbing. The end result was that the oxygen sets were more of a hindrance than a help and the main reason for this was that they had not been tested in the European Alps before the expedition left Switzerland. If they had been, both of these design faults would have been identified and corrected. It was this failure, in addition to the gross dehydration they suffered, that prevented the Swiss from climbing Everest in 1952 – a failure of applied science rather than of mountaineering.

At about 27,560ft, just to the left side of the crest of the South Ridge, a final camp was pitched and Aubert and Flory descended to the South Col. Lambert and Tenzing had a dreadful night, since they had no stove and therefore could not melt snow for drinking water. In his joint contribution to 'Forerunners to Everest' in *The Mountain World* (Allen & Unwin, 1954), Lambert commented:

We were overtaken by a consuming thirst, which we could not appease. There was nothing to drink. An empty tin gave us an idea: a fragment of ice and the candle-flame produced a little lukewarm water.

Lambert and Tenzing were grossly dehydrated.*

On 28 May they started at 6.0am as soon as the sun had warmed the tent. With nothing to eat or drink, there was no reason for delay, but as they slowly and pain-fully ascended, the wind increased in force until, after 5½ hours, they stopped 500 feet below the South Summit at a height of 28,220ft. This was higher than the height reached on the north side of the mountain in the 1920s and 1930s. At a rate of climb of 100 feet per hour, it would take them ten hours to get to the summit and five hours to descend. Like all the pre-war parties, they were climbing too slowly to reach the summit and descend in safety before dark. The descent was terrible and intermin-able. They were met by Flory and Aubert on the South Col. Here, though hungry, they could eat nothing because of their extreme thirst and this too was a repetition of what had happened on pre-war British expeditions.

On the 29th the whole party left the South Col and at 9.30am, at the top of the Geneva Spur, they met the second assault party on the way up to the col. By 4.0pm they were back at the foot of the Lhotse Face in the Western Cwm.

A second attempt on the summit

Dittert, Hofstetter, Roch and Chevalley endured an unpleasant night on the South Col and spent the next day recuperating. All were extremely thirsty, having had little or no fluid for 36 hours. In 'Forerunners to Everest' Chevalley describes how he felt:

> ... you cannot move without getting out of breath; you struggle against the congestion and disorder; you do your best to strengthen the tent ends, which the wind strains to lift up and tear to pieces; you place your boots inside your sleeping-bag; you search for something to eat (nuts, bacon – too difficult to cut – a fragment of sausage, a little jam); you would like more to drink (but Mingma Dorje cannot do much on his Meta stove); you fall asleep and the hours fly quickly by. On waking, the psychological struggle is quite painful. Your thoughts have slowed down; they are vague, perhaps euphoric; judgement still remains good, but reflection is laborious. As for your will, it persists and decision is not lacking, but the too confused situation, or the carrying out of some act which encounters insuperable obstacles, is a restraint upon it.

* By contrast, Hillary and Tenzing consumed many pints of water and lemonade at their final camp in 1953.

Unfortunately Roch's ribs, fractured earlier, had not healed and his cough got worse. Hofstetter's physical condition deteriorated rapidly too, so with Mingma Dorje the two decided to descend next day.

On the 31st Dittert and Chevalley planned to make an attempt but the Sherpas would not move. On 1st June the Sherpas, together with Roch and Hofstetter, were too weak to descend alone, so it was agreed that the whole party, strengthened by Chevalley and Dittert, should go down. One of the Sherpas, Saki, was lying in his sleeping-bag ready to die, but eventually he was persuaded to leave. At dusk, they had only reached the bivouac depôt on the Geneva Spur, but Saki was so exhausted that they all had to bivouac. Fortunately the night was fine and, having sleeping-bags, they all survived. If these had been unavailable, some would surely have died from hypothermia and more than one would probably have lost fingers or toes from frostbite. Next day all reached the Western Cwm safely and within a week they were off the mountain.

Swiss autumn expedition

On their return to Geneva the Swiss spring party found that preparations were already advanced for an autumn attempt. Only Chevalley and Lambert were available from the spring party, but five excellent new climbers were chosen. These were N Dyhrenfurth, A Spöhel, E Reiss, J Busio and G Gross. Although it would be colder in the autumn, the Swiss had done much winter climbing in the Alps and it was considered that improved equipment would combat the low temperatures. The oxygen equipment used in the spring was plainly inadequate and this was modified. In the event, however, the combination of cold, wind and oxygen lack defeated the expedition. The wind-chill effect, a combination of wind and cold, produced potentially lethal temperatures of minus 100°C on the skin, and the oxygen sets once again did not function correctly, so that climbers were moving too slowly to generate enough heat.

Arriving on 10 September in Kathmandu, they followed the spring party's route to Namche Bazar. Two porters died from hypothermia on a pass of 12,000ft, owing to inadequate clothing and shelter. Base Camp was occupied on 7 October. The Khumbu icefall was easier than in the spring and by 12 October a camp was established in the Western Cwm. From a camp at the foot of the Lhotse Face a direct route up the Geneva Spur was again made, but on 31 October an avalanche injured four Sherpas, one of whom, Mingma Dorje, died.

It was now decided to use the route up the Lhotse Face. Though less direct than the Geneva Spur, there were a number of places for camps. In the spring Chevalley had reconnoitred the traverse from the top of the face to the South Col and found it feasible. But on 5 November Gross and Busio were prevented from finding a route by intense cold and wind, the first intimation of the paralysing effect of this potentially lethal combination even on highly motivated, experienced and well-equipped climbers. Next, Lambert and Tenzing, using supplementary oxygen, started on the Lhotse Face and made a camp at 24,000ft. Chevalley, at Camp IV at 21,000ft, noted that they were 'more or less transfixed by cold the whole time'. On the 7th Lambert and Tenzing put a camp at the top of the Lhotse Face at about 25,000ft. The oxygen set used by Lambert must have been working well, for he later recorded that he was able to move fast enough to keep warm.

Over the next week the weather improved, as did Sherpa morale, but the wind had become an evil force. The temperature was so low that butter, jam and honey all froze and both food and fluid intake were restricted. The constant noise, too, of flapping tents, and the shriek of the wind across the mountains and ridges, disrupted sleep, thought and all activity.

As the weather improved on 19 November, Reiss, Lambert and Tenzing, using supplementary oxygen, climbed to the South Col, which they reached some time before their Sherpas who had no oxygen. After a monumental struggle the tents were erected, but a temperature of 72° of frost was measured, all food was frozen and only a little water could be made from frozen snow.

The highest point

On 20 November Reiss, Lambert and Tenzing set off for the South Ridge. Pierced by the gusting wind, they only got a short way up the couloir leading to the ridge, to just above 26,600ft. By midday the wind was gusting to 60mph combined with a temperature of 63° of frost, essentially equivalent to skin temperature of nearly 100° of frost. If they had persisted they would have been frozen solid. So they returned to the South Col and descended to Camp VII on the Lhotse Face where Chevalley greeted them. All night they shivered in their sleeping-bags, and next day they descended to the Western Cwm. Six days later they were off the mountain.

Reasons for the Swiss failure on Everest

In September 1952 Pugh visited the Swiss Foundation for Alpine Research in Zurich to enquire about the various problems of their spring Everest expedition. These were freely discussed with him and it emerged that there were two main reasons for the Swiss failure.

Firstly, the oxygen sets used by Tenzing and Lambert were ineffective. As we have seen, the sets used a closed-circuit system which could not cope with the extremely high rate of breathing when climbing and, as a result, the climbers felt suffocated.

Secondly, Pugh established that the Swiss became grossly dehydrated at altitude because the stoves they used were incapable of melting enough snow for water. The result was that their general physical condition was poor at extreme altitude and they suffered severely from high-altitude deterioration.

Both the Swiss attempts, in the spring and in the autumn, were foiled primarily by climatic problems of cold, altitude, wind and the failure of their oxygen sets. Also, the Swiss made a tactical error in the spring by choosing an unsuitable route from the Western Cwm to the South Col. On this route, via the Geneva Spur, there was no suitable place for a camp to break the steep 3,500ft ascent from 22,500ft to 26,000ft. Parties arrived on the col exhausted and some had to bivouac on the way up and again coming down. In the autumn a route via the Lhotse Face was chosen which allowed for two intermediate camps, but, as we have seen, adverse weather conditions and other factors precluded a successful outcome.

BIBLIOGRAPHY

R Dittert, G Chevalley, R Lambert, *Forerunners to Everest: the story of the two Swiss expeditions of 1952*. Allen & Unwin, 1954.

André Roch, *Everest 1952*. Genève. Jeheber, 1952,

André Roch, 'The Swiss Everest Expedition. Spring 1952' in *Alpine Journal 59*, 1-8, 1953.

Eric Shipton, *That Untravelled World*. Hodder & Stoughton, 1969

The Mountain World (English version of *Berge der Welt*), 17-136. Allen & Unwin, for Swiss Foundation for Alpine Research, 1954.

    René Dittert, Gabriel Chevalley, Raymond Lambert, 'Forerunners to Everest':

    Marcel Kurz, 'A Century of History'

    Elizabeth Cowles, 'North to Everest'

    Ernst Feuz, 'Events leading up to and preparations for the 1952 Everest expedition'

    The stages of the Everest expedition of spring 1952:

    René Dittert, 'The Approach. First contacts with the Buddhist world.'

    René Aubert, 'From Namche Bazar to the Base Camp'

    André Roch, 'The Khumbu icefall'

    Jean-Jacques Asper, 'The crossing of the great crevasse'

    Leon Flory, 'Three weeks in the valley of silence'

    René Dittert, 'The struggle for the South Col'

    René Aubert, 'Impressions above 23,000ft'

    Raymond Lambert, 'The attack upon the summit'

Gabriel Chevalley, 'Man at great heights'

Ernest Hofstetter, 'Provisioning and equipment'

Dr E Wyss-Dunant, 'Acclimatisation'

Augustin Lombard, 'Preliminary notes on the geology between
     Kathmandu and Everest (Eastern Nepal)'

Albert Zimmerman, 'The highest plants in the world'

E Wyss-Dunant, 'The First Swiss Expedition to Everest 1952' in *Geographical Journal*
     119, 266-279, 1953.

Chapter 18

BEYOND THE FRONTIERS
The Cho Oyu Expedition, 1952

Introduction

The Swiss having obtained permission from the Nepalese Government to attempt Everest in 1952, the British applied instead for permission to climb Cho Oyu, 25 miles west of Everest. This was granted, together with permission for Everest in 1953. The purpose of the 1952 Cho Oyu expedition was to test the ability of potential Everest members to go to great altitude, and to confirm, at altitude, the observation made in 1951 at the Medical Research Council, that an increase in oxygen uptake from two to four litres per minute was essential in order to increase performance. All other aspects of acclimatisation would also be investigated in the field.

The reason for choosing Cho Oyu was that, in 1951, while climbing a peak above Chhule, Shipton and I had seen a possible route up its south side. The northern, Tibetan side of the mountain was already well known and had been photographed during the 1921 reconnaissance. Moreover, the mountain had been visually inspected by Bourdillon and Murray from the Nangpa La and the upper part of the Kyetrak glacier in 1951, when two possible routes on the north side were identified.

When Cho Oyu had been surveyed from the north by the Survey of India, the symbols T.45 or M.1 had been allotted to it. The 1921 party was the first to discover its correct name. 'Cho' means a deity or demon, whilst 'yu' means turquoise. The letter 'O' may have been included because the name was mis-heard.

The negotiations for a possible joint Anglo-Swiss Everest expedition took a considerable time to resolve, so the decision to send a British party to Cho Oyu was not made until mid-January 1952. As a result, only six weeks were left in which to organise the expedition; lack of funds enforced extreme economy and simplicity. But some money earned by the recent reconnaissance expedition from articles and lectures was available and *The Times* contributed a further £1,000.

Shipton was confirmed as leader and chose the following as members of the party: Edmund Hillary, who had taken part in the 1951 reconnaissance, and George Lowe, his New Zealand climbing partner, who had been with him on Mukut Parbat in 1951; also from New Zealand was Earle Riddiford. Other British members were T D Bourdillon of the 1951 reconnaissance and Campbell Secord, who had been closely involved with the arrangements for that expedition but who had not, in the event, taken part; Charles Evans had climbed in Central Nepal in 1950 with

H W Tilman; A E Gregory was an experienced climber who organised climbing trips to Zermatt where he acted as a guide. Alf told me that he learned 'all about Alpine climbing by attending a Swiss climbing school at Zermatt for two months'. Ray Colledge was another experienced climber from the north of England. Dr Griffith Pugh joined the party in order to verify, in the field, the results of his London research into high-altitude medicine. Unfortunately, I was unable to go because I had to complete my National Service in the Army, but I kept in close touch with Pugh, Bourdillon and Shipton.

Although Shipton initially asked Pugh to investigate only diet, it was obvious at the Medical Research Council that, to have any hope of success in 1953, an in-depth investigation into all the problems of altitude was necessary, and this was made possible by a grant from the Royal Society.

Following his preparations in the autumn of 1951, Pugh went to Switzerland in January the following year to work on the development of new methods of measuring oxygen uptake. Later, on Cho Oyu, he managed to complete his work in the field in spite of being allowed only one porter load (70lbs) of equipment. Another potential problem was that the climbing members of the party had not been briefed about the importance of this work, so Pugh had to be very tactful and persuasive to obtain their co-operation.

In the UK the organisation was done mainly by the New Zealander Earle Riddiford, with Shipton only partially involved as he was fully occupied at the time writing a book about the 1951 reconnaissance. But before leaving for the Himalaya, Shipton visited the Swiss in Zurich, as grave concern had been expressed by them about having two large expeditions in the same area at the same time. As a result, he undertook to travel in from the south, from Jogbani.

The Swiss approached Everest from the west, via Kathmandu and, arriving earlier, had the first choice of porters in Solu Khumbu. The British expedition assembled at Jainagar, the railhead in the Darbangar district of North Bihar. On 31 March they set out at the funereal pace set by the bullock carts carrying their expedition stores, and soon became lost on a hot (156°F in the sun) dusty plain. Benighted, they were offered an elephant for transport, which did not appear. Finally, at Chesipani, the correct route was regained.

Over the next three days they walked across the Siwalik hills – covered in jungle, restless with wildlife – until on 6 April they crossed the Arun river by ferry, as we had done in 1951. It was a time of carefree enjoyment, starting at dawn at around 5.0am in order to benefit from the cool of the day; and the first meal of the day was usually taken in the shade by a stream. By midday the bulk of the march had been completed – the porters, with their immense loads, could not carry for more than

5-6 hours a day. The afternoon was spent walking in a series of easy stages and camp was made by 3.0 or 4.0pm. The daily distance covered was about 12 miles.

For Pugh, however, this was an extremely busy period, and many Sherpas mistook him for a lama, as he strode along, a striking figure, with his bright copper-coloured hair and wearing blue pyjamas; in his right hand he held a whirling hygrometer which they thought was a prayer wheel.

As no studies on food intake or energy output had ever been carried out on climbers and porters during a march-in through the Himalaya, it was important for Pugh to make the most of such a unique opportunity to study these matters. Owing to the absence of roads, one of the unusual features of the Himalayan economy was the reliance on porters for transporting goods, and this is still the case today. Sherpas have the ability to carry loads averaging 60lbs but sometimes as much as 120lbs or even more, which may be equivalent to their own body weight. These staggering loads are carried by means of head bands, with shoulder straps to steady them. A T-shaped stick, about three feet high, is used to rest the loads when standing. Where possible, conical wicker baskets are used, about 12" in diameter at the bottom and 2' 6" diameter at the top, with the open end rising to the level of the porter's head when in place, and with a band going under the load and over the forehead. The centre of gravity of the load, therefore, is as close as possible to a vertical line passing through the spine and the centre of the pelvis. This Sherpa method needs excellent balance and the development of the neck muscles from birth – a child as young as seven years old can carry 40lbs with ease. Porters carry their own food, usually ata or tsampa, eating an equivalent of 3,500 k.cal/man/day. They walk for relatively short periods and then rest. By contrast, Europeans usually walk for longer periods, climb more slowly and stop less frequently.

Shipton's party reached Namche Bazar (11,800ft) on 16 April. The Swiss had left 24 hours earlier and were already on their way to the Khumbu icefall with 200 porters. Despite this, many of the local population were extraordinarily keen to join the British party.

Attempt on Cho Oyu (26,750ft)

On 19 April, three days after arriving at Namche Bazar, seven climbers left for Chhule (15,500ft) – a small group of yak herders' buildings in the Bhote Kosi valley leading up to the Nangpa La and Cho Oyu. Three members remained at Namche to acclimatise. On the 22nd they climbed a small peak east of the Bhote Kosi and all suffered from weakness and fatigue. Next day a temporary base was established at Lunak, a settlement consisting of four stone huts – the last shelter before the Nangpa La.

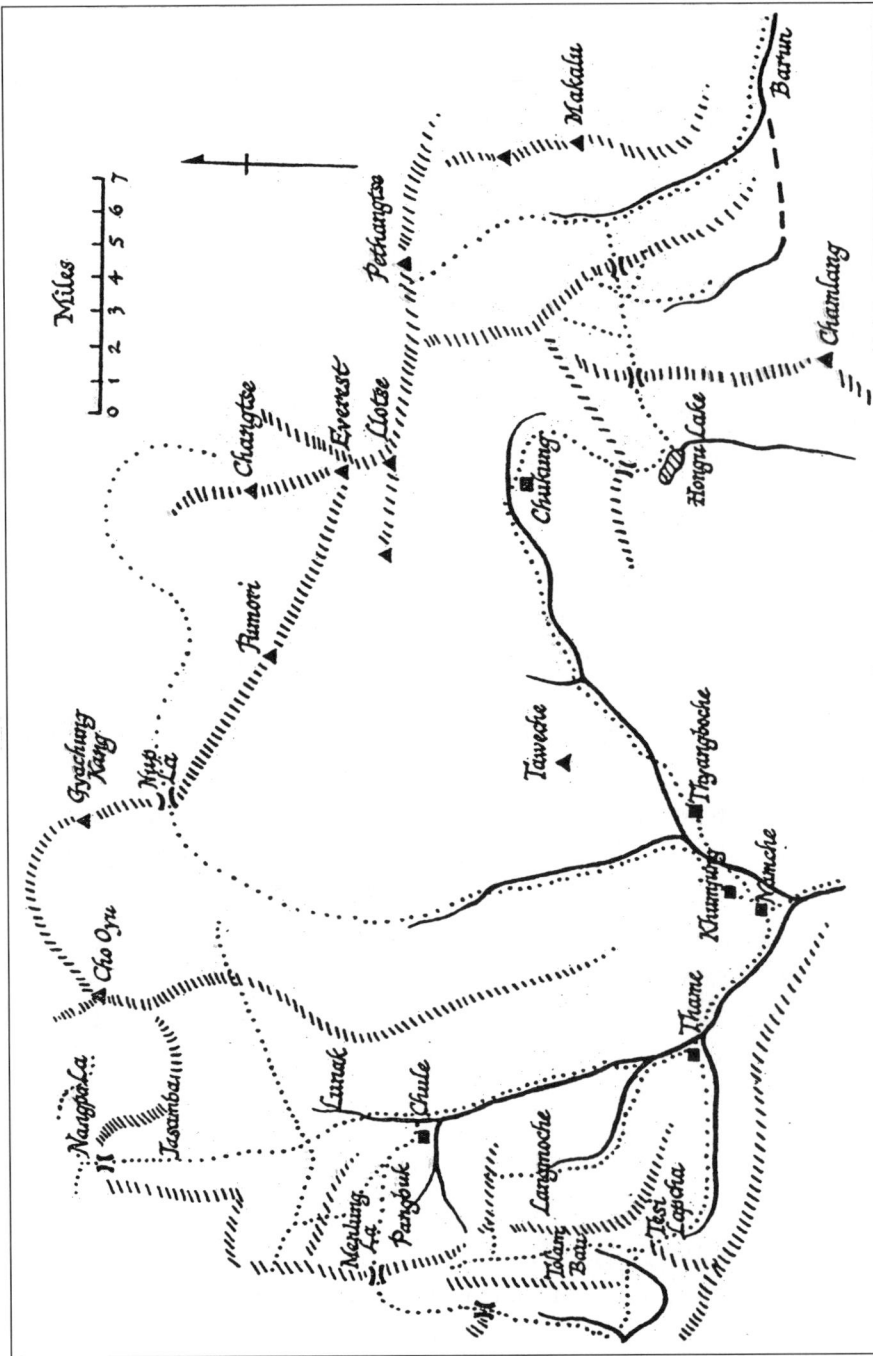

The Cho Oyu Expedition, 1952
—— Exploratory routes
Griffith Pugh's physiology camp was on the Menlung La

Traffic across the pass to Tingri in southern Tibet is usually heavy by mid-April, but in 1952, owing to exceptionally heavy winter snow, the first party across was a group of six Buddhist monks who had accompanied the expedition from Okhaldunga, followed by a large number of Tibetans who had spent the winter in Khumbu where the climate is milder and the food cheaper and more plentiful than in Tibet. They were followed by parties of Sherpas who were crossing the pass in order to buy salt at Kyetrak, the first village in Tibet and a day's march from Tingri. Other groups were making a pilgrimage to Rongbuk monastery on the north side of Everest. Men, women, children, and babies carried in conical wicker baskets, habitually set out on this long glacier trek over one of the world's highest passes, with no extra clothing, no shelter for the night and with only a few sticks of juniper for fuel.

From Lunak, Gregory and Evans moved east to the ridge that runs south from Cho Oyu and which divides the Bhote Kosi valley from the Ngozumpa glacier. Reaching a col at 19,000ft, they had to go further into the Ngozumpa basin before, on 26 April, they could gain a good view of the south face of Cho Oyu. This was a six-mile-long and 6,000ft-high wall of ice and rock which would require artificial aids to overcome. A ridge running south and west from Cho Oyu looked too formidable to climb. This was depressing news, as it meant that the only possibility of climbing Cho Oyu lay in Tibet, for which permission was not available. In the meantime, Hillary and Lowe climbed two peaks of 21,000ft to the west of the Nangpa La, and later Secord, Evans and Gregory climbed one of 18,000ft to the south. These explorations revealed that a feasible route up Cho Oyu did exist but it lay entirely in Tibet, and this was confirmed by Hillary and Lowe who climbed two further peaks in Tibet allowing them a closer view of the possible route.

The political situation in this border region was dangerous – the border between Nepal and Tibet had not yet been clearly defined and any Chinese commander in Tingri would be bound to hear from travellers from Khumbu of a British party on the Nangpa La – news that would spread rapidly to Shekar and Kampa Dzong. Shipton was unwilling to risk possible involvement with the Chinese, who might well believe him to be a spy. He had recently 'escaped' down the Yangtse Kiang river after being British Consul in Kunming, and before that he had been British Consul in Kashgar. Moreover, our exploits in the Rongshar only a few months earlier, when we had been captured by Tibetan levies and had to bribe our way free, would almost certainly be known. All these difficulties were discussed in detail on 27-29 April. Shipton's plan was to put a camp just short of the Nangpa La and send a small reconnaissance party to Cho Oyu. If any party of Chinese soldiers came up from Tingri to the Nangpa La the camp could be quickly withdrawn. This idea gained general acceptance, except from Earle Riddiford who lobbied hard for an all-out attempt on Cho Oyu. He already had gastro-enteritis and a strained back and when his lobbying failed he left the expedition and returned to New Zealand.

On the 29 April a base camp was set up at Jasamba (18,500ft) further down the Bhote Kosi valley. At this stage of the expedition there was still a considerable amount of respiratory and gastro-intestinal infection among the climbers, so it was not until 6 May that a strong but lightly-equipped party set out across the Nangpa La for Cho Oyu on the off-chance that it would be an easier climb than it looked. Secord, Evans, Bourdillon, Hillary, Lowe and Gregory put a camp at 20,000ft. A higher camp was established on a ridge giving access to the upper slopes of the mountain. Hillary and Lowe reached some difficult ice cliffs at 22,500ft, but they had to return. To mount a proper attempt would take, they considered, at least two weeks on the mountain, so they returned to the Nangpa La and Jasamba on 12 May.

The attempt on Cho Oyu was now abandoned, and unfortunately there were no other suitable peaks in the area where a high altitude could be attained. Gyachung Kang, next to Cho Oyu, was obviously too difficult, the unknown Menlungtse was in Tibet and Gaurisankar was on the border, so none of these peaks provided a viable alternative. However, a vast amount of exploratory work remained to be done in the Khumbu region, only small portions of which had been explored in 1951. Already the possibility of a map of the whole Everest region was being considered.

The party therefore split up into three groups. Hillary and Lowe decided to embark on an ambitious project which involved crossing the Nup La into Tibet, descending the West Rongbuk glacier to the main Rongbuk glacier and then attempting the East Ridge of Changtse (Everest's North Peak) at 24,500ft. Shipton, Evans and Gregory would explore the frontier ridge between the Tesi Lapcha pass and the Nangpa La and try to find another way over into the Menlung basin. These two parties would then join forces and explore east of Everest to the Barun glacier, the main glacier draining peaks east of Everest, as far as the Arun river and return to Jogbani in southern Nepal.

At the same time, the third group, Pugh, Secord, Colledge and Bourdillon, would carry out physiological work on the Menlung La at 20,000ft. I had made a note of this high point in 1951 as being a possible place for such work, as it was relatively easy to reach and, unlike the Nangpa La, not on a highway to Tibet.

Crossing the Nup La and exploration into Tibet. An attempt on Changtse.
Hillary and Lowe wanted to circumnavigate Everest by first making the formidable crossing of the Nup La; they would then descend the West Rongbuk glacier, go up the East Rongbuk, cross the Rapiu La, gain the Kangshung glacier and cross back

into Nepal near Pethangtse. To carry out this ambitious plan the first obstacle was the Ngozumpa icefall leading up to the Nup La. Shipton did not believe that they would be able to overcome such a formidable barrier. However, instead of attacking the pass directly, as we had done in 1951, they avoided the extremely difficult lower section by approaching the upper part more closely under Gyachung Kang. This route had been pointed out to them earlier by Evans and Gregory who had spotted it during their explorations on the south side of Cho Oyu and Gyachung Kang. Even so, it took Hillary and Lowe six days to reach the Nup La.

Leaving three days' food in a dump, they took with them seven days' food and decided to attempt the easy East Ridge of Changtse, the North Peak of Everest. They were now so heavily laden that they left their crampons behind on the Nup La, preferring to take the equivalent weight in food. After descending the main Rongbuk glacier, they reached the East Rongbuk in about 7½ hours.

They were now in Tibet and the Sherpas wished to pay their respects to the head lama of Rongbuk monastery, but as this would have advertised their presence to the Chinese, they were dissuaded from doing so. After ascending the East Rongbuk glacier, Hillary and Lowe placed a camp at the lower end of the gently sloping East Ridge of Changtse. Next day, after many hours of step-cutting, they reached about 22,000ft but had to turn back owing to lack of time and increasingly dangerous snow conditions. Returning, they reached the Nup La on 4 June and descended to the junction of the Guanara with the Ngozumpa. Turning east and ascending the Guanara glacier, they crossed a pass at its head (first used by us in 1951) and descended to the Khumbu glacier and the Swiss Base Camp. Here they learned that the Swiss had failed on Everest. They then went down to Pangboche where they rejoined Shipton on 8 June.

For Shipton to have agreed to this itinerary, which involved entering Tibet, when he had vetoed an attempt on Cho Oyu for the same reason, might seem strangely inconsistent. But it is possible that he saw the Nup La as such a formidable obstacle that he believed that Hillary and Lowe had little chance of crossing it. Even if their crossing were successful, a small party would attract much less attention than a full-scale expedition.

Exploration of the Tibet frontier ridge north of the Tesi Lapcha pass. The Tolam Bau glacier.

Meanwhile, Shipton, Gregory and Evans explored the complicated and tangled mass of frontier peaks between the Bhote Kosi and the Menlung basin north of the Menlung La. Unable to make progress west from Lunak, they crossed south over a subsidiary ridge into the valley west of Chhule and saw what appeared to be a 'snow plateau' south of the Menlung La. Having failed to climb onto this, they returned to the Bhote Kosi valley, descended it and went west up the Langmoche Khola; but again they failed to cross into the country beyond. Finally, they crossed the Tesi Lapcha pass and, on its far west side, found a glacier coming from the north – the Tolam Bau. This they followed north and re-discovered the 'snow plateau' that they had previously seen from a pass at its head. However, they still failed to gain access to the Menlung basin; another valley they explored turned out to be the Nangaon which led south into the Rolwaling valley. The view from a peak they climbed at the head of the Tolam Bau glacier gave them some idea of this intricate and tangled country, and showed how lucky we had been in 1951 to find the Menlung La which enabled us to cross from the Bhote Kosi valley into the Menlung basin.

For a few days Shipton had been developing a high temperature and the party returned as quickly as possible to Namche Bazar. There Shipton and Evans waited for the return of Hillary and Lowe from their Nup La-Changtse trip and Gregory left for the UK.

Exploration east of Everest. The Barun and Hongu glaciers and descent to the Arun valley.

The Barun glacier had been identified from aerial photographs taken during the 1933 Flight Over Everest. A large glacier, it drained the east side of Lhotse, the frontier ridge on which Pethangtse stands, the west and south side of Makalu and the east side of the Hongu-Barun watershed. As the Barun Khola, it joined the Arun river just south of the Nepal-Tibet frontier. Its exploration would connect two large river systems – the Bhote Kosi to the west and the Arun to the east.

Shipton decided that the Barun exploration should be carried out in two stages. The first stage would involve Evans, accompanied by Sherpas, crossing the Amphu Labtsa pass from the Imja to the head of the Hongu and placing a food dump at the Panch Pokhari lakes. He would then cross into the Upper Barun and hope to find evidence of animal grazing or human habitation. Such evidence would indicate that the lower gorge of the Barun river was passable for humans coming up from the Arun valley.

Evans left Namche Bazar on 1st June, made a food dump at the Panch Pokhari lakes, continued into the Barun and confirmed that there were human habitations lower down the Barun valley. He then returned to the largest of the five lakes to wait for the others; this trip took about ten days. In the meantime, Shipton, having recovered from his illness, met Lowe and Hillary at Pangboche on 8 June. After a short rest, and carrying three weeks' food, they all crossed into the Hongu where they re-joined Evans on 12 June.

Shipton was now in a quandary. Having written to the Himalayan Committee in London about the Swiss failure, he knew that he ought to return immediately and start organising the British attempt in 1953 – assuming that he was to be appointed leader. As we now know, this was by no means a foregone conclusion, and his decision to continue the exploration, though characteristic, did nothing to help his chances of winning the leadership. Yet the lure and excitement of exploration held him firmly in its grip and, probably as a result of these conflicting priorities, he suffered from violent mood swings which greatly upset his companions.

Shipton having decided to continue his exploration, the whole party now set out for the Barun glacier. Crossing the plateau of the Hongu glacier they climbed two peaks of 22,500ft and 21,800ft respectively which yielded good views of the whole Barun glacier stretching from the Tibet watershed to its entrance into the Barun gorge. Though mapped from the air in 1933, the whole area had never before been visited by Westerners on the ground. To the south was the vast 'plateau' peak Chamlang (24,020ft), and between Makalu, the world's fifth highest peak, and Lhotse lay a beautifully-shaped spire, Pethangtse,* on the Nepal-Tibet watershed. First noted from Tibet during the 1921 reconnaissance expedition, it made up in its graceful appearance what it lacked in height.

On 15 June Shipton and Evans with the Sherpas crossed the eastern edge of the Barun plateau and descended to the Barun glacier, whilst Hillary and Lowe climbed a peak of 21,400ft. On the 17th they all camped under the west face of Makalu and then gained the Nepal-Tibet border watershed west of Pethangtse, and looked down into the Pethang Ringmo valley; in doing so, they had linked up visually with the area seen during the 1921 expedition. They saw a good route up Pethangtse but the weather now broke and a foot of snow fell in a few hours. Avalanches started to fall off the upper slopes – the monsoon was beginning to break.

Continuing down the Barun glacier they soon emerged into a wide valley dominated by the enormous and very steep south face of Makalu, which is a confusion of icefalls and hanging glaciers. Below were many square miles of rich pasture land, with masses of alpine flowers, many of them different from those in the Khumbu valley. At Sherson they came upon a small stone hut built by yak herdsmen who, on seeing the party, fled down the valley. The Europeans must have seemed like ghosts for there was no normal route for the local Sherpas between the Khumbu and the Barun valleys. Further down, however, they came across a camp of shepherds who were unperturbed by this sudden visitation – one of them was engaged as a guide to show them down the valley to the Arun gorge.

They now entered a zone of far greater rainfall than in the Khumbu, for monsoon clouds flowed up the Arun valley from India to Tibet and deposited a lot of moisture as rain. The vegetation, too, was different, and the valleys were shaped like

* Pethangtse was climbed in 1954 by an Anglo-New Zealand expedition.

Norwegian fjords with vertical sides and a broad valley floor. Below 9,000ft, however, these changed to the narrow V-shape of a typical Himalayan gorge. Just above the junction with the Arun river, Evans, with Annullu and Da Tensing, left the party near Hatiya, went north up the Arun, crossed the river by a rope bridge, and then continued east to the Lumba Sumba range. They then crossed the grain of the country to Taplejung and continued south to Darjeeling. The others descended the Arun to the Nepal-India border.

Hillary and Lowe had to catch a boat to New Zealand on 18 July, whilst Shipton returned to the UK to assist with the preparations for the 1953 Everest expedition.

Medical research on the Menlung La (20,000ft). Confirmation of the solution to the problem of 'the last thousand feet' of Everest.

The purpose of Pugh's group of scientists on the Menlung La was to obtain data for the design of satisfactory oxygen equipment for an attempt on Everest in 1953, and to obtain information, within the limits of a mountaineering expedition, on the physiological changes taking place during the processes of acclimatisation and deterioration.

In December 1951, within a few days of the return of the Everest reconnaissance expedition bearing news that a new route on Everest did exist, Peter Lloyd, Griffith Pugh, Dr R B Bourdillon and other scientists had started to build on the preliminary work carried out earlier at the Medical Research Council laboratories. To have any chance of success, it had become clear that this work needed to be extended with much more detail and, in particular, that it should be carried out in the field at high altitude under extreme conditions. Only in this way could the solutions to the medical- scientific problems involved be shown to be consistently effective on Everest and other very high mountains, and therefore acceptable to any climbing party.

The site of the physiology camp was just below and west of the Menlung La. Its position was glorious. The elegant pink granite spire of Menlungtse dominated the western horizon, with the bare brown plains of Tibet to the north and the sharp rim of the Menlung basin, dominated by Gaurisankar, to the south. The camp consisted of one pyramid tent for equipment, with three others housing four Europeans and three Sherpas.

Pugh, Secord, Bourdillon and Colledge took part in experiments which would provide the key to the first ascent of Everest and lay the foundation for greater understanding of the effects of extreme altitude on man. A prepared track was made in the snow with a height difference, measured by barometer, of between 280 and

285 feet between the start and the finish. As this froze overnight and became soft during the day, all the exercise experiments on the track were carried out between 10am and 11am, in strictly comparable conditions of temperature. Times were recorded with a stop watch.

The most important results were those relating to flow rates of oxygen, which would, at altitude, provide an increase in climbing rate. Confirming the work done in London, Pugh showed conclusively that a rate of four litres per minute was essential to compensate both for the weight of the oxygen sets and an increased climbing rate. This was double the rate of about two litres per minute which had been used on pre-war expeditions, a rate which was insufficient to enable mountaineers at altitude to climb fast enough to reach the summit and return within a day. Some of the results of this work on the Menlung La, which lasted seven days, are shown in the table below.

	HIGH-ALTITUDE PROBLEMS	PUGH'S SOLUTIONS
OXYGEN LACK	Hallucinations Extreme shortness of breath 7-10 breaths per step Extreme fatigue Slow rate of ascent	Adequate supplementary oxygen at 4 litres/minute in open circuit sets resulted in a 'lowered altitude' in the depths of lungs; hard climbing became possible and an increased rate of ascent.
DEHYDRATION	Extreme thirst Low urine output Fluid loss from lungs	3 litres/day fluid intake to maintain good physical condition.
STARVATION	Weight loss Loss of muscle	3,000 K.Cal/day to maintain good physical condition.
COLD INJURY	Incipient hypothermia Frostbite	Increased heat production as a result of increased climbing rate. Flexible modern clothing to achieve warmth when climbing.
DETERIORATION	Mental and physical	Sleeping oxygen at 1 litre/minute to achieve a good night's sleep.

The list of contents of Pugh's report to the Medical Research Council is on the following page. The main content of the report is described in the next chapter. More details can be found in Pugh's *Report on the British Himalayan Expedition to Cho Oyu*, published in 1952 by the Medical Research Council. This seminal work was the basis on which the Everest 1953 expedition was organised.

BRITISH HIMALAYAN EXPEDITION

TO CHO OYU, 1952 By D. L. Griffith c. & Pugh

[handwritten signature]

PART I. GENERAL ASPECTS

At the end of this short period, one of the most fruitful in high-altitude mountaineering, Bourdillon and Colledge climbed a peak south of the Menlung La which
they called Pangbuk (22,500ft).* This was centrally placed at the head of the Tolam
Bau glacier. Bourdillon and Colledge then crossed into the Rolwaling valley and
over the Tesi Lapcha pass, returning to Namche Bazar, Kathmandu and the UK.

Russians and Everest, 1952

The birth of Russian mountaineering took place in 1923 with the ascent of Mt Elbrus
(18,482ft) in the Caucasus. This was not the first ascent, which was made by a British
team, with the guide Peter Knubel, in 1874. Between then and the outbreak of war
with Germany in 1940, over 25 expeditions, many with a scientific slant, took place
in the Caucasus, Pamir, Altai and Tien Shan.

The Russians' first visit to the northern, Tibetan side of Everest took place in
1952 following a training camp in the Caucasus. Base Camp was established near
the Rongbuk monastery where all the porters were paid off. In an article entitled
'Mount Everest and the Russians' in the 1994 *Alpine Journal*, Yevgeniy B Gippenreiter,
the celebrated Russian climber, gave the following account of what happened:

> ... the Russians started climbing without a period of acclimatisation. They followed
> the pre-war British route from the north. From Camp VIII at 8,200m the leader
> radioed that the assault party, being in good condition, expected to reach the top
> within the next two days, weather permitting. This was their last message. On 27
> December a search lasting 18 days had to be abandoned because of the onset of
> winter. ... No traces of the six missing men, including the leader Pavel Datschnolian,
> were found and it was assumed that they had all been swept away by an avalanche
> above Camp VIII. The following spring, while the British were climbing on the
> southern side of the mountain, the Russians resumed their search. However, the
> attempt did not produce any new information.

Gippenreiter described the Russian 1952 expedition as 'inadequately planned and
rashly implemented' and commented that it 'might well have taken place in an
attempt to gain political prestige and glory'. He added that 'at the beginning of the
fifties, Soviet climbers did not have the necessary experience to tackle such formidable
objectives and lacked suitable equipment such as oxygen apparatus.' It was only in
1958 that Russian experts started developing modern climbing gear.

---

* Pangbuk received its second ascent, by Dennis Davis, in the course of a Merseyside
Survey Party to the Tolam Bau in 1955.

BIBLIOGRAPHY

R C Evans, 'The Cho Oyu Expedition 1952' in *Alpine Journal 59*, 9-18, 1953.

Yevgeniy B Gippenreiter, 'Mount Everest and the Russians, 1952 and 1958' in *Alpine Journal 99*, 109-115, 1994.

L G C E Pugh, *Report on British Himalayan Expedition 1952*. Medical Research Council, London. Alpine Club Archives.

E E Shipton, 'The Expedition to Cho Oyu' in *Geographical Journal 119*, 129-139, 1953.

M P Ward, 'Preparations for Everest. Cho Oyu, London, Zermatt, 1952' in *Alpine Journal 100*, 222-231, 1995.

1. Telephoto of the Everest Range taken by Dr A M Kellas from the south at Sandakphu. It shows Lhotse, Everest (South Col, South Ridge and NE Ridge) and Makalu. This was one of the earliest photographs of Everest ever taken, probably in 1920 or 1921.

Above

2. The fort at Kampa Dzong in Tibet. It was near here that Kellas died, possibly from high-altitude pulmonary oedema, during the approach march in 1921. The photograph dates from 1938.

Right

3. The headstone for Kellas's grave on a hillside south of Kampa Dzong.

4. Gaurisankar (*left*) and Menlungtse, from the Chyubas range in Nepal. At one time Everest was called 'Gaurisankar', a name never accepted by the Survey of India, who had identified both peaks from a distance.

5. Tinki Dzong, visited by the 1921 expedition on their way to Everest. In the background is the north side of the main Himalayan Range.

6. Members of the 1921 Everest reconnaissance expedition. (*From L*) *Standing*: Wollaston, Howard-Bury, Heron, Raeburn. *Sitting*: Mallory, Wheeler, Bullock, Morshead. Note Norfolk jackets, nailed boots, puttees, sweaters and plus fours. No windproof clothing or down jackets were worn or available, and frostbite was common. Down jackets were used routinely on Everest only from 1951 onwards.

7. *Right*

George Ingle Finch on the 1922 expedition. Many years ahead of his time, Finch designed and wore a windproof down jacket. Unlike his contemporaries, he reached 27,000ft without suffering from frostbite or other ill effects of the intense cold at altitude.

8.   Everest 1921. The North Col (east side) from the Lhakpa La.

9.   Everest 1921. The Kangshung Face, South Col and Lhotse.

10. The famous picture of E F Norton climbing alone at 27,000ft on the north side of Everest. The photo was taken by Howard Somervell in 1924.

11. The north, Tibetan side of Everest, with North Peak in the foreground, photographed in 1936.

12. The 1951 Reconnaissance team: *clockwise from left* E Shipton, W H Murray, T D Bourdillon, H E Riddiford, E P Hillary, M P Ward.

13. The Nuptse-Lhotse Ridge with Everest, midway, peeping over the ridge. Photo taken from Thyangboche in 1951 – the first view of Everest on this approach.

14. W H Murray (*right*) and the author at Namche Bazar in 1951.

15. Taken from Pumori in 1951, this was the first photo to show the full complexity of the south side of Everest. Unlike an aerial photo taken a few years previously, which exaggerated the steepness of the Lhotse Face leading to the South Col, the photo taken from Pumori shows that the angle of the face is actually relatively mild. Although the Khumbu Icefall looks formidable, avoiding it looks even more dangerous than to go straight through it – an unusual concept in 1951. E P Hillary can be seen in the right-hand bottom corner.

16. The Khumbu Icefall, North Face of Lhotse and South Col seen during the 1951 Reconnaissance Expedition.

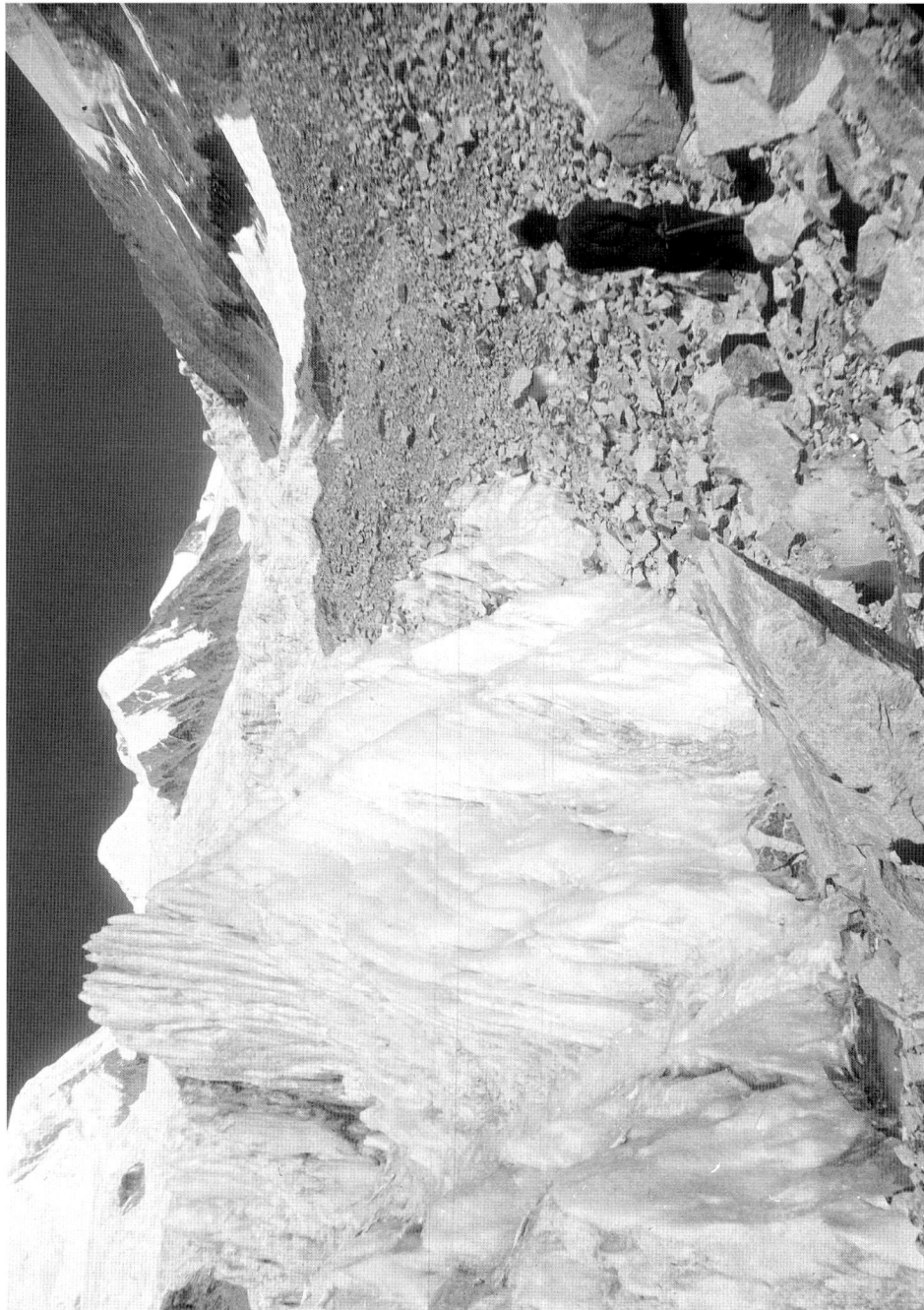

17. 1951. The upper Bhote Kosi valley, leading to the Nangpa La. T D Bourdillon in the foreground. The pundit Hari Ram crossed the Nangpa La in 1885.

18. 1951. The upper Hongu valley, with many glaciers. Ama Dablam in the background. This area was mapped by Norman Hardie in 1954 and 1955.

19. Menlungtse and the Menlung Basin where in 1951 Eric Shipton and Michael Ward saw
what they were told by Sherpas were tracks of the elusive yeti. The first 'on the ground'
identification and naming of Menlungtse was made by Shipton and Ward in 1951.
Its height and that of Gaurisankar had been known to the Survey of India for many years.

20. Kantega and Tamserku, peaks of *c.* 21,000ft, seen from the Sherpa village of Khumjung. Note the contrast between the wooded valleys on the south, Nepalese side of Everest with the bare Tibetan plains on the north side as seen from Tinki Dzong in Plate 5.

21. The Everest team a few days after the first ascent on 29 May 1953. *From left:* C W F Noyce, A E Gregory, L G C E Pugh, G C Band, T D Bourdillon, M P Ward, W G Lowe, Tenzing Norgay, H J C Hunt, E P Hillary, C G Wylie, R C Evans, Dawa Tenzing, T D Stobart and many Sherpas.

22. Everest seen from the air in 1953. The photo shows both the Tibetan and the Nepalese sides of the range and includes the North Ridge, the North Col (west side), the North Face, the Summit, the South Col, Lhotse, the Western Cwm and the Khumbu Icefall.

Right

23. Dr L G C E Pugh (1909-1994), the physiologist on the 1952 Cho Oyu and 1953 Everest expeditions. His studies laid the foundation for the first successful ascent of Everest.

Below left

24. Dennis Davis, surveyor to the 1955 Merseyside Himalayan Expedition, W of Everest. With Tashi Sherpa, he made the first ascent of Nuptse in 1961.

Below right

25. Norman Hardie, surveyor on the New Zealand Alpine Club Himalayan Expedition 1954, and on the 1955 Mount Chamlang Survey Expedition, S and E of Everest. In 1955, with three others, he made the first ascent of Kangchenjunga.

Chapter 19

THE KEY TO THE FUTURE

Preparations for the 1953 Everest Expedition
in London and Zermatt, 1952

Following Griffith Pugh's return to London after the Cho Oyu expedition, I travelled up from the Military Hospital at Shorncliffe in Kent, where I was posted as a surgeon, to see him at his laboratory in Hampstead. He was busy writing a report for the Medical Research Council and the Himalayan Committee.

He told me that two things had particularly concerned him about the expedition. Firstly, there had been no preliminary training period for the mountaineers and no acclimatisation period in the field; as an Olympic-class skier himself, he was accustomed to intensive pre-competition training schedules. Secondly, there had been an almost complete lack of hygiene precautions taken by the party, and this was associated with an abnormal amount of respiratory and gastro-intestinal infection among its members.

Pugh said that his own work on the Menlung La had gone extremely well and that he had been able to confirm as correct all the conclusions we had reached during our discussions and tests in early 1951.

Dr Griffith Pugh's report to the Medical Research Council, July 1952

Pugh's report on the Cho Oyu expedition was one of the most important in the history of scientific, high-altitude exploration. It formed the medical and scientific basis for the 1953 expedition and determined its 'shape'. Whereas on previous Everest expeditions the science had been little more than an appendage, in 1953 a scientific approach to the problems posed by 'the last 1,000 feet' was fundamental to our success. The report also gave an impetus to the fledgling sub-speciality of high-altitude physiology and medicine.

Later that year, after his visit to Zurich in September, Pugh was able to compare and contrast the performance of the British party on Cho Oyu with that of the Swiss on Everest, only 30 miles to the east, at exactly the same period. From the start, the Swiss were very active and fit, suffering little or no gastro-intestinal or respiratory infections, by contrast with the British who were very much less fit and acclimatised at the start of their attempt on Cho Oyu.

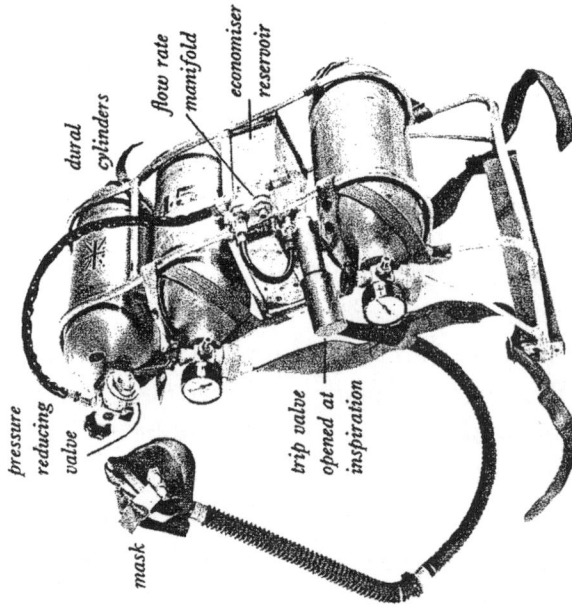

Open-Circuit
Weight with 3 cylinders 41lb, with 1 cylinder 18 lb

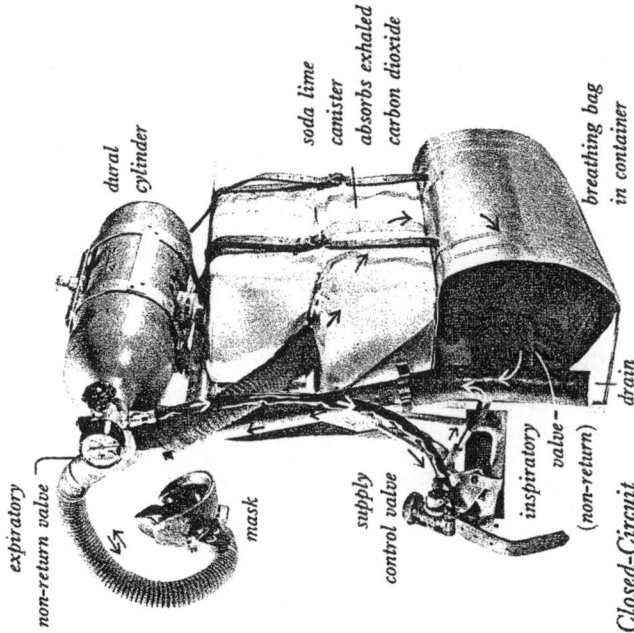

dural cylinders

flow rate manifold

economiser reservoir

pressure reducing valve

trip valve opened at inspiration

mask

Closed-Circuit
Weight with 1 cylinder 35lb, with 2 cylinders 47 lb

dural cylinder

soda lime canister absorbs exhaled carbon dioxide

breathing bag in container

expiratory non-return valve

mask

supply control valve

inspiratory valve (non-return)

drain

Closed-circuit and open-circuit oxygen sets developed for use in 1953

But despite their good health, the Swiss failed to reach the summit. This failure could be attributed mainly to their oxygen sets, which worked well at sea level but could not cope with an increased breathing rate during exercise at great altitude; here they were virtually useless. The Swiss also suffered severely from dehydration due to respiratory water loss.

All Pugh's recommendations in his report were accepted by the Himalayan Committee and put into effect and, for the first time, the use of adequate oxygen and all the other problems posed by climbing at high altitude were planned for as an integral part of the expedition.

Preparations for 1953, based on Pugh's report

In the light of Pugh's work, the Medical Research Council (MRC) was approached by the Himalayan Committee for scientific advice on the preparation and management of the forthcoming expedition, and this advice dominated the planning and conduct of the party. Dr Otto Edholm, the Director, and Griffith Pugh were asked to put the resources of the MRC's Division of Human Physiology at the disposal of the expedition and to liaise with other bodies. Four main problems had been identified by Pugh. These were high altitude, cold, nutrition and hygiene.

(a) High altitude and the use of supplementary oxygen

The most important factor leading to the successful ascent of Everest in 1953 was the use, for the first time in seven expeditions over thirty years, of adequate flow rates of supplementary oxygen. As we have seen, this followed from the work we had done in London in 1951, and from Pugh's work in the field on the Menlung La in 1952. As a result of this work, a high-altitude committee, under the chairmanship of Sir Bryan Mathews, was set up to advise on all questions relating to oxygen and the design of suitable sets. At the same time, the responsibility for the production and delivery of oxygen equipment was retained by the Himalayan Committee who appointed Peter Lloyd, a chemist and scientific civil servant, as oxygen controller and T D Bourdillon, a member of the 1951 reconnaissance, as oxygen officer. Lloyd had climbed to over 27,000ft on the 1938 Everest expedition using supplementary oxygen, and he believed in its effectiveness.

The Himalayan Committee recommended that the open-circuit set be given first priority, but that the closed-circuit set should also be developed so that a comparison could be made. The successful use of the closed-circuit set would depend on the provision of a really efficient mask which did not interfere with breathing and Dr J E Cotes of the MRC Pneumoconiosis Research Unit in South Wales provided modifications to the mask used by Pugh in 1952. Dr R B Bourdillon developed a closed-circuit set and provided sets for the expedition. The open-circuit sets were provided commercially, the principal firms involved being Normalair, Siebe Gorman and Reynolds Tubes.

It was emphasised by Pugh that, with the increased flow rates necessary to increase climbing rate and with all attempts on the summit being made using supplementary oxygen (and because 'sleeping' oxygen would also be used), much greater quantities of oxygen than were customary would have to be transported to the mountain. Also, a full training programme for both climbers and Sherpas would be necessary if the full potential benefits of oxygen were to be gained.

As we saw in Chapter 15, in the open-circuit method the climber inhales a mixture of air and oxygen, at varying flow rates, and exhales this to the atmosphere. The concentration of oxygen entering the lungs depends upon the flow rate of oxygen, the barometric pressure and the amount of air taken into the lungs each minute. A continuous supply over at least six hours would be needed, at a flow rate of four litres/minute of oxygen – a rate known to give a boost to climbing rate at altitude. At 29,000ft, this would be equivalent to the climber being at a very much lower altitude in the depths of his lungs.

Open-circuit sets had been widely used in aviation and because of their simplicity and reliability they could be adapted for mountaineering. To eliminate wastage of oxygen during expiration, a reservoir system was devised so that the flow rate of inspired oxygen could be cut off during expiration. In 1953 an RAF economiser was used for this purpose.

In the closed-circuit system there is no communication with the atmosphere. Oxygen is fed in at the rate at which it is used by the climber and the exhaled CO_2 is absorbed by soda-lime. However, economy in the use of oxygen is to a large extent counter-balanced by the weight of the soda-lime cannisters. The main advantages of the system are, firstly, that the climber breathes oxygen at a pressure above that of the oxygen at sea level and can exercise at sea-level rates, and, secondly, that the conservation of heat and water loss from the lungs is an advantage at extreme altitude; however, at intermediate altitudes climbers tend to overheat and become uncomfortable.

The main disadvantage of the closed-circuit sets was the difficulty in designing one able to handle very high rates of breathing without giving rise to feelings of suffocation due to the increased respiratory pressure. This was the main fault of the Swiss sets in 1952. Other potential problems were, firstly, the removal of surplus water (from exhaled air) which could condense after long use, freeze at altitude and impair the movement of valves; and secondly, the exchange of oxygen cylinders and soda-lime cannisters in field conditions of cold and high wind. Leakproof masks were essential.

The total amount of oxygen taken in 1953 was 198,000 litres, about sixteen times the amount used by the Swiss in 1952. About 23,400 litres were lost owing to leakage during the march-in and this severely curtailed the training programme. Only 15,600 litres remained unused after the successful ascent, not enough to mount a third assault if one had been needed. In spite of all the detailed preparations the ascent in 1953 was a close-run thing.

(b) Cold and protection from cold

In the Everest region winter conditions prevail from November to March, and very low temperatures and strong north-west winds are normal. In April, May and June the weather becomes warmer and there is less rain and snow. The start of the monsoon in the first half of June brings moist and warm weather but less snow than in the cold-weather season. In October and November, after the monsoon ends in September, there is usually a period of calm, dry but cold weather before winter snow and wind start again in November.

Mountaineering expeditions operate best in the two periods May-June and October-November, and very high-altitude climbing is usually preferable in May-June because of the warmer weather and higher barometric pressure. In 1952 few records were available of temperatures and weather conditions on Everest at altitudes above 23,000ft, but records did show that on pre-war expeditions climbers could only keep warm at 28,000ft when climbing in the sun. They could not keep warm in the shade. Before sunrise the cold was so intense that Smythe, who climbed to 28,000ft in 1933 without the help of supplementary oxygen, concluded that with the equipment and knowledge then available it would not be possible to reach the summit other than in the sun.

Every previous Everest expedition had encountered gales of great ferocity at altitude and in 1936 tents had been abandoned at the relatively low altitude of 22,400ft on the North Col because of excessive snowfall, wind and cold. Even at the lower altitudes of the Tibetan plateau (14-16,000ft) the wind cut through clothing and the wind-chill factor was a powerful component.

On the Cho Oyu expedition in the spring of 1952 records were kept of minimum night temperatures and maximum midday shade temperatures. A wind anemometer was taken but, surprisingly, very strong winds were not a problem.

The fall of temperature with altitude is of the order of 3°F for every 1,000ft of ascent (1.5°C for 300m). By extrapolation it was estimated that the minimum temperature at 28,000ft on Everest would be between −30°C and −40°C. In the autumn of 1952 the Swiss had recorded temperatures of 60-70° of frost on the South Col at 25,850ft, with winds gusting to 60mph – a potentially lethal combination.

In 1953 these figures were used by the MRC as a basis for planning the provision of protective equipment. As the temperature range was likely to be great owing to solar radiation, and because this would vary from minute to minute, all protective equipment had to be very easily adjustable.

To combat temperatures down to −40°C, with winds gusting to 60mph, tests were carried out on clothing and essential equipment at the Physiological Research Establishment, Royal Aircraft Establishment, Farnborough. The wind-resistance and permeability to water and tear-resistance of nine fabrics were also tested by experts. A cotton-nylon fabric was selected for use in both tents and windproof clothing. Waterproofing was carried out with Mistolon. Windproof outer garments were supplied by Howard Flint, a firm supplying polar equipment. Down clothing was ordered from France, as none was available in the UK at that time.

For hand protection a conventional UK assembly consisted of ventile outer mitts, woollen inner mitts and silk gloves. A limited number of large down mitts, similar in pattern to those used by the Swiss in 1952, were taken. Woollen balaclava helmets were used, as were various types of goggles and barrier cream for facial protection.

Special high-altitude boots were designed by the boot and trade association in consultation with the MRC's Division of Human Physiology. The requirements were for a boot weighing less than 5lbs which could be used on rock and ice, yet afford protection equal to that of an Arctic boot. Boots would have to be not only impermeable to melting snow, but also able to protect against intense cold. In the event they were successful in that frostbite was prevented, but the boots were clumsy, and rock-climbing to a high standard would not have been possible; luckily this was not necessary on Everest in 1953.

Studies at the Harvard Fatigue Laboratory in the United States had shown that the weight of footgear was an important factor in energy expenditure by anyone walking uphill; lifting one pound on the feet uphill was equivalent to carrying a load of 4lbs on the back. This confirmed a widely accepted principle, first suggested by Harold Raeburn many years earlier. Boots were made with Kapok insulation and micro-cellular soles devised by experts at the MRC's Division of Human Physiology.

Boots for use up to 22,000ft were also designed, but owing to inadequate briefing, it was not fully appreciated that they would become saturated with water from melting snow and foot perspiration; moreover, when the opossum fur, placed for insulation between the leather lining and the upper, became wet, it froze and proved impossible to dry out. These boots were therefore either permanently wet or frozen, and feet remained cold. To overcome this problem, the high-altitude boot was used extensively. However, throughout the 1953 expedition Tenzing wore a pair of Swiss reindeer boots used by him in 1952, and they were infinitely preferable to the British product.

Down-filled sleeping-bags were taken. The inner component weighed 3lbs and the outer 4lbs. In the light of experience on Cho Oyu and studies by the Harvard Fatigue Laboratory, the insulation of these bags was considered barely adequate and climbers would have to wear their own down clothing when sleeping. This proved to be necessary, particularly on the South Col at 25,850ft where, to conserve weight, individuals only used outer bags. Despite wearing their outer clothing, climbers remained cold at night except when using 'sleeping' oxygen. Ordinary commercial lilos were taken for use on the march-in, but on the mountain a double-layered design was used. The smaller size weighed 3lbs and the larger 4lbs, and these were satisfactory in providing comfort and insulation, especially at extreme altitude.

Tents of a number of different types were taken: the Arctic frame tent, used for the first time on the 1951 reconnaissance expedition and developed from those used by the Canadian and British Army in 'Operation Muskox' in Northern Canada in 1950, proved its value as a store and mess tent. The Meade two-man pyramid-type tent was preferred to other types, but the floor of rubberised fabric did not wear well and was insufficiently waterproof.

In December 1952 a small party consisting of John Hunt, Alf Gregory, Griffith Pugh and Charles Wylie camped on the Jungfraujoch to carry out trials of protective equipment. Temperatures as low as –20°C were encountered, and although scientifically planned user trials could not be carried out in the five days available, some guidance was obtained on the final selection of equipment.

(c) Nutrition: food and fluid intake

The Cho Oyu expedition subsisted on local food supplemented by bulk stores taken from the UK or purchased in India. In the early part of the expedition their calorie value was estimated at 3,000 k.cal/day, which was not enough to counterbalance an average energy expenditure of up to 4,500 k.cal/day, and climbers lost up to 11lbs in weight. Fluid requirements seem to have been adequately met and the average sugar intake of 12ozs/man/day proved adequate. At altitude the craving for sweet food increases and above 22,000ft climbers also develop cravings for unusual food, but a common feature is a desire for sugar. Up to 20,000ft, and with good acclimatisation, large quantities of local potatoes and rice were eaten, but if food was not palatable it was ignored. The use of pressure cookers was an important innovation and these allowed meals to be cooked at altitude which would otherwise have been impracticable owing to the reduced boiling point (178°F).

For 1953, Pugh decided that the physical condition of the party would be improved by providing a diet more consistent with European standards. A composite ration, as used by the British armed forces operating in small units, was therefore taken.

With the help of the War Office, a general purpose composite ration was worked out composed of items mainly from stock. The advantage was that this resembled a European diet, had increased palatability and simplified the making up of loads. Importantly, too, there was less chance of contamination by flies. The calorie value of a day's ration was 4,800 k.cal and it was planned that local purchases would supplement this. High-altitude rations were taken with a very high sugar content and these were supplemented by luxury items. As some items would inevitably be rejected, the calorie value of these items was higher than actually required. Overall, the food provided for the 1953 expedition was adequate and acceptable except for low fat pemmican and grape nuts. Calorie intake above 23,000ft averaged 2,500–3,000 k.cal/man/day.

The nutrition of parties at high altitude depends to a large extent on good cooking equipment. Up to about 18,000ft cooking can be done on an open fire with wood carried up from lower levels, though this is discouraged nowadays owing to the depredation of Himalayan woodlands. Above this height, all water has to be obtained by melting snow and cooking is carried out on stoves and pressure cookers. Tests on Cho Oyu showed that the production of 3-4 litres/man/day of water from snow needed ¾ pint (0.43 litres) of Kerosene.

On the 1924 Everest expedition one climber did not pass urine for 24 hours, so dehydration was severe – the result of the rapid breathing of cold, dry air at great altitude. Measurements on Cho Oyu showed that a daily water intake of 3-4 litres was necessary to prevent dehydration. This was the result of abnormally high respiratory water loss, which had first been suggested by Dr R W G Hingston in 1924, noted on Everest expeditions of the 1920s, and later by Professor Rudolf Peters of Oxford University in 1947. Despite this, no attempt had been made to provide adequate fluid intake on subsequent expeditions of the 1920s and 1930s. Up to 22,000ft climbers reported passing about 2-3 litres of urine each day, but above 26,000ft only about 500mls, enough to ensure reasonable kidney function but indicating some degree of dehydration.

In 1953, on the first 26 days of the march-in, which took the climbers up to 20,000ft, changes in body weight were only 2lbs. The daily fluid intake by Hillary and Tenzing over the two summit days was about 2,500mls, and the chloride content of their urine on their return from the summit was normal. The intake of food and fluid throughout the 1953 expedition was adequate, and this factor, combined with sufficient oxygen uptake at extreme altitude, transformed the performance of everyone on the expedition by comparison with that of mountaineers on pre-war Everest expeditions.

(d) General medical measures and hygiene precautions

In 1951 and 1952 UK parties had approached Everest directly from the south from Jogbani, a railhead at the Nepal-India border. As a result, the first week's march took place in the tropical heat of the plains and foothills. By contrast, the route chosen by the Swiss in 1952 started from Kathmandu, which is situated at 4,000ft in a relatively cool climate, and then went east in similar conditions.

In 1952 the Cho Oyu party suffered severely from gastro-intestinal infections associated with poor hygiene precautions and living in Sherpa houses. The Swiss avoided these by living in tents and by paying strict attention to hygiene. As a result, they had few such complaints and were much fitter than the Cho Oyu party. In the first few weeks at altitude the Swiss were about 80% fit, whilst the UK party on Cho Oyu were unfit by about the same amount.

In 1953 stringent hygiene precautions were imposed and the route east from Kathmandu was followed. These precautions included:

- All drinking water was sterilised by tablet or boiling.
- Contamination of food by flies was avoided by careful packing and by not camping near villages.
- Cooks were continuously supervised to ensure cleanliness in the preparation of food and utensils.
- To avoid respiratory cross-infections, lilos were not blown up by Sherpas but only by the individuals to whom they belonged.
- No Sherpa houses were used for sleeping.
- It was mandatory that the collection of water was separated by a long distance from the disposal of excreta.

In spite of these precautions some infection did occur but the acclimatisation period of three weeks in Khumbu enabled these cases to be controlled.

An acclimatisation period of three weeks between 12,000ft and 20,000ft was considered vital by Pugh. In 1952 the Swiss had acclimatised adequately, and their general state of fitness was superior to that of the UK party because throughout the year they had been able to make regular weekend ascents to over 15,000ft in the European Alps and were thus better acclimatised at the start of their expedition.

A trial of possible expedition members in Zermatt, July-August 1952

At the end of July I was asked to go to Zermatt to join a group of potential members for the 1953 Everest. Not all members of the 1952 Cho Oyu expedition had acclimatised well and Shipton asked Alf Gregory to assess the form of a number of other possible Everest candidates. Besides myself, there was Tony Streather, an officer serving in the Gilgit Scouts, who had recently climbed Tirich Mir (25,290ft) during a Norwegian expedition to the Hindu Kush. John Jackson and Jack Turner had just returned from the Himalaya, and Alf Gregory himself had been a member of the Cho Oyu expedition.

We spent a pleasant but frustrating two weeks in appalling weather climbing some classic peaks such as the Weisshorn. Despite his proven ability to acclimatise, Tony Streather was not chosen for the 1953 party because his technical expertise was not considered as good as that of the others. This was a mistake. Streather's subsequent performance on Kangchenjunga, K2 and other peaks was outstanding.

It was decided that both Pugh and I should take part in the 1953 expedition to make certain that all the scientific principles were correctly applied. As both Shipton and later Hunt were ignorant of these, this was of considerable importance.

The change in leadership, July-September 1952

After his return to London from the Cho Oyu expedition, Campbell Secord, a member of the party, wrote to the Himalayan Committee complaining about Shipton's leadership. Responding to this, and before Shipton's return from the Himalaya, the Committee invited additional reports from Gregory and Pugh. Their main criticisms were that the equipping of the party had been haphazard, that standards of hygiene had been poor, that no real attempt had been made to allow members to acclimatise properly and that Shipton had shown little interest in the important scientific programme.

In 1952 the members of the Himalayan Committee were Claude Elliott, President of the Alpine Club, whose climbing days were long past and who had never been to the Himalaya; Lawrence Kirwan, Director and Secretary of the Royal Geographical Society, who was not a mountaineer, his main interest being in the archæology of the Sudan. Claremont Skrine, also a non-mountaineer, had been in the Diplomatic Service as British Consul in Kashgar; he had travelled widely in Central Asia and had written an excellent book *Chinese Central Asia* on his explorations and time in Kashgar. George Lowndes, more a plant-hunter than a mountaineer, was a former Colonel in the Garhwal Rifles and had travelled with Tilman to Annapurna in 1950. James Wordie, another non-mountaineer, was a notable Arctic explorer and President of the Royal Geographical Society. Basil Goodfellow, a senior executive at Imperial Chemical Industries, was Honorary Secretary of the Alpine Club and had travelled, but not climbed, in the Himalaya. Harry Tobin, a co-founder of the Himalayan Club, had been transport officer with the Bavarians attempting Kangchenjunga in the 1930s and had been a Colonel in the Bombay Pioneers. The only currently active mountaineers were Lawrence Wager, Professor of Geology at Oxford, who had climbed to 28,000ft in 1933, and Peter Lloyd, a chemist, who had been on Nanda Devi in 1936 and to 27,000ft on Everest, using supplementary oxygen, in 1938; in 1950 he had climbed in the Nepal Himalaya with Tilman. T S Blakeney, the salaried Assistant Secretary of the Alpine Club, recorded the Minutes.

The main issue was Shipton's leadership, for the Committee felt that he had shown inadequate drive both in preparing for the expedition and in pressing home the attempt on Cho Oyu. They failed to acknowledge, however, the political disaster that might have followed if some, or all, of the party had been captured by Chinese soldiers sent up from Tingri. It is clear that, in the field, Shipton and the majority of the party had felt that this was an unacceptable risk. Only Earle Riddiford was vehemently opposed to that view.

A number of possible replacements for Shipton were considered, and three of these were soldiers. J O M Roberts was a Gurkha officer who had done a great deal of Himalayan exploration and climbing. Charles Wylie was also a Gurkha officer who, as a POW in the Second World War, had survived the infamous Burma Railway camps; he had climbed in the Himalaya. The third possible candidate was John Hunt of the 60th Rifles, who was stationed at SHAPE Headquarters. He had Himalayan and some Alpine experience. 'Preference was expressed for military officers on the grounds that they could most readily be released and could be expected to have organising capacity.'

Goodfellow, who had climbed with Hunt in the Alps, wrote to him expressing the Himalayan Committee's doubts about Shipton's organising ability and commitment to the job of leader; it appears that both Goodfellow and Elliott wrote to Hunt saying that they would like him to become organising secretary, and possibly deputy leader, or even leader. Whether these letters had the blessing of the whole Committee is open to question.

On 28 July Shipton, who had by now returned to the UK, was invited to attend a meeting of the Committee to give an account of the Cho Oyu expedition and discuss the organisation for 1953. It was clear to him, at this stage, that they assumed he would lead the 1953 expedition. However, he himself had doubts about his own fitness, partly because of the seeming intractability of the problem of Everest and partly because he feared the inflated publicity, the competitiveness and the need for a large expedition – all things he disliked.

Shipton was asked to leave the meeting while the question of the leadership was discussed and, on his return, and despite his misgivings, he accepted the Committee's unanimous view that he should be leader for 1953; he proposed Charles Evans as deputy leader. The Committee concurred.

However, according to T S Blakeney, the Assistant Secretary, in a memorandum on the *Everest Expedition Leadership for 1953* compiled in 1967 from notes made at various meetings, what the Committee really wanted was an alternative to Shipton, but they had not the guts to say so. Blakeney wrote:

> The meeting of July 28 was a disaster ... [When] Shipton was confronted with the leadership question for 1953 he expressed doubts about himself for the job; he said (a) that he had to consider his own career – he was out of a job and needed to get one; (b) he suggested that newer blood was needed for Everest; (c) he admitted that he preferred small parties. In the face of all this, it was a gross mistake that he should have been talked into accepting the leadership ... When the meeting broke up, he remarked to Colonel Lowndes, and I overheard it, that it would need a fanatic to get up Everest – and Shipton was in no sense a fanatic.

After this meeting Shipton went to Norway for two weeks which, coming so soon after his tardy return from Nepal, together with his manifest doubts about returning to Everest, seemed extraordinarily stupid if he really wanted to be offered the leadership. In effect, he was backing away from a crucial decision that neither he nor the Himalayan Committee wanted to take.

Elliott wrote to Hunt about the Committee's decision, on the understanding that Shipton needed a deputy leader, and indicating that Hunt might be chosen as that deputy. He seems to have overlooked the fact that Shipton had already nominated Charles Evans, a better climber and a good organiser, for that position. Moreover, Evans well understood the science of extreme altitude.

Over the next few weeks the whole question of Hunt as organising secretary or deputy leader was discussed ad nauseam – and on 22 August Shipton and Hunt met at the Royal Geographical Society. Shipton, who still believed that he was leader, thought he was interviewing Hunt for the post of organising secretary, whilst Hunt thought he was being interviewed for the deputy leadership; not surprisingly, there was no meeting of minds. As Shipton wrote in his autobiography *That Untravelled World*, '... it was clear to both of us, and admitted, that our approach to the enterprise, both practical and temperamental, was so fundamentally different that we would not easily work together. We parted, however, on friendly terms.'

On 11 September the Himalayan Committee met again at the Alpine Club. Two strong supporters of Shipton – Kirwan and Wager – were away on holiday. Shipton and Charles Wylie attended by invitation. Wylie had no idea that Hunt or anyone else was being considered as leader. They were both asked to withdraw while individual committee members had their say.

The current view of the Committee was strongly in favour of Hunt as leader –
above base camp – with Shipton and Hunt as co-leaders up to that level. Shipton
returned to the committee room and this proposal was put to him. Blakeney recorded
what followed:

> When Shipton was confronted by Elliott & Co., he refused to accept joint leadership
> and was not prepared to appoint Hunt as deputy leader, though Hunt might become
> the Secretary and Organizer of the expedition, and have a place in the party in the
> field. If the Committee thought it in the best interests of the Expedition, he was
> prepared to resign the leadership, but if Hunt was appointed leader he felt it would
> be impossible for himself to remain in the party, as he thought his qualifications
> were only employable as leader.

After further discussion Shipton's resignation was accepted and it was decided that
Hunt should be offered the leadership.

After the intense disagreements over the leadership, many people thought that
Eric Shipton had been treated badly, and still do to this day. Lawrence Kirwan summed
up a widely-held view: 'If ever there was a case of the right thing done in the wrong
way, this was it.' But, as Peter Steele wrote in his biography of Shipton, '1953 was
probably Britain's last chance to be first on the summit of Everest. Many people felt
that national prestige could not be compromised by taking chances, and that John
Hunt was the nearest they could foresee to a leader who could guarantee success.'
However, when Peter Steele asked Edmund Hillary, George Lowe, Alf Gregory,
Charles Wylie, Jack Longland, Raymond Greene and myself whether we thought
that Eric Shipton could have delivered victory, all of us agreed, with varying degrees
of conviction, that, given such a strong team, he probably could. As Hillary put it,
'with Eric's leadership, bumbling though it might have been at times, we would still
have done it.' My own view was that, since every previous Everest expedition,
including the two Swiss attempts, had had the benefit of excellent climbers, good
leadership and efficient organisation, it was the independent contribution made by
the Medical Research Council to the 1953 expedition that was the prime reason for
its success, not the change in leadership.

Charles Wylie started work as organising secretary in September, and began the
very considerable task of planning for the expedition. Meanwhile, the Committee
had followed up the work that Pugh started in 1951-52 by setting up an 'oxygen sub-
committee' under Pugh and Bourdillon. They recommended and it was agreed that
the expedition was to be based on scientific principles worked out by the MRC, the
most important single factor of which was the mandatory use of double the amount

of supplementary oxygen, 4 litres/minute, at great altitude, rather than half that quantity which had been used on pre-war expeditions.

John Hunt did not take up active leadership until the end of October. He still needed to choose a team and make an overall plan for the expedition. The team he chose was based on members of the Everest reconnaissance expedition of 1951 and the recent Cho Oyu expedition. His plan was a detailed one, allowing for three attempts on the summit on successive days; it covered every aspect of the expedition and was based on the scientific content worked out by the Medical Research Council.

BIBLIOGRAPHY

T S Blakeney, *Memorandum on the Everest Expedition Leadership for 1953*.
    Unpublished archival material. Alpine Club Library, 1967.
R W G Hingston, 'Physiological difficulties in the ascent of Mount Everest' in *Alpine Journal 35*, 22-38, 1925.
Normalair, Instruction manual.
    This describes the open-circuit oxygen apparatus, with instructions for use.
    In addition, there are, on separate typed sheets, instructions for the use of the
    closed-circuit apparatus by Dr R B Bourdillon. Alpine Club Library 1953.
L G C E Pugh, *Report on the British Himalayan Expedition to Cho Oyu 1952*.
    Medical Research Council, Alpine Club Archives 1952.
L G C E Pugh, *Report of Cho Oyu 1952 and Everest 1953 Expeditions*. Unpublished
    archival material. Alpine Club Library 1953.
H L Roxburgh, 'Oxygen equipment for climbing Mount Everest' in *Geographical Journal 109*, 207-216, 1947.
Peter Steele, *Eric Shipton. Everest and Beyond*. Constable 1998.
M P Ward, 'Preparations for Everest. Cho Oyu, London, Zermatt 1952' in *Alpine Journal 100*, 222-232, 1995.
Michael P Ward, James S Milledge, 'Griffith Pugh: Pioneer Everest Physiologist' in
    High Altitude Medicine and Biology, Vol 3, No 1, 2002.

Chapter 20

SCIENCE AND SUCCESS
The First Ascent of Everest, May 1953

Introduction

In the years immediately following the Second World War, very few British mountaineers were available who had had any Himalayan experience. By contrast, owing to the work of the Medical Research Council from 1951 onwards, our understanding of the effects of cold and extreme altitude, so central to success, was of a totally different dimension to that of both the pre-war expeditions and the Swiss in 1952. By the time John Hunt took over the leadership in October 1952 all the main problems to do with climbing at high altitude had been solved. Charles Evans, who had been on Cho Oyu, played a pivotal role in 1953, as he was a climber, along with Bourdillon, Griffith Pugh and myself, who thoroughly understood the medical breakthrough that had been made.

Hunt's original selection of party members, which he restricted to mountaineers from Britain and the Commonwealth, did not include Edmund Hillary or George Lowe because they were living in New Zealand and he would not be able to meet them before the start of the expedition. Fortunately, however, Evans and Gregory persuaded him to change his mind and both the New Zealanders joined the expedition.

Charles Wylie, after harrowing experiences in the war, had regained his health by climbing and trekking in the Himalaya. His organisational skills and knowledge of the Nepalese people and language were outstanding. It was his urging and leadership at a critical stage in the expedition, when he led fourteen Sherpas from Camp VII to the South Col, that enabled vital stores to be placed there for the summit attempts. Wylie had been taught to climb by G Kempson at Marlborough College, as had Hunt and myself.

Wilfrid Noyce was a scholar-mountaineer who taught classics at Charterhouse. One of the UK's best pre-war mountaineers, he had a gift for languages and had been in the intelligence service in India. During his local leaves he climbed in Kashmir and Sikkim, and wrote *A Climber's Guide to Sonamarg in Kashmir* when he was an instructor at the Aircrew Mountain Centre there in 1944. It was one of my great regrets that I did not ask him to join the 1951 Everest reconnaissance expedition.

Tom Bourdillon was incensed by the way that Shipton had been treated by the Himalayan Committee members and wanted nothing more to do with them,

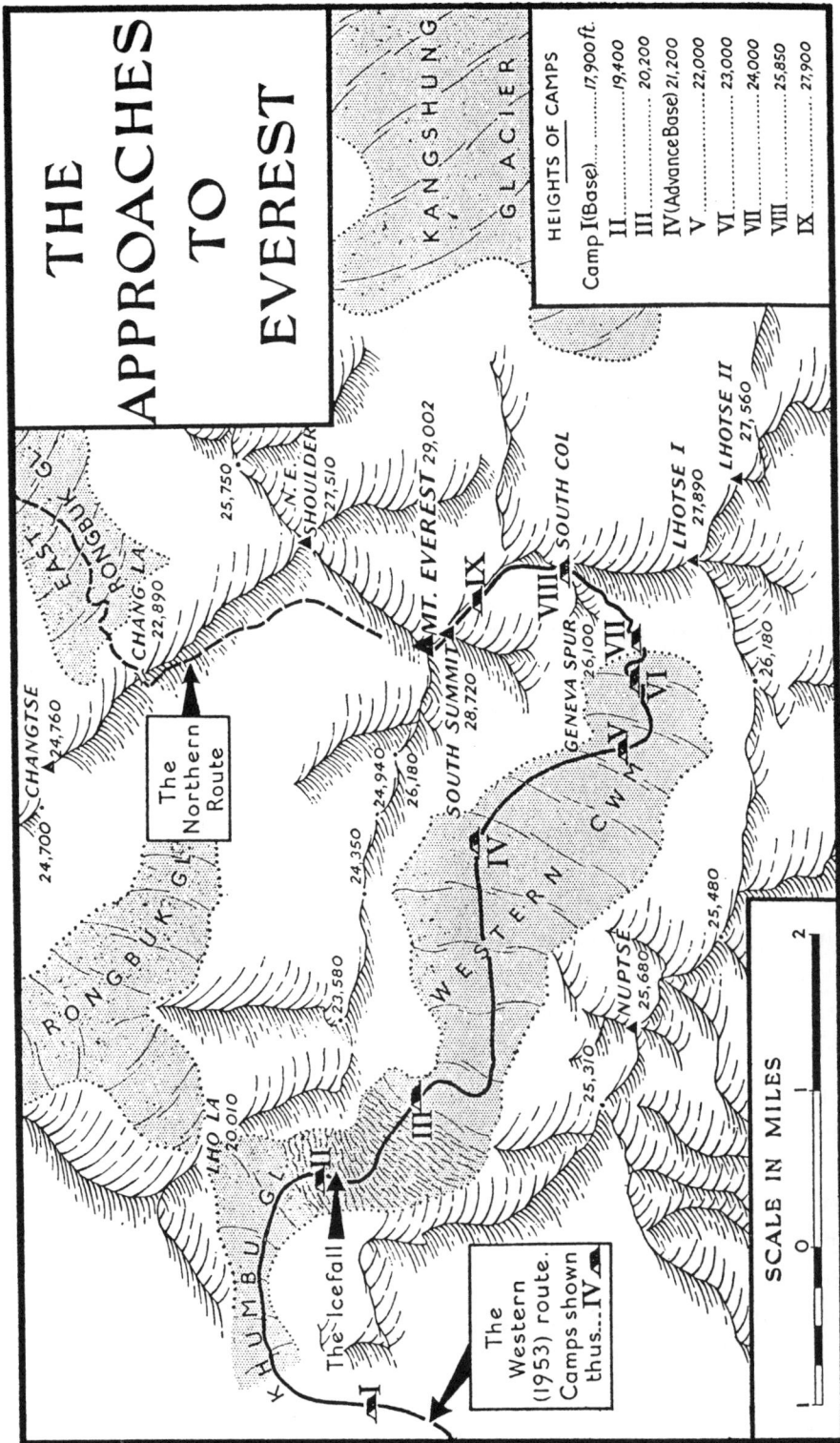

THE APPROACHES TO EVEREST

HEIGHTS OF CAMPS

Camp I (Base)	17,900 ft.
II	19,400
III	20,200
IV (Advance Base)	21,200
V	22,000
VI	23,000
VII	24,000
VIII	25,850
IX	27,900

The Northern Route

The Western (1953) route. Camps shown thus...IV

SCALE IN MILES

KANGSHUNG GLACIER

RONGBUK GLACIER EAST

CHANG LA 22,890

CHANGTSE 24,760

24,700

N.E. SHOULDER 27,510

MT. EVEREST 29,002

25,750

SOUTH SUMMIT 28,720

SOUTH COL

GENEVA SPUR 26,100

LHOTSE I 27,890

LHOTSE II 27,560

26,180

24,940

24,350

26,180

23,580

RONGBUK GL.

LHO LA 20,010

WESTERN CWM

NUPTSE 25,680

25,480

25,370

KHUMBU GL.

The Icefall

Routes to the North and South sides of Everest

but he was persuaded by Shipton to change his mind and join the 1953 team. Alf Gregory had been on Cho Oyu in 1952, whilst George Band, who would later make the first ascent of Kangchenjunga with Joe Brown in 1955, was an outstanding mountaineer from Cambridge University. Michael Westmacott was his Oxford counterpart and they were both ex-presidents of the mountaineering clubs of their respective universities.

Griffith Pugh's main concern was to make certain that his scientific recommendations were complied with. As a result, the amount of illness during this expedition, compared with those of the 1920s and 1930s, was negligible. While fulfilling my own role as Medical Officer, I was able to do a lot of climbing during the expedition as well as helping Pugh with his scientific work.

Tom Stobart was an experienced cameraman who had filmed in many countries. James (Jan) Morris, *The Times* reporter, was an inspired choice even though he was no climber and had never been to Nepal. He understood the country and our expedition as if by osmosis and wrote entertainingly and perceptively about both.

Tenzing Norgay, who had done so well with the Swiss in the spring and autumn of 1952, was born in Kharta in Tibet, but raised at Thame in Khumbu. He had already taken part in five Everest expeditions (three with the British and two with the Swiss) and had climbed to over 28,000ft. He had also climbed Nanda Devi East with the French in 1951. He came initially as sirdar but was later made a full climbing member of the team. Tenzing and Charles Wylie chose the porters.

The march-in through Nepal

The expedition left Kathmandu in two groups, the larger party a day in front of the smaller one which consisted of Wylie, Pugh and myself. While the first party had a carefree trek to Namche Bazar, our own march-in provided a unique opportunity to study medical problems in the Nepalese population of hills rising to 12,000ft and also to extend Pugh's work of 1952 on acclimatisation.

The main diseases of the Nepalese foothills were those of a third world country with poor standards of public health. Malaria was naturally prevalent at lower altitudes, as were a number of undiagnosed 'fevers'. Goitre was endemic, occurring in about 60% of the population. Only the fit survived in Nepal at that time.

On most days during the march-in Pugh and I carried out a number of simple yet important experiments on ourselves, concerned with finding out the maximum heart rate and the maximum oxygen uptake on exercising. This was done by marking out by means of an altimeter a height of between 300ft and 500ft on the path ahead. We would then ascend this as fast as possible, measuring heart rate and collecting exhaled air in a Douglas bag.* At the top, a sample was taken from the bag into a vacuum flask, which was sealed and analysed later in the UK. This experiment was usually repeated two or three times a day. We calculated that on the summit of Everest, without supplementary oxygen, the climber would have to breathe (or pant) near to his maximum to take in enough oxygen to remain conscious at rest. When climbing, he could only move very slowly, with rests every few paces, confirming what we knew already from accounts of pre-war expeditions. Surprisingly, the heart is remarkably little affected by extreme altitude. This may be due to the increase, at altitude, in the number of extra blood vessels supplying the heart with oxygen.

We started these experiments on the long climb from the valley of the Sun Kosi, which cuts through the Himalaya by the Nyalam valley, a few days out of Kathmandu, up to the Chyubas ridge. At Dolaghat the river is crossed by a bridge and the path then climbs about 4,000ft to the crest of the ridge. We followed this crest for two days, and had exceptional views of the Himalaya 50-60 miles away to the north. Everest was not visible, but the Gaurisankar-Menlungtse group, that I had explored with Shipton two years before, glowed pink against the dark blue sky at dawn. As we walked along the ridge we were hit by a ferocious hailstorm, with stones as large as golf-balls. Leaving the ridge beyond Risingo, we continued across the grain of the country, arriving at the first Sherpa village of Chyangma at 6,900ft (now Bhandar). We then crossed the Salpa Bhanyang pass (now Lamjura pass), 12,000ft, into Solu, the southern district of Solu Khumbu. Further experiments were completed during this ascent, ending at a cluster of prayer flags fluttering gaily on the crest of the pass. Descending to Junbesi (8,800ft) where *kukris*, the characteristic knives carried by the Gurkhas, are made, the country changed to a harsher, rockier, colder and less forgiving land. We then dropped down steeply to the Dudh Kosi river that drained the whole of the Everest region, and turned north up a deep, steep-sided valley to Namche Bazar where we camped on a saddle outside the village.

The simple preventative measures of avoiding houses and being careful over water and cooking worked well and there were few respiratory or gastro-intestinal complaints. On 26 March the main party descended to the Dudh Kosi again, before climbing a diagonal zigzag path to the grass meadow at 12,800ft on which Thyangboche monastery is perched, surrounded by rhododendron and birch. Here, a day later, we re-joined the main group. High winds were blowing snow off all the peaks 10,000ft above us, and we were too early for Everest, but the acclimatisation period would get us fit for our battles at extreme altitude.

---

* A large bag, now made of polythene, into which air is exhaled and collected over a set period – say ten minutes. A portion of air is later removed from the bag and analysed.

THE ROUTE TO THE TOP

MT. EVEREST

IX (behind ridge)

LHOTSE

VIII

NORTHERN ROUTE

Geneva Spur

VII

NUPTSE

WEST SHOULDER

VI

V

IV

Lho La

III

II

The route to the top, showing Camps II – IX

Acclimatisation period and the Khumbu icefall

Before leaving Thyangboche we checked the oxygen bottles and found that a number of them had leaked. We immediately telegraphed Lieut Col J O M Roberts, who was due to bring up the second consignment from Kathmandu, and asked him to check the bottles before doing so.

Although no formal survey was carried out on this expedition, there still remained a number of gaps in our geographical knowledge, particularly to the south and west of Everest, an area I had partially explored in 1951.

We now divided into three parties. Evans, Bourdillon, Band and Westmacott set out to test the oxygen apparatus, in particular the closed-circuit sets, and whilst doing so, they explored the Mingbo valley to the south of Ama Dablam where, in 1951, Hillary and Shipton thought, wrongly, that they had found a hidden valley. In 1953 a 19,000ft peak was climbed from which two passes could be seen leading from the Mingbo valley into the Hongu, the next valley east. The northern pass had been crossed in 1951. The southern pass, the Mera La, was reached by this 1953 party who then had a clear view of the Lower Hongu glacier and valley. The second party – Hunt, Gregory, Lowe and Tenzing – went up the Imja glacier north of Ama Dablam and parallel with the Lhotse-Nuptse ridge. Open-circuit sets were tested and Chukhung peak (19,200ft) was climbed.

The third party – Noyce, Hillary, Wylie and myself – explored the complicated peaks to the south and west that I had visited in 1951. Going west up the Chola Khola valley we reached a pass at the hub of three converging ranges. By climbing a nearby peak at 19,200ft we were able to see a valley running south to Thyangboche. We then climbed another, higher peak, Kang Cho (20,000ft), and confirmed that the glacier to the north of it was the Guanara down which we had descended in 1951 before attempting the Nup La icefall. By climbing these two peaks we had 'sorted out' one of the pieces in the jigsaw of the western part of the Everest region, and in the autumn Charles Evans returned to complete a photo-survey of the whole region which was later incorporated into the 1961 map of the Everest region. Throughout the acclimatisation period Pugh continued with his medical research and worked on the oxygen sets.

Another group – Hunt, Bourdillon, Noyce and myself – returned up the Imja valley and climbed a peak, Ambu Gyabjen, below the north face of Ama Dablam. Both closed and open circuit sets were tested and these tests demonstrated how hot the climber became when the closed-circuit set was used at intermediate altitudes below 19,000ft: it was only above 22,000ft that they became bearable in this respect. We then crossed the Imja into the lower part of the Khumbu valley, climbing on the way another peak, Pokalde (19,000ft).

Hunt did not climb this peak as he was not feeling well, and when I examined him I found that he had 'crackles' in both lungs. This indicated fluid in the alveoli, but as he had no temperature or cough and improved on going to lower levels, it seems certain (with hindsight) that he had a mild sub-clinical attack of high-altitude pulmonary oedema. In 1953, this condition was not known to medical science, though many years previously a few cases had been recorded in a little-read medical journal.

The second period of acclimatisation coincided with the arrival of Jimmy Roberts from Kathmandu. The oxygen cylinders he had brought with him were immediately checked and found to be intact. Evans and Wylie, both of whom spoke Hindi and Nepali, trained selected Sherpas in the use of the oxygen sets. The Sherpas were delighted with this 'English air'. With Gregory and Tenzing, Evans and Wylie then went up the Imja glacier and climbed a solitary peak, Imja Tse, 20,254ft (Island Peak), which is now a standard 'trekking' peak. In the acclimatisation period we climbed six new peaks between 19,000 and 20,000ft.

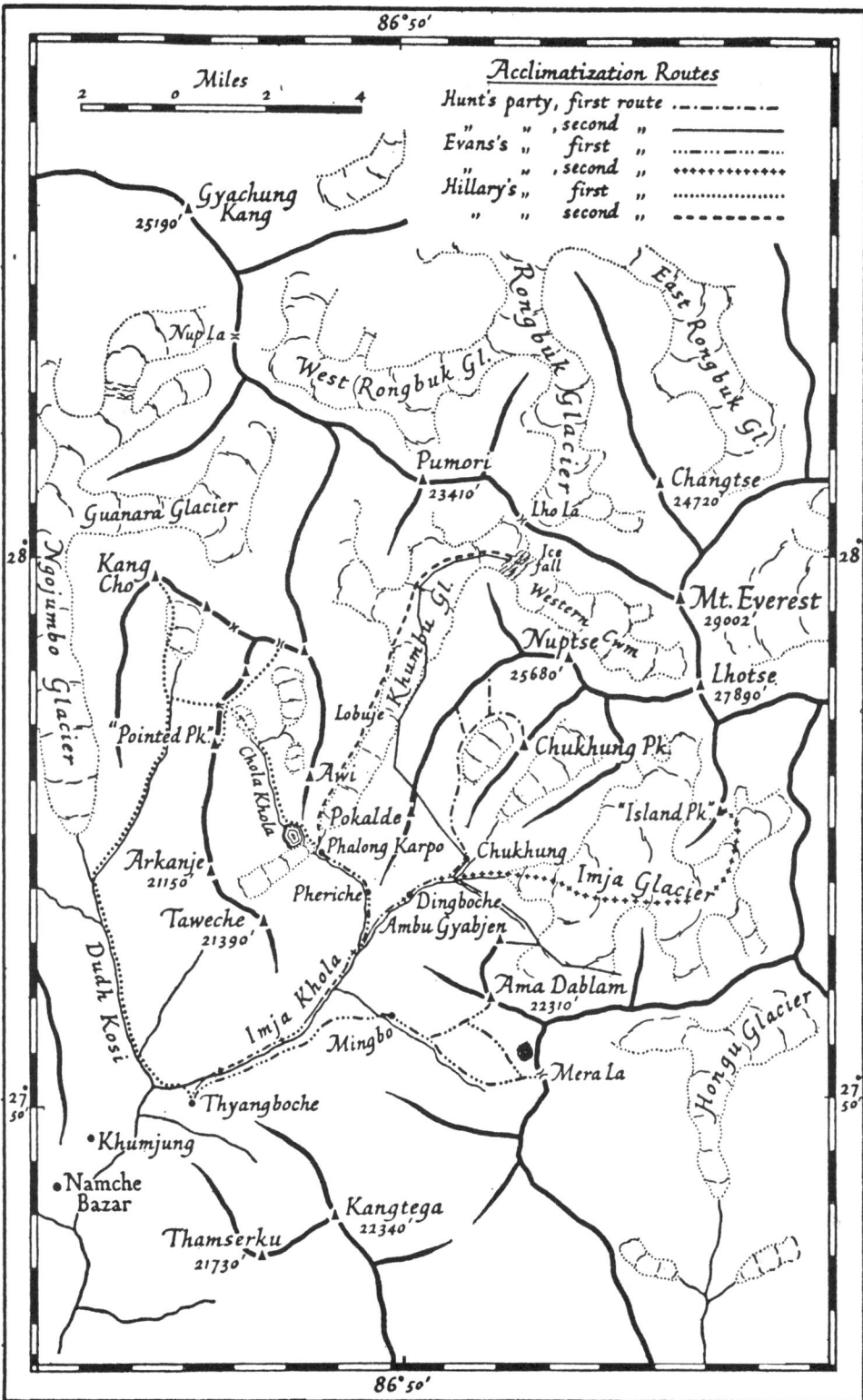

Royal Geographical Society

Routes followed by parties during the acclimatisation period

● Position of Silver Hut, 1960–61

In the meantime, Hillary, Pugh and Stobart established Base Camp at the foot of the Khumbu icefall. They were joined by the rest of the party and work started on finding a route through the icefall – the most dangerous and technically difficult part of the expedition. Eventually a route, always dangerous and ever-changing, was made through the chaotic, tottering ice pinnacles and moving crevasses. The monster crevasse that had guarded the entrance to the Western Cwm in both 1951 and 1952 had gone, to be replaced by a 30ft cliff of ice which was climbed initially by an ice crack down which we hung a rope ladder. Many of the crevasses were crossed by using aluminium ladders or tree-trunks brought up from Namche Bazar. Although a temporary camp was established in the icefall, this was so dangerous that few slept in it. It was a great relief when Camp III in the Cwm was established on 22 April and we could climb through the icefall without stopping there overnight.

Over the next few days stores were ferried up the icefall to Advanced Base Camp (Camp IV) at the head of the Western Cwm. On 2 May Hillary and Tenzing made an experimental 'run' from Base Camp (17,900ft) to Camp IV (21,200ft), using 4 litres/ minute of open-circuit oxygen, and returning the same day. Both were very satisfied with the way the sets worked, the boost that they gave to their climbing rate, and how fresh they felt after a long day's climb which, without supplementary oxygen at this flow rate, would have left them exhausted. It was the first indication of just how effective the use at great altitude of an adequate flow rate of oxygen would be.

John Hunt's assault plan

On 7 May John Hunt outlined his plan for the attempts on the summit. This involved two attempts from a secure and well-provisioned camp on the South Col (25,850ft) which would be carried, using supplementary oxygen. Although the closed-circuit set had not been working 100% all the time, when it did work well the boost it gave, despite its weight, was formidable.

Hunt's plan was for Bourdillon and Evans, using closed-circuit oxygen, to climb direct from the South Col to the summit and return in one day – a 3,000ft ascent and descent – without an intermediate camp. Hillary and Tenzing would be the second assault party, using open-circuit supplementary oxygen at 4 litres per minute. This flow rate would give a height of about 20,000ft in the depths of their lungs, but a high camp at about 27,800ft would be provided for them because their climbing rate would be slower than that of the other pair, using closed-circuit oxygen, who would be climbing at the equivalent of sea-level.

After Hunt had outlined this plan there was an awkward silence, for the obvious flaw to the plan was the risk it posed to Bourdillon and Evans in making a summit bid without an intermediate camp on the South Ridge. In case of the failure, or partial failure, of their oxygen sets, which they had already experienced, they would be at grave risk, it seemed to me, of being at one moment at the equivalent of sea-level and the next at 28,000ft. This could result in unconsciousness and coma, with no place of relative safety – a tent – within reasonable reach to provide shelter. The obvious solution would be to provide for the first party the high camp at 27,800ft which was planned anyway for use by Hillary and Tenzing, and leave it in place for the second party. The change in the plan would be negligible, but despite strong representations from myself, and also from Alf Gregory who insisted that the first assault had no prospect of success and would serve no useful purpose, Hunt felt it was not possible to make this change. In the event, both Evans and Bourdillon had to turn back from the South Summit at 28,720ft owing to a malfunction of their sets; and on the South Col (25,850ft) during the descent, Bourdillon collapsed and nearly became unconscious as his set suddenly malfunctioned again; luckily by this time he was close to a tent and was revived by Evans.

The second party obviously had a much better chance of success, as a high camp at 27,800ft would be provided for them and their open-circuit sets were more rugged and reliable than the closed-circuit sets to be used by Bourdillon and Evans. There was insufficient oxygen to allow for a third attempt.

One possible explanation for this controversial plan was that Hunt never really intended the first party to make a full-scale bid for the summit. This was the impression gained by Hillary, who described Hunt's plans for the two summit bids in his autobiography, *View from the Summit*, in the following terms:

> He was proposing that Charles [Evans] and Tom Bourdillon should use the powerful closed-circuit oxygen equipment to make a thrust for the South Summit at 28,700 feet. The final push to the top would be made by Tenzing and myself, using the more reliable open-circuit oxygen. The terms 'first assault' and 'second assault' which became attached to these two endeavours were completely misleading. Charles and I agreed with John's recommendations and I was left in no doubt that the final summit assault would be the responsibility of Tenzing and myself.

When reviewing Hillary's book in the *Alpine Journal*, George Band disagreed with this interpretation: 'At the time, I think the rest of us felt that both assaults would be serious attempts to reach the main summit.'

Many years later, on 11 May 1991, in a television programme transmitted on Channel 4, John Hunt was asked about this very point. Speaking of the first assault, by Bourdillon and Evans, he said:

I had in mind the prospect, although I didn't say it to them, that the second assault would be the one that would succeed and I regarded *their* first attempt more as a reconnaissance, but of course if they *could* make it, God bless them. What I *did* say to them was that they were not to go on beyond the South Summit unless things were in their favour. Had they time to go all the way to the top and back, all the way back to the South Col? Was there enough oxygen? ...

This would seem to suggest that Hillary's impression of Hunt's true intentions was substantially correct.

The other point I made in response to Hunt's outline of his plan concerned his own fitness for the role he had assigned to himself. According to James Morris in his book *Coronation Everest*, I said 'I think it's a great mistake that you're going so high yourself ... You've done too much already. You shouldn't go with the support team. I feel this very strongly.' The reason that I said this was that Hunt was already showing signs of high-altitude deterioration and I feared that he might get very ill. My own view was that Wilfrid Noyce, who seemed quite impervious to fatigue and altitude, should take his place. But Hunt could not be persuaded.

The Lhotse Face

Although the ultimate problem of Everest was 'the last thousand feet', the Lhotse Face was a substantial preliminary 'mountain' of 4,000ft, rising from the head of the Western Cwm to the South Col. It was clear that the Swiss, in 1952, had 'shot their bolt' by the time they reached the South Col. So important was the ascent of the Lhotse Face that, in addition to Pugh, both Hunt and Evans had been to Zurich to get guidance on this problem from the Swiss, which was freely given. When climbing the Lhotse Face, we followed the route used by them in the autumn of 1952, rather than their spring route up the Geneva Spur on which it had been impossible to put an intermediate camp.

A reconnaissance of the Lhotse Face was made between 2nd and 6th May, and Camp VI on the face was established. Both types of oxygen set were tried out, and the closed-circuit set, which at lower altitudes had made climbers overheat, was now, at over 22,000ft, able to keep them nicely warm rather than overheated.

On 10 May George Lowe, with four Sherpas but without supplementary oxygen, began preparing the Lhotse Face, cutting a staircase of steps and fixing ropes. He based himself at Camp VI (23,000ft) at the foot of the face and on the 14th climbed to Camp VII at 24,000ft. However, so much snow fell over the next few days that it obliterated his steps and, despite great efforts without supplementary oxygen by Lowe and others including myself, a high point of only 25,000ft was reached. At this altitude we got progressively colder because we were moving so slowly, and though not frostbitten, we suffered a degree of non-freezing cold injury to both hands and feet.

This was a critical point on the expedition and it was decided that to increase climbing rate and consequent heat production, supplementary oxygen should be used by a fresh climber, Wilfrid Noyce, who had not been worn out already by work on the face. On 20 May Noyce, using open-circuit oxygen, left Camp V (22,000ft) and climbed to Camp VII (24,000ft) where he spent the night; the next day, with the Sherpa Annullu also using supplementary oxygen, he reached our highest point by midday. Starting the leftward traverse to the South Col, they stopped for food at 12.50pm. Annullu now led, kicking steps in the firm snow until they started climbing towards the top of the Geneva Spur, a broad crest of snow.

The South Col, a wind-polished ice field measuring about 400 yards square, now lay 300 feet below them. Some yellow canvas rags flapping from bare tent poles were all that remained of the Swiss tents. The col was strewn with oxygen bottles and food boxes. Already it was becoming 'the world's highest rubbish dump'. Annullu seized a fine Swiss rucksack containing felt boots, for Tenzing had told him that the first Sherpa reaching the South Col could have his share of the booty to be found there, and although Annullu had to leave his oxygen cylinder behind, he descended proudly with his newly-won prize.* Noyce commented to me that he was able to enjoy the climb back up to the top of the Geneva Spur, instead of having to endure a battle for survival – such was the beneficial effect of adequate oxygen uptake.

By 6.0pm they were safely back at Camp VII where they were met by Wylie, Tenzing and Hillary. The Lhotse Face had been climbed, and the first loads could now be carried to the South Col. So vital was this stage that Wylie, who was to lead the Sherpas up the face, had the help of Hillary and Tenzing, each using supplementary oxygen, to boost morale and cut steps.

At 8.30am on 22 May all set off, with Hillary and Tenzing in the lead using supplementary oxygen. Slowly they zigzagged up the Lhotse Face and then traversed across to the South Col. Wylie's oxygen gave out just before the col, but the Sherpas, who were not using oxygen, had to be encouraged and with a considerable effort Wylie helped carry the load of one of them. At last all the loads were dumped in this inhospitable place. Hillary and Tenzing and five Sherpas returned to Camp IV that night. Wylie and the rest of the Sherpas reached Camp VII on the Lhotse Face.

---

* In an article in the 1993 *Alpine Journal* entitled 'Some Words on Everest 1952' André Roch described how his rucksack inadvertently got left behind on the South Col.

Fortunately no snow fell for several days, which made the route up the Lhotse Face to the South Col easy to follow, with crampon marks and steps clearly visible. The change in the weather, coupled with the use of adequate oxygen, meant that this critical part of the expedition was a success and all was now in place for the two attempts on the summit.

First ascent of the South Summit, 28,720ft, using closed-circuit oxygen sets
On 23 May Bourdillon and Evans set off from Camp IV at the head of the Western Cwm using closed-circuit oxygen. They were heavily laden with loads of over 50lbs each, including their oxygen sets, an extra soda-lime cannister each, and their personal gear. Thanks to the patient work of Bourdillon, these oxygen sets, though clumsy-looking and heavy, had begun to justify themselves.

In effect, the climbers were getting the same amount of oxygen as they would normally have used at sea-level, and therefore they could move as fast and exercise as energetically as they did at sea-level, while carrying a heavy load. Another advantage was that, because the environmental temperature was always below freezing, the heat generated by the absorption of CO_2 by soda-lime kept the climbers warm but not too hot at this altitude; and being cut off from the outside air, they lost very little fluid and heat from their lungs and were therefore less dehydrated.

If anything went wrong with the either of the sets, however, the climber would suddenly 'ascend' from sea-level to the altitude at which he was actually climbing – and near the summit of Everest he could expect to lapse into coma or even die. This meant that any fault in the set had to be diagnosed and repaired immediately, and both climbers had had much practice in doing that.

Accompanying them in support were Hunt and two Sherpas, Da Namgyal and Balu, using open-circuit sets. From the Cwm they climbed slowly to Camp VII (24,000ft) and slept the night using 'sleeping' oxygen from the Swiss Draeger cylinders. Next day they continued to the top of the Lhotse Face and traversed across to the South Col. After 5½ hours Hunt left the two Sherpas to follow in their own time and tied himself on to Bourdillon and Evans's rope. At 4.0pm they reached the top of the Geneva Spur and descended to the South Col. Here the wind suddenly increased to nearly gale force. Evans and Hunt mistakenly took their masks off to pitch the tent while Bourdillon kept his on. For over an hour they fought the wind to put up a Pyramid tent which was kept in place by climbing ropes attached to its apex, a job that can normally be done in three or four minutes. This struggle exhausted them, particularly Hunt and Evans who, by taking off their masks, were not using extra oxygen and got very cold. The Meade tent was less trouble to put up and into this the Sherpas crowded.

Warm soup and coffee at last stopped the violent attacks of shivering from which they had begun to suffer. This had a sinister implication for it meant that the temperature of their bodies, normally at 37°C, was falling to dangerous levels and they were nudging hypothermia. By extrapolation, the outside temperature that night must have been somewhere between −25°C and −30°C. Next day, 25 May, they were so exhausted that there was no question of starting. Bourdillon and Evans worked on the oxygen sets for four hours, between 2.0pm and 6.0pm. They noticed that everything took three times as long and they immediately forgot where they had put things. All went for a short walk on the col in the afternoon, when the sun came out and the wind dropped. Though the weather was fine and they could have made an attempt, the day's rest helped them, for Bourdillon and Evans, using sleeping oxygen, slept between 10.30am and noon. That night all used sleeping oxygen again from 7.30pm until 3.0am – and woke when the oxygen ran out.

Their work on the sets highlighted one of the problems of the closed-circuit system. The re-breathing bags were full of ice and, as a result, some of the valves became frozen, which blocked the flow of the oxygen. This occurred because, when warm air from the lungs was exhaled into the bags, the water in this exhaled air froze as it circulated in the apparatus while exposed to the cold wind. The iced-up valves had to be melted with boiling water. By nightfall both the open and closed-circuit sets were working. The large thermos flasks were filled with water for the morning start and these, together with the soda-lime cannisters, were taken into sleeping-bags to be kept warm.

At 5.0am on 26 May they started to get ready, but at 6.0am, as soon as they left the tent, they found that a valve had frozen. This they thawed using a candle. Evans put on his set again but, after a few minutes, he felt as if he was going to die – the oxygen feed was stuck in the closed position and no oxygen was coming through. Eventually Bourdillon fixed this and at 7.30am they finally started – about half-an-hour after Hunt and Da Namgyal, both of whom were using open-circuit oxygen. Balu was too exhausted to start at all.

In spite of their late start, and loads weighing over 50lbs, Evans and Bourdillon overtook Hunt and Da Namgyal at the start of the couloir leading up to the South Ridge. Leaving these two behind, they kicked steps in the snow to the top of the couloir and on the ridge they climbed steadily to the site of Lambert's tent at about 27,400ft. This 1,400ft ascent took 1½ hours, which was very fast going. Here they stopped. Except for some clouds the sky was clear, with little wind; the orange tents of the camps on the South Col and the Lhotse Face showed up clearly a thousand feet below. They continued easily up the ridge, keeping either to the crest or just below it on the left. At 28,000ft, after passing a prominent shoulder, they came to a ridge composed entirely of snow, and at 11am reached a slight hollow at about

28,100ft. They had reached this point after only 3½ hours' climbing from the South Col. This was at a rate of 700ft/hour – an almost Alpine rate of climbing – and twice as fast as the open-circuit users.

The comparative shelter of the hollow enabled each of them to change to a second bottle of oxygen and soda-lime cannister. These would last about 5 hours, and if all went well the last thousand feet to the summit should take 1 to 1½ hours at their present climbing rate. It all looked good. They also brought out a flask of lemonade to drink – but it had frozen and the glass had broken, so they threw it away.

For ten minutes after starting again all went well; then suddenly Evans had an attack of shortness of breath, but examination of his set showed no obvious fault, so they concluded that the soda-lime cannister had got wet and was not absorbing carbon dioxide which, as a result, was building up within the set. The ridge now steepened and they started climbing on the east or Kangshung side of the ridge, but here the snow was soft and deep, so they returned to the crest – a firm rocky backbone rising in a series of steps separated by ledges. At last they reached the foot of a steep slope leading to the South Summit. Cutting steps up this, they reached its small corniced dome at 28,720ft – the highest men had ever been. It had taken only 5^ hours from the South Col and the time was about 1.10pm.

The final part of Everest lay before them. It looked difficult, with a broken ridge leading to the final obstacle – a step about 30 feet high – which we could see with binoculars from the Western Cwm. Beyond was a ridge, with cornices jutting over the Kangshung Face, leading to the summit.

Because of the undetected fault in his set, Evans had had to make an unprecedented effort to keep up with Bourdillon and this had slowed them both down. It would, they reckoned, take between two and three hours to reach the summit, and the amount of oxygen in their cylinders would last only that long before giving out. If this happened on the summit they would become disoriented from sudden oxygen depletion and be unable to climb down safely. In effect they could get to the summit but not get back, or they could return safely to the South Col.

They took off their sets on the South Summit and immediately became light-headed and started to pant. Bourdillon went down to the gap beyond the South Summit. On his return at 1.30pm they decided, with heavy hearts, to turn back. It was a wise decision. Bourdillon told me later that he was sick with disappointment at not having provided sets that were effective enough for the climb. He was also regretful, as was Evans, that there was no top camp where they could have repaired their sets in shelter and, if necessary, spend the night. The fact that one *was* provided for Hillary and Tenzing and 'carried' by Lowe and Gregory, indicated that it could have been provided for the first party, though this might have involved logistical difficulties. Later, however, Bourdillon wrote in the *Alpine Journal*:

We were not likely to be able to carry to the top camp enough supplies for more than one summit party, and thus the other party had to start from the col. The open circuit, while more reliable, gave very little chance of reaching the summit from the col and was therefore to be used by the pair taking two days for the assault. The closed-circuit was still unproven at these altitudes and was to be used by the pair starting from the S.Col. Thus if it failed completely, it would not have wasted invaluable weight at the top camp; if it worked fairly well it might result in steps and information useful to the second party; and if it continued to work as well as it had done on the Lhotse Face it gave a good chance of reaching the summit from the S.Col.

The other point they made to me, at Camp IV on their return, was that they really thought the difficulties of the final ridge and the 30-foot step might be too great at the extreme altitude for *anyone* to climb them. This thought, however, they kept to themselves.

On their descent Bourdillon, who was fresher, came last, but they slipped a lot, and on one occasion Bourdillon's ice axe was torn out of his grasp and he had to climb back up some way to retrieve it. At the 'Lambert' campsite, they made a solemn pact to treat the couloir leading from the ridge to the South Col with extra care. 'We knew we were too tired to be safe, but we had to get down.' At the steepest part of this couloir they fell again and slid to the bottom. As Evans commented, on each slide they were meticulously polite to each other, apologising profusely. At last they reached the South Col, to be welcomed by Lowe and Gregory with hot tea. It was 4.30pm – they had taken three hours to descend from the South Summit.

At the same time that the first ascent of the South Summit was being made, the support group of Hunt and Da Namgyal, using open-circuit oxygen, carried loads for the proposed camp at 28,000ft for Hillary and Tenzing to use. They set off from the South Col at 7.0am and, going very slowly, struggled up the couloir and the South Ridge as far as the site of the Lambert camp. Here they stopped for half-an-hour before going up another few hundred feet. Hunt felt ghastly, gasping and fighting for breath and feeling claustrophobic. He was obviously acutely short of oxygen, probably because his outlet valve had become blocked with ice, as the water in the expired air froze as it left the mask.

Neither Hunt nor Da Namgyal could go any further, and they dumped their loads of oxygen, tent, food and kerosene at 27,300ft. Their descent needed a great effort of concentration. In the gully Da Namgyal slipped twice and on the South Col both had to be given oxygen before they began to feel better and could walk normally. Everyone on the South Col had a very bad night, but the wind died down in the morning so that on the 27th Evans and Bourdillon, with Ang Temba, started down without using supplementary oxygen. However, it soon became obvious that

Bourdillon could not ascend the 300 feet to the top of the Geneva Spur, so they returned to camp and Evans put him on open-circuit oxygen. Hunt, who was not fully aware of the severity of his condition, had originally intended to remain on the South Col to support the second assault, but when he saw that Evans needed someone to help him get Bourdillon down to camp VII, he gave up the idea of staying on the col and, despite his exhaustion and wish to remain, accompanied the descending party. This released both Gregory and Lowe to support Hillary and Tenzing on their summit bid.

The first ascent of Everest, 29,028ft, using open-circuit oxygen sets

On 25 May, a rest day on the South Col for Bourdillon and Evans, Hillary and Tenzing left Camp IV at 21,200ft in the Western Cwm, and using open-circuit oxygen at 4 litres per minute, climbed to Camp VII at 24,000ft where they arrived feeling fresh and fit. That night, using sleeping oxygen at 1 litre per minute, they slept for up to nine hours. It was a deep refreshing sleep, only interrupted when their oxygen ran out in the morning.

Next day, 26 May, with Gregory, Lowe, Ang Nyima, Pemba and Ang Temba – the second support party – they all reached the South Col. Hillary and Tenzing were carrying 38lbs each and used oxygen at 4 litres per minute when leading and making the trail, and 2 litres per minute when following, as recommended by Griffith Pugh. It took them 3½ hours and all arrived fresh, having filmed part of the way.

On the col all removed their oxygen sets and found that they could walk uphill without undue fatigue. They met Bourdillon and Evans at the foot of the couloir; both were exhausted and were helped to their tent. Lowe filmed this. Later, Hillary and Lowe walked without supplementary oxygen to look down the Kangshung Face, but it was hard work walking into the wind.

That night a gale started, and despite using sleeping oxygen Hillary had one of the most uncomfortable nights he had ever experienced on the mountain. He felt cold all the time, despite wearing all his clothes in his sleeping-bag. These consisted of a string vest, wool vest, shirt, two Shetland pullovers, down jacket, long wool underpants, down trousers, windproof trousers, two pairs of socks, high-altitude boots, wool gloves and ear muffs. Only the outer sleeping-bag was used; to save weight, the inner was not taken to the col. As Pugh had observed beforehand, this would be barely sufficient to maintain body temperature, and if the temperature on the col had been lower than –25°C, it is doubtful if that amount of insulation would have been adequate. Gregory felt cold all the time at this altitude and it was obvious that clothing and protection were only just adequate to prevent hypothermia and frostbite on the South Col and above.

On 27 May they had the greatest difficulty in getting Hunt, Evans and Bourdillon off the col. Hunt, though using supplementary oxygen, was in a particularly bad way. Both Hillary and Tenzing felt well and spent the day on the South Col eating and drinking as much as they could – neither used oxygen and both felt reasonably fit. Lowe and Gregory used the oxygen mask alone – a modification of the Mathews gauze mask used on the 1933 expedition – which helped them to lose less heat from their lungs. It also checked the development of arguments about trifles which otherwise were inclined to occur at this altitude.

That night sleeping oxygen was used from 8.0pm to 2.40am. They all slept fairly well but felt cold. The temperature outside remained at about –25°C. On the morning of 28 May the preparations for carrying the high camp were long and protracted in the high wind, and tempers became frayed. Only one of the Sherpas, Ang Nyima, was well enough to help carry the camp, and at one stage Lowe felt that everything was falling apart. However, at 8.45am Lowe, Gregory and Ang Nyima left the South Col carrying 45lbs each and using oxygen at 4 litres per minute. They cut steps up the couloir leading to the South Ridge and turned their oxygen down to 2 litres per minute when following the leader. After a bit Lowe even began to enjoy the 'uphill movement of limbs'. Though conscious of the weight on his back he was not fatigued by it. On reaching the ridge, they took some photographs and then continued uphill, quite easily, to the place at about 27,300ft where Hunt and Da Namgyal had dumped their loads. Here each added 10lbs to his own load, making a total weight of about 50-55lbs each. From then on it was very hard work, and they reached the site of Camp IX (27,800ft), in good condition, at 2.30pm after 5¾ hours' climbing.

In the meantime, Hillary and Tenzing had left the South Col about an hour later – between 9.30 and 10.0am. Hillary was carrying 49lbs and Tenzing 44lbs, and they used 4 litres per minute of oxygen, catching up with their support party at the site of the highest Swiss camp at 27,200ft. About 100 feet higher they came to the stores left by Hunt and Da Namgyal. Here Hillary took on extra food. His load was now 63lbs, but he increased his flow rate of oxygen to 5 litres per minute and in the next 30 minutes climbed to 27,800ft. Despite his very heavy load, this increase in flow rate made an appreciable difference. 'I felt more energetic,' he told me, 'Everything went more easily, like changing gear.' At 2.30pm the whole party reached the site of Camp IX at 27,800ft on the side of the South Ridge.

As Lowe, Gregory and Ang Nyima were confident of being able to descend without supplementary oxygen, they left their part-empty cylinders at Camp IX, and descended to the South Col, which they reached at 6.0pm. Here, despite the use of sleeping oxygen between 8.30pm and midnight, they slept badly and felt cold.

At Camp IX Hillary and Tenzing took off their oxygen sets and spent 2½ hours, from 2.30-5.0pm, clearing a platform. To do this they had to hack stones out of the ice, and could only make a divided platform, one level of which was six inches above the other. They anchored the guy ropes of the tent to oxygen bottles, as there were no suitable rocks. An uncomfortable night followed, with Hillary sitting on the upper 'shelf' and Tenzing lying on the lower. They had enough sleeping oxygen at 1 litre per minute to last for 3 hours. They used this over two periods, one just after dark and the other before dawn, and while using oxygen they dozed uneasily. For an evening meal they made themselves a mixture of soup, followed by a tin of apricots, jam, nuts, biscuits and sardines, and drank as much as they could.

On 29 May, at about 3.0am, Hillary looked at the thermometer he had put outside the tent; it recorded –27°C. Soon afterwards, as dawn was breaking, they brewed up tea, ate some biscuits and left at 6.30am, using 4 litres per minute and carrying about 30lbs. It was a fine day. As their camp was just below the ridge, they had to kick steps up the crest in firm snow. Moving continuously and together along the narrow, hard snow-edge, they reached the 400ft slope leading to the South Summit. This looked steep, avalanche-prone and potentially very dangerous. On their way, Hillary had noticed a resistance to his breathing, as the expiratory valve, protected by a 'snout' of rubber, had got partially frozen. He cleared his own as well as Tenzing's. About halfway up this snow slope, Hillary turned to Tenzing and asked if he thought they should continue in such dangerous snow conditions. After a short discussion, Tenzing replied, 'Just as you wish', so they carried on.

At 9.0am they reached the South Summit at 28,720ft – the high point achieved by Bourdillon and Evans two days before. Here both sat down and had a drink from their water bottles. They left one oxygen bottle for their return and carried about 20lbs from then on. They also decided to use a flow rate of 3 litres per minute from that point to the summit in order to conserve oxygen. Looking along the next part of the ridge, they could see the crux – a 30ft rock step. The narrow ridge to its foot did not look easy either, with cornices overhanging the Kangshung Face on their right, and the SW Face, to their left, falling steeply to the Western Cwm a vertical mile below. Hillary led off along the ridge, partly cutting steps and partly kicking them. They moved one at a time. Suddenly Tenzing lagged behind – his mask valve had blocked again with ice, but once Hillary had freed it for him he gained immediate relief. Soon they reached the foot of the great black rock step, later known as the 'Hillary Step'. It looked formidable, but then Hillary saw that there was a crack, or chimney, between the rock and the snow-and-ice plastered to its vertical right-hand face. This was where the heat from the rock had melted the snow, and it was wide enough to take a climber. Hillary crawled into it and by jamming his cramponed feet against the ice and his body against the rock, he was able to inch his way up it. This method of 'chimneying', using both back and feet, is very exhausting and must have required a lot of oxygen which he turned up temporarily. Eventually he landed, gasping, at the top. The crux had been overcome. Hillary belayed the rope around his ice axe in the firm snow and brought Tenzing up. It is most unlikely that either could have performed this piece of exhausting climbing if they had not been using adequate supplementary oxygen. After a short rest they continued – nothing was going to stop them now – but both began to feel very tired. Hillary cut steps around one snow hump after another. Then he noticed that there were no more humps and he could see the bare brown plains of Tibet stretching endlessly into the distance. About 40ft above and to the right was a cone of snow. A few more blows with the ice axe, a few more steps kicked in the snow and they were on the top of Everest. It was 11.30am and had taken 2½ hours from the South Summit. Hillary's first feeling was relief rather than triumph. Both removed their oxygen sets, with no immediate feeling of light-headedness or dizzyness. Hillary took a photograph of Tenzing, with the four flags – United Nations, Nepal, India and the British – fluttering from his ice axe. Then he took a series of photos looking down each of the four main ridges. The most important of these was the one looking down to the North Col, which they could see clearly, with the North Peak beyond and the main Rongbuk and East Rongbuk glacier below. This would prove to the sceptics that Everest had in fact been climbed. Before they left the summit they looked at all the other peaks around – an unrivalled and unique panorama.

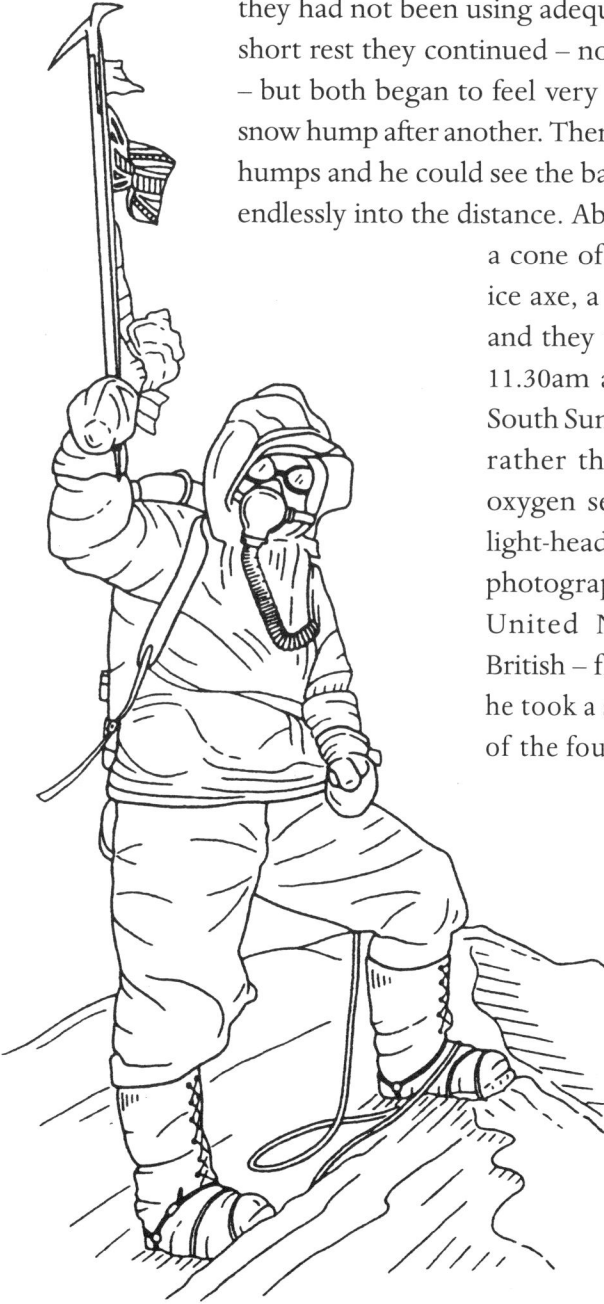

Tenzing on the summit of Everest
Sketch by E J Hatch, after the photo by Edmund Hillary

Makalu and Lhotse – the world's fifth and eighth highest peaks – were clearly seen. Kangchenjunga, the world's third highest – 80 miles away on the Sikkim-Nepal border – dominated the horizon to the east. Cho Oyu had sunk below them, as had a myriad peaks in the Everest region of up to 23,000ft and above. The peaks to the north, on the Tibetan side of Everest, looked quite flat. After five minutes without supplementary oxygen, Hillary became clumsy-fingered and put on his mask. Tenzing, in the meantime, had buried some sweets and biscuits as an offering to the Buddhist gods of Everest, which lies on the border of Buddhist countries. After some Kendal Mint Cake, they left at 11.45am, using 2 litres per minute of oxygen, and rapidly reached the top of the rock step, down which they slithered, and were on the South Summit by 1.0pm. The snow on the far side was still in a dangerous condition and it was a great relief to reach their camp on the ridge an hour later at 2.0pm. Here they stopped for about an hour and brewed up some tea and lemon juice. Also they dumped their nearly-empty oxygen bottles and some partially-filled ones, continuing on 2 litres per minute and carrying loads of about 30lbs. They climbed down the ridge, feeling tired but taking it steadily. At the top of the couloir leading to the South Col their fatigue increased and they realised with dismay that they would have to cut steps down this. Hillary started and continued for 2-3 rope lengths, after which Tenzing found some firm snow and they kicked steps down the rest of the way. When they reached the bottom of the couloir they met George Lowe coming towards them with hot soup. Lowe described their meeting in a letter to his sister:

> Ed unclipped his mask and grinned a tired greeting, sat on the ice and said in his matter-of-fact way, 'Well, we knocked the bastard off!'. It was not quite matter-of-fact, he was incredulous of what they had done ... Tenzing, though tired, was all smiles and I congratulated them both enthusiastically, and Ed's reply was 'It was a wonderful climb, if you had been there you would have done the same.'

Then their oxygen suddenly ran out and the wind started to increase. It was no place for prolonged congratulations, so they walked slowly over the slippery, burnished surface of the col without supplementary oxygen and every slight ridge had them panting. At the South Col camp they found Noyce looking very strong and all crammed into a tent where they answered innumerable questions and drank as much tea as possible. Darkness fell, and there followed another really miserable and windy night. Despite the use of sleeping oxygen they shivered and remained cold. Dawn brought some relief but they felt so terrible that it was all they could do to get out of their sleeping-bags, pack their rucksacks and leave their tents, which they left behind on the South Col.

On 30 May, despite using oxygen at 4 litres per minute, both Hillary and Tenzing took a long time to climb the 300 feet or so upwards from the col to the top of the Geneva Spur, from which a downward traverse led to the top of the Lhotse Face. Finally they reached Camp VII where Charles Wylie was ready with hot drinks and some food. They decided to continue down to Camp IV at the head of the Cwm, where Hunt and the rest of the party were waiting for news; and this they did, getting stronger as they descended. A short way above Camp IV Tom Stobart started filming. As George Lowe followed them down, he gave the thumbs up sign and waved his ice axe in the direction of the summit. Hillary later commented:

> What a thrill it was to be able to tell them that all their efforts amongst the tottering chaos of the icefall, the disheartening plunging up the snowy inferno of the Western Cwm, the difficult technical ice work on the Lhotse Face and the grim and nerve-racking toil above the South Col had been fully rewarded and that we had reached the top.

Both Pugh and I were aware that if we wished to get an accurate account from climbers we had to take a history as soon as possible after their return. If we delayed, they would tend to favour their own performance in many subtle and different ways. Having taken clinical histories from tens of thousands of patients over forty years, I can vouch for this. The brain is exquisitely sensitive to oxygen lack at altitude, so that climbers' accounts and impressions often show a lack of insight into their own physical and mental condition. Bizarre and obsessional behaviour is not uncommon. Undoubtedly this is a factor in many deaths at altitude. It may also explain discrepancies in individual accounts of the same episode. I took histories at Camp IV, often within an hour of each and all individuals returning from the South Col, the South Summit and the Summit. The accounts by Evans, Bourdillon and Hillary are copied almost verbatim from my diary.

In the early evening, while the light was still good, I examined both Hillary and Tenzing as thoroughly as I could and took a very detailed 'clinical' history of the whole period of the ascent. Of particular interest were the following points:

(1) Hillary carried 63lbs from 27,300ft to 27,800ft, and to do this he had to increase his oxygen flow rate from 4 litres to 5 litres per minute. As he told me, it was like changing gear – everything went more easily. Above the South Col he used 4 litres per minute on average, though on the final day he used 3 litres per minute. Because, by then, he was not carrying so much weight and wished to conserve oxygen, less oxygen was used on the descent and sleeping oxygen was used as much as possible.

(2) Hillary passed urine on the summit of Everest. This showed that he was not dehydrated, which was confirmed by clinical examination in the Western Cwm. In fact he drank about 2,250mls on 28 May and 3,000mls on 29 May. This was close to the daily intake of 3,000mls recommended by Pugh.

(3) Food intake over the assault period was barely adequate, but over this short period it was less important than adequate fluid intake. However, Hillary had lost a great deal of weight when I examined him and even a few days afterwards looked almost emaciated. By contrast, Tenzing, who had spent most of his life at high altitudes in Tibet and Nepal, was much fitter, lost less weight, and showed fewer signs of physical deterioration.

(4) Sleeping oxygen at 1 litre per minute promoted sleep, produced a feeling of warmth, and increased recovery from fatigue. It therefore helped to combat high-altitude deterioration in all those going above the Western Cwm.

(5) Clothing insulation was only just adequate for all those going to and above the South Col.

It is difficult to fault the prescience of Pugh who recommended the measures that enabled Everest to be climbed and the mountaineers to return in such good physical and mental condition. After the successful ascent, we quickly descended to Base Camp and James Morris sent a coded cable to the British Embassy. As is well known, this reached London on the night before the Coronation of Queen Elizabeth II.

Reasons for success

One factor that contributed to our success was topographical, the southern Nepalese route having a number of advantages over the northern Tibetan approach. On the south side the main technical difficulties occurred low down, in the Khumbu icefall, between 18,000 and 20,000ft; whereas on the north side, difficult and dangerously sloping and overlapping rock strata lay above 28,000ft, imposing severe physiological problems. By contrast, the strata above the South Col at 26,000ft were favourable to climbing. Finally, the slopes of the Lhotse Face leading to the South Col were avalanche-free, unlike the avalanche-prone slopes below the North Col.

But the main reason for our success in 1953 was that, during the previous two years, from 1951 to 1952, every factor that had resulted in thirty years of failure on Everest was identified, investigated and countered, both in the laboratory and in the field, by the Medical Research Council's Division of Human Physiology, backed by the Royal Society and by other scientists.

All this vital work, carried on with initially minimum support from the Alpine Club or the Royal Geographical Society, defined the way that the 1953 expedition was organised. Because the solutions to all the important problems, a process initiated

E P Hillary on 30 May 1953, 24 hours after the first ascent of Everest.
Hillary was more exhausted than Tenzing, who was better acclimatised.

in early 1951, had been confirmed in the field in 1952, this gave them credibility and they were embraced by the whole party, if not with enthusiasm at least with the knowledge that any hope of success depended upon their correct application. Of paramount importance was the use of adequate flow rates, four litres per minute or more, of supplementary oxygen when climbing and a lower rate when sleeping. Oxygen also proved life saving in enabling exhausted climbers to leave the South Col. Almost equally important was adequate fluid intake, to prevent dehydration and fatigue, together with good protective clothing, to prevent hypothermia and frostbite. Because of their good physical and mental condition, climbers at extreme altitude in 1953 were no longer 'sick men climbing in a dream' but capable of overcoming all obstacles, including the all-important psychological ones.

For the first time, detailed and comprehensive scientific methods were applied to the problems of Everest. This marked out our party as different in its approach from all the previous Everest expeditions, each of which had been well organised but without this extra dimension. It was good science, applied by everyone who took part, that got us to the summit.

BIBLIOGRAPHY

R B Bourdillon, T D Bourdillon, E Harris, 'The closed circuit oxygen apparatus' in *Alpine Journal 59*, 238-246, 1953/54.

T D Bourdillon, 'Oxygen apparatus on the mountain' in *Alpine Journal 59*, 247-263, 1953/54.

R C Evans, 'The first ascent of the South Peak of Everest' in *Alpine Journal 59*, 173-234, 1953/54.

R C Evans, *Eye on Everest*. Dobson, 1955.

A E Gregory, The Picture Book of Everest. Hodder & Stoughton, 1954.

E P Hillary, 'The last lap' in *Alpine Journal 59*, 235-237, 1953/54.

E P Hillary, *High Adventure*. Hodder & Stoughton, 1955.

E P Hillary, *View from the Summit*. Doubleday, 1999.

J Hunt, *The Ascent of Everest*. Hodder & Stoughton, 1953. New edition 1993.

J Hunt, E P Hillary, 'The Ascent of Mount Everest' in *Geographical Journal 119*, 385-399, 1953.

G Lowe, '1st June 1953: Base Camp' in *Alpine Journal 98*, 27-33, 1993.

B Mathews, 'A discussion on the physiology of man at high altitude' in *Proceedings of the Royal Society 143*, 1-42, 1954.

James Morris, *Coronation Everest*. Faber & Faber, 1958.

W H Murray, *The Story of Everest*. Dent, 1953.

C W F Noyce, *A Climbers' Guide to Sonamarg, Kashmir*. Himalayan Club, Delhi, 1944.

C W F Noyce, *South Col: one man's adventure on the ascent of Everest, 1953*. Heinemann, 1954.

N E Odell, 'South Summit versus South Peak' in *Alpine Journal 59*, 367-368, 1953/54.

L G C E Pugh, 'Scientific aspects of the expedition to Mount Everest 1953' in *Geographical Journal 120*, 183-192, 1954.

L G C E Pugh, M P Ward, 'Some effects of high altitude on man' in *Lancet*, 1115-1121, 1956.

Various authors, 'Everest' in *Himalayan Journal 18*, 9-66, 1954.

M P Ward, 'The contribution of medical science to the first ascent of Mount Everest' in *Alpine Journal 98*, 37-51, 1993.

M P Ward, 'The first ascent of Mount Everest 1953: the solution to the problem of the last thousand feet' in *Journal of Wilderness Medicine 4*, 312-318, 1993.

M P Ward, 'The first ascent of Mount Everest' in *British Medical Journal 306*, 1455-1458, 1993.

M P Ward, 'Verbatim reports taken within a few hours of returning to the Western Cwm from all those who ascended to the South Col, to the South Summit and to the Summit of Everest' in *M P Ward Archive*, 1953.

Chapter 21

FILLING THE LAST BLANKS ON THE MAP OF THE EVEREST REGION

Introduction

The first ascent of Everest in 1953 revealed how much of the area south of the mountain remained to be explored and mapped. The northern, Tibetan side had been well mapped during the three expeditions between 1921 and 1924 and during the 1935 reconnaissance expedition.

Although some preliminary explorations of the southern, Nepalese side of Everest had been carried out in 1951 and 1952, large areas remained virtually unknown, unvisited, and unmapped. These were the mountain ranges south of Namche Bazar, the south and east quadrant of the Everest region, where the glaciers drained into the Arun valley, and the complicated border area west of Namche Bazar between the Tesi Lapcha pass and the Menlung basin. Finally, a revised height of Everest needed to be computed.

Once all these problems had been solved, it was possible to make the first comprehensive map of the region, covering both the north and the south sides of the mountain. This was compiled and drawn by G S Holland of the Royal Geographical Society and published in 1961.

South and south-west of Everest, 1953: the Lumding Khola, Inukhu Khola and Hongu Khola

At the beginning of the 1953 expedition Jimmy Roberts brought up extra oxygen bottles from Kathmandu, arriving at Base Camp on 17 April 1953. He then had six weeks' leave at his disposal before returning to his Gurkha battalion, and he used this time to fill in one of the last gaps on the map of the Everest region.

Roberts was working from the most recent map of the Khumbu – a 1926 ¼-inch Survey of India map – which did not go beyond glacier level. This map showed that the country immediately south of Everest was drained by three rivers – the Imja, the Hongu and the Inukhu. The exploration carried out on the 1951 expedition had confirmed that only a few of the Everest glaciers drained into the Imja Khola, which ran east-west, parallel to and just south of the Lhotse-Nuptse wall. Yet the size of the Hongu Khola and Inukhu Khola did not seem adequate to account for the drainage of this vast array of glaciers and peaks south of Everest, and this indicated that either a river existed which had not been identified or the Inukhu Khola, in particular, was larger than expected. Roberts' main task was to solve that riddle.

Another major piece of important exploration needed to be carried out in the extensive range that borders Khumbu to the south, shutting it out from Solu and the rest of Nepal. The only way to approach the range was from the the south – that is, to descend the Dudh Kosi river for twelve miles, south of Namche Bazar, and then to go west into the Lumding Khola from Ghat. Roberts initiated this piece of exploration in the spring of 1953 and it was completed by Charles Evans in the autumn of the same year.

Roberts took with him four Sherpas, including Sen Tensing who had been on the 1951 Everest reconnaissance and many other expeditions. Climbing up west from Ghat, they crossed the Moro La (14,000ft) into the Lumding Khola. In April this pass was snow-covered; on its westward side it led to a broad valley running north and south. To the north, above a 2,000ft rock step, the main Lumding glacier drained Numbur (6,958m) and Karyolung (6,530m).* But bad weather and winter snow made further exploration impossible, so Roberts returned to Ghat.

He now struck east, crossing a pass above the village of Chaunri Kharka. Descending to the valley of the Inukhu Khola, he found a large river with what appeared to be the same volume of water as the Dudh Kosi which they had just left. This indicated that it probably did drain a very considerable area. Following this river north to a yak pasture, Lusamba, Roberts came to a flat glacial plain where the 1924-26 Survey of India map wrongly showed a ridge of peaks including the main peak – Mera (6,470m). Once Roberts and his Sherpas had been able to establish that this range did not exist, it was easy to go east again and, by crossing an 18,000ft pass to the north of Mera peak, descend into the Hongu Khola, the next valley to the east. At the head of this (Hongu) valley were the Panch Pokhari lakes which had been visited by the 1951 and 1952 expeditions.

Roberts returned to the Inukhu Khola and went north to its head, where he reached a pass, the Philibu La, from which a very steep valley dropped west to Thyangboche monastery. He turned back on 20 May. With Sen Tensing he then made the first ascent of Mera peak from the Hongu, by its northern flank.

They then went north again up the Hongu Khola to the Panch Pokhari lakes, crossed the Amphu Labtsa pass into the Imja Khola and reached Thyangboche monastery from the north.

* Where metric heights are given, these are intended to conform to the maps by Ted Hatch on pages 274 and 276 and with the back end paper. Other instances of metric measurements reflect modern usage.

Roberts had proved by this exploration that there was no 'extra' river, but that the Inukhu Khola drained a much larger and wider area of country than had hitherto been recognised; the 1961 map of the Everest region was adjusted accordingly.

The Guanara glacier, west of Everest; the Lumding Khola and peaks south of Namche Bazar, 1953

At the beginning of June, after the members of the 1953 expedition had left Namche Bazar to return to Kathmandu, Charles Evans stayed on in Khumbu for three weeks before travelling to Darjeeling, where he stayed with the Hendersons whom he knew from his army leaves during the war. On his return, at Raxaul on the Nepal-India border, he met Professor Christoph von Fuhrer-Haimendorf of the School of Oriental and African Studies in London, who was well known for his work on the social anthropology of the hill people of north-east India. He was about to start on a study of the Sherpa population, on which he later wrote a widely-acclaimed book. They trekked together to Khumbu where Evans, taking advantage of the clear autumn skies, carried out a photo-theodolite survey of the peaks around the Guanara glacier, west of Everest and south of Cho Oyu and Gyachung Kang; and between the Ngozumpa glacier and the Dudh Kosi valley to the west. This joined up the explorations of 1951 and 1952. In the course of this work he made the second ascent of Kang Cho (6063m), the first having been made by Wilfrid Noyce, myself and others during the acclimatisation period in 1953.

Left
Charles Evans. (*John Merton RA*)

In 1953, after Everest, Charles Evans carried out some difficult but essential exploration west and south of Everest to fill in two 'blanks on the map' of the region.

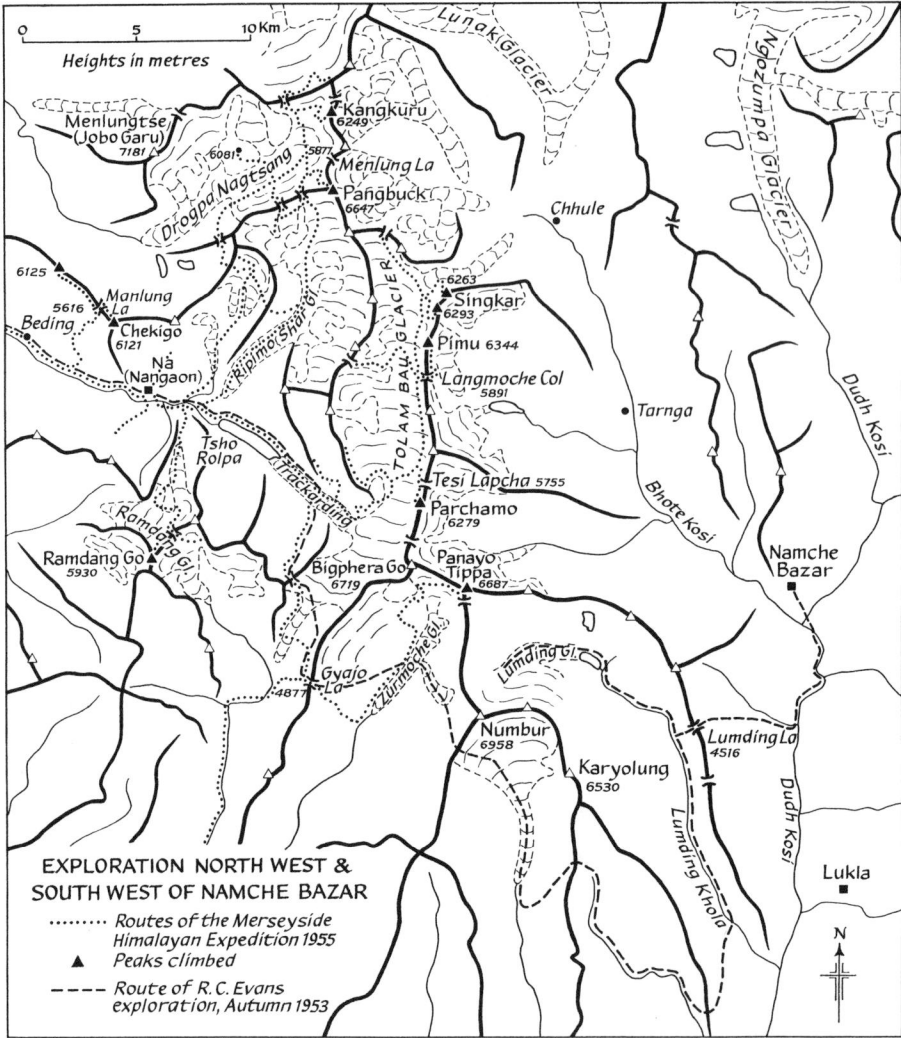

Evans then decided to explore the ranges south of Namche Bazar, using the same route as the one Roberts had followed, going west from Ghat into the Lumding Khola. From this valley he could find no way out of the Numbur-Karyolung cirque of peaks to the north, so he turned south down the Lumding Khola as far as Thangu, a small hamlet. From here he went west and north into the Dudh Kund valley on the south side of Numbur. Ascending a glacier, he managed to break out west again by a 5,500m pass and descended to a small village, Samsa. Going north up this valley to the Zurmoche glacier, he was stopped by a steep ice wall from crossing into the Bhote Kosi valley that runs north to the Nangpa La. Instead, he crossed west over a ridge running south from the peak Bigphera Go (6,719m) and descended onto a glacier that ran north into the mixture of snowfields and glaciers west of the Tesi Lapcha pass, which was crossed by the 1951 expedition. At last Evans was on familiar ground, for the main route west from Namche Bazar to Kathmandu crosses this pass and descends to the Rolwaling and Rongshar valleys.

These two explorations, by Roberts and Evans, filled in two blanks on the map of Khumbu and the Everest region. By the end of 1953, not only had Everest been climbed, but all the main valleys, peaks, glaciers and passes had been seen, many photographed, and a great amount of aerial and ground survey work completed. Also in 1953, two expeditions, one Scottish, the other Indian, failed to climb Pumori (7165m). Finally, in 1954, the height of Everest was determined at 29,028ft (8,848m) by B L Gulatee of the Survey of India. However, the south-east quadrant of the Everest region remained unmapped, together with the ranges north of the Tesi Lapcha pass and the Menlung basin.

The south-east quadrant of the Everest region: the Barun, Iswa, Choyang and Hongu valleys, 1954 and 1955

The south-east quadrant was the last substantial area of the Everest region to be mapped, and this was done mainly by Norman Hardie, a New Zealand civil engineer, in the course of two expeditions, in 1954 and 1955.

The area is contained within two ridges that run from the summit of Lhotse. The first is the border ridge between Nepal and Tibet which runs east through Pethangtse (6,738m), Makalu II (7,678m), the Makalu Col, Makalu (8,485m) and then drops gradually towards the Popti La before plunging into the Arun gorge. The second ridge runs more or less due south from Lhotse to Baruntse (7,168m), and then west towards Ama Dablam (6814m); it then turns due south to Mera peak (6,470m) and Naulekh (6,363m).

Within this area there are five main valleys: the Barun close to the Tibet border, the Iswa and Choyang running east, and the Sangkhua and Hongu running south. The Inukhu valley is smaller than these and separates the Hongu from the main valley of Khumbu in which lies the Dudh Kosi river.

In 1880 the pundit Sukh Darshan Singh (G.S.S.) ascended the Arun valley from Nepal, crossed the border by the Popti La and entered the Kharta valley in Tibet before being turned back. In 1921 on the first Everest reconnaissance expedition, Howard-Bury looked over the border from Tibet, near the peak Pethangtse, and glimpsed the tangled mass of peaks that make up this south-east quadrant. The Barun glacier, the largest in the region, was identified on the '1933 Flight Over Everest' and depicted on the 1952 Milne-Hinks map.

In 1951 Shipton and Hillary circumnavigated Ama Dablam and visited the Panch Pokhari, the five lakes at the head of the Hongu valley; whilst in 1952, during the Cho Oyu expedition, Shipton, Evans, Hillary and Lowe crossed from the Imja to

Exploration south and east of Everest in 1954 and 1955 by Norman Hardie the Hongu and then to the Barun valley, which they descended to the Arun valley. In the autumn of 1953, J O M Roberts explored the Inukhu valley for the first time. In none of these exploratory journeys was any formal survey carried out.

The 1954 New Zealand Alpine Club Himalayan Expedition ascended the Arun valley and then split into groups. The main group went west over a pass into the lower Barun valley which they ascended, establishing a base camp near the start of the south ridge of Makalu, then being attempted by a Californian party. Whilst exploring the Upper Barun glacier, C J McFarlane, a member of the survey team, was badly concussed after falling into a crevasse and, in the course of his rescue, Hillary, the leader of the party, broke three ribs. In the meantime a smaller group had left the Arun gorge to explore the Choyang valley, but to do this they had to cross into the Iswa further north and follow the crest of the ridge between these two heavily forested valleys. Eventually they reached the head of the Choyang, and crossed north into the Iswa and then into the Barun valley.

The third group, which included Norman Hardie, surveyed the Iswa from bottom to top, the south and east sides of Chamlang peak (7,321m) and the complicated group of peaks to the south. They followed an indistinct yak track up the floor of the Iswa valley, but being shut in by its precipitous walls and cloud cover, they found that the compass was of more use than the photo-theodolite. Reaching the head of this valley they obtained a good view of the ice bulges on the south face of Chamlang which emphasised that no easy route existed on that face. Able to use a theodolite for the first time, Hardie surveyed the head of this valley and reached a pass on a ridge running south from Chamlang, which gave good views of the complicated middle part of the Hongu valley to the west.

Meeting up with members of the Choyang party, they then crossed into the Barun by an easy pass between Peak 6 and the east ridge of Chamlang. Joining up with the Barun party, they made a reconnaissance to the Tibet frontier ridge north of Makalu II. They also attempted to climb to the col between Makalu and Makalu II. Unfortunately at this stage Hillary became so ill that both he and McFarlane had to be evacuated to Kathmandu. The remaining members continued their exploration and survey and Hardie completed an enormous amount of work. He climbed Pethangtse (6,739m), an elegant cone-shaped peak on the border ridge, a number of other peaks and crossed into the Upper Kangshung basin, thus joining up with the areas explored by the 1921 Everest reconnaissance expedition.

Hardie now concentrated on mapping the Barun-Imja divide and reached a ridge running north from Ama Dablam. A few days later he climbed a peak, Cho Polu, and after returning to the Barun-Imja divide, managed to cross this by a difficult pass descending into the Upper Imja glacier. He reached Khumjung, the highest village in the valley, a few days later.

The last area to be visited in 1954 was the Barun plateau, a region of level snowfields between the Barun and the Hongu. Evans surveyed the area. The edge of this plateau was ringed with peaks. To the north, was Baruntse (7,168m) which the party climbed. They then crossed into the Hongu valley and some left by crossing the Amphu Labtsa pass at its head to the Imja glacier, whilst others went south, climbing Naulekh (6,363m). Returning up the Hongu, this group crossed onto the small snow plateau in the Upper Mingbo valley which was subsequently, in the winter of 1960-61, used by the Silver Hut expedition as a base for a high-altitude scientific party. They then descended to Pangboche and Thyangboche.

In 1955 Norman Hardie, with George Band, Joe Brown and Tony Streather, took part in the first ascent of Kangchenjunga. After that successful expedition, Hardie went west, crossing passes in the Lumba Sumba range and in north-east Nepal. He reached the Arun valley, which he descended before going west again; after crossing the Hongu and Inukhu rivers, he reached the Dudh Kosi river which he ascended to Namche Bazar. Here he stayed for some time before returning to the Nepal border where he met another New Zealander, A J MacDonald. From mid-September, Hardie and MacDonald crossed into the Inukhu valley by Lukla and surveyed this valley, visiting all its remote corners. From the Mera La, about halfway along its east side, they crossed into the mid-Hongu. From here, in fine weather, MacDonald climbed a peak commanding good views of the Hongu and Upper Iswa valleys. He also reached a col on the Iswa-Hongu divide that had been ascended from the east in 1954.

Meanwhile, Hardie descended the Hongu valley and climbed a pass giving access to the Sangkhua valley to the south and east. The upper slopes of this valley provided fine grazing for yaks belonging to the inhabitants of the west side of the Arun valley. Hardie then went north up the Hongu again and crossed the Amphu Labtsa pass into the Imja Khola. Later, he met Macdonald who had tried to climb Mera peak but had been foiled by new snow. Crossing over to Namche Bazar, MacDonald climbed two more peaks on the Inukhu-Dudh Kosi divide for survey reasons.

These two expeditions, in 1954 and 1955, achieved an enormous amount of surveying in a highly complicated and unmapped part of the Everest region. Unlike the northern, Tibetan side of Everest, where the approach valleys were relatively shallow and bare, those on the south, Nepalese aspect had near-vertical sides, and fell very steeply into gorges, while the lower parts were densely forested. This made travel in them much more difficult and hazardous, with afternoon cloud shortening survey time. That such a large area was mapped in the course of only two expeditions reflects great credit on Norman Hardie, an outstanding mountaineer and surveyor, whose feats can be compared with those of Wheeler and Morshead on Everest in 1921, and of Spender in 1935.

Exploration to the west and south of Everest, 1955: the Tolam Bau glacier, Menlung basin and the Sarmoche valley

One of the most complicated glacial areas to be visited by mountain survey parties was that surrounding the Tolam Bau glacier, west of Everest, between the Tesi Lapcha pass and the Menlung basin. In 1955 this area was surveyed by a party led by Alfred Gregory, and the map produced by plane tabling was drawn by Dennis Davis.

The party came mainly from the north of England and after a preliminary period at Nangaon in the upper part of the Rolwaling valley, moved to the Tolam Bau glacier. This was just west of the Tesi Lapcha pass and from the plateau at its head, first visited in 1952 during the Cho Oyu expedition, a number of peaks were climbed. The next glacier to the west, the Ripimo Shar, was then explored, and it was possible to cross over in two places onto the Menlung glacier, first explored in 1951. This glacier was followed north until the brown plains of Tibet could be seen from a ridge falling east from the peak Menlungtse, identified by us in 1951.

On their return to Nangaon, the party split, with some returning to the UK. Others continued their exploration in the mountains south of the Rolwaling valley, and after climbing some more peaks, left for Kathmandu via the Sarmoche valley. In addition to surveying work and mapping, 19 peaks between 20 and 21,000ft were climbed in one of the most successful and productive of the expeditions in the Everest region.

The previous year, in 1954, Raymond Lambert had crossed a pass, the Hadengi La, above Beding in the Rolwaling valley and entered the Menlung basin. Shipton and I had visited the Tibetan side of this pass in 1951. Lambert then traversed the Menlung La and Dingjung La from west to east, descending to Chhule. From there his party went north over the Nangpa La and attempted to climb Cho Oyu, reaching 7,700m, before being stopped by bad weather.

The first comprehensive map of the Everest region. The modern height of Mount Everest.

With the opening of Nepal in 1950 surveyors were allowed to within 30-40 miles of Everest, and a small Indian survey team reached Namche Bazar in 1953. Between 1952 and 1954 a new and sophisticated survey network was set up by B L Gulatee, then in charge of the geodetic and research branch of the Survey of India. From the main network already established in India, a chain of six quadrilateral figures was extended north towards the Nepal Himalaya, ending in an eight-sided figure. From points on this, Everest was observed on numerous occasions at distances between 24 and 47 miles. As a result of this work a position of latitude, N 27° 59' 15.83" and longitude, E 86° 55' 49.51" was fixed. The height of Everest was calculated at 29,028ft (±5ft), 8,848m. This superseded the original height, 29,002ft, computed in 1849-50, and a further survey computed between 1880 and 1902 from Darjeeling, when a height of 29,141ft (8,882m) was calculated. This last height was never accepted either by scientists or by the general public.

The height 8,848m is now the generally acccepted height of Everest. However, this will always be an approximation as the top is a snow dome and therefore liable to alteration due to snowfall, wind, and melting resulting from solar radiation.

Between 1954 and 1955 the Fédération Française de la Montagne published a 1:50,000 map of the area between Makalu and Everest, whilst in 1957 Erwin Schneider, the Austrian cartographer, drew a map at 1:25,000 of the south side of Everest. In 1963 this was extended and reissued at 1:50,000.

In 1960 Chinese surveyors under Professor Wang Wenying covered the north side of Everest and accepted the 1954 Indian survey's position and height. It was on that expedition, on 25 May at 4.20am, that Wang Fu-chou, Konbu, and Chu Yin-hua reached the summit – the first ascent from the north, Tibetan side of the mountain.

In 1961 the first comprehensive map of the whole Everest region, from Rongbuk to Namche Bazar, and from the Tesi Lapcha pass to the Barun valley, was drawn by G S Holland of the Royal Geographical Society. A broader definition of the Everest region extends from the Rongshar valley to the Arun valley, and from Tingri in the north to just south of Ghat in the Dudh Kosi valley to the south, and this larger area is covered by the basic map used in the present monograph (see pages 320-327).

The 1961 Holland/RGS map is based on the Survey of India control, while the height of Everest was determined by B L Gulatee in 1954. The 1961 map incorporated the following material:

a. Mount Everest and the group of Chomo Lungma 1:63,360, from the photographic survey by Major E O Wheeler, RE, 1921. Published by the RGS and Alpine Club, 1925 (with unpublished eastward extension).
b. Mount Everest and environs 1:126,720. Survey of India 1930.
c. The Northern Face of Mount Everest 1:20,000, from a photogrammetric survey by Michael Spender, 1935. RGS 1936.
d. Photogrammetric survey by Michael Spender 1:50,000, 1939. An unpublished plotting of the area north of Everest, covering the greater part of Wheeler's area and extending north-eastwards to the region of 'Dent Blanche'.
e. The Southern Face and region south of Mount Everest 1:50,000. Compiled and drawn by H F Milne from photographs, including those of the Mount Everest Flight 1933. RGS, 1952 (limited publication).
f. Photographs taken by Charles Evans, 1953.

g. New Zealand Alpine Club Expedition 1954 and Chamlang Survey Expedition 1955 1:50,000. A draft map plotted from photographs by Norman Hardie (unpublished).

h. Esquisse topographique de la région de l'Everest et du Makalu 1:50,000. Expéditions Françaises à l'Himalaya 1954-55.

j. Mahalangur Himal: Chomolongma-Mount Everest 1:25,000, from the photogrammetric survey by Erwin Schneider, International Himalayan Expedition 1955. Deutscher Alpenverein and Österreichischer Alpenverein 1957.

k. Merseyside Himalayan Expedition 1955 1:68,500 (unpublished). A survey in the Rolwaling Himal to the west of Tesi Lapcha.

l. Photographs taken by Erwin Schneider, 1955.

m. Survey of India 1:255,440, sheets 71L (1932), 71P (1929), 72I (1932) and 72M (1930).

Two Survey of India maps seem to be missing from this list: These are:

i. Preliminary map. Mt Everest detachment 1921, 11,255,440ft.

ii Mt Everest reconnaissance map. 1928 edition 1:255,440.

Both these maps are based on Wheeler's 1921 photosurvey, and can be found in the map room of the RGS. In 1975 Holland's 1961 map was revised, extended and further detail added. This is now the landmark map of the Everest region against which all others are judged.

Further maps up to 1992

A large scientific and mountaineering expedition was mounted in 1975 by the Chinese, who brought the Survey a major step forward by putting a tripod on the summit of Everest on 27 May. From 13 control points at heights between 5,600m and 6,300m and at distances from the summit between 7km and 12km, a height (excluding the thickness of the snow cover, which is variable) of 29,029ft ($\pm$1ft), 8,848.13m, was computed above the mean sea-level of the Yellow (China) Sea about 2,000 miles away. It was also calculated that Everest was rising at a mean rate of 0.15mm each year.

In 1977 Chinese cartographers from Lanzhou University, working under Professor Chen Jiaming, printed a map of the Everest region in Chinese from survey work carried out between 1966 and 1975. In 1984 Bradford Washburn, Director of the Museum of Science in Boston, wished to increase the accuracy of the maps in the Everest region, so that glaciologists and geologists could have a large-scale, 1:10,000 detailed base with 20m contours on which to work. To this end he obtained

permission to overfly Everest at 12,000m. The resulting map at 1:50,000 was published by the National Geographic Society in 1988. It was drawn by the Swiss Federal
Office in Berne and place names were decided in consultation with Nepalese and
Chinese cartographers. The second edition was published in 1991, showing the
names and dates of the different routes made on Everest up to that date. The larger-
scale maps will be found in the map archives of the Royal Geographical Society.

A re-examination of the height of Everest was made in 1987 by an Italian party
using Global Positioning Systems (GPS) and Electronic Distance-Measuring (EDM)
lasers. These established conclusively that Everest was the world's highest peak by a
large margin, with K2 (Mount Godwin Austen) in the Karakoram the second highest
at 28,250ft.

Professor Roger Bilham of the Department of Geophysics at the University of
Colorado carried out a major repositioning of a number of GPS stations in Nepal in
1991. He set up four new stations at Lukla, Namche Bazar, Pheriche and Kala Pattar
respectively, as well as one at the ruined monastery at Rongbuk which had been
destroyed by the Chinese. His main finding was that Everest seemed to be rising in
one block rather than in segments.

In 1992 two prisms for the reflection of laser beams were placed on the summit
on 12 May, a day when over 30 people crowded onto the summit. Measurements
were made by EDM lasers from a new station at Thyangboche in Nepal by a small
survey team backed by the Boston Science Museum and its Honorary Director
Bradford Washburn and his wife. In September of the same year, after prisms had
been placed on the summit by Italian climbers, an Italian-Chinese party measured
the height of Everest from six stations, three in Tibet and three in Nepal, each within
eight miles of the peak. The result of these Sino-Italian surveys was published in a
major article in GPS World, and the new Everest altitude was reported to be
8,848.65m.

The summit of Everest is a dome of snow and in one photo taken in 1993 an
oxygen bottle and prayer flags are visible in the snow, perhaps a dozen feet below
the present surface on the vertical NE face of the summit snows. Presumably they
had been left on the surface and became buried by successive snowfalls. Extra snow
appears to be added to the summit during each monsoon. This settles but some
gets blown away by the ferocious winter winds that blast the summit. Winds of
165mph were recorded by Washburn when he flew over Everest in a Lear Jet in
December 1984. The direction of the prevailing wind, which is parallel to the NE
ridge and at right angles to the ridge between the south and main summit, probably
explains why no cornices have been reported on the NE ridge overlooking the
Kangshung Face, whilst there are large ones on the ridge between the south and
main summits overhanging this face.

The most recent height, calculated in 1999

In 1999 the height of Everest, using Global Satellite Positioning was re-calculated at 29,035ft, 8,850m.

TABLE OF PRINCIPAL ESTIMATIONS OF THE HEIGHT OF MOUNT EVEREST

Date	Observer	Height		Comment
		Ft	m	
1847	Armstrong	28,799	8,778	Isolated observation
1849	Nicholson	29,002.3	8,840	From 6 stations in the plains
1892-1903		28,994	8,837	Change in heights of control stations
1905	Burrard	29,141	8,882	Re-computation. Mean of 6 values.
1922	De Graaff Hunter	29,149	8,885	Adjustment to Burrard's 1905 value.
1922	De Graaff Hunter	29,079	8,863	Allowing for geoid height and refraction adjustment, sometimes given as 29,080.
1929	Bomford	29,050	8,854	New value for geoid height
1933	The Times Atlas	29,141	8,882	
1952-54	Gulatee	29,028	8,848	Geoidal height
1975	Chinese	29,029.24	8,848	Beacon on summit
1987	Desio	29,107	8,872	Orthometric height
1992	Italian/Chinese	29,022	8,846.10	using GPS

(*From* J R Smith, *Everest. The Man and the Mountain*)

BIBLIOGRAPHY

R C Evans, *Notes of exploration south of Namche Bazar*.
   These were compiled by M P Ward from notes taken from R C Evans
   in the autumn of 1953. M P Ward archive, 1954.

A E Gregory, 'The Merseyside Himalayan Expedition, 1955' in *Alpine Journal 61*, 54-59, 1956-57.

B L Gulatee, 'Mount Everest. Its height and name' in *Himalayan Journal 17*, 131-142, 1952.

B L Gulatee, 'The height of Mount Everest – a new determination, 1952-1956' in *Survey of India technical paper No 8*, 1954.

B L Gulatee, 'The height of Mount Everest – a new determination' in *Himalayan Journal 19*, 174-175, 1954.

N Hardie, A section in 'New Zealand Alpine Club Himalayan Expedition' (Edited by E P Hillary) in *New Zealand Alpine Journal 16*, 5-53, 1955.

N Hardie, *In Highest Nepal*. Allen & Unwin, 1956.

N Hardie, 'Mount Chamlang Survey Expedition' in *Himalayan Journal 26*, 86-93, 1957.

G S Holland, C R Crowe, 'A new map of the Mount Everest region' in *Geographical Journal 128*, 54-57, 1962.

R Lambert, C Kogan, *White Fury*. Hurst and Blackett, 1956.

H Macinnes, 'The Creagh Dhu Himalayan Expedition, 1953' in *Alpine Journal 60*, 58-61, 1955.

N Parrekh, 'An Attempt on Pumori' in *Himalayan Journal 18*, 150-156, 1954.

G Poretti, C Marchesini, A Brinat, 'GPS Surveys Mount Everest' in *GPS World*, 33-36, October 1994.

J O M Roberts, 'South of Everest' in *Himalayan Journal 18*, 59-64, 1954.

Erwin Schneider, Forward to the map of the Mount Everest area in *Mount Everest: formation, population and exploration of the Everest region* by Toni Hagen, G O Dyhrenfurth, Christoph von Fürer-Haimendorf, Erwin Schneider. Translated by E Noel Bowman. Oxford University Press, 1963.

J R Smith, *Everest. The Man and the Mountain*. Whittles Publishing, 1999.

Unattributed article, 'Mount Everest now poses an even bigger challenge' in *The Times*, page 17, November 13, 1999.

M P Ward, 'Sagarmatha – Mount Everest – Chomolungma Map'. National Geographical Society Review in *Geographical Journal 155*, 433-435, 1989.

M P Ward, 'Mapping Everest' in *Cartographic Journal 31*, 33-44, 1994.

M P Ward, 'Exploration and Mapping South-East of Everest in 1954 and 1955' in *Alpine Journal 104*, 197-201, 1999.

Chapter 22

THE MYSTERIES HAVE GONE

Introduction

Following the first ascent of Everest in 1953, it was inevitable that attempts would be made to reach the summit without the help of supplementary oxygen. Given that European climbers, born and bred at sea level, had been able to climb to within a thousand feet of the summit, and that Sherpas, who live permanently at high altitude, had reached a similar height carrying loads of 20lbs or more, mountaineers felt that it should be possible to break through this height barrier and reach the summit of the highest mountain without using supplementary oxygen.

Medical scientists were not so sure. In 1875 two out of three balloonists who had ascended rapidly to 28,000ft, died from oxygen lack; yet other balloonists, who had reached the same altitude, survived. No supplementary oxygen was used on either occasion, and although both crews were at rest, this result did indicate that the oxygen uptake by at least some of the balloonists had been just adequate for survival.

The decompression chamber experiment in 1946, Operation Everest I, showed that after 32 days' acclimatisation, it was possible for volunteers to survive at rest at an altitude equivalent to the height of Everest without supplementary oxygen. Whether they could also climb (ie exercise effectively) at this altitude, when oxygen intake would need to be greater, was doubtful. This area of uncertainty was the main reason why the Medical Research Council considered that adequate supplementary oxygen was necessary to ensure success on Everest in 1953.

Another important difference between balloonists and mountaineers was that, whereas the former had to withstand a sudden lack of oxygen, the latter would be exposed to oxygen deprivation over a much longer period and could therefore become to some extent acclimatised to it. In 1953 Edmund Hillary, while resting on the summit of Everest, was able to remove his oxygen mask for as much as ten minutes before getting light-headed.

After investigations were carried out on a number of scientific expeditions to great altitude, notably the Silver Hut expedition of 1960-61 which wintered at 19,000ft in the Everest region, the possibility of an ascent without supplementary oxygen became more likely. On that occasion the barometric pressure, which pushes oxygen through the walls of the lungs into the blood, was recorded frequently, and supplemented data from the 1953 expedition. It was confirmed that barometric pressure at this very high altitude was higher than expected compared with standard altitude tables. It became clear, therefore, that an ascent to the summit of Everest without supplementary oxygen might just be possible.

In 1960-61 an experiment at 24,500ft on the Makalu Col by John West and myself showed that on the summit of Everest, at 29,028ft, there was likely to be a natural uptake of oxygen at about 1 litre per minute. This would be just enough to enable a climber to move up slowly with pauses for rest. We concluded theoretically, therefore, that on the summit of Everest, the barometric pressure would be high enough and the intake of naturally available oxygen great enough for climbers to be able to move slowly without the help of supplementary oxygen.

Breaking the final barrier, 1978

The first mountaineers to climb the last few metres to the summit of Everest without using supplementary oxygen were two Chinese mountaineers, Wang Fu-chou and Chu Yin-hua, and a Tibetan, Konbu. The circumstances of their ascent were so bizarre that for many years they were not believed. However, in 1980, when I was at a symposium on Tibet in Beijing, I met Wang Fu-chou and also Shih Chan-chun who led the 1960 expedition and was currently Vice-President of the Chinese Mountaineering Association. I believed the story he told me.

Briefly, on 24 May 1960 three Chinese mountaineers and a Tibetan, using supplementary oxygen, left their top camp at 8,500m on the north, Tibetan side of Everest and managed to climb the 'Second Step', which took them three hours. Here, Liu Lien-man became so exhausted that he could go no further. The other three continued, but at 8,835m their oxygen ran out just as night was falling. Discarding their sets, they carried on, with frequent halts and suffering from hallucinations – a sure sign of oxygen lack. At last, at 4.30am, they reached the summit in the dark, 19 hours after leaving camp. After a few minutes' rest they buried a page of Konbu's diary, and a bust of Chairman Mao. Slowly they descended to about 8,700m where it was light enough to take some photos using a ciné camera. After re-joining Liu Lien-man, they reached Base Camp on 30 May. Wang Fu-chou suffered from severe frostbite and lost some of his fingers and toes. He told me that their survival had been 'a very close-run thing'.

In 1963 the final barrier was breached a little further. On 22 May two Americans, Tom Hornbein and Willi Unsoeld, using supplementary oxygen, traversed Everest by ascending the previously unclimbed upper part of the West Ridge and descending by the normal South Ridge route. Just below the South Summit they met their support party who, using oxygen, had climbed Everest from the South Col on the same day. All survived a bivouac, without supplementary oxygen, at 8,700m. But Barry Bishop, despite being fully clothed as were the others, lost fingers and toes due to frostbite. His peripheral tissues cooled to the environmental temperature which was many degrees below freezing. All survived, however.

The final barrier was broken in 1978 when Reinhold Messner and Peter Habeler, two Austrian climbers, climbed Everest from the south without using supplementary oxygen. Their background, training methods and approach to mountaineering were different from the majority of those who had previously climbed Everest. Having climbed together since 1966, both were exceptional athletes who had become mountaineering legends after ascending some of the hardest routes in Europe in less than half the usual time taken. In 1975 they had transferred their rapid 'Alpine style' to the Himalaya, climbing Hidden Peak (26,470ft, 8,068m) in the Karakoram in three days without porter support.

In 1978 Habeler and Messner joined an Austrian expedition which was aiming to climb Everest from the south using supplementary oxygen. The party was a formidable one, all its members being experienced Himalayan climbers. It was led by Wolfgang Nairz, with Oswald Oelz as climbing physician and with two excellent British cameramen, Leo Dickinson and Eric Jones. The expedition successfully climbed Everest using supplementary oxygen on 3 May 1978.

Three days later, on 6 May, Habeler, Messner and three Sherpas reached the South Col (25,850ft) without using supplementary oxygen, the Sherpas returning to camp on the Lhotse Face. Eric Jones also reached the South Col and was able to film the two Austrians. On 7 May most of the day was spent melting snow to prevent dehydration. On 8 May they woke at 3.0am, made coffee and started at around 6.0am. Messner was wearing silk underwear, a fleecy pile undersuit, a complete down suit, double-layer boots of insulated neoprene, three pairs of gloves, two hats and goggles.

After four hours of climbing up the couloir and the South Ridge, they reached a camp site at 8,500m, and rested for 30 minutes. On the South Summit they put on a rope for the first time. From here to the summit both felt as if they were climbing on 'automatic pilot' with little appreciation of danger or anything else. They also had a feeling of euphoria, though physically they felt quite finished. Despite hallucinations, they managed to climb the Hillary Step, though not without difficulty. The last 100ft to the summit took one hour, with both climbers collapsing in the snow every few feet. After a few minutes on the summit they returned rapidly and Habeler glissaded most of the way from the South Summit to the South Col, where he arrived totally exhausted and with a frostbitten nose. Messner followed half an hour later suffering from snow blindness. Their ascent had taken 8 hours, yet their descent took 1 to 1½ hours only. On 9 May they reached the Western Cwm and were at Base Camp by 10 May. On 11 May Reinhard Karl and Oswald Oelz climbed Everest using supplementary oxygen.

Both Habeler and Messner were born and raised in the South Tyrol at altitudes between 1,000 and 2,000 metres, thus acquiring since birth a certain degree of acclimatisation to oxygen lack. Their technical climbing ability was exceptional, and they had an outstanding record of first, often solo, ascents on hard routes. Their speed and skill, which derived from economy of movement, gave them an extra margin of safety on difficult ascents, and before 1978 both had already climbed many high Himalayan peaks without using supplementary oxygen.

They had trained seriously for 10 years before attempting Everest. Both were true athletes in the modern sense of the word, and the first mountaineers to treat the sport as an athletic challenge. Messner began hill running in 1975, frequently ascending hills around Bolzano at a rate approaching 1,700 metres an hour (5,000ft/hour), and Habeler could match that. By contrast, the average climbing rate at low altitudes of the members of the 1953 Everest expedition was 700 metres an hour (2,000ft/hour) – less than half the speed of the Austrians.

Messner had trained himself to take exercise over long periods whilst fasting,* thus increasing his dependence on stored body fat. On their ascent of Everest in 1978 they reduced the amount that they carried to a minimum, each taking just a short length of rope, some food, bivouac sack and climbing equipment – in all about 20lbs. They realised that their oxygen demands were directly related to their total weight and every added ounce could militate against success. The pattern of their ascent was determined by their oxygen uptake.

Over long periods, mountaineers climb at their preferred and comfortable rate of ascent and, at this rate, the amount of oxygen used is roughly 50% of their maximum uptake. As altitude increases, in order to keep moving continuously and to keep in thermal balance and not to cool down (risking hypothermia and frostbite), the climber will approach his maximum oxygen uptake until, at about 24,000ft, continuous climbing becomes impossible. Thereafter he stops every so often to pant in order to restore his oxygen deficit. He then moves on again. In other words, over a certain altitude his progress becomes slower and more intermittent, and without supplementary oxygen he tends to cool at extreme altitude. A rate of two minutes' climbing to half a minute's rest is common, but the higher the altitude the shorter the active periods, and the rest periods become correspondingly longer.

At 28,850ft, over the last 50 metres to the summit, Messner described their progress: 'We can no longer keep on our feet while we rest ... every 10-15 steps we collapse into the snow to rest, then crawl on again.' This description is very similar to that of Norton at 28,000ft in 1924: 'Our pace was wretched. My ambition was to do twenty consecutive paces uphill without a pause to rest and pant, elbow on bent knee ... Every five or ten minutes we had to sit down for a minute or two and we

---

* This strategy does have some disadvantages at altitude where an increased carbohydrate uptake is to be preferred.

must have looked a sorry couple.' Of course, Hillary and Tenzing, who used supplementary oxygen, did not suffer from such a dramatic fall-off in performance.

From the summit, both Habeler and Messner descended to the South Col in 1-1½ hours – very much more rapidly than the time achieved by Hillary and Tenzing. Overall, their performance, without using supplementary oxygen, was better than that of both Hillary and Tenzing using open-circuit oxygen and Bourdillon and Evans using closed-circuit oxygen. However, it is impossible really to make a fair comparison between performances in 1978 and 1953 because climatic conditions would not have been the same on both occasions.

Survival at extreme altitude

It is a remarkable coincidence that when humans are well acclimatised to oxygen lack, they are just able to reach the summit of Everest, the highest point on earth, without the help of supplementary oxygen. A critical factor in achieving this is the fact that barometric pressure in the Himalaya, which are near the equator, is higher than that predicted by the standard atmosphere tables. Another critical factor is the extreme over-breathing required, which washes out large quantities of carbon dioxide (the waste product from muscle metabolism) and increases the affinity for oxygen in the blood. Even so, the maximum oxygen uptake on the summit of Everest is about one litre per minute – just enough to enable the climber to walk slowly, with many halts.

Acclimatisation and deterioration

When people born and brought up at sea level are transported to 17,500ft and above for long periods, they deteriorate mentally and physically despite good living conditions. The members of the 1960-61 Silver Hut expedition, wintering in the Everest region at 19,000ft, showed signs of high-altitude deterioration by the end of three months. Acclimatisation was initially so good that the author and three companions were able to make the first ascent of the 'Matterhorn of the Himalaya', Ama Dablam – a peak just under 7,000m – by a route of the highest Alpine standard, Grade VI. In addition, the author and another medical scientist climbed a lower but technically even more demanding peak, Rakpa (c 6,000m), overcoming continuous snow and ice slopes of 60°-70°. The completion of these two difficult climbs at high altitude without supplementary oxygen was a demonstration of how very effective acclimatisation could be. However, this initial success was short-lived. Later in the expedition deterioration set in, and for this reason the party's attempt to climb Makalu (8,485m) without supplementary oxygen was unsuccessful.

An unusual amount of illness also occurred on Makalu, with Hillary suffering from transient stroke, whilst others developed pulmonary thrombosis, high-altitude pulmonary oedema and, despite adequate protective clothing, severe frostbite caused by heat production becoming insufficient to counter the low environmental temperature. The data, both physiological and medical, produced by the Silver Hut expedition emphasised how very rigorous and dangerous a long-term stay at extreme altitude can be.

Barometric pressure and maximum oxygen uptake

It has been suggested that the outstanding achievements of Habeler and Messner could be attributed to a higher maximum oxygen uptake than that occurring in most other climbers. This increase is found in world class marathon runners and cross-country skiers and is dependent on both training and genetic factors.

But in 1986 Oswald Oelz, the climbing doctor on the 1978 Austrian Everest expedition, who, using supplementary oxygen, climbed Everest a few days after Messner and Hebeler, carried out a series of studies on these two, and on four other mountaineers who had reached 8,500m without supplementary oxygen. His findings suggested that all were good athletes in medium-to-good training and with high powers of endurance. There was no evidence that any of them had an exceptionally high maximum oxygen uptake, as occurs in marathon runners, but that, after years of training, they had developed the ability to work continuously closer to their maximum oxygen uptake than mountaineers who were not in such good training. In other words, they had more oxygen available for working muscles than the majority of mountaineers, and were able, as a result, to move faster and for longer periods at high altitude.

Oelz considered that their success depended on shrewd assessment, high motivation and exceptional powers of endurance. Being very good and economical climbers, they had been able to use the available oxygen to the best possible advantage and not to waste it on extraneous movement. They always allowed themselves plenty of time to acclimatise and then when the time was right and the weather good, they struck with maximum force and speed.

All the limiting factors on the performance of man at extreme altitude are still not known. One of these factors is barometric pressure, upon which oxygen pressure in the depths of the lungs depends. Over the years, and in particular on the 1953 and 1960-61 expeditions to Everest, it had been shown that oxygen pressure for a given altitude was higher than expected in the equatorial regions than it was elsewhere. Everest lies at 28°N.

Barometric pressure was measured for the first time on the summit of Everest on 25 October 1981 by Dr C Pizzo of the American Medical Research Expedition led by Professor J B West. A reading of 253mm Hg was recorded and this was confirmed as correct in 1997. If Everest had been at the latitude of Mount McKinley

(63°N), the highest peak in North America, the barometric pressure would have been much lower at 233mm Hg. At that low pressure an ascent without supplementary oxygen would have been inconceivable.

Oxygen transport

Exercise performance at great altitude is extremely sensitive to the amount and pressure of oxygen in the depths of the lungs (alveolar PO_2). A fall of only 3mm Hg will reduce maximum oxygen uptake by 5%; therefore, even small daily variations in barometric pressure caused by weather can greatly affect performance at extreme altitude. Seasonal variations, too, which are larger than daily ones, will have a marked effect. On the summit of Everest the barometric pressure may vary from 255mm Hg in summer to 243mm Hg in winter, and a decrease in maximum oxygen uptake of 25% can result. Partly for this reason and partly for climatic reasons, a winter ascent of Everest without supplementary oxygen was not made until 1987.

Other factors that play an important part in limiting exercise at extreme altitudes are, firstly, loss of water from the lungs, which can lead to severe dehydration and exhaustion, and, secondly, loss of heat from the lungs. Both of these result from the excessive panting that occurs at great altitude. A third factor is the cost, in terms of oxygen used by the breathing muscles, which will be working near to their maximum. It used to be thought that loss of heat due to excessive panting would limit ascent to great altitude. This has not been borne out by events. A considerable loss of heat does indeed occur, but the respiratory tract acts as a heat exchanger, warming up inspired cold air so that not too much heat is lost on expiration. Loss of fluid from the lungs, caused by excessive panting, means that a fluid intake of 2-3 litres/day is necessary, and as this is hardly ever achieved, some degree of dehydration and resulting poor physical condition appears to be inevitable if long periods are spent at great altitude.

The amount of oxygen used by the muscles employed in breathing is greatly increased at extreme altitude by panting. About 10% of the oxygen uptake may be used in this way at rest, but when climbing, this may increase to such an extent that almost all the oxygen taken in may be used for breathing and little is left over for activating the climbing muscles. Remarkably, the normal heart seems relatively little affected by high altitude.

The best-known adaptation to altitude is the increase that naturally occurs in the number of red blood cells per unit volume of blood. This increase, and the resultant increase in haemoglobin, improves the oxygen-carrying capacity of the blood so that, up to a height of 5,300m, a fully acclimatised man has the same oxygen content in the blood as he would have at sea level, and this compensates for the decreased saturation of the blood with oxygen. However, the extent to which there is benefit to be gained from increasing the haemoglobin is limited and thrombotic episodes or vascular spasms have been reported. These are the result of increased sludging of the blood associated with increased numbers of red cells, dehydration due to respiratory water loss, periods of inactivity and possibly cold as well. The question arises, therefore, whether this, the best-known of all adaptations, may not be as beneficial as it was once considered to be. Changes also occur in both the tissues and the cells, and these play a particularly important role in those born and living at high altitude.

One way to improve the transfer of oxygen from the blood in the capillaries (minute blood vessels) to the cells would be to increase the number of functioning capillaries. This occurs naturally during exercise training but does not necessarily occur at altitude. However, at altitude the degree of tortuosity of the capillaries increases, which has much the same effect.

The size of the muscle fibres decreases at altitude, and together with the increased tortuosity of capillaries, results in more oxygen being delivered to the cells because of the shorter distance that it has to travel between capillary and muscle fibre. Muscle contains a pigment, myoglobin, which aids transfer of oxygen at low barometric pressures and this also increases at altitude.

The final links in the chain of oxygen transport are the mitochondria which are inside the cells. Here oxygen is converted into energy. However, in acclimatised man at altitude, the number of mitochondria appears to decrease. Genetic factors also play a part, particularly in those who are born and live at altitude. Very recently it has been demonstrated that mountaineers who can climb above 8,000m without supplementary oxygen may have a greater preponderance of certain genes concerned with changes in the lung vessels at altitude. Many enzymes that help the production of energy within the cell are increased. These changes in tissue enzymes are consistent with the assumption that the muscles are improving their ability to increase energy production in the face of oxygen deprivation.

Survival and death

Survival at extreme altitude depends to a large extent on the ability to take in enough oxygen in order to exercise and thus keep in thermal balance. Above about 24,000ft, climbers without supplementary oxygen are unable to move continuously and have to stop frequently. Heat output falls and they tend to cool. It is the heat from the sun, either directly or reflected from the snow, that keeps them in thermal balance. On occasion, however, heat gain, even at these altitudes, may be so great that clothes may be temporarily discarded. However, at night, or if the sun is blotted out by cloud, the temperature falls rapidly and within a short time temperature variations of 70°C have been recorded. It is therefore not surprising that cold injury, whether generalised hypothermia or localised frostbite, is so common at great altitude.

Despite being fully clothed and protected by a tent, a mountaineer at high altitude may die from exhaustion caused by a combination of hypoxia and hypothermia. The use of supplementary oxygen minimises these effects and may be life-saving. Over a thousand ascents of Everest have now been made using supplementary oxygen, while only a fraction of that figure have been accomplished without its help, many of them involving fatalities. The mortality rate on expeditions to the world's highest peaks up to the time of their first ascent was of the order of 5% of mountaineers at risk. On early Everest expeditions of the 1920s and 1930s the mortality rate was high, owing to the parties' inexperience of great altitude and lack of awareness of the potentially lethal combination of oxygen lack and cold. But by 1953, when Hillary took on an extra load at over 27,000ft, knowledge had so far advanced that he was able to do this, without risk, simply by turning up his oxygen flow rate to 5 litres per minute. He said it was 'like changing gear' and it gave him the extra boost he needed.

Because of the expertise gained by the Medical Research Council in 1951-52, we had a much better idea of the climatic, medical and physiological hazards of high altitude. The result was that the first ascent of Everest in 1953 was not only successful but was unmarred by deaths or serious injury.

The edge of the possible

Everest has now been climbed by an exceptionally athletic and well-trained European climber in 24 hours and by a Sherpa, Babu Chhiri, in a similar time. He took under 17 hours from base camp to the summit, on which he spent 21 hours without supplementary oxygen – an example of the beneficial effect of genetic adaptation allied to training, for he had climbed Everest on many previous occasions. But even for those who are extremely fit, acclimatised and highly motivated, to climb Everest without supplementary oxygen is to be on a physiological knife-edge; the penalty for failure is high. As more and more difficult routes are attempted at great altitude, often in winter and without supplementary oxygen, the mortality rate is likely to remain high.

Climbing at extreme altitude without supplementary oxygen is potentially extremely dangerous. The balance is in favour of the climber in good, sunny, calm weather, a high barometric pressure, with no wind, good training and acclimatisation. By contrast, bad weather, low barometric pressure, a high wind, poor physical condition and poor acclimatisation all tip the balance against him. As we saw in May 1996, when five climbers including two highly experienced Himalayan leaders lost their lives on Everest, sudden and vicious weather on the world's highest peaks can strike with great speed, ferocity and vigour. When that happens, the upper slopes of Everest are no place for man.

The thirteen main routes on Everest

Each successful ascent of Everest relies heavily on knowledge gained by previous expeditions. The result of these advances is that all the main faces and ridges of Everest have now been climbed.

	Route	Year of First Ascent
1	South-East Ridge from South Col	1953
2	North Ridge by North Col	1960
3	West Ridge by Hornbein Couloir	1963
4	South-West Face	1975
5	West Ridge Direct	1979
6	North Face from North Col	1980
7	North Face by Hornbein Couloir	1980
8	South Pillar	1980
9	South-West Face by Central Pillar	1982
10	East Face by Central Pillar	1983
11	North Face by the Great Couloir	1984
12	East Face and South-East Ridge	1988
13	North-East Ridge (incomplete to summit)	1988

Some but not all of these routes have been climbed without supplementary oxygen. For details of all expeditions and ascents of Everest, as well as routes on Lhotse, Nuptse, Changtse and surrounding peaks, see *Mount Everest Massif* by Jan Kielkowski, published by Explo Publishers, Poland. First edition in English, 1993. Second (enlarged and updated) edition, 2000.

Envoi

Over the last fifty years, I have been privileged to be involved in every aspect of research into cold and altitude, as well as in the exploration of the great ranges of High Asia. I hope that this monograph will help to throw new light on the main problems the solution of which led to the successful exploration, first ascent and mapping of Mount Everest, and on how these events have affected so many subsequent achievements in the realms of both high-altitude mountain exploration and high-altitude medicine.

BIBLIOGRAPHY

B C Bishop, 'Wintering in the High Himalayas' in *National Geographic 122*, 503-548, 1962.

P Habeler, *The Lonely Victory*. Simon and Schuster, 1978.

T Hornbein, *Everest. The West Ridge*. Sierra Club, 1965.

Jan Kielkowski, *Mount Everest Massif*. Explo Publishers, Poland, 1993. Second edition (enlarged and updated), 2000.

R Messner, *Expedition to the Ultimate*. Translated by Audrey Salkeld. Kaye & Ward, 1979.

O Oelz, H Howard, P E di Prampero, et al, 'Physiological profile of world class high altitude climbers' in *Journal of Applied Physiology 60*, 1731-1742, 1986.

S Patel, A Peacock, 'Who will cope at high altitude? Is it in the genes?' in the Newsletter of the *International Society for Mountain Medicine 11*, 5-8, 2001.

L G C E Pugh, 'Physiological and medical aspects of the Himalayan Scientific and Mountaineering Expedition 1960-61' in *British Medical Journal 2*, 621-627, 1962.

Shih Chan-chun, 'The conquest of Mount Everest by the Chinese mountaineering team' in *Alpine Journal 66*, 28-41, 1961.

Walt Unsworth, *The Mountaineering History* (3rd edition). The Mountaineers/Bâton Wicks, 2000. (With Addendum: Ascents of Everest 1990-1999)

M P Ward, 'The Himalayan Scientific Expedition 1960-61 (A Himalayan Winter, Rakpa Peak, Ama Dablam, Makalu)' in *Alpine Journal 66*, 343-364, 1961.

M P Ward, 'The descent from Makalu 1961 and some medical aspects of high-altitude climbing' in *Alpine Journal 68*, 11-19, 1963.

M P Ward, J S Milledge, J B West, *High Altitude Medicine and Physiology*. Arnold, 2000. (Especially chapter entitled 'Limiting Factors at Extreme Altitude'.)

J B West, *Everest: The Testing Place*. McGraw-Hill, 1985.

J B West, S Lahiri, K H Maret, et al., 'Barometric pressure at extreme altitudes on Mount Everest – physiological significance' in *Journal of Applied Physiology 86*, 1188-1194, 1983.

J B West, 'Barometric pressure on Mount Everest: new data and physiological significance' in *Journal of Applied Physiology 86*, 1062-1066, 1999.

The Obituary of Babu Chhiri Sherpa in *The Times*, Wednesday, 2 May 2001.

APPENDIX

Offprint from *The Geographical Journal*, Vol 158, No 1, March 1992, reprinted by kind permission of the Royal Geographical Society.

Author's Note:

The photographs and map which make up this Appendix had never before been published when, in 1992, Peter Clark and I wrote a paper for *The Geographical Journal* of March 1992 entitled 'Everest, 1951: cartographic and photographic evidence of a new route from Nepal'. The photographs yielded much more information about the southern, Nepalese side of Everest than had been obtained previously, either by native surveyors working for the Survey of India or by C S Houston and H W Tilman during their expedition to Solu Khumbu in the autumn of 1950. The discovery of these photographs and the Milne-Hinks map, described in detail in this offprint, was, in fact, critical to our success in 1953.

The 1950 Anglo-American trekking expedition of which Houston and Tilman were members was an informal affair which had not initially set out to identify a possible route up Everest from the south; but naturally, once in the area, Houston and Tilman tried to obtain as much information as was possible in the limited time available to them. As our paper explains, they managed to reach a point on Kala Pattar (about 18,000ft), not without difficulty, from which they took the first ground photograph of Everest's southern aspect; but their vantage point was not high enough for an accurate assessment to be made. In his autobiography *The Evidence of Things Not Seen*, W H Murray records asking Tilman what he thought about a route from the south. "His reply was unequivocal, characteristically terse: 'Impossible. No route.'"

It seems likely that this mistaken conclusion reached by such a well-respected mountaineer lay behind the initial rejection by the Himalayan Committee of our proposed reconnaissance of this approach in 1951. Fortunately, its negative reaction was ignored by Bourdillon, Murray and myself, so certain were we that the newly-discovered photographs and maps, which had lain unnoticed for so long in the archives of the Royal Geographical Society, provided evidence of a viable new route up the south side of Everest.

Offprint from:

THE GEOGRAPHICAL JOURNAL

ROYAL GEOGRAPHICAL SOCIETY
LONDON

The Geographical Journal, Vol. **158**, No. 1, March 1992, pp. 47–56

Everest, 1951: cartographic and photographic evidence of a new route from Nepal

M. P. WARD AND P. K. CLARK

Consultant Surgeon, St Andrews Hospital, London E3 3NT and Keeper, Royal Geographical Society, London SW7 2AR

This paper was accepted for publication in October 1991

Until 1949 topographical information about the Nepal Himalaya was almost non-existent. Following a less than optimistic report by an Anglo-American trekking party to Sola Khumbu, in 1950, on the possibility of a new route up Everest, research in the archives of the Royal Geographical Society, in early 1951, revealed ground and aerial photographs of the Nepalese side of Everest taken between 1921 and 1950. These photographs, combined with the RGS (Milne-Hinks) map, 1933–45, of the Tibetan and Nepalese side of the mountain showed a possible 'line' to the summit. This paper describes an important period in Himalayan exploration, the existence and importance of much of the information has neither been recognized nor credited in the literature.

KEY WORDS: Nepal, Everest, new route.

UNTIL 1949, TOPOGRAPHICAL information about Nepal was negligible and relied upon reports from the Pundits, in particular Hari Ram (M.H. or No. 9) (Waller, 1990) and native surveyors of the Nepal Detachment of the Survey of India, who between 1924 and 1927 surveyed 129 500 square kilometres, and produced a quarter-inch map of the whole country. Neither European surveyors nor travellers were given permission to enter Nepal, nor was photography allowed. As a result, the Nepal Himalaya remained virtually unknown except for the position of the major peaks. The quarter-inch Survey of India maps gave fair detail up to glacier level, but it was not until 1929 that it was thought that representation of the glaciated regions of the Himalaya should be improved to meet the requirements of glaciology (Mason, 1929). However, this did not apply to the quarter-inch Nepal sheets as the Survey there ended in 1927.

Very little extra information was available about the Nepalese side of Everest beyond the quarter-inch maps and the knowledge that in 1907 Natha Singh, a native surveyor, had been allowed to visit the Upper Dudh Kosi river to sketch the southern slopes of Everest. He managed only to delineate the southern end of the Khumbu glacier.

In 1930 Sola Khumbu and the Rolwaling valley were visited by a retired Nepalese Army Officer,

Major Lal Dhwoj, and his botanical survey was continued, in 1933, by another Nepali, K. N. Sharma. An Indian, M. L. Bannerji, made five visits to East Nepal between 1948 and 1955, but no sketch maps of the Khumbu region were produced (Ward, 1992).

No mountaineering parties were allowed to visit Sola Khumbu until 1950, when an Anglo-American trekking group that included the American mountaineer C. S. Houston and the British Himalayan explorer H. W. Tilman visited Namche Bezaar. With no maps they had difficulty in finding the Khumbu glacier but ascended to Kalar Pattar at about 5182 metres, from which point they took the first ground photograph of the southern aspect of Everest (Tilman, 1951, 1952). Their assessment of a possible route up Everest from this side was not at all optimistic and neither followed up their visit with a climbing reconnaissance.

In early 1951 a thorough search of the photographic and map archives of the Royal Geographical Society was carried out, and a considerable amount of topographical information was obtained, which showed a possible new route to the summit. Information came from photographs taken on the 1921, 1935, and 1936 Everest expeditions, the 1933 'Flight over Everest' expedition, clandestine flights over Everest in 1945 and 1947, and the photo taken by the Anglo-American party in

1950. Finally an R.G.S. map, at 1:50000 scale of both the Tibetan and Nepalese side of Everest compiled between 1933 and 1945 by A. R. Hinks FRS, the Secretary of the R.G.S. and H. F. Milne, chief draughtsman of the R.G.S. was examined in detail. Part of this map is shown in Figure 1.

The evidence
Photographs: The following is a selection of the more important photographs.

PLATE I

Taken by H. W. Tilman from near Kalar Pattar (5182 metres) in 1950, the photograph shows the Lho La, with North Peak (Changtse) in Tibet behind. To the left of the Lho La is Khumbu Tse. Pumori and Lingtren peak are further left, out of the picture. Tilman's contention was that the skyline ridge from the south summit of Everest fell directly to the South Col. In fact other photographs show that this ridge, the South West Ridge ends in a buttress that falls into the Western Cwm. The South Ridge itself is out of sight, and is an easy-looking ridge going to the South Col, and was the 'line' to the summit.

PLATE II

Taken by L. V. Bryant, on the 1935 Reconnaissance Expedition to the north side of Everest, from the col between Pumori and Lingtren peak, the photograph looks east straight into the Western Cwm, over the ice fall. The mark B indicates the height in the Cwm similar to that from which the photograph was taken, approximately 6100 metres.

The height of the ice fall is approximately 1000 metres and although little can be seen of the floor of the Western Cwm this appears relatively level. Another photo was taken by Mallory on the 1921 Reconnaissance Expedition from the same position, but gives less detail.

PLATE III

This photograph was taken by E. G. H. Kempson on 11 June, 1936 whilst on the 1936 Everest expedition, from the Lho La. J. M. L. Gavin (Gavin, 1990) was with Kempson on this occasion and confirmed that a good view of the ice fall and upper part of the Khumbu Glacier was obtained. The photograph shows the ice fall in profile and the buttress of Nuptse that bounds it to the south. It indicated that the option of climbing this buttress to avoid the ice fall would be a difficult undertaking, and this was confirmed on the 1951 Everest Reconnaissance, when a good and close view of this face of Nuptse was obtained from the buttress on Pumori.

PLATE IV

This is an aerial photograph, taken possibly in 1945.

Almost the whole of the north face of Lhotse is shown, from the summit to the Western Cwm. The South Col, Geneva Spur and summit of Lhotse are clearly visible in excellent detail: a good 'line' can be seen to the South Col either up what became known as the 'Geneva Spur' or traversing from the upper part of the face to the South Col. Both these 'lines' were confirmed on the 1951 Reconnaissance Expedition, when a good view of this face was obtained from a buttress at about 6100 metres on Pumori. Plate IV is composed of three photos joined in a mosaic fashion. There are two collimation marks on the right and one on the left, which indicates that this photo was taken with an official camera. TA series of aerial photographs of Everest was taken on an unofficial flight over Everest in 1945 by a Mosquito XIX aircraft of No. 684 Squadron and was given to the photographic archives of the R.G.S., in early 1951, by B. H. Farmer, who had been an Air Survey Liaison Officer with the army in India. In this batch there were three photographs each with collimation marks, two wrongly labelled as being of Everest; the mountain that was photographed was Makalu some kilometres to the east. It is possible that Plate IV comes from this series.

PLATE V

This is the third photograph of the 1945 series. It has collimation marks and shows the whole of the South Ridge of Everest in some detail, from the summit to the South Col, including the Hillary Step. There is no obvious difficulty along the whole ridge.

PLATE VI

This photograph was taken on the 1933 'Flight over Everest'. 'All available photographs taken on this flight have been transferred to the Archives of the Royal Geographical Society (Mumford, 1990)'.

It is one of a pair and each photo is taken from a slightly different angle and height. Some spot heights are shown and peaks and ridges to the north and west of Everest were named and delineated by H. F. Milne (Holland, 1990). In 1951 the most important feature was the straight ridge extending from the South Summit of Everest (8763 metres) towards the Western Cwm. This, the South West Ridge, is shown in profile in Tilman's Plate I.

The more gentle ridge falling to the South Col, up which the mountain was climbed, is closer to the camera in this photo and out of sight in Plate I. Details are hazy, but other photographs (Plate V) from the clandestine flights in 1945 and 1947 were much clearer.

Much of the country to the north and west of Everest covered by the quarter-inch Survey of India, sheet 72I is shown and this was the first

EVEREST, 1951

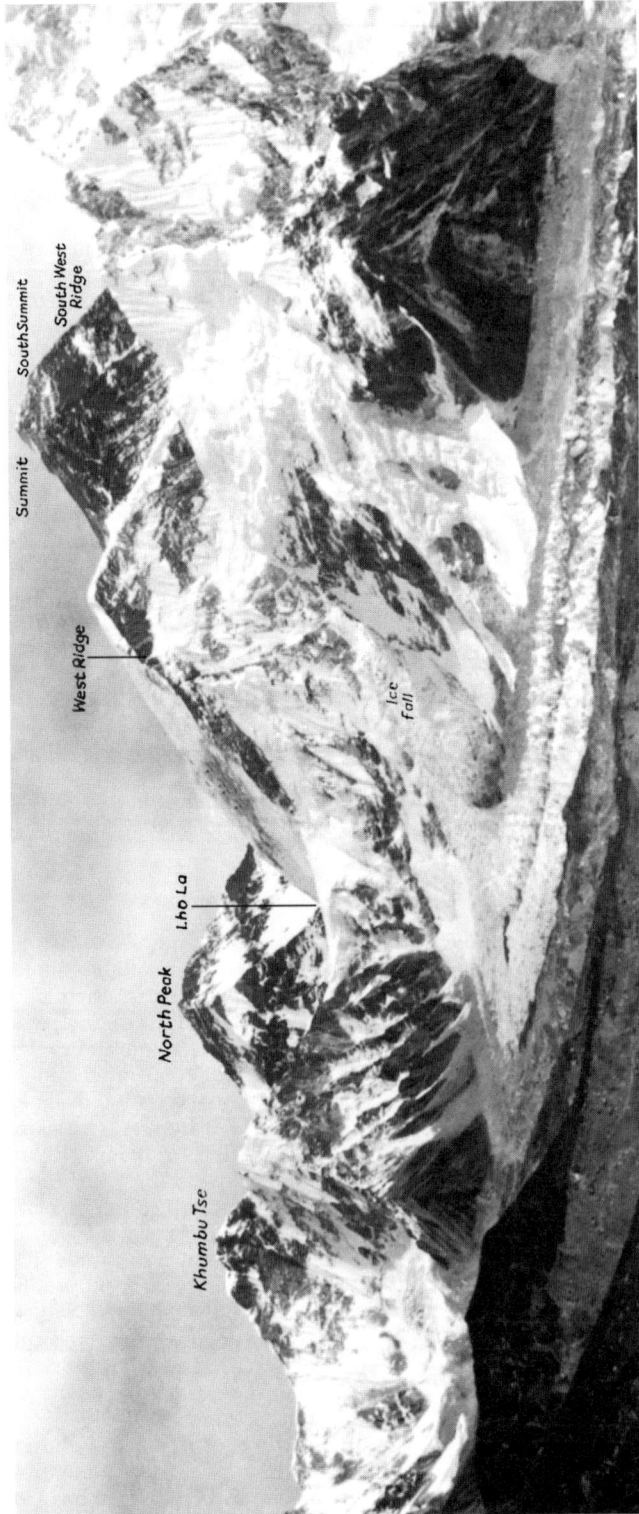

PLATE I *The south side of Everest, taken from near Kalar Pattar*

Summit
South Summit
South West Ridge
West Ridge
Ice fall
Lho La
North Peak
Khumbu Tse

Fig. 1. An extract from the Milne-Hinks map, 1933–45

PLATE II *The Western Cwm and ice fall, taken from the col between Pumori and Lingtren Peak, by L. V. Bryant in 1935*

PLATE III *The ice fall and buttress of Nuptse, taken from Lho-La, by E. G. H. Kempson in 1936*

EVEREST, 1951

PLATE IV *The North Face of Lhotse. taken from the air by pilots of 684 Squadron in 1945*

PLATE V *The South Ridge of Everest, taken by pilots of 684 Squadron in 1945*

PLATE VI *The South Ridge of Everest; taken on 'Flight over Everest' Expedition*

general photograph ever taken of this region. The delineation of these ridges was probably based on stereo-pairs (Hinks, 1933; Salt, 1934).

These photographs were taken by a hand-held camera on the 1933 'Flight over Everest' Expedition (Clydesdale and McIntyre, 1936). Not all the identifications are correct, the position of the Rongshar Chu being wrong. This photograph encouraged us, in 1951, to leave the Everest region by exploring west towards Gaurisankar (Tibetan name – Jobo Tseringma 7162 metres), wrongly identified by Schlagintweit in 1855 and 1857 as Mt Everest (Odell, 1935), and Menlungtse (Tibetan name – Jobo Garu 7192 metres). According to archival material (Archives RGS, Sept 1953) Milne intended to draw a map of the whole Everest region based on his 1933–45 map, but this project was never achieved. If this was the case the delineation of the peaks and ridges may have been a preparation.

OTHER PHOTOS

A number of aerial photographs were taken by Flight-Lt K. D. Neame, of No. 34 Squadron, in 1947 on an unofficial flight over Everest (Neame, 1955). These also show the South Ridge, South Col, and North East Ridge clearly, as well as the upper part of the North Face of Lhotse. Some are in the front of Shipton's book on the Everest Reconnaissance of 1951, but without attribution (Shipton, 1952), others are in the Archives of the Royal Geographical Society, to which they were given by Neame in 1948.

Map: Milne-Hinks Everest region 1933–45 This was drawn between 1933 and 1945, and is based on Spender's photogrammetric survey of the north side of Everest completed in 1935 (Ruttledge, 1937; Spender, 1936) and the 'Flight over Everest' expedition in 1933 (Salt, 1934). At 1:50000 with numerous spot heights and great detail, it covers the north side of Everest and a large stretch of country to the south and east (see Fig. 1). It confirmed that a ridge (South West) fell from the south summit of Everest to the Western Cwm, and another ridge (South) went to the South Col. On this map heights were compiled from ground survey and photographs, both ground and aerial. The flight path of the first flight of the 1933 'Flight over Everest' expedition came north up the Hongu Khola and Hongu glacier, the plane then flew over Lhotse, and the summit of Everest, but not the Western Cwm, before turning south-east and returning along the south flank of the Makalu group (Salt, 1934). The 'unofficial' second flight on this expedition flew over the Lhotse-Nuptse Ridge, the Western Cwm, and near the summit of Everest and some vertical photographs were taken, as well as obliques and a cine film. A few of the oblique photographs may be found in the photographic archives of the R.G.S. On the map the topographical features and spot heights of the whole south side of Everest are remarkably accurate. Yet no Everest expedition of that date, all of whom had kept to the north, Tibetan side of Everest had had a view into the Western Cwm, and certainly none had seen the west face of the South Col, the north face of Lhotse or the south-west face of Everest. All the topographic details depicted of the south side of Everest must therefore have been taken from photographs on the 1933 'Flight over Everest', and are the result of the cartographic and mathematical skills of A. R. Hinks, allied to the drawing skills of H. F. Milne, and the whole linked to the 1935 photogrammetric survey of Spender of the north side of Everest.

It is a very remarkable compilation both artistically and topographically. A photostat copy of this map was taken on the 1951 Everest reconnaissance, (*Geogrl J* 117, 1951: 363). On the back of this photostat is a pencil sketch, in Shipton's hand, showing the relative position of the South (in fact South West) ridge of Everest, the steep North Ridge of Nuptse, the curve of the Khumbu glacier, and the position of the hanging glaciers on either side of the ice fall. This drawing fits perfectly with the photograph taken by Shipton when, with Hillary, he went to about 6100 metres on Pumori and looked for the first time on the expedition into the Western Cwm. It was probably drawn that evening or next day, on descent to Base Camp to show the rest of the party the position of the main features at the entrance to the Cwm, there being in 1951, no instant camera photographs. It is of historic interest as the first sketch map of this mysterious valley whose whole length, dimensions and features were thus seen for the first time from the ground in Nepal. The Milne-Hinks map was first lithographed in 1952 and exhibited at the 17th International Geographical Congress meeting in Washington DC the same year, and was further exhibited at the Sir George Everest Bicentennial at the Royal Geographical Society in 1990.

Discussion
The combined evidence of all the photographs available in early 1951 and the Milne-Hinks RGS map showed a possible climbable new 'line' up the southern Nepalese side of Everest, once the ice fall the most dangerous part of the route could be overcome. Shipton and those who planned the 1951 Reconnaissance Expedition were well aware of this cartographic and photographic evidence although no full account of it was published at the time or subsequently. However, such evidence alone is not sufficient to assess whether a route on any mountain is feasible, and ground inspection is mandatory. This was the *raison d'etre* for the 1951 Reconnaissance

Expedition, which climbed through the ice fall. The slopes of the west side of the South Col and the north slope of Lhotse were clearly visible from both the entrance to the Western Cwm and the slopes of Pumori, and confirmed the possible 'line' of ascent seen in the photographs. Using this route, the two Swiss expeditions of 1952 made the first ascent of the South Col and climbed to within 300 metres of the summit on the South Ridge, before being defeated by the effects of altitude and cold. This outcome was exactly similar to the experience of all British expeditions to the Tibetan side of Everest between 1921 and 1938, namely that 8500 metres

was an altitude barrier. The solution of this altitude problem by Dr Griffith Pugh and his colleagues at the Medical Research Council in London and on the Cho Oyu Expedition in the Everest region in 1952 helped Hillary and Tensing to make the first ascent of Everest in 1953 (Pugh, 1952).

Acknowledgements

The authors wish to thank the following for their help in preparing this paper: George Holland; Ian Mumford; W. H. Murray; J. M. L. Gavin; Christine Kelly; Rachel Duncan; B. H. Farmer; and K. D. Neame.

REFERENCES

Archives, 1953 Royal Geographical Society, September.

Clydesdale, Marquess of and McIntyre, D. F. 1936 *The pilots book of Everest.* London: William Hodge.

Gavin, J. M. L. 1990 *Pers. comm.*

Geogrl J., 1951 **117**: 363.

Hinks, A. R. 1933 Photographs from the Mount Everest Flight. *Geogrl J.* **82**: 54–60.

Holland, G. 1990 *Pers. comm.*

Jefferies, M. and Clarbrough, M. 1985 *Sagarmatha, mother of the universe; the story of the Mount Everest National Park.* Auckland: Cobb/Horwood Publications.

Mason, K. 1929 The representation of glaciated regions on maps of the Survey of India. *Professional Paper No. 25.* India: Dehra Dun.

Mumford, I. 1990 *Pers. comm.*

Neame, K. D. 1955 *'Alone over Everest'. Mountain world.* London: Allen and Unwin.

Odell, N. E. 1935 The supposed Tibetan or Nepalese name of Mount Everest. *Alpine J.* **47**: 127–9.

Pugh, L. G. C. E. 1952 *Report on the Cho Oyu Expedition.* London: Medical Research Council.

Ruttledge, H. 1937 *Everest. The unfinished adventure.* London: Hodder and Stoughton.

Salt, J. S. A. 1934 Plotting the vertical photographs of the second Mount Everest Flight. *Geogrl J.* **83**: 101–18.

Shipton, E. E. 1952 *The Mount Everest Reconnaissance Expedition, 1951.* London: Hodder and Stoughton.

Spender, M. 1936 Photographic surveys in the Mount Everest region. *Geogrl J.* **88**: 289–303.

Tilman, H. W. 1951 Explorations in the Nepal Himalayas. *Geogrl J.* **117**: 263–74.

——, 1952 *Nepal Himalaya.* Cambridge: C.U.P.

Waller, D. 1990 *The Pundits: British exploration of Tibet and central Asia.* Lexington, Kentucky: University Press.

Ward, M. P. 1992 Everest 1951: exploration from Nepal. *Alpine J.* (forthcoming).

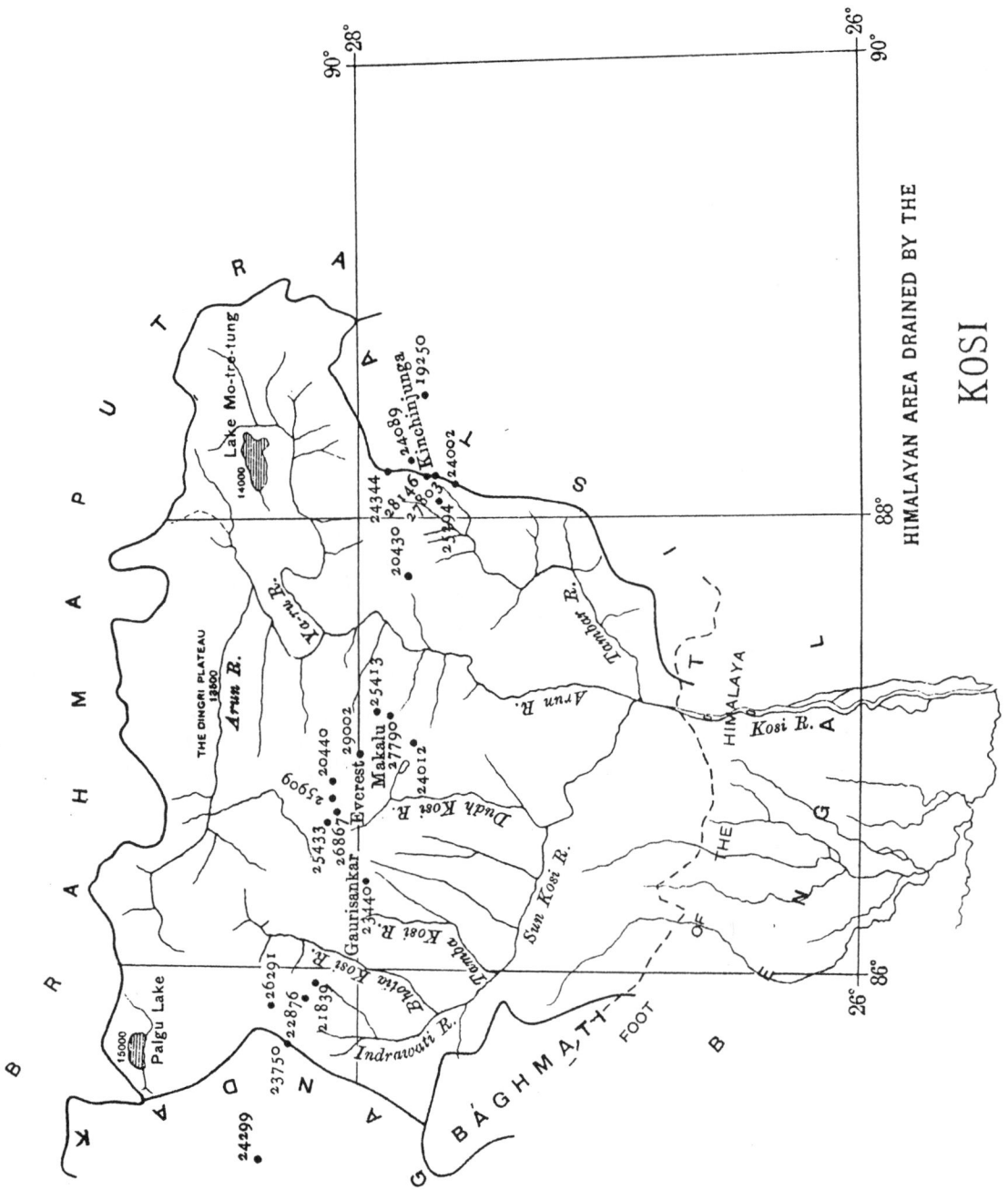

From S G Burrard and H H Hayden,
A Sketch of the geography and geology of the Himalaya mountains and Tibet, 1907-08.

General Topography of the Everest Region

Introduction

The Everest region is situated between two of the Himalaya's steepest and deepest gorges, which carve their way through the main Himalayan range midway between Lhasa, capital of Tibet, and Kathmandu, capital of Nepal. The eastern gorge has been formed over millions of years by the great Arun river, whose main western tributary rises north of Everest in southern Tibet on the lower slopes of Shisha Pangma (Gosainthan). The main eastern tributary rises near Kampa Dzong, an important administrative centre on the way to Lhasa from Darjeeling and India.

About fifty miles to the west of the Arun gorge is the even narrower gorge of the Nyalam river (Po Chu), which also rises north of the Himalaya. It joins the Kosi river in Nepal.

The northern boundary of the Everest region is Tingri, its main village, while its southern boundary, fifty miles to the south, is the junction of the Solu and Khumbu provinces of north-east Nepal. This area of about 25,000 square miles contains four of the world's highest peaks – Everest, Lhotse, Makalu and Cho Oyu – and innumerable others over 23,000ft.

Many millions of years ago the Tibetan plateau was the floor of a sea named Tethys, but with the northward movement of India into Asia this sea was gradually elevated, crumpled and crushed, draining mainly to the south. With the gradual emergence of the Himalayan range, these rivers carved great gorges, 'the sword slashes of Buddha', through the range; the gorges of the Arun and Nyalam are two of these. As a result of their geological history, all the glaciers and rivers of the Everest region, whether they drain to the north, east, south or west, eventually run south into the Kosi river (see map on opposite page) and then into the Ganges which ends in the Bay of Bengal. Paradoxically, the 'water parting' of the two great rivers, the Tsangpo in southern Tibet and the Ganges of India, is not located in the main Himalayan chain but is in a relatively low range just south of the 'Tsangpo trench' and north of the main Himalayan range and Everest.

The exploration and mapping of this immensely tangled and complicated mountain region of Everest was carried out initially by 'pundits' – secret native explorers employed by the Survey of India – some Survey officers and by mountaineers with a scientific interest who took part in the expeditions to Everest, starting in 1921.

A feature of the north, Tibetan, side of the region is that the mountains rise from the Tibetan plain at 14–16,000ft, the valleys being wide and bare, with little vegetation, making surveying much easier. By contrast, the southern, Nepalese, side has much narrower, deeper and steeper valleys, thick vegetation and forest.

Surveying and exploration was much more difficult there, took longer, and had to be carried out piecemeal.

Everest, the mountain

Located half in Tibet and half in Nepal, Everest is topographically complex. Its north, Tibetan side is split by a shallow, wide, north ridge that falls to the North Col between the main mountain and the North Peak (Changtse). The North Face is bounded by the West Ridge and the North Ridge and falls to the head of the main Rongbuk glacier. The North-East Face lies between the North Ridge and the North-East Ridge, and at its foot is the upper basin of the East Rongbuk glacier, out of which the Rapiu La, at the foot of the North-East Ridge, gives access to the Kharta Chu glacier beyond. Further to the east is the Kangshung glacier at the foot of the East Face. The ice cliffs of the east side of the South Col and the East Face of Lhotse also fall to the Kangshung glacier. Returning to the west side of the mountain, the West Ridge falls to the Lho La and continues along the Nepal-Tibet frontier ridge, consisting of the Lingtren peaks and Pumori. The circuit finally ends at the Nup La, at the head of the West Rongbuk glacier.

The southern, Nepalese side of the mountain has a high, secret, hidden valley, the Western Cwm, guarded at its western end by a steep, active, dangerous, 1,000ft-high icefall. The Western Cwm itself is ringed to the north by the West Ridge rising to the summit of Everest; the eastern end is blocked by the South Ridge of Everest, the slopes leading to the South Col and the North Face of Lhotse. To the south there is the steep north wall between Lhotse and Nuptse, and the North Face of Nuptse.

The Everest region, north side

The main feature of the north side of Everest is the Rongbuk glacier made up of the east and west Rongbuk, with other subsidiary glaciers. This ends short of Rongbuk monastery. The subsidiary glaciers drain peaks including Khartaphu and Kharta Changri, whose far eastern side glaciers, ending in the Kama and Kharta valleys, fall to the Arun valley just north of the Nepal-Tibet border. The lower parts of these valleys are dense with vegetation, as the monsoon clouds coming up the Arun valley from India deposit much rain. The dividing line of the Doya La has tropical vegetation on the south side of the pass, with vegetation suited to the dry Tibetan plateau only a few yards away to the north.

To the west of Everest are two high peaks, Cho Oyu and Gyachung Kang. Their northern sides drain to the Kyetrak glacier, on the north side of the Nangpa La, an easy though high (5,716m) glacier pass between southern Tibet and North-East Nepal, which is used at all times of the year except the winter months. At the snout of this glacier, and close to the village of Kyetrak, a small steep track goes west to the Phuse La (crossed by the 1921 expedition) which is at the head of the Rongshar valley. This is a very narrow and little-used gorge, which was traversed for the first time from Tibet to Nepal by members of the 1951 Everest reconnaissance expedition. The next gorge to the west, that of the Nyalam river, is the main route between Nepal and Tibet and was traversed in the 17th century by Jesuit priests. This now has a road, though one frequently cut by landslides.

Most of the northern, Tibetan side of the Everest region was mapped by H T Morshead and E O Wheeler during the 1921 expedition, and their work was extended by Michael Spender in 1935.

The Everest region, south side

The whole of the Nepalese side of the region is infinitely more complex than the north, Tibetan side. The main feature is the Dudh Kosi river which drains most of this large area and joins the Kosi river.

The Dudh Kosi is formed by two main tributaries that join just below Namche Bazar, the main village of Khumbu, which lies on a shelf a thousand feet above the junction. To the south of Namche Bazar is a group of peaks dominated by Numbur and Karyolung, first explored by J O M Roberts and R C Evans in late 1953. The main western tributary of the Dudh Kosi, the Bhote Kosi, rises from the Nangpa La on the Nepal-Tibet border, which was crossed by the pundit Hari Ram (M.H., No. 9) in 1885. The frontier ridge between Nepal and Tibet runs west of the Bhote Kosi and then north from the Tesi Lapcha pass, which separates the Bhote Kosi from the Rolwaling valley.

On the west side of this frontier is the Menlung basin dominated by the peaks Gaurisankar (often mistaken, in the past, for Everest) and Menlungtse. The first exploration of this region was made during the 1951 reconnaissance by Eric Shipton and the author. The east side of the frontier ridge was explored in 1952 by members of the Cho Oyu expedition. To the north, the frontier ridge turns east and west just south of the peak Jobo Rabzang and is crossed by the Nangpa La.

To the east of the Nangpa La are two border peaks, Cho Oyu and Gyachung Kang, on whose south side is a vast cirque of glaciers draining to the Ngozumpa glacier, which has the Nup La on its east side, communicating with the West Rongbuk glacier in Tibet.

East of the Ngozumpa glacier is the Khumbu glacier draining the Western Cwm, and the lower part of Everest. This was visited for the first time in autumn 1950 by C S Houston and H W Tilman. Draining this south side of the Lhotse-Nuptse wall is the Imja glacier, whose river the Imja Khola, joins with the stream from the Khumbu glacier to form the main eastern tributary of the Dudh Kosi.

Running almost due south from Lhotse is a ridge of peaks that effectively divides the rivers and glaciers of the Khumbu region into a western group, draining into the Dudh Kosi, and an eastern group, the Barun, Iswa and Choyang, running into the Arun valley. This south-east block was surveyed for the first time by air in 1933, and on the ground by Norman Hardie in 1954 and 1955. The Arun valley was first ascended through Nepal, and the Popti La crossed into Tibet as far as the Kharta valley by the Pundit Sukh Darshan Singh (G.S.S.) in 1880.

The Nepal-Tibet frontier
This frontier runs east from the Rongshar gorge along the crest of Gaurisankar (Menlungtse is wholly within Tibet) to just north of the Tesi Lapcha pass. Here it turns north to just south of the peak Jobo Rabzang before going east again to the Nangpa La. Continuing east over the summits of Cho Oyu and Gyachung Kang, it drops to the Nup La and continues along the frontier ridge to Pumori and drops again to the Lho La. It then follows the West Ridge of Everest to the summit, and turns south to the South Col before ascending to the summit of Lhotse. It continues east to Pethangtse, rising to Makalu II and then Makalu, before finally falling to the Popti La and the Arun valley.

Events in the Mapping of Everest
Filling the last Blanks on the Map of the Everest Region

1708–18	A map of Tibet was commissioned by the Chinese Emperor in 1708. It was produced by Jesuit missionaries and completed in 1718.
1733	First European map of Tibet with Everest (Tchoumour Lancma) depicted. Published in Paris by J B B d'Anville.
1845–56	Spot heights of the most prominent Himalayan peaks were taken from the Indian plains by surveyors working for the Survey of India.
1868–80	A route survey of the Everest region was carried out for the Survey of India by Pundits Hari Ram and and Sukh Darshan Singh.
1903–04	The identification of Everest was made on the ground from Nepal and Tibet by Henry Wood of the Survey of India.
1907	The lower Khumbu glacier was visited by Natha Singh of the Survey of India.
1921	A survey of the Tibetan side of the Everest region including Everest itself was made by E O Wheeler, H T Morshead, Lalbir Singh Thapa, Gujjar Singh and Turubaj Singh on behalf of the Survey of India during the 1921 British reconnaissance expedition.
1924	A further survey of the Tibetan side of Everest was made by Hari Singh Thapa for the Survey of India.
1924–27	A map of Nepal was produced by the Nepal Detachment of the Survey of India.
1933	An aerial photographic survey of the Western Cwm and Barun glacier was made by the Houston–Westland 'Flight Over Everest' expedition.
1933–45	The first map of both the Nepalese and Tibetan sides of Everest was produced by H F Milne and A R Hinks of the Royal Geographical Society (RGS).
1935	A survey of the Tibetan side of Everest was carried out by Michael Spender for the RGS.
1951	A route survey covering an area west of Everest and the Menlung Basin was carried out by M P Ward for the RGS.
1952–54	B L Gulatee estimated the height of Everest as 8,848m (modern estimation 8,850m).

1953 (Spring)   A preliminary survey of the Inukhu Khola and mountains south of
                  Namche Bazar was carried out by J O M Roberts for the RGS.

1953 (Autumn)   A route survey of mountains south of Namche Bazar, west of
                  Everest, was carried out by R C Evans for the RGS.

1954   A survey of the Tolam Bau glacier, west of Everest, was carried
                  out by Dennis Davis for the RGS.

1954–55   A survey of the south-east quadrant of the Everest region, including
                  Makalu, Barun, Iswa and Hongu Khola, was carried out by Norman
                  Hardie for the RGS.

1955–58   Maps of Everest were drawn by French and Austrian surveyors.

1961, 1975   The first comprehensive map of the Everest region, showing both
                  the Tibetan and the Nepalese sides, was drawn by G S Holland of
                  the Royal Geographical Society in 1961 and revised in 1975.

1988, 1991   An aerial map of Everest was created by Bradford Washburn for
                  the National Geographic Society and revised in 1991.

LIST OF MAPS OF THE EVEREST REGION

Most of these can be found in the map room of the
Royal Geographical Society (RGS), London

1. Pictorial Map of Everest Region. Tibetan. In *Geographical Journal Vol 12*, 1898.
2. Mt Everest Area, 1955-56. Scale 1:25,000. Mahalungur Himal-Chomolongma. Erwin Schneider. Wien. Kartographische. Analt Freytag.
3. Mt Everest Region, 1960. Scale 1:100,000. Drawn by G S Holland. RGS, 1961.
4. Mt Everest Region, 1971. Drawn by Graphic Art, Kathmandu. Dept of Tourism. Ministry of Industry and Commerce. Shows Everest trek.
5. Mt Everest Region, 1973. Scale 1:100,000. G S Holland RGS, 1973.
6. Mt Everest Area, 1975. Scale 1:50,000. Chumulangma Feng. Ti–Chu–Tu. Lanchou, China. [Chinese]
7. Mt Everest Region, 1975. New Edition. G S Holland Scale 1:100,000. Heights in metres. Contains glossary of Nepali, Sherpa and Tibetan terms. RGS, 1975.
8. Mt Everest Region, 1976. Scale 1:100,000. Covers Nepalese approaches to Everest. Produced for the British Army and Royal Nepalese Army Expedition. Printed in the UK by the Ministry of Defence, 1976.
9. Mt Everest Area, 1988. Scale 1:50,000. Drawn by John B Garver. 'Sagarmatha–Mt Everest–Qomolangma' Boston Museum of Science. Bradford Washburn. National Geographic Society, Washington, 1988. Cartographic work and reproduction by Swiss Federal Office of Topography.
10. As above, 2nd Edition (1991). Scale 1:25,000. On the reverse side are routes of first ascents.
11. Mt Everest Area. Geology 1921. From surveys by A M Heron. Scale 1:750,000. Geological Survey of India. Accompanying article on the 1921 Everest Expedition in *Geographical Journal 59*, 1922.
12. Mt Everest 1921. Photographic survey. Scale 1:63,360. (3 sheets) Survey of India, 1922.
13. Mt Everest Region 1921. Scale 1:253,440. Map showing original surveys made by Mt Everest detachment 1921. Survey of India, 1921.

14. Mt Everest Region 1921. Scale 1:750,000. Map to show route of Mt Everest Expedition 1921. RGS, 1922.

15. Mt Everest Region 1921. Scale 1:100,000. Map from photographs and sketches made on 1921 expedition. RGS, 1922.

16. Mt Everest 1922. Scale 1:63,360. Map from photographic survey. Survey of India, 1922.

17. Mt Everest 1924. Scale 1:126,720. Map from surveys made by Major E O Wheeler in 1921, with additions by the 1924 expedition. RGS, 1924.

18. Mt Everest 1924. Scale 1:63,360. Tracing of original surveys made by Hari Singh Thapa, the surveyor attached to the 1924 Everest Expedition. RGS, 1924.

19. Mt Everest 1925. Map of Mt Everest group drawn by Charles Jacot-Guillarmod. RGS, 1925.

20. Mt Everest 1928. Scale 1:253,440. Survey of India, 1928.

21. Mt Everest 1930. Scale 1:126,720. Survey of India, 1930. Facsimile, 1990.

22. Mt Everest 1933. Mount Everest Flight, 1933. A plot from vertical strips flown by the Marquess of Clydesdale and Flight Lieut. McIntyre.

23. Mt Everest 1933-46. The southern face and region south of Mt Everest from photographs taken on Mt Everest flight, 1933. Drawn by H F Milne. RGS. Lithographs printed by the War Office in 1952.

24. Mt Everest 1934. Mt Everest group drawn by Charles Jacot-Guillarmod. Reprint of 1925 map showing positions of Camps III, IV, V and VI on the north (Tibetan) side of the mountain during the 1933 expedition.

25. Mt Everest 1936. Scale 1:20,000. The North Face of Mt Everest based on photogrammetric surveys by Michael Spender. RGS, 1936.

26. Mt Everest 1958. Scale 1:50,000. 'Esquisse Topographique de la Région de l'Everest et du Makalu dressée par P. Bordet'. (Expéditions Françaises à l'Himalaya). Institut Géographique National, Paris, 1958.

27. Mt Everest 1965. Scale 1:50,000. Khumbu Himal. Freytag Bernot und Artaria, Vienna, 1965.

28. Mt Everest 1990. Scale 1:50,000. Image map prepared in Digital Mapping Centre, New Delhi. Survey of India, 1990.

29. Mt Everest. Geological 1925. Sketch map of Mt Everest from surveys done on the 1921 and 1924 expeditions, with additions by N E Odell. RGS, 1925.

30. Mt Everest. Geological 1958. Scale 1:50,000. 'Esquisse Géologique de la Région de l'Everest et du Makalu'. (Expéditions Françaises à l'Himalaya 1954-55). Institut Géographique National, Paris, 1958.

31. Mt Everest. Geological 1958. Scale 1:250,000.
     'Esquisse Géologique de la Région de l'Himalaya, de l'Arun et de la Région de
     l'Everest'. (Expéditions Françaises à l'Himalaya 1954-55).
     Institut Géographique National, Paris, 1958.

32. Nepal Series 1992-99. Scale 1:50,000 and 1:25,000. Survey Department of HM
     Government of Nepal, with Finnish International Development Agency.

33. Survey of India Series. Scale 1:63,360, 1:126,720, and 1:253,440 which will
     include Everest region.

34. Lucette Boulnois, *Bibliographie de Nepal, Vol 3. Sciences Naturelles. Tome 1.*
     'Cartes du Nepal dans les Bibliotheques de Paris et de Londres'.
     Editions du Centre National de la Récherché Scientifique, 15 Quai Anatole-
     France, 75700 Paris. 1973.

35. W R Fuchs, *Der Jesuiten Atlas der Kanshi Zeit Monumenta Serica.*
     Monograph, Series IV. Fujen University, Beijing, 1943.

36. J B Du Halde, *Déscription Géographique Historique ... de Empire de la Chine et
     de la Tartarie Chinoise, Vol 4.* Paris Le Mercier, 1735.

37. M P Ward, 'Mapping Everest' in *Cartographic Journal, Vol 31, No 1*, 33-44, 1994.

38. Nepal, China, Tibet. Scale 1:200,000. Soviet General Staff. Sheets G-45-III
     and H-45-XXXIII, 1977. [In Russian]

39. Mt Everest Region. Scale 1:200,000. Tingri–South of Namche Bazar.
     Arun Valley–Rongshar Valley and Shisha Pangma.
     Drawn by E J Hatch, RGS 2000. To accompany
     Everest: A Thousand years of Exploration. A monograph by M P Ward.

40. Mt Everest (1991) 2nd Edition. Scale 1:50,000. Sagarmatha.

41. Mt Everest Region 1921-1954. A series of maps showing routes on Mt Everest
     and in the Everest region. All are in either the Michael Ward Map Archive or
     the RGS Map Archives.
     (1) 1936 Expedition. Drawn by J M L Gavin.
     (2) 1921, 1922, 1924 Expeditions. Drawn by M P Ward.
     (3) 1952 Cho Oyu Expedition. Drawn by W G Lowe.
     (4) 1952 Cho Oyu Expedition. Drawn by A E Gregory.
     (5) 1953 Exploration south of Namche Bazar. Drawn by R C Evans.
     (6) 1952 Cho Oyu Expedition. Routes of L G C E Pugh, R C Evans and others.
          Drawn by M P Ward.
     (7) 1954 New Zealand Expedition SE of Everest. Drawn by W G Lowe.
     (8) 1952 Swiss routes on Everest. Drawn by Swiss expedition members.
     (9) 1954 Swiss route in the Menlung Basin and on Cho Oyu.
          Drawn by R Lambert.
     (10) 1933, 1935, 1936. Routes on Everest. Drawn by M P Ward.

(11) 1952 Cho Oyu. Routes drawn by M P Ward.

(12) 1950 (UK–US), 1951 (Everest Reconnaissance), 1952 (Swiss Spring and Autumn Expeditions). Drawn by M P Ward.

(13) 1951 (Everest Reconnaissance), 1952 (Cho Oyu), 1953 (First Ascent), 1954 (SE of Everest). Drawn by E P Hillary.

(14) 1953 (April). Routes South and East of Everest. Drawn by J O M Roberts.

(15) 1921, 1922, 1924, 1935, 1936, 1938, 1950, 1951, 1952, 1953 routes on Everest. Very large scale. Drawn by M P Ward.

(16) 1933, 1936, 1938 routes on Everest. Drawn by M P Ward.

(17) 1951 (Reconnaissance), 1952 (Cho Oyu), 1953 (First Ascent), 1954 (East of Everest). Drawn by E P Hillary.

(18) 1935 (Reconnaissance). Drawn by C B M Warren.

(19) 1936 Everest. Drawn by C B M Warren.

(20) 1935 Everest (Reconnaissance). Drawn by M P Ward.

(21) 1938 Everest. Drawn by Peter Lloyd.

(22) 1952 (Swiss) Everest. Drawn by André Roch.

(23) Mt Everest Upper Slopes. 20-metre contours.
    A. Route of First Ascent 1953. Drawn by M P Ward.
    B. Routes in 1922 and 1924 (north side). Drawn by C B M Warren.
    C. Routes in 1933, 1935, and 1938 (north side). Drawn by C B M Warren.
    D. Routes in 1952 (Swiss). Drawn by André Roch.

42. Mt Everest. Summit (1990). Scale 1:5000. Five-metre contours. Bradford Washburn. Boston Science Museum.

43. Mt Everest (1990). Scale 1:5000. Orthoptic map. Contours at 20-metre intervals. Bradford Washburn. Boston Science Museum.

44. Mt Everest Region (1875). 'Pundit Map'. RGS.

45. Everest and Deodanga (1857). Showing Survey of Nepal Himalaya from Indian Plains (including Everest). RGS.
Probably the first time a mountain appeared under the name 'Everest' and in its correction position on any official map.

46. Mount Everest. In *Mount Everest: formation, population and exploration of the Everest region* [by] Toni Hagen, G O Dyhrenfurth, Christoph von Fürer-Haimendorf, Erwin Schneider. Translated by E Noel Bowman. Oxford University Press, 1963. For an account of the geological evolution of Mount Everest, see the chapter by Toni Hagen entitled 'Evolution of the highest mountain in the world' in the above book.

47. Marcel Kurz (1959). Everest information, maps and photos in *Chronique Himalayenne* and Supplement (1963). Swiss Foundation for Alpine Research, Zurich.

MOUNT EVEREST REGION

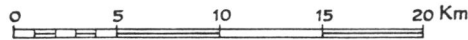

```
0        5        10       15      20 Km
```

Heights in metres

NAMES: *Where possible older and more established
names have been used
The spellings on published maps can vary depending
on country of origin.*

HEIGHTS: *The heights used for the immediate Everest
region come mainly from the National Geographic map
1:50000 (1988). Beyond that the heights for Nepal come
where possible from the Nepal (Finnmap) 1:50000 survey
(1996-97), the Austrian 1:50000 (1981), and RGS 1:100000
(1975) maps. Heights for Tibet come from the Soviet
1:200000 (1970-74) maps, Chinese maps and trekking
information.*

*Drawn by Ted Hatch for Michael Ward to accompany
his monograph EVEREST: A Thousand Years of Exploration*
                                                    2000

Scale and information
for the following sections of map,
pages 320-327.
Reduced from original map of 1:200 000

86°

Selung
5470

Men Chu

Lalung La
4791

5630

Yamabo
5739

Sepa La)(
5034

Nyenang La
4852

28°
30'

6180

Kangjaru Gl.

6049

5794

Zigaozong

Koryag pu

Talung

Nashing

6197 Kangbure

Dale

Ngora

Yalep

Langtang Ri
7205

7292 Porong
Ri

7365 Yebokangal
Ri

Gya

Tarjeling

Po Chu

Risum
7050

7703

Kangxi Co

Changdong

6182

Gosainthan
(Shisha Pangma)
8027

Phola
Gangchen
7486

Pungpa Ri

Gong Co
(Tashi
Tso)

5897

6257

Tashigang

Karra

6404

Goldum
6632

Nyanang Ri
7119

Kung
Tso

6599

6743 Phemtang
Ri

Sumo
5502

Kyunga
Ri

6484

6240

Karijue
5629

5510

Pelgyeling
Gompa

5871

Phemtang
Karpo Ri
6865

5753

Sugasong

+

Kang La
5460

Lanshisha
Ri

6412 Gurkarpo
Ri

6889 6733

Ta

Dorle Pahad
(Longpo Gang)

6979

Eiger Pk

Gyalsten
6151

Tara
Tso

Phu Chu

5738

Gangchempo
6378

Dorle Lakpa
6966

Nyalam

Kang Chu

Lapche

Urkinmang
6143

Jugal
(Yangri) 6535

Karbu
Bumri
5306

6637

Phurbi Chyachu

6075

Ladanbesi

Choksum

Thasing

Panch
Pokhari
4656

Kharane
Tippa

5581

6109 Chhoba
Bamare

Tharpu

5510 Kharape Tippa

Po Chu

5901

5918

Risang
Gumb

Tembathan

Lomn

Zom
Khola

28°

Dram
(Khasa)

Kodari

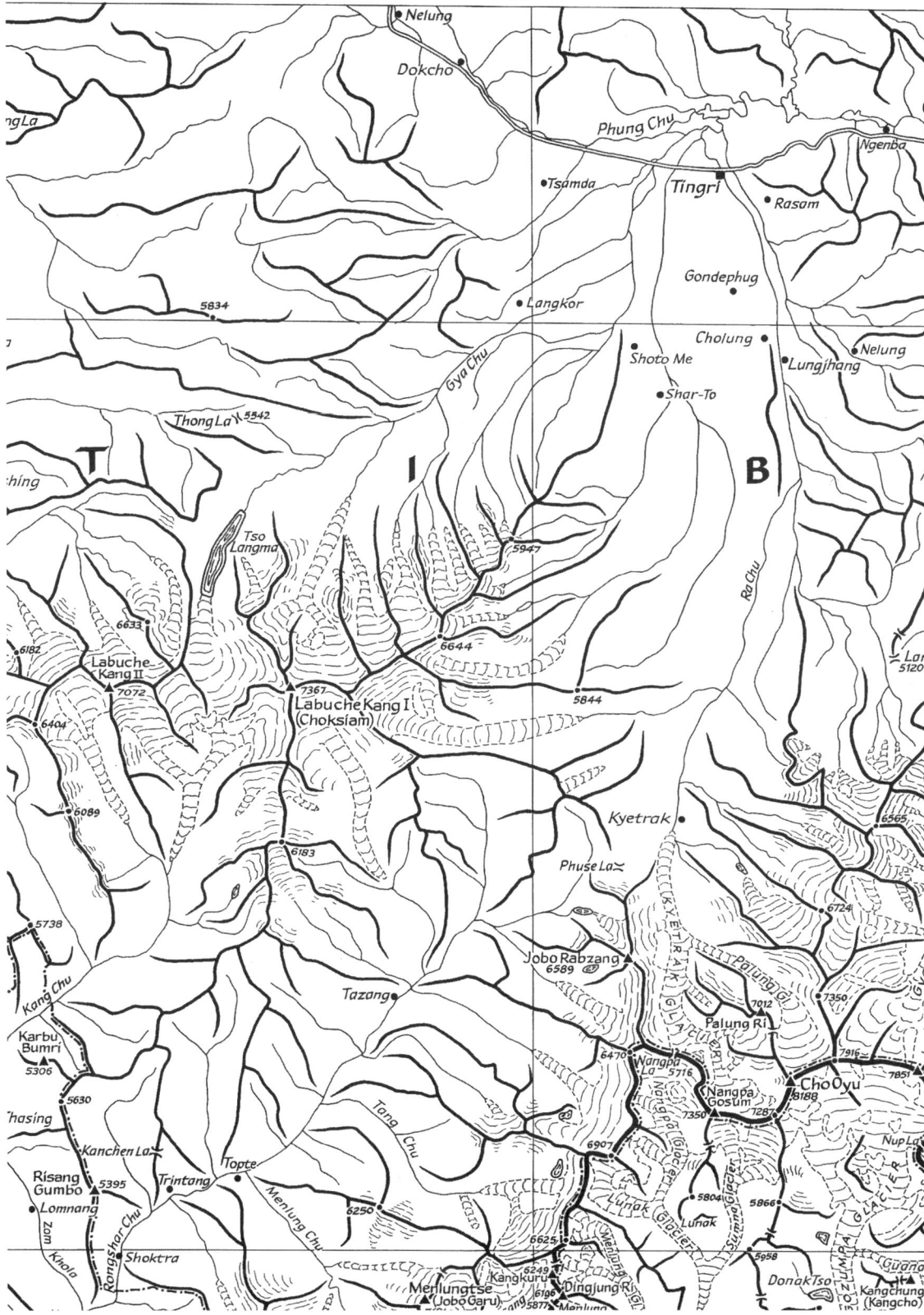

86°30'

Nelung

Dokcho

Phung Chu

Ngenba

Tsamda

Tingri

Rasam

Gondephug

5834

Langkor

Cholung

Nelung

Shoto Me

Lungjhang

Thong La 5542

Shar-To

T

I

B

Tso Langma

5947

Ra Chu

6633

6182

6644

Lan 5120

Labuche Kang II 7072

7367

Labuche Kang I (Choksiam)

5844

6404

6089

6183

Kyetrak

6565

Phuse La

6724

5738

Jobo Rabzang 6589

Kang Chu

Palung Ri

Karbu Bumri 5306

Tazang

7012

7350

5630

Palung Ri

7916

Thasing

Kanchen La

6470

Nangpa La 5716

Cho Oyu 8188

7851

Risang Gumbo 5395

Trintang

Topte

Nangpa Gosum

7350

7287

Nup La

Lomnang

Tong Chu

Menlung Chu

6250

6907

Lunak

5804

5866

Zom Khola

Rongshar Chu

Shoktra

6625

5958

Donak Tso

Kangchung (Kangcho)

Menlungtse (Jobo Garu)

Kangkuru

6249

6196

Dingjung Ri

Menlung Ri

Menlung

5877

86°30'   87°

Phung Chu

Ngenba   •Memo   Tsakor   Phung Chu

•Tsamda   Tingri   •Rasam   •Trakkar

•Langkor   Gondephug   •5501

Cholung   •Nelung   LamarLa   •Gara   Trongkar
Shoto Me   •Lungjhang   4890
•Shar-To   Nyo Chu   •Nyum

B   Ding La   E   Peruche
5000   (TashiDzom)

•5947   Palung   Ding Chu   Passum
•5691

Ra Chu   •Kuyul
Zommug   Rongbuk Chu

Lamna La   •Chhoubu   •Chosang
5120
•5844   •Rap

Kyetrak•   •6565   Gyachung Chu   •6270   •6623

Phuse La   Rongbuk
Monastery   Passang
6724   Rong Chu   Fall Col
6067

Jobo Rabzang   Qianjing   •6646   •7093
6589   7012   7350   6742   Lixin   7003   Kharta
Palung Ri   7916   6622   •Shiguang   7113   Dongfang Changri
6470   Wangpa   7851   Gyachung   6975   Ri-ring   6977   Khartaphu
La   5716   Kang   6956   Tongqiang   7283
Nangpa   7287   Cho Oyu   Khartse
Gosum   8188   8188   Nup La   West Rongbuk Gl.   6849   Lhakpa La   6550
7350   5844   Lingtren   Khumbutse   Changtse
6907   7029   Nup   Lingtren   7583   Rapiu La
5804   5866   6396   6749   Pumo Ri   North Col   Lho La   6548
Lunak   Chumbu   7165   7066   6026
6625   5958   6870   Changri La   Kala   West Cwm
6249   Guanora   5720   Pattar   MOUNT EVEREST
Kangkuru   Donak Tso   5575   8850
Dingjung Ri   Kangchung   6159   Gorakshep   South Col
6196   (Kangcho)   5656   Nuptse
5877

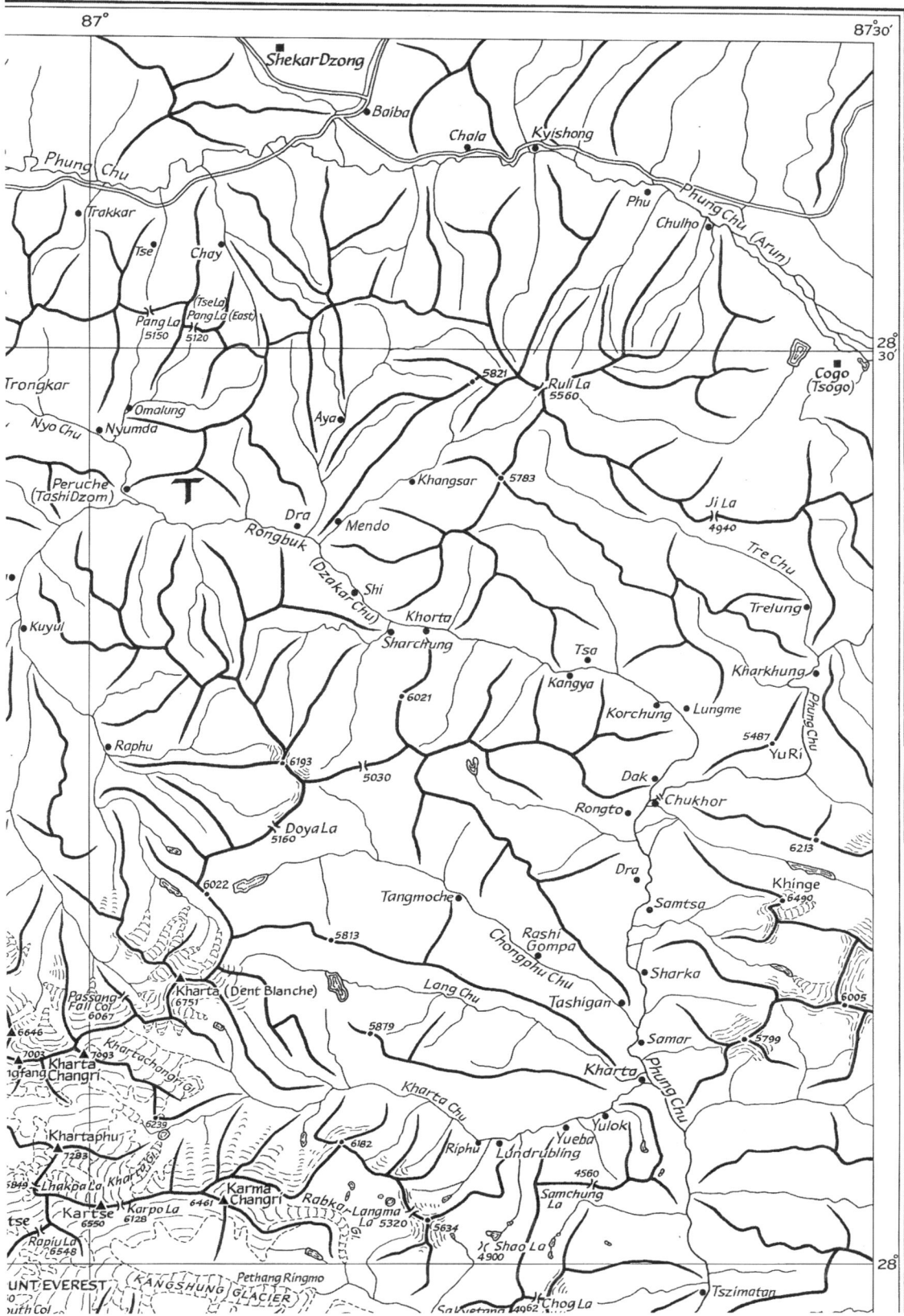

87°

87°30'

Shekar Dzong

Baiba

Chala

Kyishong

Phung Chu

Trakkar

Phu

Chulho

Phung Chu (Arun)

Tse

Chay

(Tse La)
Pang La (East)
5120

Pang La
5150

28°
30'

Cogo
(Tsogo)

Trongkar

Omalung

5821

Ruli La
5560

Nyo Chu

Nyumda

Aya

Peruche
(Tashi Dzom)

Khangsar

5783

Ji La
4940

Tre Chu

T

Dra

Mendo

Rongbuk

Trelung

Shi

(Dzakar Chu)

Khorta

Kharkhung

Kuyul

Sharchung

Tsa

Kangya

Korchung

Lungme

6021

5487

Yu Ri

Raphu

6193

5030

Dak

Phung Chu

Rongto

Chukhor

Doya La
5160

6213

6022

Dra

Khinge
6490

Tangmoche

Samtsa

5813

Rashi
Gompa

Chongphu Chu

Sharka

6005

Passang
Fall Col
6067

Kharta (Dent Blanche)
6751

Lang Chu

Tashigan

6646

5879

Samar

5799

7003

7093

Kharta

Phung Chu

fang
Changri

Kharta Chu

Kharta

Khartachongri

Yulok

Khartaphu
7283

6239

6182

Riphu

Yueba

Lundrubling

4560

5849

Lhakpa La

Karma
Changri

Samchung
La

Kartse
6550

Karpo La
6128

6461

Rabka

Langma
La 5320

5634

Shao La
4900

Rapiu La
6548

tse

Pethang Ringmo

Tszimatan

UNT EVEREST

KANGSHUNG GLACIER

Chog La

uth Col

Sakyetang 4962

28°

Gangchempo
6378
Urkinmang
6143
Dorje Pahad
(Longpo Gang)
Gyalsten
6151
Tara
Tso
Phu Chu
5738
Dorje Lakpa
6966
Nyalam
Lapche
Karbu
Bumri
5306
Jugal
(Yangri)
6535
6637
Phurbi Chyachu
Thasing
6075
Ladanbesi
Kharane
Tippa
5581
Choksum
Chhoba
Bamare
6109
Risang
Gumbo
Lomn
Panch
Pokhari
4656
Tharpu
Kharape Tippa
5510
5901
5918
Zam
Kholo
Tembathan
Po Chu
Dram
(Khasa)
Chaduk
Bhir
5940
Hum
Ghumthan
Kodari
Ama
Bamare
5328
Lamabagar
(Choksham)
Lidi
Tasithan
Tatopani
Gunsakot
Baiephi Khola
Pangarpu
Nimlung
Paku
Bhote Kosi
Chaku
Deodunga
4426
Chetche
Tselaphu
3981
Tasin
Bigu Gompa
Ruphtang
3747
3319
Tinsang
La
Alampu
Khartal
Loding
Amatal
Jaga

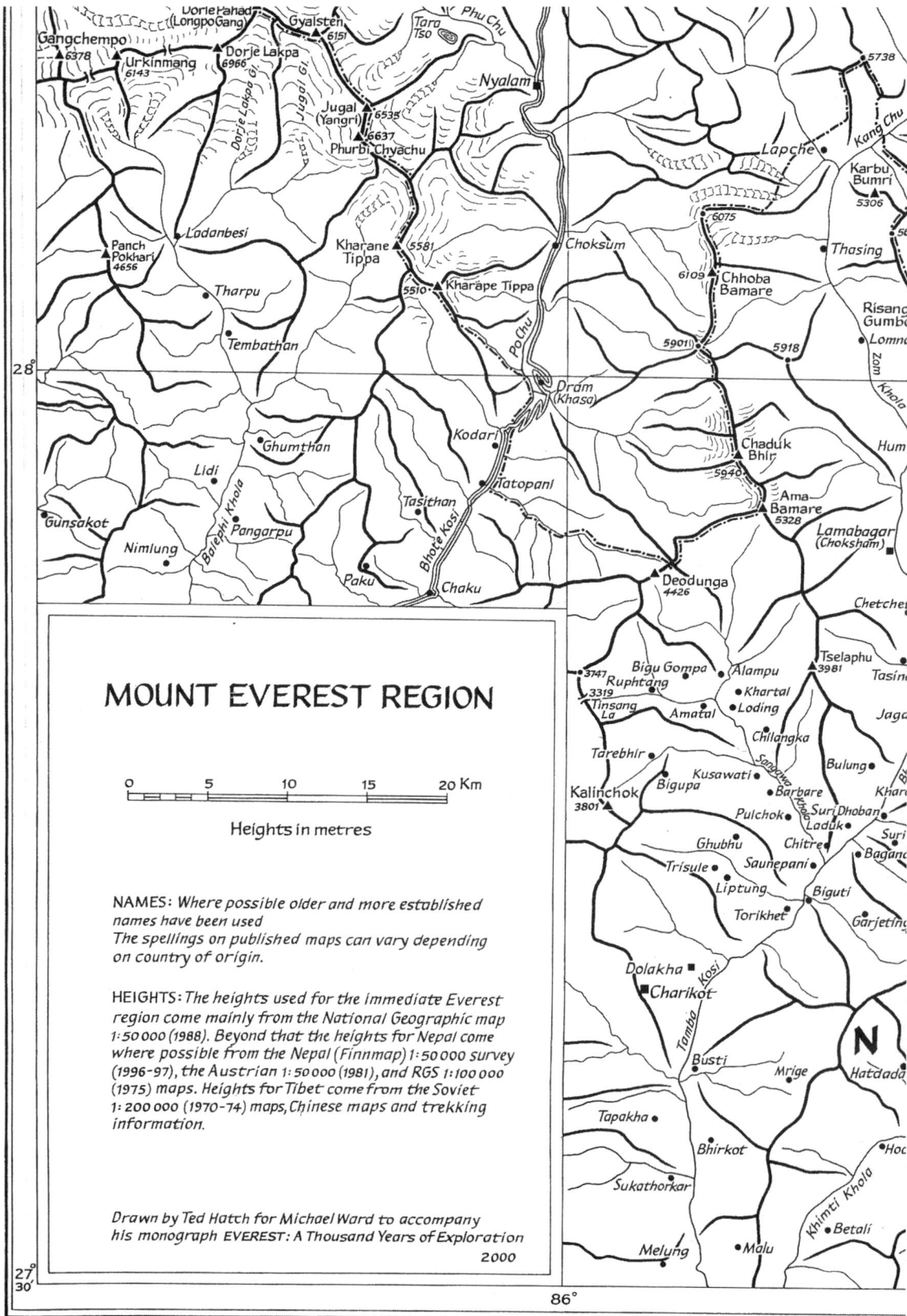

MOUNT EVEREST REGION

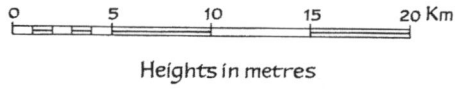

```
0        5        10       15      20 Km
```

Heights in metres

NAMES: *Where possible older and more established
names have been used
The spellings on published maps can vary depending
on country of origin.*

HEIGHTS: *The heights used for the immediate Everest
region come mainly from the National Geographic map
1:50 000 (1988). Beyond that the heights for Nepal come
where possible from the Nepal (Finnmap) 1:50 000 survey
(1996-97), the Austrian 1:50 000 (1981), and RGS 1:100 000
(1975) maps. Heights for Tibet come from the Soviet
1:200 000 (1970-74) maps, Chinese maps and trekking
information.*

*Drawn by Ted Hatch for Michael Ward to accompany
his monograph EVEREST: A Thousand Years of Exploration*
                                                    2000

Chilangka
Tarebhir
Kusawati
Bulung
Kalinchok
3801
Bigupa
Barbare
Khar
Suri Dhoban
Pulchok
Laduk
Suri
Ghubhu
Chitre
Bagan
Trisule
Saunepani
Biguti
Liptung
Torikhet
Garjeting
Dolakha
Tamba Kosi
Charikot
N
Busti
Mrige
Hatdada
Tapakha
Bhirkot
Hoo
Sukathorkar
Khimti Khola
Melung
Malu
Betali

27°
30'

86°

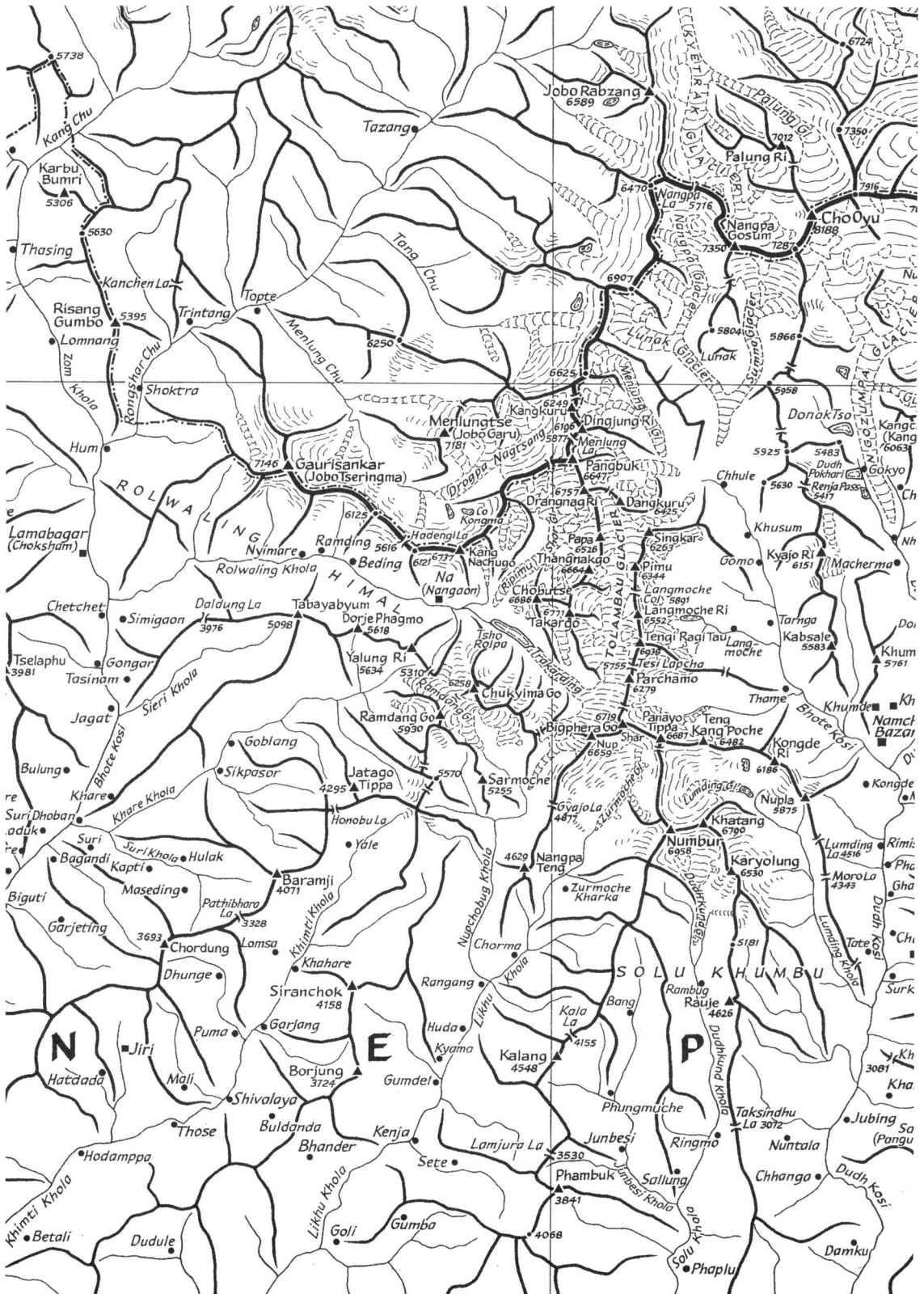

5738

Kang Chu

Karbu
Bumri
5306

5630

Thasing

Kanchen La

Risang
Gumbo 5395
Lomnang

Zom Khola

Rongshar Chu

Shoktra

Trintang

Topte

Tazang

Menlung Chu

6250

Tang Chu

Jobo Rabzang
6589

Palung Gl

7012

Palung Ri

7350

6724

6470
Nangpa
La 5716

Nangpa Glacier

Nangpa
Gosum
7350
7287

Cho Oyu
8188

7916

Lunak Glacier

5804
5866

Lunak

6907

6625

5958

Sumna Glacier

Gokyo
Donak Tso

Kang
Kang

6063

ROLWALING

Hum

7146 Gaurisankar
(JoboTseringma)

6125

Lamabagar
(Choksham)

Nyimare
Ramding
5616

Beding

Rolwaling Khola

HIMAL

Chetchet

Simigaon

Daldung La
3976

5098

Tabayabyum

Dorje Phagmo
5618

Tselaphu
3981
Tasinam

Gongar

Sieri Khola

Yalung Ri
5634

Jagat

Bhote Kosi

6249
Kangkuru

Menlungtse
(Jobo Garu)
7181

Dingjung Ri
6196
5877 Menlung

Pangbuk
6447

Droppa Nagrsong

Co
Kongma

Drangnag Ri
6757

Dangkuru
6425

Papa
6526

Singkar
6263

Pimu
6344

Langmoche
(Col) 5891

Langmoche Ri
6552

TOLAMBAU GLACIER

Khusum

Chhule

5630

5483
Dudh
Pokhari

Renjo Pass
5417

5925

Gomo

Kyajo Ri
6151

Macherma

Tarnga

Kabsale
5583

Khum
5761

Hadengi La

5616
6121
6737

Kang
Nachugo

Na
(Nangaon)

Pipimu

Thangnakgo
6664

Chobutse
6686

Takardo

Tisho
Rolpa

Trakading

Ramding Go
6258

Chukyima Go

5310

Tengi Ragi Tau
6938

5755 Tesi Lapcha

Parchamo
6279

Lang-
moche

Thame

Bhote Kosi

Khumde

Khumjung

Namch
Bazar

Kongde

Ramdang Go
5930

Jatago
Tippa
4295

Honobu La

Yale

Bigphera Go
6719

Nup
6659

Panayo
Tippa
6687

Teng
Kang Poche
6482

Kongde
Ri
6186

Nupla
5875

Goblang

Sikpasor

5570

Sarmoche
5255

Gyajola
4877

Zurmoche Gl

Lumding Gl

Khatang
6790

Lumding
La 4516

Rimi

Pha

Gha

Suri Dhoban
aduk

Khare

Khare Khola

Suri

Bagandi
Kapti

Suri Khola

Hulak

Maseding

Pathibhara
La 3328

Baramji
4071

4629 Nangpa
Teng

Zurmoche
Kharka

Numbur
6958

Karyolung
6530

MoroLa
4343

Lumding Khola

Dudh Kosi

Biguti

Garjeting

3693

Chordung

Lomsa

Dhunge

Khahare

Siranchok
4158

Khimti Khola

Chorma

Chorma Khola

SOLU KHUMBU

5181

Dudhkund Khola

Tate
3081

Chu

Surk

N

Jiri

Hatdada

Puma

Garjang

Mali

Those

Shivalaya

Buldanda

Borjung
3724

Gumdel

E

Rangang

Huda

Kyama

Likhu Khola

Kalang
4548

Kala
La
4155

Bang

Rambug

P

Rauje
4626

Phungmuche

Taksindhu
La 3072

Jubing
(Pangu

Hodamppa

Bhander

Kenja

Sete

Lamjura La
3530

Lamjura La

Junbesi Khola

Junbesi

Salung

Ringmo

Nuntala

Chhanga

Dudh Kosi

Betali

Dudule

Likhu Khola

Goli

Gumba

4068

Phambuk
3841

Solu Khola

Phaplu

Damku

Jobo Rabzang 6589
Palung Ri
7012
7350
6724
KYETRAK GLACIER
PALUNG GLACIER
Gyachung Kang
Rong Chu
6270
6623
Passang Fall Col 6067
Qianjing 6646
Lixin 7113
7003
Kharta 7093
Dongrang Changri
6742
Shuguang 6622
Ri-ring 6975
6956
Tongqiang 6977
Khartaphu 7283
Cho Oyu 8188
Nangpa La 5716
Wangpa 6470
Nangpa Gosum 7287
7350
7851
7916
Nup La 5844
West Rongbuk Gl.
7029
Lingtren Nup 6396
Lingtren 6749
Chumbu 6870
RONGBUK GLACIER
Lhakpa La
6849
Kartse 6550
612
Khumbutse 7583
Changtse
North Col 7066
Lho La 6026
Rapiu La 6548
Pumo Ri 7165
Changri La 5575
Kala Pattar 5575
Gorakshep
MOUNT EVEREST 8850
Nuptse 7861
South Col 8386
Lhotse 8501
7590
7444
6738 Pe
Shartse
6907
6625
6249
Kangkuru Tse Garu 6196
Dingjung Ri 5877
Nagtsang
Menlung La
Pangbuk 6447
Drangnag Ri
Dangkuru 6425
5804
Lunak
5866
5958
DonakTso
5925
5483
Dudh Pokhari
Renjo Pass 5417
5630
Chhule
Gokyo
Chugima
5368
Kangchung (Kangcho) 6063
5656
6159
Guanara
5720
Lobuche 6135
West Cwm
5817
Mehra 5535
Chukhung 5857
Island Pk 6173
Cho Polu 6695
5732
Pokalde
Tshola Co
6423
Khusum
Nha
Taweche
6495
Dingboche
Baruntse 7168
Amphu Labtsa
5787
West Col
Hongu Gl.
6143
Pyramid Pk 6764
6833
Kyajo Ri 6151
Macherma
Dudh Kosi
Dole
Khumbila 5761
Phorche
Thyangboche Monastery
Ama Dablam 6828
Pangboche
Mingbo La 5866
Hunku 6119
6420
Singkar 6261
Gomo
Pimu 6344
Langmoche Col 5891
Langmoche Ri 6552
Tarnga
Kabsale 5583
Langmoche
Thame
Khumde
Khumjung
Namche Bazar
Dudh Kosi
6573
Kangtega 6783
Tamserku 6618
Pk41 6648
Chamlang 7321
Papa 6526
Thangnakbo
Chobutse 6686
Takardo
6771
6757
Tesi Lapcha 5755
Tengi Ragi Tau 6938
Parchamo 6279
Kang Poche 6482
Teng 6687
Panayo Tippa
6719
Kongde Ri 6186
Kongde
Monjo
Kyashar (Pk43) 6770
Khare
Mera La 5413
6281
Bigphera Go
Nup Shar 6659
Chukyima Go
Sarmoche 5255
Gyajo La 4871
Numbur 6958
Khatang 6790
Nupla 5875
Lumding La 4516
Rimishung
Phakdingma
Ghat
6370
Kusum Kangguru
Lungsamba
Mera 6470
Gonglha
Urpa
6213
4629 Nangpa Teng
Zurmoche Kharka
Karyolung 6530
Moro La 4343
5181
Tate
Chaunrikharka 5808
Lukla
Tashing Dingma
Naulekh 6363
5067
norma Khola
SOLU KHUMBU
Rambug
Rauje 4626
Bang
Kala La 4155
Kalang 4548
P
Phungmuche
Dudhkund Khola
A
Surke
Zair Pass 4580
5329
5444
4679
L
5489
5275
jura La 3530
Junbesi
Ringmo
Taksindhu La 3072
Nuntala
Jubing
Khari La 3081
Kharte 4259
Salu La (Pangum La) 3178
Cherem
Surkie La 3085
4256
Miklakharka
Phambuk 3841
Sallung
Chhanga
Dudh Kosi
Inukhu Khola
Khiraule
Chheskam
4068
Solu Khola
Phaplu
Damku
Bun
Gudel
4097

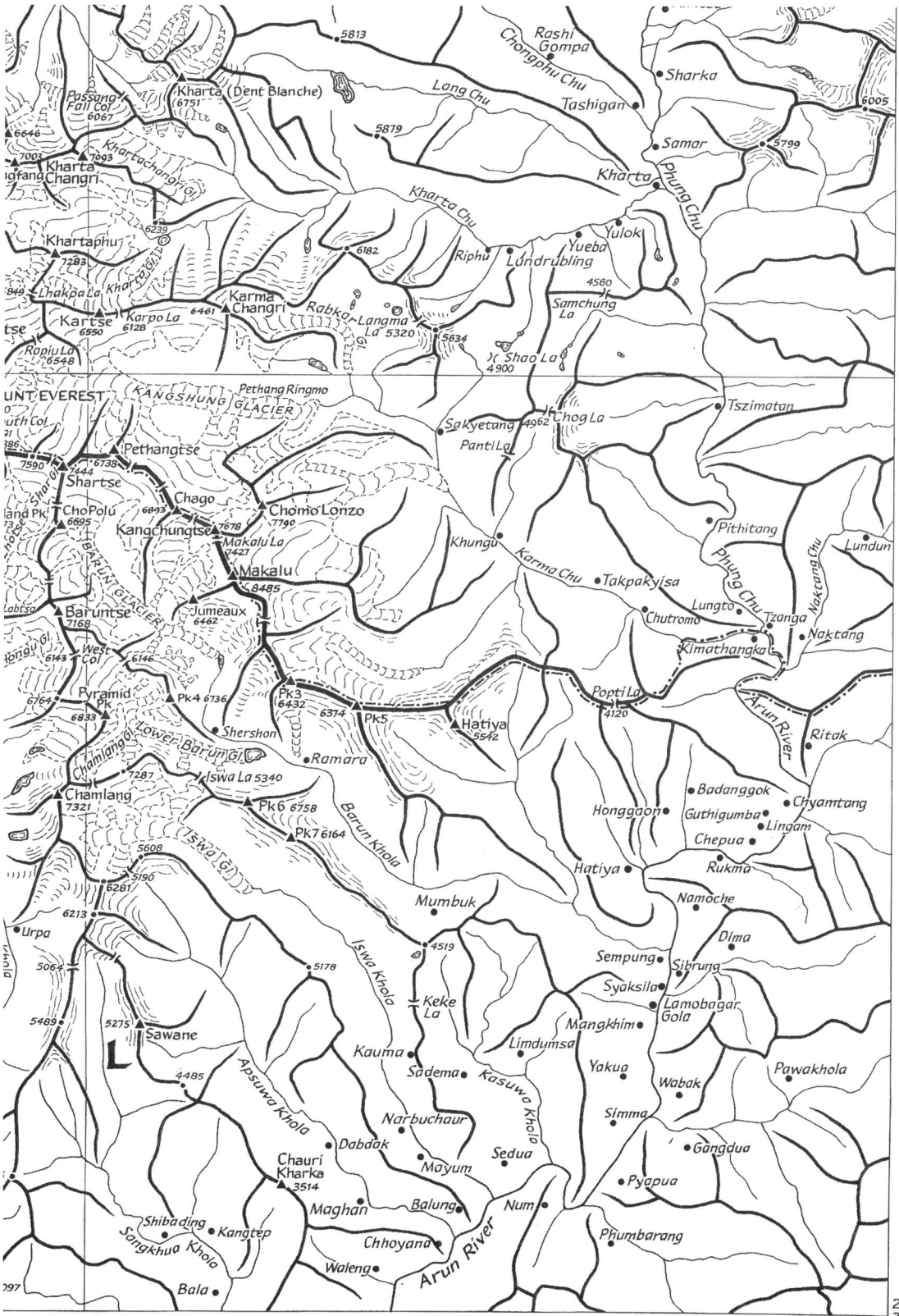

Rashi Gompa
Chongphu Chu
Sharka
5813
Lang Chu
Tashigan
6005
Passang
Fall Col
6067
Kharta (Dent Blanche)
6751
6646
5879
Samar
5799
7003
Kharta
gfang
Changri
7093
Khartachangra
Kharta
Phung Chu
6239
Khartaphu
7293
Kharta Chu
6182
Riphu
Yueba
Lundrubling
Yulok
849
Lhakpa La
Karma
Changri
4560
Kartse
6550
Karpo La
6128
6461
Rabka
Langma
La 5320
Samchung
La
tse
Rapiu La
6548
5634
Shao La
4900
28°

MOUNT EVEREST
KANGSHUNG GLACIER
Pethang Ringmo
Sakyetang
4962
Chog La
Tszimatun
uth Col
Pethangtse
Panti La
386
7590
Shartse
7444
6738
land Pk
ChoPolu
6695
Chago
6893
Chomo Lonzo
7790
Khungu
Pithitang
Lundun
Kangchungtse
7678
Makalu La
7427
Karma Chu
Takpakyisa
Phung Chu
Naktang Chu
abtsa
Makalu
8485
Lungto
Tzanga
Naktang
Baruntse
7168
Jumeaux
6462
Chutromo
Kimathangka
iongu Gl.
6143
West
Col
6146
Pk3
6432
Popti La
4120
Arun River
6764
Pyramid
Pk
6833
Pk4 6736
6314
Pk5
Hatiya
5542
Ritak
Shershon
Ramara
Chamlang Gl.
Lower Barun Gl.
7287
Iswa La 5340
Badanggok
Chyamtang
Chamlang
7321
Pk6 6758
Honggaon
Guthigumba
Lingam
Pk7 6164
Chepua
5608
Rukma
5196
6281
Hatiya
Namoche
6213
Mumbuk
Dima
Urpa
Barun Khola
4519
Sempung
Sibrung
5064
5178
Syaksila
Lamobagar
Gola
5489
5275
Sawane
Keke
La
Mangkhim
Yakua
Wabak
Pawakhola
L
4485
Iswa Khola
Kauma
Limdumsa
Apsuwa Khola
Sadema
Kasuwa Khola
Simma
Narbuchaur
Chauri
Kharka
3514
Dabdak
Sedua
Gangdua
Maghan
Mayum
Balung
Num
Pyapua
Shibading
Kangtep
Chhoyana
Phumbarang
Sangkhua Khola
Waleng
Arun River
Bala
097
87°
27°
30'
87°30'

© E.J. HATCH 2000

Short Biography of the Author

Michael Ward CBE, MD, FRCS,

Education:	Marlborough College, Wilts.
	Peterhouse, Cambridge (Ironmonger's Company Exhibition).
1950-1952	RAMC, Captain.
1951	Everest Reconnaissance Expedition, Member and Medical Officer.
1952-Present	Alpine Club, Vice-President (1968-69), Hon Member (1992-present).
1953	Everest Expedition (first ascent), Member and Medical Officer.
1954	Hunterian Professor, Royal College of Surgeons of England.
1957	Marriage to Felicity Ewbank. One son, Mark.
1960-61	Himalayan, Scientific and Mountaineering Expedition (Silver Hut) in Everest region.
	Leader of first ascent of Ama Dablam, 6,828m, with B C Bishop, M B Gill, W Romanes.
1964, 1965	Medical research and mountain exploration, Bhutan-Tibet border, leader.
1964-1993	Consultant Surgeon, City and East London Area Health Authority (Teaching).
1975-1993	Lecturer in Clinical Surgery, Royal London Hospital Medical College.
1980-1981	Medical research and mountain exploration in Mt Kongur region of Pamir/Kun Lun, Chinese Central Asia. Leader of the 1980 reconnaissance and leader of the 1981 British Mt Kongur expedition, when the first ascent of Mt Kongur (7,719m) was made by P Boardman, C J S Bonington, A Rouse, J R Tasker.
1982	Founder's (Royal) Medal, Royal Geographical Society.
1985-1986	Royal Society/Chinese Academy of Sciences, Tibet Geotraverse. Member and Medical Officer.
1986-1995	Cambridge Alpine Club, President.
1993-94	Master, The Worshipful Society of Apothecaries of London.

PUBLICATIONS

Text Books	*Mountain Medicine: a clinical study of cold and high altitude.* Crosby Lockwood Staples, 1975.
	High Altitude Medicine & Physiology (jointly with J S Milledge, J B West), 3rd Edition, 2000. Arnold.
Other	*The Mountaineer's Companion*, edited by Michael Ward. Eyre & Spottiswoode, 1966.
	In this Short Span: a mountaineering memoir. Gollancz, 1972 Articles on medical research in the *British Medical Journal*, the *Lancet*, *Wilderness and Environmental Medicine* (formerly *Journal of Wilderness Medicine*) and *High Altitude Medicine and Biology*. Articles on mountain exploration in the Himalaya and Central Asia in the *Alpine Journal* and the *Geographical Journal*.

Index

Note: The page numbers marked 'bibliography' refer to the pages on which an author's name appears in the bibliography at the end of the chapter. Numbers in italics indicate drawings, maps or other illustrations. Heights vary between the metric and imperial forms, as explained on page vii of the preliminary pages.

Phuse La

KYETRAK GLACIER

Palung Gl.

Jobo Rabzang ▲
6589

7012
Palung Ri

6724

7350

6470
Wangpa La
5716

Nangpa Gosum ▲
7350   7287

7916

Cho Oyu ▲
8188

7851

Gyachung Kang ▲

Nangpa Glacier

6907

Lunak Glacier

Sumna Glacier

Nup La
5844

7029

63

Chumbu ▲
6870

6625

5804
Lunak

5866

5958

NGOZUMPA GLACIER

G

Guanara
5720

6249
Kangkuru ▲
6196

Dingjung Ri ▲

DonakTso

Kangchung (Kangcho)
6063

6159
5656

Char

ru

5877
Menlung La ▲

Rl Gl.

5925

5483

5368

Lobuche
6135

agtsang

Pangbuk ▲
6647

Chhule

Dudh Pokhari

Gokyo

6757
Drangnag Ri ▲

Dangkuru ▲
6425

5630
Renja Pass
5417

Chugima

6423

TOLAMBAU GLACIER

Papa ▲
6526

Singkar ▲
6263

Khusum

Nha

Thangnakgo ▲
6664

Pimu ▲
6344

Gomo

Kyajo Ri ▲
6151

Macherma

Tawec
6495

Chobutse ▲
6686

Langmoche Col 5891

Langmoche Ri ▲
6552

6771
Takargo ▲

Trakarding

Tengi Ragi Tau ▲
6938

Tarnga

Langmoche

Kabsale ▲
5583

Dole

Khumbila ▲
5761

Phorche

Thyang Mo

kyima Go

5755
Tesi Lapcha

Parchamo ▲
6279

Thame

Khumde

Khumjung

Namche Bazar ■

6719
Bigphera Go ▲

Panayo Tippa ▲
6687

Teng Kang Poche ▲
6482

Khumde ■

Dudh Kosi

Nup Shar
6659

Bhote Kosi

Kongde Ri ▲
6186

Tamserku ▲
6618

rmoche

Aina Gl.

Konade ●